Street of the Knights, Rhodes old town

Blue Guide

RHODES &
THE DODECANESE

Robin Barber

A & C Black · London

W W Norton · New York

First edition 1997

Published by A & C Black (Publishers) Limited
35 Bedford Row, London WC1R 4JH

A CIP catalogue record of this book is available from the British Library.

ISBN 0–7136–4093–6

Published in the United States of America by
WW Norton and Company, Inc
500 Fifth Avenue, New York, NY 10110

Published simultaneously in Canada by
Penguin Books Canada Limited
10 Alcorn Avenue, Toronto
Ontario M4V 3B2

ISBN 0–393–31582–7 USA

The author and the publishers have done their best to ensure the accuracy of all the information in Blue Guide Rhodes and the Dodecanese; however, they can accept no responsibility for any loss, injury or inconvenience sustained by any traveller as a result of information or advice contained in the guide.

Robin Barber was born in Chapel en le Frith, Derbyshire, in 1940. Formerly Head of the Department of Classical Archaeology at Edinburgh University, he is an MA (Classics) and PhD of St Andrews University and holds the Oxford Diploma in Classical Archaeology. He has travelled in Greece for over 30 years, five of which were spent there, first as Greek State Scholar (for research in Aegean archaeology), then as Assistant Director of the British School at Athens. He has done fieldwork in Crete and the Cyclades and published numerous articles on Greek art and archaeology. His book *The Cyclades in the Bronze Age* appeared in 1987 and, in Greek translation, in 1994. He is also author of *Blue Guide Greece* and *Blue Guide Athens*. Among particular Greek enthusiasms, he would count the poems of G. Seferis, the rebetika songs of Sotiria Bellou, and walking in the countryside.

Maps and plans © A&C Black, drawn by Julian Baker, Derby
Illustrations © Jaideep Chekrabarti, 1997
Cover photograph: doorway on Sími by Andy Keate/Edifice
Printed in Great Britain by William Clowes Ltd., Beccles and London

Preface

At the extreme edge of the Aegean world, straggling off the southwestern coast of Turkey, the Dodecanese have distinctive characteristics most of which ultimately derive from their position on the map. Even their name (twelve islands) is a curiosity, when there are fourteen major islands and other smaller ones.

The climate is warm and inviting from Spring well into the Autumn, and winters are mild. Not without their share of starkly barren mountains, there are surprisingly green and fertile areas on most of the islands and, on Rhodes and Kos, luxuriant forests. Flowers, their colours flaring against the whiteness of the houses, and insect life abound. Rhodes, after all, is the 'Island of Roses'. The coasts, in places steep and forbidding, in others relax into sweeping sands and shingle beaches. In major tourist centres you can find the trappings of modern tourism; off the main routes, these islands represent the Greece of your imagination—rural, sea-washed, by turns gentle and dramatic, and people whose friendliness and hospitality are exceptional, even by the standards of a nation famed for these qualities. The variety of landscape and scenery and, in smaller islands the lack of traffic, make the Dodecanese an ideal area for quiet leisure.

Two historical events in particular have shaped the character of these islands, both periods of occupation. The first, from 1309–1522, was by the crusader Knights of St John, after their expulsion from the Holy Land; the other, from 1912–47, by the Italians, in the course of their conflict with Turkey. The Knights left a legacy of massive castles, and the magnificent medieval 'old town' of Rhodes, and introduced western European elements into the architecture and arts of the period, modifying the powerful Byzantine tradition. The Italian legacy is more complex—some massively distinctive public buildings, spacious streets but also a sense of local pride and identity forged by resistance to the imposition of alien authority. Blue and white, the Greek national colours, are even now preferred for houses on Kálimnos, the most vociferous in opposition. Between these two was a third and longer occupation, by the Turks, whose mosques and fountains give an eastern feel.

Most of the islands have their Classical site and the area was important throughout antiquity. Some of these are spectacular: the sanctuary of Athena on the acropolis at Lindos on Rhodes or the walls of ancient Nisyros. The presence of Byzantium is strongly sensed and there are many fine churches, often with impressive frescoes. Traditions that have survived until recent times are embroidery and sponge fishing, the latter having played a vital role in the economic rise and decline of the area.

Of the individual islands **Rhodes** is rightly celebrated for the splendour of its medieval architecture and the evocative old town. Its museums and galleries match the island's leading role in the Dodecanese. Although the north is studded with large hotels, it is easy to escape into the countryside, to find quiet beaches, to enjoy the sleepy villages and rich inland scenery, and to explore ancient sites, Byzantine churches and medieval castles.

Kos, though smaller, has similar attributes: there are several castles, with a particularly fine one in the main town, Early Christian basilicas and mountain villages, cool amid their greenery. Some of the island's fine beaches and resorts supply the needs of mass tourism—'home comforts' and watersports.

Rugged **Kárpathos**, long and narrow and lying between Rhodes and Crete, is no smaller than Kos but much less well known. Its southern port (Pigádhia), set on the sweep of a wide and beautiful bay, has acquired plenty of hotels and tourist facilities. But the inland villages, cupped in the folds of the mountains, are unspoilt and enticing. In the centre and north where the going is rough, you can feel a real explorer and the isolated village of Olimbos, where traditional dress and customs survive, is unmissable.

Neighbouring **Kásos**, tiny and neglected but with some fine houses, built by its sea-faring families, has a delightful scatter of villages in its broad coastal plain, two fascinating caves and a population whose friendly welcome sets them firmly in the Greek tradition of *filoxenía* (hospitality to the stranger).

Just to the north of Rhodes, little **Khálki** is a rugged island, with some elegant houses in its port, an ancient acropolis where the medieval castle was later built, and good rough walking to inland monasteries.

Several hours by boat to the east of Rhodes, in a fold of the mainland, **Kastellórizo** is an outpost, much easier to reach from Turkey, though there is no crossing. With a turbulent history, the island makes up for depopulation with the enthusiasm of its inhabitants both resident and émigré to maintain and rebuild its traditional houses and way of life. Monuments include a castle and a fine ancient tomb.

Heading northwards from Rhodes, the sparkling and spectacular neo-classical architecture of the town of **Sími**, covering the hillsides round the port, is astonishing for such a small and barren island but reflects its former wealth from sponge-fishing and shipbuilding. Many of the houses have been restored as accommodation for visitors. The interior is good for energetic walkers who can seek out remote beaches or some of the numerous churches, often painted.

Sleepy **Tílos** arouses great affection in its adherents. The intriguing craggy outline conceals the softer side of its interior, a large and fertile plain, reaching to the sea at two points. The inland village is delightful, with a castle towering above, its fine Classical gateway, of shining marble, still intact. From there you gaze north to the volcanic saucer of **Nísiros** and spot the distant houses of Nikiá village perched high on the crater's rim. The volcano draws visitors to the island: they may stay longer for its lush fertility and remarkable ancient fortifications.

Out on a limb to the west of Nísiros is **Astipália**, more like the islands of the Cyclades than the Dodecanese. Its isolation contributes greatly to its charm, the white houses of the town tumbling down to the port, with little traffic and places to explore on foot.

Beyond Kos, the local giant, is **Kálimnos**, home of the sponge industry, now almost defunct. An island of contrasts, Kálimnos has a tourist belt on the west coast but the bustling town, theatrically situated above the harbour, makes few concessions to outsiders. The island's bare and barren mountains (including the mass of offshore **Télendos**) contrast sharply with the green and tree-clad valleys and it has some fine Byzantine and medieval monuments, not to mention a famous 'prehistoric' cave.

Léros to the north, formerly an Italian naval base and with public buildings to match, has overcome the opprobrium of recent years caused by conditions in its mental hospital to become a popular destination for people who like fine scenery and a quiet island setting. The island has impressive architecture in contrasting styles, a dominant castle and pervasive historical atmosphere.

Little **Lipsí** is a badly kept secret but the island has retained its quiet and friendly rural charm. **Pátmos**, the furthest north of the Dodecanese, is known above all for its imposing monastery and the Revelation of St John but the charming upper village, the opportunities for uninterrupted walking along its myriad tracks to beaches, to the multicoloured rocks of Lámbi or the pleasant rural outposts of the monastery, give the island a unique blend of sobriety and charm.

A new Blue Guide devoted exclusively to Rhodes and the Dodecanese allows, for the first time, detailed description of this attractive and fascinating region of Greece, which has previously received only limited coverage as part of *Blue Guide Greece*. The topographical and social variety of the islands and the interest of their art, architecture and history, together with the increased pace of research in all these areas, have given additional encouragement to the production of such a book.

Acknowledgements

In spite of the fact that my name appears on the title page, the research, writing and production of this book has been a joint effort. Fieldwork and research has been undertaken on my behalf by **Eleanor Loughlin** (Kárpathos, Kásos, Kastellórizo, Khálki, rural Rhodes) and **Jamie Morton** (Astipálaia, Kálimnos, Kos, Léros, Lipsí, Pátmos). Without their enthusiastic and able assistance *Blue Guide Rhodes and the Dodecanese* would never have appeared. My own contributions are coverage of the other islands and parts of islands, the introductory articles, additional information and editing.

In addition I am extremely grateful to Dick Elliott who has once again put at my disposal the fruits of his long acquaintance with Greece, offering suggestions and corrections of detail, as well as writing the section on the flora of the islands, and parts of the introductory article on Art and Architecture.

Prof. Norman Ashton of the University of Western Australia and Mr Nicholas Pappas helped to amplify the entry on Kastellórizo (and sent me copies of their recent books on the island), Ann Thomas researched the information on sailing in the Dodecanese and checked up other details on my behalf. I am most grateful for hospitality extended by the Ephorate of Prehistoric and Classical Antiquities on Rhodes and, in particular, to Toula Markettou for her help and generosity. I thank, too, the following for information, advice and help of various kinds: John Chapple, Richard Clogg, Gemma Davies, Glenys Davies, Martin Davies, Olga Filaniotou, Carole Hillenbrand, Ruth Macrides, Paul Magdalino, Chris and Christa Mee, Anna Nika, Vasso Patsiadha, Stelios Stefanakis, Lyn Rodley, Judy Tither and Penny Wilson-Zarganis.

R.L.N. Barber
1997

The Guide

The practical information provided at the beginning of the volume aims (i) to help the reader plan and arrange a trip in advance, and (ii) to travel effectively within the Dodecanese on arrival. These two parts are linked by information for travellers who wish to approach the islands via Athens. There follows further information about the practicalities of life in Greece and about various aspects of Greek food, language and customs.

A good deal of emphasis has been placed on providing sources of information, both in Greece and abroad, since these are the only means of getting completely up-to-date information. For each island at least one travel agent has been listed, with telephone/fax number. Even on the smaller islands, local agents are normally well-organised and, in addition to booking local and international tickets, will assist with finding accommodation, hiring cars, booking excursions, changing money and making telephone calls. Their services are strongly recommended. Some islands also have local tourist offices, though the hours can be erratic in smaller centres.

The introductory essays on history and art and architecture offer the visitor a complete overall view of the history and culture of the Dodecanese and help to avoid needless repetition of information within the main text.

The entries for each island give, first, a vignette of the character of the place, then a summary of its geography and history. These are followed by descriptions of the main centres and possible excursions which take in the most interesting or attractive features.

The following symbols are used on the maps in this guide:

mosque

mount

castle/fortification

site

cave

church/monastery

main road

footpath/rough road

Contents

Practical Information

Sources of information

Before you go

Information on any topic connected with visiting Greece can be obtained from the **National Tourist Organisation of Greece** (NTOG); in Greek Εθνικός Οργανισμός Τουρισμού (EOT), which has offices in **London** (4 Conduit Street, W1R 0DJ; tel. 0171 499 9758, 0171 499 4694, fax 0171 287 1369), **New York** (645 Fifth Ave., Olympic Tower, NY 10022; tel. 212 421 5777, fax 212 826 6940), **Los Angeles** (611 West Sixth St., Suite 2198, California 90017; tel. 213 626 6696, fax 213 489 9744) and **Chicago** (168 North Michigan Ave., Suite 600, Illinois 60601; tel. 312 782 1084, fax 312 782 1091). There are also branches in **Canada** (1300 Bay St., Toronto, Ontario M5R 3K8; tel. 416 968 2220, fax 416 968 6533 and 1233 Rue de la Montagne, Suite 101, Montreal, Quebec H3G 1Z2; tel. 514 871 1535, fax 514 871 1498) and **Australia** (51–57 Pitt St., Sydney, NSW 2000; tel. 612 241 1663/4/5; 612 252 1441, fax 612 235 2174), as well as other countries. Leaflets about Rhodes, Kos and the Dodecanese, also Athens and other parts of Greece, and the regularly revised booklet, *General Information About Greece*, are available.

Two excellent English-language travel monthlies—*Greek Travel Pages* and *Hellenic Travelling*, published in Athens but available outside Greece, from BAS Overseas Publications Ltd, Unit 1C, 159 Mortlake Road, Kew, Surrey TW9 4AW—are invaluable for planning travel both to and within Greece, since they contain an extremely wide range of information, giving details of air, rail and bus travel, hotel information (not below C category) and much other useful matter (customs, shop hours, etc.).

For inter-island boat travel the best source is R.F. Poffley, *Greek Island Hopping*, 1995 (regularly updated), although it is essential to bear in mind that routes and frequencies change continually and certainty about timetables is impossible until you are on the spot.

British Sunday (and some evening) newspapers, and the New York Sunday Times, are useful for information about cut-rate travel to Greece.

For **accommodation**, the detailed and comprehensive *Guide to the Greek Hotels*, published annually in mid-March by the Hellenic Chamber of Hotels and available through EOT, gives information about hotels of all categories, with prices.

Advance booking from Britain is most simply done by purchasing a package tour or dealing with a travel agent who has specialist knowledge of and contacts in Greece (see below). Bear in mind that virtually all travel agents will steer you towards establishments with which they already have connections: this can be an advantage in terms of reliability. Choosing and booking accommodation yourself is more difficult, but not impossible. It is easiest with hotels in higher categories which have staff who speak English, and which accept credit card deposits. The best method is to take advantage of the postal booking service provided by the **Hellenic Chamber of Hotels** (publisher of the *Guide to Greek Hotels*). The address is XENEPEL, 24 Stadhíou, Athens 105 64 (tel 01 323 6962; fax 01 322 5449, 01 323 6962). Another possibility is to contact one of the travel agents listed below under individual islands.

For **maps**, Stanfords, of 12 Long Acre, Covent Garden, London, WC2E 9LP; tel, 0171 836 1321, fax. 0171 836 0189, has a good selection, although it is difficult to find thoroughly reliable maps, particularly of the islands, either in England or in Greece. Most islands have maps, of varying quality, available locally. Official maps of the Dodecanese compiled by the Statistical Service and the Army Geographical Service are restricted because of the status of this part of Greece as a frontier zone.

For other background information, see bibliography below.

In the Dodecanese
The National Tourist Organisation has an office in **Rhodes**, at Papágou/Arkhiepiskópou Makaríou, Rhodes; tel. 0241 23655, 23255, 27466; fax 0241 26955. There are local information offices in several islands (see individual entries), mostly open only in season, for on-the-spot advice. Advance information can sometimes be obtained by writing to the town hall (Dhimarkhíon; Δημαρχείον), or contacting one of the travel agents listed under individual islands.

Newspapers
The useful *Rodos News*, giving mainly tourist information, is published occasionally in season and is available free in Rhodes, from the EOT and other outlets. The *Athens News*, a regular English newspaper, is published daily in Athens and is available throughout Greece; another English paper is the weekly *Greek Times*.

Travel agents
Every island has at least one agent (see under individual islands). In addition to booking domestic and international air **tickets**, agents will normally help you find **accommodation**, arrange **car hire** or book places on local **excursions**, change **money** and provide **telephone** facilities.

General information

Prices
These change, and relative values alter so frequently with fluctuations in the exchange rate that prices are rarely quoted in the following pages, though some general estimates of costs in comparison with those prevailing in the UK are given. At present (1996) the exchange rate is favourable to visitors from western Europe and the USA and Greek prices seem reasonable, sometimes cheap.

Season
Climatically the best months to visit Greece are April to mid-June and September

to October. In July and August the average maximum temperature is 32°C, minimum 22°C). The Dodecanese are at the hotter end of the temperature scale and summer daytime temperatures are often in the high 30°s, although these are moderated near the sea or in the mountains of the larger islands. March and November and later months often have surprisingly warm days with long hours of sunshine, but in the earlier part of the year the sea is rarely warm enough for bathing. Equally it can be rainy with chilly evenings until well into April.

Health
Climate and unfamiliar food may cause problems. Elementary precautions are obvious: avoid overexposure to the sun (which burns even when a breeze makes it seem cool), and too much oily food. It is a good idea to carry one or two patent remedies. Rice and lemon juice are good for upset stomachs; chemists can advise on other medicines. Dog bites need immediate treatment by a doctor.

Although Greece has a reciprocal arrangement with the National Health Service (take form E111, available from post offices, if you wish to take advantage of this) and emergency treatment will be given freely, a private insurance policy is advised since the reciprocal system may involve lengthy bureaucratic procedures.

Equipment
Most people require sunglasses in Greece, even in winter. A sun-blocking lotion, a sunhat, and care in exposing yourself to the sun are important, especially in the summer. It is best to have some form of mosquito repellant, though you may not need it: small electrical devices are available from all chemists and supermarkets. A pocket compass can be useful, since many directional indications in the Guide are given by compass points. A light pair of binoculars is good for watching wildlife and for spotting footpaths and elusive monuments. A torch is useful. If travelling informally you might consider taking a small camping stove for hotel-room breakfasts, etc. It is a good idea to carry washing powder, a few clothes pegs and a strong piece of string for a temporary clothes line.

Weights and measures
The French metric system of weights and measures adopted in Greece in 1958, is used with the terms substantially unaltered, thus μέτρο, χιλιόμετρο (khiliómetro), etc. Some liquids are measured by weight (κιλό, kiló), not in litres. The standard unit of land measurement, the *strémma*, is equal to one-tenth of a hectare.

Time and calendar
Greece uses Eastern European Time (two hours ahead of GMT, except for a few weeks in the year when clocks are changed on different dates); π.μ. = a.m. and μ.μ. = p.m. All movable festivals are governed by the fixing of Easter according to the Orthodox calendar.

Public holidays
Official public holidays in Greece are: New Year's Day; 6 January (Epiphany; *Blessing of the Waters*); Katharí Dheftéra ('Clean Monday'), the Orthodox Shrove Day; 25 March (Independence Day); Orthodox Good Friday; Easter Monday; 1

May; Ascension Day; 15 August (Assumption of the Virgin Mary); 12 October (Anniversary of Liberation in 1944); 28 October ('Okhi' Day; rejection of Italian ultimatum in 1940); Christmas Day; 26 December (St Stephen). For the pre-Lenten Carnival, see below under Manners and Customs.

Travelling formalities

Passports
Passports are the only travel documents necessary for American, Australian, Canadian and EU nationals to travel in Greece (note that British Visitors' Passports are no longer available or valid). In the UK, application forms are available from any post office. Passport requests may take some time to process and several weeks should be allowed. If you wish to stay in Greece for longer than three months, you must apply at the end of that period, and not before, for a *permis de séjour* (άδεια παραμονής, ádhia paramonís) from the Aliens' Bureau, Leofóros Alexándras 173, Athens; elsewhere from the local police station. You may be required to submit proof of financial self-sufficiency.

Customs
Normal EU regulations on import/export of goods, alcohol, tobacco, etc. apply. If you bring in valuable items (especially electronic equipment) these may be entered in your passport and re-export required (or else payment of import tax) at the end of the period of stay. This restriction always applies to private cars. To keep a foreign-registered car in Greece for more than four months, you must apply for a permit from the appropriate customs department (Od. Frantzí 14, Athens; tel. 01 922 7316).

The Dodecanese have some special duty concessions on items such as alcohol and umbrellas (note the number for sale in Rhodes!), but these are no longer very significant.

Currency
Drs 100,000 in Greek currency may be imported by foreign nationals but the amount of travellers' cheques etc. is not limited. Foreign banknotes of more than US $1000 must be declared on arrival. Any foreign currency, in whatever form, whose re-export may be desired on departure, must be declared on arrival. Declaration is also necessary if you wish to deposit foreign currency in a foreign exchange account in Greece belonging either to yourself or to a third party. The export limits are Drs 20,000 for foreign visitors; foreign currency up to US $1000, unless provision has been made on arrival (see above).

Getting to the Dodecanese

Whether you travel with a package or independently—and, if the latter, whether you go directly to the Dodecanese or via Athens and mainland Greece—for most travellers, the best method of travel will be by **air**.

Package tours can take in one or more islands. Almost all tour operators offer holidays in Rhodes and Kos, with flights available from most major regional British airports. One tour operator with a good reputation for the Dodecanese, particularly the smaller islands (and winner of a recent *Observer* award for the most honest brochure!), is *Laskarina Holidays* (tel. 01629 824881 for a brochure). Also *Grecofile Filoxenia*, tel. 01422 375999 (specially Léros).

If you want **independent travel**, and consequently greater freedom to organise your movements, there are **scheduled air routes** to Athens (by **British Airways** (tel. 0345 222111), **Olympic Airways** (tel. 0171 409 3400 or 0171 409 2477 for budget travel) and **Virgin Airlines** (tel. 0293 747747) via London; or via Brussels, Amsterdam, or Zurich using various British airlines and/or Belgian, Dutch or Swiss national carriers. These can be continued to Rhodes or Kos, also Astipália, Léros, Kárpathos, Kásos and Kastellórizo by Olympic Airways (Kárpathos, Kásos and Kastellórizo may require a change in Rhodes). Rhodes is also serviced by planes of **Air Greece**. There are no scheduled flights direct to the Dodecanese,

Scheduled flights are often much cheaper out of season and are probably best booked through a good travel agent. Increased competition on the London–Athens route seems to be leading to some reduction in fares. The cheapest scheduled fares usually apply when the ticket is booked well in advance and no change at all is permitted to the dates or times of travel. As there are frequent changes in fare structures, current information should be sought from the airlines. Travel at weekends is more expensive than on weekdays.

If seats are available on the **charter flights** which are mainly geared to package holidays, they may be sold on a 'flight only' basis, through most travel agents or via newspaper advertisements. These flights are direct to the Dodecanese (Kos or Rhodes, occasionally Kárpathos) from a large number of airports. You are however restricted as to season (May to early October) and dates (strictly week-to-week, usually one or two; possibly three or four). Seats are most easily and cheaply obtained early and late in the season; for high season travel you need to book early.

The tour operators mentioned above will also make arramgements for individually planned holidays.

Changing planes in Athens
Since almost all domestic flights in Greece are by Olympic Airways, which has exclusive use of the West Terminal at Athens airport, if you arrive from abroad by any other airline you will have to change terminals for an onward connection within Greece. There is a bus service between the East and West terminals.

Travellers in transit via Athens

Athens airport
Athens Airport is at Ellinikó, 9.5km SE of the city on the coast. There are three terminals, separately approached, one of which is exclusively for charter flights. All scheduled services of foreign airlines use the East Terminal, while Olympic Airways (international and domestic) operate from the West Terminal.

Transport to central Athens and Piraeus

Express bus no. 91 (blue and yellow double-decker) connects all terminals with central Athens (Síntagma and Omónia Squares), every 30 minutes from 06.00 to 21.00, less frequently at other times. Express bus no. 19 connects the terminals with Piraeus (Karaïskáki Square, near the port), every one or two hours from 05.00 to 20.20. There is a direct Olympic Airways bus from the West Terminal to the town terminal in Od. Singroú. Other local bus services pass close to the entrance of the West Terminal. The East Terminal is some distance from the main road. There are **taxi** ranks at each. The fare to central Athens is about Drs 1500 in normal hours: it will be higher during the night and drivers are entitled to make a small charge for luggage carried in the boot.

The main port of Athens is at **Piraeus** (usually referred to in the accusative, 'Piraiá'), 25 minutes from Athens by the Electric Railway (the most central station is below Omónia Square), rather longer by bus (no. 040, green, from Od. Filellínon, near Síntagma Square; every 15 minutes from 05.00 to 24.00, otherwise every hour), or taxi (about Drs 1200).

Tourist information

In Athens there are **National Tourist Organisation of Greece** (NTOG/EOT) offices at 2 Karayeóryi Servías, Síntagma Sq (within the National Bank of Greece); 4 Stadhíou; in the booking hall of the Omónia Underground station; and at the airport. The EOT publishes (weekly, free) *The Week in Athens*, in English and French.

Also in Athens, **telephone information** (any topic) is provided by the Tourist Police (tel. 171) and ELPA, the motoring organisation, (tel. 174). English is spoken.

Hotels

Athens has numerous hotels in all classes. Several of the higher class hotels are around Síntagma Square and in Leofóros Singroú, more modest hotels are around Omónia. Pláka (streets near Síntagma), Thissíon and the area south of the acropolis (Od. Mitséon etc.) are also places worth trying. The Hellenic Chamber of Hotels (publisher of the *Guide to the Greek Hotels*), 24 Stadhíou (tel. 01 3236962) offers a postal booking service. Their desk next to the EOT information counter in the National Bank of Greece in Síntagma (2 Karayeóryi Servías; tel. 01 3237193) offers an on-the-spot service.

Youth hostels

The Greek Youth Hostel Association is at 4 Odhós Dhragatsaníou. There are hostels at 1 Ayíou Meletíou (170 beds; open all year); 2 Alexándras (220 beds; July-Sept only); 20 Ioulianoú (82 beds); 5 Kipsélis (180 beds); 4 Patissíon. In Athens also are the YWCA (11 Odhós Ameríkis) and the YMCA (28 Odhós Omírou), maximum stay ten days, meals extra.

Taxis

In Athens the minimum fare is Drs 200: surcharges operate from a public transport terminal (Drs 200 airport, Drs 60 bus or railway station), during night hours (rural tariff) and at holiday periods (a flat Drs 70 on top of the fare). Outside the city boundary, a higher tariff applies (at present Drs 82 per km).

Radio taxis are reliable and the supplement modest, although the telephone lines are often very busy. Some Athens firms are Ikaros 3214058; Radio Taxi 5132316; Omónia 5021131, 2921910.

By rail
You can travel by rail either through former Yugoslavia (passenger services not operating at time of writing), or by train to an Italian port (Venice, Ancona, Bari or Brindisi) followed by a boat crossing to Greece, arriving at either Igoumenítsa (on the coast opposite Corfú), Pátras (followed by a bus journey of about three hours to Athens) or Piraeus. Timetable and other information about rail travel is available from **British Rail Travel Centres** (best at the larger stations) or BR International enquiries, tel. 0171 834 2345. For sea crossings consult one of the larger travel agents.

In **Athens** the international Lárissa **railway station** can be reached/left by bus 405 from/to Leof. Alexándras, trolley 1 from/to Leof. Amalías or Panepistimíou (passing close to Omónia and Síntagma).

By car
The shortest overland route is c 3150km (1950 miles), via southern Germany, Austria and Yugoslavia (not practicable at present) and takes an absolute minimum of four days. Alternatively, car ferries may be used from one of the Italian ports mentioned above. (The Brindisi route is the fastest, but not necessarily the most pleasant.) **Motorail services** from a Channel port or Paris to southern France or Italy (Milan best) reduce the strain of driving. The services (including route and customs information, and bookings) provided by the AA (tel. 0345 555577) and RAC (tel. 0345 3332220) are essential.

The Athens office of the excellent **Greek motoring organisation (ELPA)** is at the Pírgos Athinón (Vasilíssis Sofías/Mesogeíon 2–4; tel. 01 779 1615, fax 01 778 6642). There are reciprocal arrangements with the organisations of other countries.

By bus
The bus is the least comfortable but no longer a particularly cheap method of getting to Greece. Vehicles travel either direct (not at present) from a Channel port, or via one of the Adriatic ferries. There may or may not be night stops *en route*. The cost of food and accommodation should be taken into account. You should be certain to choose a reliable operator. Information may be obtained from the **National Express** enquiry service (tel. 0990 808080), **Eurolines** (tel. 01582 404511, Mon–Fri 09.00–17.00), student travel agencies, or newspaper advertisements (see above). The journey takes about 3–4 days.

Getting to the Dodecanese from Athens

By sea
Once in Greece (Athens or the islands) you can continue your journey by sea, which is usually the only form of transport *between* islands. If you want to research island ferries in detail a useful book is R.F. Poffley, *Greek Island Hopping,*

published by Thomas Cook and updated annually. In Greece the best source of information for major routes is the daily shipping and financial newspaper *Naftemborikí* (ΝΑΥΤΕΜΒΟΡΙΚΗ) although other newspapers carry lists of departures from Piraeus and Rafína, and (in Athens) there is a recorded telephone announcement of sailings on 143. For local services based in the islands the local Port Office (Limenarkhíon or Limenikós Stathmós; ΛΙΜΕΝΑΡΧΕΙΟΝ or ΛΙΜΕΝΙΚΟΣ ΣΤΑΘΜΟΣ) is the only reliable source. Travel agents will promote the boats with which they are most closely associated and omit to tell you about others.

For overnight travel (and longer day trips) berths (in shared two or four-berth cabins) are a great advantage. Most cabins are either first, second or tourist class: all are usually quite satisfactory, although the higher grades naturally are rather better situated and have better facilities; and tourist class may be best avoided on older vessels. You can often get a cabin on boarding the boat but this is not true of the busy summer months when prior booking is essential. There is no additional charge for a berth: you simply pay the fare appropriate to your chosen class. Make sure that the agent enters a cabin and berth number on your ticket.

The larger islands (Kos, Rhodes) have fast direct services (mostly overnight and with cabins) from Piraeus. Islands of intermediate size usually have at least one daily service from Piraeus in season. The smallest islands are served least frequently (as little as once a week direct in winter, sometimes even less). Kastellórizo must be approached via Rhodes (or another island on the circuit of the *Nísos Kálimnos*; see below). Kásos and Kárpathos are reached via the Cyclades and Crete, or Rhodes. Note that services are less frequent outside the high summer months, and substantially reduced in winter.

Within the Dodecanese the *Nísos Kálimnos* (or a substitute) normally calls at all the islands south of Kálimnos in a twice weekly circuit. Otherwise there are connections (daily in season; less frequently in winter) between Rhodes (town) and Sími; Rhodes (Kámiros Skála) and Khálki; Kos (Kardhámaina) and Nísiros; as well as excursion boats (in season) linking them and other islands. Such day trips can be used for one way journeys, if you wish, though they may be somewhat more expensive than regular services. **Hydrofoils** based on Rhodes and Kos connect most of the islands in season.

By air

There are flights once or twice daily (more to Rhodes) to Astipália, Kos, Léros, Kárpathos (via Rhodes or Crete), Kásos (via Rhodes or Crete) and Kastellórizo (via Rhodes). Kárpathos and Kásos have direct flights two or three times a week. In season seats must be booked well in advance. Capacity is very limited for most islands other than Kos and Rhodes, all of which are served by much smaller aircraft.

Book via travel agents, or (Athens) **Olympic Airways**' excellent telephone service (tel. 01 966 6666) which allows also provisional reservations against a specified time limit. Tickets can be collected from any Olympic office or affiliated travel agent. Addresses of Olympic offices in the islands are given below. **Air Greece** tickets (Athens–Rhodes route only) can be booked by phone in Athens (tel. 01 324 4457/8) or, on Rhodes, through travel agents or at the airport.

Travel on the islands

Buses
Bus services are described under individual islands. Only Rhodes and Kos have town services and, in the smaller islands, even the village buses are very limited. To make the most of your time, it is essential to investigate the times and frequencies as soon as you arrive.

Taxis
Taxis (normally metered) are plentiful in towns but less readily available in the countryside, and the smaller islands may have only one or no taxi at all. Charges are reasonable; about Drs 82 per km in rural areas). Tip by rounding up to the nearest Drs 50; a little more if it has been a long journey.

Taxis are well worth using for excursions: if there is no meter, you negotiate the fare in advance. Price lists are sometimes displayed at ranks. The charge for taking you to your destination, waiting a reasonable time and then bringing you back, is less than for two quite separate trips.

Car hire (self-drive)
There are numerous car hire companies in Greece (details available in the main Sources of Information and from the National Tourist Organisation): major firms include Hertz, Avis, Budget, Holiday Autos. The larger airports have representatives of some companies. Hire cars can be found even on quite small islands, but the vehicles of local operators are not always well kept, and insurance is usually third party only and quite restrictive. Be sure to check before you sign.

Hire in Greece is relatively expensive (in 1996, about £210–280 per week for a small car, with unlimited mileage and inclusive of all taxes, in the high season). Three-day unlimited mileage rates are also available; otherwise the cost is calculated by adding a charge per kilometre to a modest daily rate—this may be the cheapest option if you want the car for convenience rather than covering long distances. It is probably advantageous (though in no way essential) to arrange hire before leaving home: this is easy with international companies. Some travel firms offer inclusive packages with flight, and car on arrival; others provide the option of car hire at a reduced rate. On the spot, reductions can often be negotiated at quieter periods. When calculating rates from hire company leaflets, be sure to include taxes (usually high—about 20 per cent) and any charges for additional insurance cover which is required.

The above remarks apply to the Greek mainland and, in the Dodecanese, to Rhodes and Kos. On small islands, hire is normally arranged on the spot, with the dealer or through a local travel agent, inclusive daily rates are the norm and firms charge from about £27 per day.

Motorcycles, **scooters** and **bicycles** can be hired locally.

Motoring
Driving (on the right) is conducted in a competitive spirit which can be alarming to the visitor and accords Greece the dubious distinction of one of the highest

accident rates in Europe. The Greek motoring organisation ELPA has some representatives on the larger islands only.

Walking

This is a great pleasure in the countryside though it is virtually impossible to
plan walks in any detail, since large scale maps showing footpaths are not generally available. Directions may be sought locally (for useful words, see below on
finding archaeological sites). *Landscapes of Rhodes* (see Bibliography) suggests
some routes on the island; other sources are mentioned in the text below. In
most islands, distances are quite small and directions can be sought locally.

Excursion boats

Apart from boats linking the islands, most islands have local excursion boats in
season, to neighbouring islands, local beaches or other places of interest.

Sailing

Sailing is popular in this part of Greece. Vessels can be hired, with or without
crew, and flotilla holidays are also available. Some useful addresses are: *Yacht
Agency Rhodes (International) Ltd*, PO Box 393, 85100 Rhodes, Greece, tel. 0241
30504/5; 22927; fax 0241 23393; email yar@c+nrhodes (large variety of
yachts for charter; comprehensive range of charts, pilot books and chan-
dlery); *Sunsail International*, The Port House, Port Solent, Portsmouth,
Hampshire, PO6 4TS, tel. 01705 219847; fax 219827; Greek base: Apollonos
12, Palaión Fáliron, 175 61 Athens, Greece, tel. 01 983 6465, 981 9024, 981
5376; fax 01 983 9330. (Sunsail runs a flotilla of 12 Oceanis 320 and Oceanis
350 on two-week cruises out of Kos round islands of the Dodecanese. Some
sailing experience is necessary. The same organisation runs the Kéfalos Club,
based on their hotel at Kéfalos on Kos, which is orientated towards sailing and
windsurfing. The same boats are also available for one-week hire within the
flotilla area, with or without a skipper). *Nautical Club of Rhodes* (Naftikós Omilos
Rhódhou; ΝΑΥΤΙΚΟΣ ΟΜΙΛΟΣ ΡΟΔΟΥ) Plateía Koundouriótou 9; tel.
0241 23287 (dinghy sailing): *Fun and Action*, Rení Koskinoú, Rhodes, tel. 0241
62102 (windsurfing, also at other locations).

Various **watersports** are available on some other islands (see below).

Accommodation

Hotels (Ξενοδοχεία; Xenodhokhía). Lists of hotels can be found in various
Sources of Information (*Greek Travel Pages*, *Hellenic Travelling*, also NTOG
leaflets). The most comprehensive is the *Guide to the Greek Hotels*. Other publications tend not to list hotels in categories below C.

There are six official categories: L, A–E. The de Luxe hotels compare
favourably with their counterparts in other countries. In all hotels of Class A,
most of Class B, many of Class C (especially in Athens) and some of Class D a
proportion of rooms (sometimes all) have a private bath or shower. Class C, at
present the most numerous, is also the most varied. Most Greek hotels do not
have restaurants, unless they are chiefly catering for tourists. Hotels classed D or

E have no public rooms and sometimes only cold water, though their standard of cleanliness and service may well be adequate for a short stay. (F/A = Furnished Apartments.)

Rooms for rent are always to be found in tourist centres. Extremely varied in character and quality, they are often the most economical and pleasant places to stay. On-the-spot inspection is essential. This type of accommodation may include self-catering facilities.

Charges for hotels and rooms are fixed annually by the Government or local authorities. Hoteliers may not exceed the maximum permitted figure; the charge appropriate to each room, quoted with service and taxes included, is displayed on a notice fixed usually to the inside of the door. Central heating or air conditioning is always extra. Considerable reductions can be obtained in November-March.

Despite the official categorisation, hotels can still vary widely. Here, as elsewhere, many hotels are geared to package tours and coach groups rather than to the unexpected overnight guest. Some hotels can legally insist on demi-pension terms, thus tying the visitor to their usually unimaginative restaurants. It is difficult to get single rooms; single occupation of a double room is often charged at the full price, especially in high season.

Charges vary considerably within each category, so that a cheap B-class hotel can be less expensive than a dearer C. It is thus worth investigating establishments which seem at first sight likely to be too expensive. In 1996 (also applicable winter 1996/97), the price range for a twin room in a good C class hotel, with private bath, was about Drs 5000–8000 (£15–£24) (accommodation only). It is advisable to inspect the accommodation before making a definite agreement. Hoteliers are always willing to show rooms and respect an adverse decision.

Booking (see also above Before you go section). In Athens, the Hellenic Chamber of Hotels has a desk next to the National Tourist Organisation information counter in the National Bank of Greece in Síntagma (2 Karayeóryi Servías; tel 3237193), providing an on-the-spot service (Mon–Sat, mornings only). Travel agents will also book hotels or apartments and can, of course, accept deposits. Booking is easiest for accommodation in the higher categories (not below C). Other establishments may agree to hold rooms for you without deposit but are unlikely to give you any leeway if you arrive late at a busy time of year.

Although you can have difficulty finding accommodation on the spot in busy resorts in height of summer, it is rare for the traveller to be completely stranded. In many places people meet boats (and sometimes flights) with offers of rooms (including photographs!). Such accommodation may well be adequate, but can also turn out to be far away or have other disadvantages. If so, you can always decline, or move the next day. Otherwise local travel agents or information offices will always help find accomodation. In remoter areas, the village café is the best source of information.

This information is presented in the following way. The official tourist board category (if any); the name of the hotel; the number of twin-bedded/double-bedded rooms; special facilities; price range; telephone and fax numbers; months open, if seasonal; price range for F/As, where these are offered in addition to normal hotel rooms. The abbreviation NPA=no price available.

The hotels listed in this guide are given as a general indication only of the range of accommodation available throughout the Dodecanese, and should **not** be regarded as the personal recommendations of the author.

Youth hostels

The central office of the Greek Youth Hostel Association is at 4 Odhós Dhragatsaníou, Athens. The GYHA is affiliated to the International Youth Hostels Federation and its hostels may be used by members of any affiliated association. There are many other so-called youth hostels not belonging to the organisation, and which must be investigated on the spot.

Camping sites

These are quite common in the islands (see below), usually unlicensed. The National Tourist Organisation provides a list of official sites.

Food and drink

Places to eat

Places of refreshment are of several types, although in small villages and islands, the functions of all of them are often combined into one.

Cafés (kafenéia) are numerous, serving coffee, soft drinks, and a limited range of alcoholic drinks. The traditional Greek kafeneíon (καφενείον) is an austere establishment usually thronged with male patrons for whom it is both local club and political forum. Coffee (καφέ) is always served in the 'Turkish' fashion with the grounds. It may be drunk heavily sweetened (variglikó), medium (métrio) or without sugar (skhétto). Cafés displaying the sign ΚΑΦΕΝΕΙΟΝ–ΜΠΑΡ (café-bar) also serve drinks.

Zakharoplasteía, properly speaking, are confectioners, selling a wide range of traditional and modern cakes and sweets. Often now they also have the function of a superior type of café or tea-room, serving also alcoholic drinks, and the largest also substantial cold dishes. They are only evident in larger towns.

Occasionally still found is the **galaktopoleíon**, or dairy. It offers the simplest kind of meal, consisting of milk, coffee, bread, butter, honey, etc. Such establishments are becoming rare, while others of a more western type (tea-rooms, fast-food canteens) increasingly common.

The **ouzerí** serves mezédhes (several small dishes, often including seafood such as octopus and shrimps), traditionally with ouzo but most offer also wine, beer and soft drinks. They can be relatively expensive but are often colourful and provide good food.

The distinction between restaurants (εστιατόρια: estiatória) and tavernas (ταβέρνες) is nowadays often unclear. In general, the **tavérna** is less formal, patronised for a convivial evening rather than for lunch and, partly at least, out of doors. A table, once occupied, is often kept for the evening. The **restaurant** is for lunch, which may however last until the early evening. An **exokhikó kéntro** (εξοχικό κέντρο; 'rural centre') combines the functions of café and taverna in a country or seaside setting.

Lunch is usually taken between 13.00 and 15.00 (earlier on Sunday) and dinner (generally the more important) between 20.00 and 23.00 (summer 21.00 and 01.00, or considerably later), though hotels catering particularly for foreigners have a more Western timetable. Restaurants display a menu, showing their category (L, A–D) and the prices of each dish, both basic and with tax and service included. There are usually translations into English. Fixed-price and table d'hôte meals are rare. A service charge is added by law so that any small gratuity to the waiter (on the plate) is a recognition of personal service. The wine boy (mikrós), however, if there is one, receives only what is left for him on the table (about 5 per cent).

Dining out

In the larger centres a few restaurants and de luxe hotels provide an international cuisine. Well-prepared Greek dishes, however, are far preferable to foreign dishes. The basic ingredients are usually excellent and, since all Greeks eat out frequently, you will be well advised always to choose establishments crowded with locals, where the food will be better (and cheaper) and the atmosphere livelier.

Restaurants and taverna meals of comparable standard are considerably cheaper than in Britain. The pattern of meals is also less stereotyped, sharing of portions being quite usual. It is advisable to order each course separately unless you do not mind all the dishes ordered arriving together. It is usual to visit the kitchens to choose food and, in waterside tavernas, fish can be selected from the ice and then weighed, the price appearing on the menu per kilo.

The oily content of most Greek food is too exuberant for some tastes, though many cooks now take care to appease foreigners' palates, and the local wine is a good counter-agent. Frozen foods (still relatively rare in Greece) must be indicated by law on the menu with the letters KAT.

Good table wines (unresinated, *arretsínoto*), both red and white, are obtainable in bottle everywhere and some of the better-known have a nation-wide distribution. *Retsína*, the resinated white wine, characteristic particularly of Attica and the Peloponnese but obtainable everywhere, has lost some of its former popularity as other wines have improved. It can always be obtained in bottle, but the traditional can or jug from the barrel is to be preferred, when available. Beer (of Bavarian type) is brewed in Greece and other lagers are brewed under licence or imported. The ordinary water is usually safe, but mineral waters from spas such as Loutráki are ubiquitous and may be preferable in some places.

Food

The favourite Greek apéritif is *oúzo*, a strong colourless drink made from grape-stems and flavoured with aniseed; it is served with *mezé/mezédhes*, snacks consisting of anything from a simple slice of cheese or tomato or an olive to pieces of smoked eel or fried octopus.

As in Italy a Greek meal can begin with a foundation course of rice, such as *piláfi sáltsa*, or of pasta (*makarónia*), perhaps baked with minced meat (*pastítsio*) or with *tirópita* (cheese pie). Alternatives are soup or hors d'oeuvre, the latter being particularly good. *Taramosaláta* is a paste made from the roe of grey mullet and olive oil. *Tzatzíki* is composed of chopped cucumber in yoghurt heavily flavoured with garlic.

The main course may be meat (κρέας, kréas), or fish or a dish on a vegetable base, baked (τού φούρνου, too foúrnu), boiled (βραστό, vrastó), fried (τηγανιτό, tiganitó), roast (ψητό, psitó), or grilled (σχάρας, skháras). The chef's suggestions will be found under πιάτα της ημέρας (piáta tis iméras; dishes of the day). Moussaká consists of layers of aubergines, minced beef, and cheese, with butter and spices, baked in the oven. Many foreign dishes may appear in transliteration, e.g.: εσκαλόπ (escalope), Σνίτσελ Χόλσταϊν (Schnitzel Holstein), Μπιντόκ αλα Ρους (Bintók a la Russe), Κρέμ Καραμελέ (crème caramelle), Σαλάτ ντέ φρουῖ (salade de fruits).

Many sweets have Turkish names, and 'shish kebab' is frequently used as a synonym for souvlákia, pieces of meat grilled on a skewer. Also cooked in this fashion is kokorétsi, which consists of alternate pieces of lamb's liver, kidney, sweetbreads, and heart, wrapped in intestines. When not grilled, meat is often stewed with oil in chunks (κοκκινιστό; kokkinistó). Of Greek cheeses, the ubiquitous féta (goat's cheese) is better eaten, peasant-fashion, with black pepper, oil and rígani (oregano) than on its own.

Sweets are elaborate and varied, though more often taken separately than as a course of a meal. Among the most popular are baklavás, composed of layered pastry filled with honey and nuts; kataïfíwheat shredded and filled with sweetened nuts; and galaktoboúreko, pastry filled with vanilla custard.

The following **menu** contains a number of the simpler dishes to be found.

ΟΡΕΚΤΙΚΑ (Orektiká), Hors d'oeuvre

Διάφορα ορεκτικά (dhiáfora orektiká), Hors d'oeuvre variés

Ταραμοσαλάτα (taramosaláta), see above

Ντολμάδες Γιαλαντζή (dolmádhes Yalantzí), Stuffed vine leaves served hot with egg-lemon sauce

Ντολμαδάκια (dolmadhákia), Cold stuffed vine leaves

Ελιές (elliés), Olives

ΣΟΥΠΕΣ (Soúpes), Soups

Σούπα αυγολέμονο (soúpa avgholémono), Egg and lemon soup

Σούπα άπο χόρτα (soúpa ápo hórta), Vegetable soup

Μαγειρίτσα (maghirítsa), Tripe soup generally with rice (Easter speciality)

Ψαρόσουπα (psarósoupa), Fish soup

ΖΙΜΑΡΙΚΑ (Zimárika), Pasta and Rice dishes

Πιλάφι σάλτσα (piláfi sáltsa), Rice with sauce

Σπαγέτο σάλτσα με τυρί (spagéto sáltsa me tirí), Spaghetti, with sauce and cheese

Μακαρόνια (makarónia), Macaroni

ΨΑΡΙΑ (Psária), Fish

Στρίδια (strídhia), Oysters

Συναγρίδα (sinagrídha), Sea bream

Μπαρμπούνια (barboúnia), Red mullet

Μαρίδες (marídhes), Whitebait

Αστακός (astakós), Lobster

Γαρίδες (garídhes), Scampi (Dublin Bay prawns)

Καλαμαράκια (kalamarákia), Baby squids

Κταπόδι (ktapódhi), Octopus

Λιθρίνια (lithrínia), Bass

ΛΑΔΕΡΑ (ladherá), Vegetables or ΧΟΡΤΑ (khórta), Greens

Πατάτες τηγανιτές (patátes tiganités), Fried potatoes

Φασολάκια φρ. βουτ. (fasolákia voútiro), Beans in butter

Μπισέλλια (biséllia), Peas

Ντομάτες γεμιστές (domátes yemistés), Stuffed tomatoes

ΑΥΓΑ (Avgá), Eggs
Ομελέττα Ζαμπόν (Omelétta Zambón),
Ham omelette
Αυγά Μπρουγέ (avgá 'brouillé'),
Scrambled eggs
Αυγά α λα Ρούς (avgá 'á lá Russe'),
Eggs with Russian salad

ΕΝΤΡΑΔΕΣ (Entrádhes), Entrées
Αρνάκι φασολάκια (arnáki fasolákia),
Lamb with beans
Μοσχάρι (moskhári), Veal
Σικοτάκια (sikotákia), Liver
Κοτόπουλο (kotópoulo), Chicken
Χήνα (khína), Goose
Παπί (papí), Duck
Τσουτσουκάκια (tsoutsoukákia),
Meat balls in tomato sauce
Κοτολέττες χοιρινές (kotolettés
khirinés), Pork cutlets

ΣΧΑΡΑΣ (skháras), Grills
Σουβλάκια άπο φιλέτο (souvlákia
ápo filéto), shish kebab (see above)
Μπριζόλες μοσχ. (brizóles moskh.),
Veal chops
Κεφτέδες Σχάρας (keftédhes skháras),
Grilled meat balls
Γουρουνόπουλο ψητό (gourounópoulo
psitó), Roast sucking-pig
Παιδάκια χοιρινά (paidhákia khiriná),
Pork chops

ΣΑΛΑΤΕΣ (salátes), Salads
Ντομάτα σαλάτα (domáta saláta),
Tomato salad
Μαρούλι (maroúli), Lettuce
Ραδίκια (radhíkia), Radishes
Κολοκυθάκια (kolokithákia), Courgettes
Αγγουράκι (angouráki), Cucumber
Αγκινάρες (ankináres), Artichokes
Μελιζάνες (melizánes), Aubergines
(eggplants)
Πιπεριές (piperiés), Green peppers
Ρώσσικη (Russikí), Russian

ΤΥΡΙΑ (tiriá), Cheeses
Φέτα (féta), Soft white cheese of goat's
milk

Κασέρι (kasséri), Hard yellow cheese
Γραβιέρα (graviéra), Greek gruyère
Ροκφόρ ('Roquefort'), Blue cheeses
generally

ΓΛΥΚΑ (gliká), Sweets
Χαλβάς (halvás), halvás
Μπακλαβάς (baklavás), see above
Καταίφι (kataïfi), see above
Γαλακτομπούρεκο (galaktoboúreko),
see above
Ρυζόγαλο (rizógalo), Rice pudding
Γιαούρτι (yiaoúrti), Yoghurt

ΦΡΟΥΤΑ (froúta), Fruits
Μήλο (mílo), Apple
Μπανάνα (banána), Banana
Αχλάδι (akhládhi), Pear
Πορτοκάλι (portokáli), Orange
Κεράσια (kerásia), Cherries
Βύσσινα (víssina), Black cherries
Φράουλες (fráoules), Strawberries
Δαμάσκηνα (dhamáskina), Plums
Ροδάκινα (rodhákina), Peaches
Βερύκοκα (veríkoka), Apricots
Πεπόνι (pepóni), Melon
Καρπούζι (karpoúzi), Water-melon

MISCELLANEOUS
Ψωμί (psomí), Bread
Βούτυρο (voútiro), Butter
Αλάτι (aláti), Salt
Πιπέρι (pipéri), Pepper
Μουστάρδα (moustárdha), Mustard
Λάδι (ládhi), Oil
Ξίδι (Xídhi), Vinegar
Γάλα (ghála), Milk
Ζάχαρι (zákhari), Sugar
Παγωτό (paghotó), Ice Cream
Λεμόνι (lemóni), Lemon

ΑΝΑΨΥΚΤΙΚΑ (anapsiktiká), Soft
drinks
Νερό (neró), water
Ένα ποτήρι (éna potíri), a glass
Ένα μπουκάλι (éna boukáli), a bottle
Παγωμένο (pagoméno), iced
Καφέ (café), coffee
Ελληικό (ellinikó), Greek (see above)

Φίλτρο/γαλλικό (fíltro/gallikó), filter coffee
Εσπρέσσο (esprésso), espresso
Καπουτσίνο (kapoutsíno), capucchino
Νές (nés), Nescafé
Φραπέ (frappé), frappé
Με/χωρίς γάλα/ζάχαρη (mé/khorís gála/zákhari), with/without milk/sugar
Τσαï (tsáï), tea

Τσαï του βουνού (tsáï tou vounoú), mountain (herbal), tea
Χαμόμηλο (khamómilo), camomile
Πορτοκαλάδα (portokaládha), orangeade
Λεμονάδα (lemonádha), lemonade
Κόκα-Κόλα (kóka-kóla), Coca-Cola
Χυμός (khimós), fruit juice (may or may not be freshly pressed)

Wine
Wine (Κρασί; krasí) in Greece is generally good, and stronger than French wine. The two basic categories are resinated and unresinated. *Retsína*, flavoured with resin from pine trees, is most characteristic of the south and, to the experienced palate, varies as much in taste and quality as do unresinated wines. Although a great amount is bottled, *retsína* is better drunk young from the cask. Rosé varieties, called *kokinélli* (κοκκινέλλι), are locally much sought after. There is a large variety of wines, white (άσπρο, áspro), red (μάνρο, mávro, literally 'black'), or rosé (kókkivo, literally 'red').

There are good draught red wines from Nemea, Rhodes and Corfu. It is invidious to recommend bottled wines from the vast range available but some of the following may be sampled: Hymettus (red and white), Santa Elena (white), Pallíni (white), Vílitsa (white), Zítsa (white, semi-sparkling), Sámaina (white), Castel Daniélis (red), Tsántali (white, rosé), Náoussa (red), Robólla (white). The latter three are rather more expensive but no Greek wine is costly by British standards. The wines of the Carrás estate are also good.

In the Dodecanese the wines of Rhodes are particularly well known. The champagne of the island is pleasant; Chevalier de Rhodes is an excellent red.

Services and facilities

Emergency services
Police, tel. 100; **fire**, tel. 199; **ambulance**, tel. 166. Local services on each island have their own numbers.

Consulates
British Consul, British Embassy, 1 Od. Ploutárkhou, Athens; tel. 01 723 6211–19; British Vice-Consul, 23 Od. 25 Martíou, Rhodes; tel. 0241 27247, 27306. **USA Consul**, USA Embassy, 91 Leofóros Vasilíssis Sofías, Athens; tel. 01 721 2951–9, 721 8400–1. **Australian Consul**, 37 Dhimitríou Soútsou St., 115 21 Athens; tel. 01 644 7303. **Canadian Consul**, 4 l. Genadhíou St., 115 21 Athens; tel. 01 723 9511, fax 01 724 7123.

Banks and changing money
There are numerous **banks** (standard hours 08.00–14.00 (13.30 Fridays); closed Saturday and Sunday); some branches in tourist centres have longer hours

and weekend opening). Cash machines are still fairly thin on the ground except in larger centres, but can be used to get money with recognised credit cards or an appropriate local account. **Bureaux de change** are operated by some **travel agents**, and **hotels** will often change money, though it is advisable to ensure that the proper rate is being offered and that commission charges are not excessive. **Post offices** may also be used (very useful in out-of-the-way places).

Travellers' cheques are undoubtedly the easiest way of carrying funds. Major credit cards are accepted by a fair number of establishments but are sometimes regarded with suspicion, especially in more remote places. If you require an **emergency transfer** of funds, banks can be unhelpful and slow, but there are other providers such as *Western Union* (UK enquiries 0800 833 833) or, for Girobank account holders only, *Eurogiro* (0151 966 2794).

Postal services

Most post offices (Ταχυδρομείο: Takhidhromío; yellow signs) open at 07.30, close at 14.00, and do not open at weekends. Some in larger centres have longer and weekend opening. Letter boxes (γραμματοκιβότια) are yellow. Postage stamps are obtainable at some kiosks and shops as well as post offices (10 per cent surcharge). A transit period of 4–5 days to the United Kingdom is normal but there are often considerable delays to post (especially postcards) in the summer season and internal mail is not exempt from problems. The charge for Express letters is reasonable and usually ensures delivery in the UK two days after posting. A registered (συστημένο) letter is 'éna sistiméno grámma'. Correspondence marked POSTE RESTANTE (to be called for) may be sent to any post office and collected by the addressee on proof of identity (passport preferable). A small fee may be charged. The surname of the addressee should be clearly written, and no 'Esq.' added. Parcels are not delivered in Greece. They must be collected from the post office, where they are subject to handling fees, full customs charges, and often to delay.

Telephones

Card-phone cubicles are ubiquitous and the most convenient way of making all calls, including international. Cards (THΛΕΚΑΡΤΑ, tilékarta) of 100 or 500 units (at present Drs 13 per unit) can be bought from many shops and kiosks. Long-distance calls can also be made from most hotels, many kiosks, and any other establishment which has a meter (μετρητή: metrití) attached to the telephone. The meter records the number of units and payment is made accordingly. The charge per unit is fixed—lowest at OTE, slightly higher at kiosks and shops, highest in hotels. The cheap rate periods are 22.00 to 06.00 (UK), 23.00 to 08.00 (USA) and 22.00 to 08.00 (Greece). International calls are, at present charges and exchange rates, about 25 per cent higher than in the UK. There is international direct dialling. Otherwise, for Greek long-distance calls, dial 132: international 161; telegrams: domestic 155, international 165. Police 100. Time 141 (in Greek).

Local calls can be made from most other phones, in shops, kiosks etc., on payment of the small charge.

The Greek telephone and telegraph services are run by a public corporation, the OTE (always referred to by its acronym 'ό' té'), which is quite separate from the postal authority. Only major offices have a 24-hour service. Offices are listed individually where separate establishments exist; otherwise they may be in a local kafeneío.

The availability of card and metered phones means that it is not usually necessary to visit an OTE centre to make a long-distance call (either domestic or international).

Shops

Shops are open in summer 08.00–13.30 and 17.30–20.30 on Tuesday, Thursday and Friday; 08.00–14.30 only, on Monday, Wednesday and Saturday. In winter 08.30–13.30 and 17.00–20.00 on Tuesday, Thursday and Friday; 08.30–14.30 on Monday, Wednesday and Saturday. Supermarkets have a special status, opening 08.00–21.00 daily, except Sunday. Some kinds of shop (e.g. dry cleaners) never open in the evening or on Saturdays. In rural areas— indeed anywhere outside the major cities—the hours are more flexible.

The **períptero** (περίπτερο), or kiosk, developed from a French model, is a characteristic feature of Greek life. Selling newspapers, reading matter, postcards, cigarettes, chocolate, toilet articles, roll film, postage stamps, etc., some kiosks are open for about 18 hours a day.

Foreign newspapers are obtainable in the larger islands on the day following publication at about three times the home price; and less regularly elsewhere. For *Athens News*, see above, under sources of information.

Duty chemists rotas are listed the press, in shop windows or may be discovered by dialling 173 on the telephone. In smaller communities the pharmacist, if there is one, will always dispense in an emergency.

Archaeological authorities

Ephorate of Prehistoric and Classical Antiquities, Plateía Aryirokástrou, Rhodes. *Ephorate of Byzantine Antiquities*, Od. Ippotón, Rhodes

Museums, archaeological sites, churches, etc.

Ancient remains of any significance are usually signposted and the sites enclosed. An admission charge is normally made, the amount varying with the importance of the place concerned. Students are allowed free entry on production of an ISIC (International Student Identity card), supported by proof of nationality of an EU member state (the latter rarely requested).

Opening hours of sites and museums vary in accordance with the season, the importance of the antiquities and local conditions. Museums (but not sites) are closed on Mondays. For smaller sites/museums, it is advisable to reckon on opening hours of 08.30–13.00, for absolute safety. In fact the closing time is usually about 15.00 and, at the more important centres, as late as 17.00 for museums and 19.00 for sites. The National Tourist Organisation in Athens provides an information sheet on opening hours, as do the sources of information (above). Museums not belonging to the state do not conform to these arrangements.

Sites and museums are closed on 1 January, 25 March, Good Friday morning, Easter Day and Christmas Day. Hours are restricted on Christmas Eve, New Year's Eve, 2 January, 5 January, the last Saturday of Carnival, Thursday in Holy Week, Easter Tuesday. At major sites, where the number of visitors can detract considerably from your pleasure in the tourist season, it is highly desirable to begin your visit at opening time in the morning, before the large parties arrive. The antiquities can then be viewed at reasonable leisure and the surroundings enjoyed.

In general photography (hand cameras) is free on archaeological sites, and allowed (except where unpublished material is on display) in museums on purchase of a second ticket for the camera. ΑΠΑΓΟΡΕΥΕΤΑΙ (apagorévetai) means forbidden. Set fees (not cheap) are charged for using tripods, etc.

The Greek Antiquities Service treats its visitors' safety as their own responsibility. The very nature of archaeological sites ensures the maximum number of objects that can be tripped over: excavation trenches are often unfenced, and heights unguarded by railings. It is particularly dangerous to move about while reading or sighting a camera.

Assistance beyond that given in the text can usually be canvassed on the spot with the use of the following vocabulary: '*yiá*' (towards) '*ta arkhaía*'('ancient things'), '*to kástro*' (any fortified height), '*tis anaskafés*' (excavations), '*to froúrio*' (medieval castle). Licensed guides are available on some major sites.

Orthodox churches (sometimes open) can be visited at any reasonable hour. When they are closed ask for the key which is usually with the priest in the nearest village, sometimes in a nearby house. Visitors should be respectably dressed: women are expected to wear skirts (often provided on the spot).

Antiquities. The regulations to protect Greece's heritage are strictly enforced. Importation of antiquities and works of art is free, but such articles should be declared on entry so that they can be re-exported. Except with special permission, it is forbidden to export antiquities and works of art (dated before 1830) which have been obtained in any way in Greece. If a traveller's luggage contains antiquities not covered by an export permit, the articles are liable to be confiscated and prosecution may follow. Note that the use of metal detectors is strictly forbidden in Greece and it is an offence to remove any object, however seemingly insignificant, from an archaeological site.

Diving and underwater photography are not permitted in most parts of Greece (leaflet from the NTOG) and attempts to locate, photograph or remove antiquities are strictly forbidden.

Manners and customs

When making an appointment it is advisable to confirm that it is an 'English rendezvous', i.e. one to be kept at the hour stated. The siesta hours after lunch (often late, up till c 19.00) should not be disturbed by calling or telephoning.

Attention should be paid to the more formal conventions of Greeks: the handshake at meeting and parting is de rigueur, and inquiry after the health taken seriously. The correct reply to καλώς ωρίσατε *kalós orísate* (welcome) is καλώς σας βρήκαμε *kalós sas vríkame* (glad to see you). To the inquiry τί κάνετε, *ti kánete* (how do you do?) or πως είσθε; *pos ísthe* (how are you?) the reply should be καλά ευχαριστώ, και σεις *kalá efkharistó, ke sis* (well, thank you—and you?)—or έτσι καί έτσι *étsi ke étsi* (so-so).

General greetings are χαίρετε *khérete* (greetings, hallo), γειάσας *yásas* (hello, goodbye—lit: your health) and στο καλό *sto kaló* (keep well), both useful for greeting strangers on the road. Περαστικά, *perastiká* is a useful word of comfort in time of sickness or misfortune meaning 'may things improve'.

Except in the centre of Athens it is still customary to greet shopkeepers, the company in cafés, etc., with καλημέρα *kaliméra* (good day) or καλησπέρα *kalispéra* (good evening). Σας παρακαλώ *sas parakaló* (please) is used when asking for a favour or for information, but not when ordering something which is to be paid for, when θά ήθελα *tha íthela* (I should like) is more appropriate. The Greek for yes is *ne* or, more formally, *málista*, for no, *ókhi*. Addío (goodbye, so long) in Greek has none of the finality of its Italian origin.

In direct contrast to English custom, personal questions showing interest in a stranger's life, politics and money are the basis of conversation in Greece. You should not be offended at being asked in the most direct way about your movements, family, occupation, salary and politics, though you will usually find discussion of the last singularly inconclusive.

By Greek custom the bill for an evening out is invariably paid by the host; the common foreign habit of sharing out payment round the table is looked upon as mean and unconvivial, and visitors valuing their 'face' will do it discreetly elsewhere. A stranger is rarely allowed to play host to a native.

It is not good manners to fill a wine-glass, nor to drain a glass of wine poured for you, the custom being to pour it half full and keep it 'topped up'. Glasses are often touched with the toast εις υγείαν σας, your health (generally shortened in speech to the familiar *yásas* or *yámas*, or, to a single individual, *yásou)*; the glasses are then raised to the light, the bouquet savoured, and the wine sipped before drinking (thus all five senses have been employed in the pleasure).

When visiting a Greek house you may formally be offered preserves with coffee and water. Strictly to conform to custom the water should be drunk first, the preserves eaten and the spoon placed in the glass, and the coffee drunk at leisure. Payment must, of course, never be offered for any service or hospitality. An acceptable way of reducing an obligation is by making a present to a child of the house. Equally hospitality should not be abused; those offering it frequently have less resources than their foreign guest—even the proverbially poor student.

The 'Volta', or evening parade, universal throughout provincial Greece, has no fixed venue in Athens. Fasting is taken seriously in Lent.

Carnival after three weeks' festivities reaches its peak on the Sunday before Clean Monday with processions and student revels. It is particularly celebrated in Pátras, Náoussa, and, in Athens, in Pláka. Procession of a shrouded bier (Epitáfios) takes place on **Good Friday**; there is ceremonial lighting of the Paschal candle and release of doves, in front of churches at midnight preceding **Easter Sunday**; the conventional greeting is *Chrístos anésti* (Christ is risen) and the reply *Alíthos anésti* (He is risen indeed). This is followed by candlelight processions and 'open house'. The roasting of Paschal lambs and the cracking of Easter eggs take place on the morning of **Easter Day**. These ceremonies are performed with official pomp in the capital. **Okhi Day** commemorating the Greek 'no' (όχι) to the Italian ultimatum of 1940, is celebrated with remembrance services and military processions, especially in Thessaloníki.

Language

A knowledge of ancient Greek is a useful basis, but no substitute for the study of modern Greek. Apart from the unfamiliarity of modern pronounciation, many of the commonest words (e.g. for water, wine, fish) no longer come from the same roots. Fluency in modern Greek adds greatly to the ease and pleasure of travelling—even brave attempts can be of some practical help and will certainly help you make contact with ordinary people and win you friends. English is understood everywhere on the main tourist routes.

A knowledge of the Greek alphabet, at least, is highly desirable, since otherwise some street names, bus destination plates, etc. may be unintelligible. A successful introduction to modern Greek is D.A. Hardy, *Greek language and people* (BBC publications, 1983 and many reprints; cassettes available but not essential).

The Greek alphabet now as in later classical times comprises 24 letters: Αα, Ββ, Γγ, Δδ, Εε, Ζζ, Ηη, Θθ, Ιι, Κκ, Λλ, Μμ, Νν, Ξξ, Οο, Ππ, Ρρ, Σσ (ς when final in lower case), Ττ, Υυ, Φφ, Χχ, Ψψ, Ωω.

Vowels
There are five basic vowel sounds in Greek to which even combinations written as diphthongs conform: α is pronounced very short; ε and αι as *e* in egg (when accented more open, as in the first *e* in there); η, ι, υ, ει, οι, υι have the sound of *ea* in eat; ο, ω as the *o* in dot; ου as English *oo* in pool. The combinations αυ and ευ are pronounced *av* and *ev* when followed by loud consonants (*af* and *ef* before mute consonants).

Consonants
Consonants are pronounced roughly as their English equivalents with the following exceptions: β = *v*; γ is hard and guttural before *a* and *o* like the English *g* in hag, before other vowels approaching the *y* in your; γγ and γκ are usually equivalent to *ng*; δ = *dh* as in this; θ as *th* in think; before an *i* sound λ resembles the *lli* sound in million; ξ has its full value always, as in ex-king; ρ is always rolled; σ (ς) is a sibilant as in oasis; τ is pronounced half way between *t* and *d*; φ = ph or f; χ akin to the Scottish *ch*, a guttural *h*; ψ = *ps* as in lips. The English sound *b* is represented in Greek by the double consonant μπ, *d* by ντ. All Greek words of two syllables or more have one accent which serves to show the stressed syllable. The classical breathing marks are never written and have no significance in speech. In the termination ον, the *n* sound tends to disappear in speech and the ν is often omitted in writing.

Transliteration
On the subject of Greek place-names, Colonel Leake wrote 150 years ago 'It is impossible in any manner to avoid inconsistency'. Many recent writers on Greece have tried to make a virtue of 'the avoidance of pedantry', but even pedantry is preferable to chaos, and some measure of consistency must be attempted, even if doomed to incomplete success. Modern Greek is not the same language as ancient Greek, and in any case many modern places in Greece have names derived from Albanian, Turkish, or 'Frankish' roots. The most acceptable

compromise is gained by using one set of rules for modern place-names, and another for those of ancient times.

Names of modern localities have been transliterated in accordance with the phonetic system codified by the Permanent Committee on Geographical Names (E. Gleichen and J.H. Reynolds, *Alphabets of Foreign Languages*, P.C.G.N. for British Official Use, London 1951, pp 52–56), used by NATO and by professional and archaeological journals. Though this results sometimes in visual ugliness, and for those with a knowledge of Greek increasing irritation (disguising the familiar apparently unnecessarily: thus Khloí, for Chloë) it has three merits: a great measure of alphabetical consistency for indexing; easy cross-reference to most official maps and to original excavation reports; and the possibility for non-Greek speakers of producing a recognisable approximate pronunciation. Where the result has seemed intolerably *outré* and where there is a recognised and familiar English version (e.g. Rhodes), this has been used, at least in all subsidiary references.

Ancient names have been given in the traditional English form used by classical scholars and archaeologists, preferring the purely English form where this exists (e.g. Aristotle, Homer), and the Latin form where this has become accepted everyday English usage: e.g. Boeotia, not Boiotia; Plato, not Platon. In other instances the form nearest to the ancient Greek has generally been preferred (with k for κ, rather than the misleading c), and (e.g.) Sounion rather than Sunium.

This duality, though producing inconsistencies between ancient and modern (e.g. respectively ch and kh for χ), highlights the pitfall that the modern place bearing the equivalent of a Classical name is not necessarily in the location of its ancient counterpart. Where they are coincident, some compromise is necessary: Christians should remember the Beroea of St. Paul but, when travelling there, think of the modern town as Vérria.

It should be pointed out that, until the recent designation of demotic Greek as opposed to katharévousa (formal Greek) as the state language, place-names had often both a katharévousa and a demotic form (αι Αθήναι, η Αθήνα for Athens). Formal versions of place-names may occasionally linger on old signs. Neither modern form is necessarily the ancient form: thus, Thorikos, anciently ή Θόρικος has become ο Θορικός. In addition **all** place-names, like other nouns, decline; this often produces a change of stress as well as of inflexion. Some places have their more familiar spoken form in the accusative (given, where thought desirable, in the text), though they appear on maps in the nominative; places ending in -on usually drop the 'n' in speech, sometimes the whole syllable. Street names are in the genitive when called after a person, e.g. Ermoú (of Hermes), also in the genitive when leading to a place, e.g. Patissíon (to Patíssia).

As in English, a church may be spoken of by the name of its saint in the nominative or genitive. In the vexing instance where the Greek name is in itself a transliteration from Roman characters, each example has been treated on its apparent merits. Thus Βερανζέρου (which in Greek pronunciation bears little resemblance to the Fr. *Béranger*) has been rendered Veranzérou; Βύρωνος similarly has been rendered Víronos by sound since Lord Byron properly appears in Greek literary criticism as Μπάϋρον. Names of modern Greeks have been rendered where possible as their owners transliterated them, or as arbitrary custom has demanded.

No consistency can be attempted in the language or spelling of hotel names, since they are often chosen quite arbitrarily themselves. What is displayed on the building may well not correspond with the name listed in the hotel guide—only experience can help in the realisation that (e.g.) Ilios, Helios and Soleil designate the same hotel (Ηλιος), or that Mont Blanc and Lefkón Oros are one and the same.

In this book, at its first mention, a place-name is given also in Greek, where the difference from English may make this an aid to reading maps and road signs. On main roads signposts are printed in Greek and Roman characters (but inevitably not in a consistent transliteration). Ancient names, if accented, have been given their modern stress, where this may be a help in asking directions. Breathings are only printed for ancient Greek. Accents on initial vowels are not given, in accordance with modern practice.

FURTHER READING

Books about The Dodecanese

Guides to and books about individual islands are normally mentioned in the main text; books listed here have a wider relevance.

S. Dietz (ed.), *Archaeology in the Dodecanese* (National Museum of Denmark, 1988).

N. Doumanis, *Myth and memory in the Mediterranean: the Italian Dodecanese*, Macmillan (Australia), forthcoming (1997).

P. M. Fraser and G.E. Bean, *The Rhodian Peraea and islands* (OUP, 1954).

Pauline Johnstone, *A guide to Greek island embroidery* (HMSO, 1972; with good references in the fields of embroidery, costume and folk arts).

Chr. Karouzos, *Rhodes* (Hesperos, Athens, 1973).

R.E. Kasperson, *The Dodecanese: diversity and unity in island politics* (Chicago University Press, 1966).

E. Kollias, *The Knights of Rhodes: the palace and the city* (Ekdotike Athenon, 1991).

G. Konstantinopoulos, Αρχαία Ρόδος (Cultural Foundation of the National Bank of Greece, Athens, 1986).

R. Matton, *Rhodes*, (Collection de l'Institut Français d'Athènes, Villes et paysages de Grèce, 1959).

G. Merker, *The Hellenistic sculpture of Rhodes* (Studies in Mediterranean Archaeology no. 40, Göteborg, 1973).

N. Rochford, *Landscapes of Rhodes* (Sunflower Books, London, 1994, rev. ed.; good for walks).

M.D. Volonakis, *The island of Roses and her eleven sisters*, London, 1922.

A. Ταρσούλη, Δωδεκάνησα, Athens, 1947–1950; a major source of information, with many illustrations).

Articles on all aspects of Dodecanesian history, ethnography, art and archaeology can be found in the Greek periodical Δωδεκανησιακά Χρονικά.

Art, archaeology and history of Greece

Prehistory. Sinclair Hood, *The arts in prehistoric Greece* (Pelican History of Art,
1978).
History. A.R. Burn, *A traveller's history of Greece: the Pelican history of Greece*
(Pelican, 13th rev. edn, 1982).
R. Clogg, *A concise history of Greece* (Cambridge University Press, 1992).
C. Foss and P. Magdalino, *Rome and Byzantium* (Elsevier-Phaidon, Making of the
Past series, 1977).
A. P. Kazhdan *et al.* (eds), *The Oxford Dictionary of Byzantium* (Oxford University
Press, 1991).
Peter Lock, *The Franks in the Aegean* (Longman, 1995).
A. Luttrell, *The hospitallers in Cyprus, Rhodes, Greece and the West* (London, 1978).
W. Miller, *The Latins in the Levant* (J. Murray, 1908).
Art and archaeology. C.M. Robertson, *A shorter history of Greek art*
(Cambridge University Press, 1981).
A.W. Lawrence, *Greek architecture* (Pelican History of Art, 1968).
R.R.R. Smith, *Hellenistic sculpture: a handbook* (Thames and Hudson, World
History of Art series, 1991).
D.E. Strong, *Roman art* (Pelican History of Art, 1976).
F. Sear, *Roman architecture* (Batsford, 1982).
D. Talbot Rice, *Art of the Byzantine era* (Thames and Hudson, 1963).
A.P. Kazhdan et al. (eds.), as above.
R. Krautheimer, *Early Christian and Byzantine architecture* (Pelican History of
Art, 1975).
L. Rodley, *Byzantine art and architecture: an introduction* (Cambridge University
Press, 1994).
Archaeological sources. R.J. Stillwell (ed.), *The Princeton encyclopaedia of
Classical sites*, (Princeton University Press, 1976); useful summary descriptions
of ancient sites and areas (including individual islands), with good references.
British School at Athens/Society for the Promotion of Hellenic Studies,
Archaeological Reports (an annual, and somewhat technical, survey of recent
discoveries in Greece and its ancient colonies). Enquiries to the Secretary,
Hellenic Society, 31-34 Gordon Square, London WC1H 0PY.
There are several articles in English (published in the Annual of the British
School at Athens) which may be of interest to those wanting more detail about
the nature and location of ancient sites in the islands: R.M. Dawkins in vol. 9
(1902–3) 176–210 (Karpathos). Dawkins and A.J.B. Wace in vol. 12 (1905–6)
151–174 (Astipalaia, Tilos, Nisiros, Leros). G.E. Bean and J.M. Cook in vol. 52
(1957) 58–146 (pp. 116ff. refer to Tilos, Nisiros, Kos, Kalimnos, Kalolimnos,
Leros, Lipsi). R. Hope Simpson and J.F. Lazenby in vol. 57 (1962) 154–175
(Karpathos, Saria, Kasos, Simi, Nisiros, Kos, Kalimnos). Hope Simpson and
Lazenby in vol. 65 (1970) 47–77 (Patmos, Arki, Lipsi, Leros, Kos, Simi, Tilos,
Karpathos, Kasos, Kastellorizo). Hope Simpson and Lazenby in vol. 68 (1973)

127–179 (Rhodes, Khalki, Alimnia, Astipalaia, Sirina, Kasos, Karpathos and Saria).

Fauna. T. Akriotis and G. Handrinos, *The Birds of Greece* (A&C Black, 1997).

Flora. A. Huxley and W. Taylor, *Flowers of Greece and the Aegean* (Chatto and Windus, 1977).

Sailing in Greece. Particularly recommended are Rod Heikel, *Greek waters pilot*, 1995 (regularly updated). Rod Heikel's *Tetra* charts. UK bookshop: Captain Watts, 7 Dover St., London W1X 3PJ; tel. 0171 493 4633, fax 0171 495 0755.

Booksellers. *Alsos Books*, 14 Ashbridge Street, London NW8 8DH; tel. 0171 724 6774; fax 0171 724 5294, is recommended for all books about Greece, and particularly for obtaining works published in Greece. Also *Zeno*, 6 Denmark St., London, WC2H 8LP; tel. 0171 240 1968; fax 0171 836 2522.

The Dodecanese

The modern nomós, or administrative region, of the Dodecanese consists of 14 independently governed islands in the southeastern Aegean, as well as some smaller satellites. These 14 are Astipálaia, Kálimnos, Kárpathos, Kásos, Kastellórizo, Khálki, Kos, Léros, Lipsí, Nísiros, Pátmos, Rhodes, Sími and Tílos. They are divided into the four eparkhíes (sub-regions), of Kálimnos, Kárpathos, Kos and Rhodes. The total population (1991 census) is 163,476.

The name

In antiquity the eastern Aegean islands between Samos and Crete (excluding all the Cyclades) were known as the Sporades ('the scattered islands'), and the term is still used, though the group to which most of the Dodecanese belong constitute the Southern Sporades (the Northern being Skíathos, Skópelos, Alónissos and Skíros).

The term 'Dodecanese' meaning 'twelve islands' is patently a misnomer today. It is found in Byzantine sources, but with a significance which is never clear. On occasion then it included, or even consisted of, the Cyclades and, in the 10C AD, certainly excluded Rhodes and Sími, which belonged to a different administrative division (*thema*). A more definitive usage was adopted in 1908 when it was applied to a genuine Dodecanese of 12 islands which had been given special privileges during the period of Ottoman control of the islands (1523–1912). These privileges, originating in the 16C, consisted of taxation of the community as a whole at a fairly modest level rather than by assessment of each individual inhabitant; and freedom from the permanent residence of Turkish officials.

The 12 islands thus 'privileged' were Astipálaia, Ikaría, Kálimnos, Kárpathos, Kásos, Kastellórizo, Khálki, Léros, Nísiros, Pátmos, Sími and Tílos. Of this list, Ikaría is not part of the modern nomós. On the other hand Rhodes and Kos, which are not included, are now the most important from the point of view of size, economy and population. Their very significance is, of course, the reason for their exclusion from the Ottoman Dodecanese, when they were a rich source of revenue and commercial advantage and were the obvious seats of civilian and military administration. Accordingly no privileges of release from tax or supervision were allowed. In this book, the term is used with its present-day meaning.

Geography

In remote geological time, these islands were joined to the mainland of Asia Minor, which is always visible to the east and in places (Kastellórizo) is as close as 2.5km. Although they do not differ greatly in physical character from other parts of the southern Aegean, in some details of flora, fauna and climate, the Dodecanese are closer to Asia Minor than to mainland Greece or the rest of the archipelago.

Their present lack of contact with Asia Minor is due to the political situation rather than the natural logic of communications and resources. In antiquity these islands were closely associated with the mainland. In the Archaic period the Dorian *hexapolis* (see below) included both island and mainland states and its headquarters was on the mainland. In the Classical and Hellenistic periods

Rhodes (and to a much lesser extent other islands) exercised direct control over a substantial area of the mainland (the Rhodian 'Peraia')—in Caria, and Lycia, south of the River Maeander, though the extent of this territory varied from period to period. Under this system, many mainland communities were incorporated as official components (demes) of the Rhodian state. In the 4C BC the Carian dynasty at Halikarnassos influenced the affairs of the islands. In Byzantine times, mainland and island communities were administratively united and, under the Ottoman Empire, there was no barrier to communications.

Until the Greeks were expelled from Asia Minor in the compulsory exchange of population after 1922 contact was close and regular and the people of Sími, for example, kept flocks on the mainland and crossed over regularly to tend them. Nowadays connections are limited almost entirely to tourist excursions, although in summer these take place from most islands which are within easy reach.

It should be noted that the emphasis laid on the role of Rhodes in the history of the Dodecanese reflects a genuine position of political and commercial authority, although there is undoubtedly more to be learnt about the histories of the smaller islands, which might change the picture in some details.

Prehistory to c 1075 BC

The earliest signs of life in the Dodecanese have been located in the Kharkadhió cave on Tílos, where the petrified bones of small elephants and some other species have been found. These date to the Pleistocene/Upper Palaeolithic, c 45,000 BC, when the islands were still joined to the mainland of Asia Minor.

Human settlement is first attested in the Neolithic period with finds from the same site on Tílos, from caves on Rhodes, Léros, Kálimnos, Kos, Alimniá and elsewhere. Some of these continued in occupation into the Early Bronze Age, when open sites are also found. Finds from the Seraglio on Kos and from Assómatos on Rhodes show Anatolian relationships and may represent some movement into the area by groups of people from the mainland of Asia Minor in the late third millennium: a similar trend has been observed in the Cyclades. In the second millennium BC the palace culture of Minoan Crete was highly influential on the Dodecanese. There may even have been some settlers. Finds from Ialysos and Triánda on Rhodes in particular have demonstrated that relationship, especially in architectural style and pottery.

The eruption and explosion of the volcanic island of Thira, to the northwest, c 1500 BC (or perhaps 1628 BC as suggested by some new scientific evidence) must have affected the Dodecanese; perhaps more than any other part of the Aegean in the light of recent finds. Excavations on Rhodes (Triánda) have shown thick layers of volcanic ash covering the site. It seems likely that here, as on Crete and elsewhere in the Aegean, the psychological and physical damage caused by the volcanic catastrophe led to a decline in local culture and opened the way for the expansion of the authority of the mainland Greek Mycenaeans into the area.

From the later 15C BC Minoan influence is replaced by Mycenaean as is again shown by finds from Triánda, from the Seraglio on Kos and by Mycenaean tombs on other islands. In the second millennium Minoan and Mycenaean culture is also well represented at sites on the coast of Asia Minor such as Miletus and Kolophon.

Homer mentions three cities in Rhodes—*Lindos, Ialysos* and *Kameiros* (*Iliad*, II, 656). These three, together with *Kos, Nisyros, Syme, Karpathos, Kasos* and the *Kalydnian Islands* (perhaps Kálimnos and its satellites) all contributed ships to the Greek fleet which sailed to Troy.

Dark Ages and Archaic Period 1075–479 BC

Archaeological evidence, supported by a variety of traditions and legends, shows that there were migrations of Greeks from the mainland eastwards across the Aegean in the 'Dark Ages' following the collapse of the Mycenaean palace civilisation. It would have been during this period that speakers of the Dorian dialect of Greek arrived and became dominant in the Dodecanese. In the early history of the southeastern Aegean the three cities on Rhodes mentioned above, together with *Kos*, and *Knidos* and *Halikarnassos* on the coast of Asia Minor, formed the so-called Dorian *hexapolis* (unit of six cities; the term is used by Herodotus). Their meeting place was the mainland Sanctuary of Apollo at Knidos.

In the Archaic period, the cities of Rhodes in particular attained great prosperity, trading with the Near East and North Africa. Rhodians shared in the Greek foundation of the trading emporium *Naukratis* on the Nile Delta in the late 7C, and Rhodian mercenaries fought in Egypt for the Pharaoh Psammeticus II (594–589). Colonies were founded on the southern coast of Asia Minor, in Sicily (*Gela*) and in northern Spain.

Much less is known about the other Dodecanesian islands at this time. Some of them certainly participated in some of the colonial foundations and, accordingly, perhaps also in trading and other enterprises. Politically they were most likely subordinate to Rhodes or one of the mainland cities, as was the case in Classical and later times (see below). In the 6C BC tyrants were often established, amongst whom Kleoboulos of Lindos (fl. 580 BC) is a prominent example. The prosperity and energy of this period is reflected in the emergence of local art styles (see below, Pottery).

Classical period 479–323 BC

In the great wars between Greece and Persia which dominated the first 20 years of the 5C, some of the islands (Kos, Nísiros) were controlled by the Persians through Artemisia, Queen of Caria; others were allied with Athens and most ended up as members of the Delian League and appear in the Athenian tribute lists. In the Peloponnesian War, fought in the last 30 years of the century between Athens and Sparta, allegiances changed frequently according to the military situation and/or the political dominance of pro-Athenian or pro-Spartan parties in various states.

In 408 and 366 BC respectively important *synoikisms* (unions of the populations of formerly independent cities or settlements) took place on Rhodes and Kos. On Kos a new town was laid out, probably in the area of the earlier city of *Kos-Meropis*, but incorporating also the inhabitants of the site of *Astypalaia* in the south of the island. In 408 the three ancient cities of Rhodes united to found a new capital. The overall layout, attributed to Hippodamos of Miletus, the most famous town-planner of antiquity, and making use of the characteristic grid plan which is associated with his name, has been traced. Its planning was highly praised by Strabo and it became noted for its fine buildings and sculptures.

As a result of these developments the control of smaller by larger islands was intensified, especially through their formal incorporation as demes (see above). In the case of Rhodes (and to a much lesser extent Kos) this also applied to her area of influence (Peraia) on the mainland.

In the early 4C BC the Athenians defeated the Spartans at the battle of Knidos (394), after which the influence of Athens in the area was in the ascendant. Most islands were members of the Second Athenian Confederacy but were subject to pressure from Mausolus, king of Caria who, for example, placed a Carian garrison on Rhodes. The later 4C BC was marked by the ascendancy of the kingdom of Macedon and the campaigns of Alexander the Great, whom the Rhodians opposed at the siege of Tyre. After Alexander's victory at Halikarnassos in 334, he controlled the Dodecanese.

Hellenistic and Roman periods 323 BC–c 330 AD

In the wars of succession that followed Alexander's death (323 BC) at the beginning of the Hellenistic period, the islands were subject to the Ptolemies of Egypt. In the 3C the area in general and Rhodes in particular, as a major commercial and naval power, was very prosperous. In both politics and art, the island controlled the Dodecanese: communities on other islands continued to be incorporated in the city of Rhodes and more mainland centres became her subjects. In the 2C BC the Rhodians led the islands into alliance with Rome, providing frequent military support, supporting her, for example, against Philip V of Macedon and Antiochus the Great, king of Syria, and being rewarded with new possessions on the mainland. Rhodes became head of a Nesiotic League which gave her control of many islands in the Cyclades.

Subsequently, however, Rhodes' support of Perseus and his defeat at Pydna led to confiscation of her external territories and in 166 the Romans declared Delos a free port, dealing a heavy blow to Rhodian, and Dodecanesian, trade. The islands followed the fortunes of Rhodes, which regained Roman favour in the wars against Mithridates of Pontus (1C BC) but lost it again through support for Julius Caesar. After 43 BC the Rhodian fleet was destroyed, an event which adversely affected also the prosperity of dependent islands.

Under the early Empire Rhodes was formally recognised as an important centre. Under Diocletian (284–305) it became capital of the province of the Islands. St. Paul went there during his second or third journey (*Acts*, xxi, 1).

Early Christian and Byzantine period c AD 330–1453

The Early Christian period can either be reckoned to begin with the birth of Christ, or from AD 330, when the Emperor Constantine moved his capital from Rome to the Greek city of *Byzantium*, renaming it *Constantinople*. The Empire divided into Eastern and Western branches in 395. Under Constantine Christianity became the official religion of the Roman empire and it is from this point that older architectural forms and artistic media start to be adapted to suit Christian rites and beliefs. The term Byzantine is often applied to the Eastern Empire after the reforms of Heraclius in AD 629.

The early history of this period in the Dodecanese is shadowy although the widespread discovery of Early Christian basilicas is significant, and we know that Rhodes had a bishop from the 4C AD and that he became a Metropolitan with authority over 12 of the dioceses of the archipelago. In general Dodecanesian history followed that of the Eastern empire. From the 6 to the 9C, a Dark Age, the area was under pressure from Persia and the islands were subject to raids by Saracens and others. Patmos seems to have been completely deserted at this time. The empire was split by the iconoclast controversy. Some of the castles in the Dodecanese which have a Byzantine phase may belong to this or the following period.

From the mid 9C, the authority of Constantinople was restored. In the 10C Rhodes and Syme, at least, belonged to the theme of *Cibyra* (the southwest coast of Asia Minor from Miletus to Seleucia); some, at least, of the others to a sub-command based on Kos, which later became the full theme (*thema*) of the Aegean Sea. In 1054 occurred the schism which irrevocably split the Eastern and Western churches. In 1088 the Emperor Alexius Comnenus specified Patmos as the site of the monastery of St John, which remains to this day subject to the jurisdiction of the Ecumenical Patriarch of the Orthodox Church in Constantinople.

During the reign of the same emperor came the appearance in the Aegean of the Crusaders, on their way to free the Holy Land from Turkish control; and of representatives of the mercantile republics of Italy, in particular the Venetians and the Genoese, the former of whom were given important privileges in the Dodecanese, where they continued in some places to exercise control even after the establishment of Ottoman rule. The armies of the Fourth Crusade forcibly established a 'Latin' empire in Constantinople (1204), far from the Holy Land. This lasted until 1261. In the Late Byzantine period, the time of the Palaiologue dynasty, the empire came under increasing pressure until Constaninople fell to the Ottomans in 1453.

The Knights of St John 1309–1522

In 1309 Rhodes was captured, after two years' siege, by the Knights of St John. The island became their base for two centuries' domination of the Dodecanese. The Knights of St John of Jerusalem (in other contexts known as the Knights of Rhodes or, later, the Knights of Malta), were originally Hospitallers, charitable brotherhoods founded for the care in hospital of the poor and sick. They originated c 1048 in a hospital which merchants of Amalfi had built in Jerusalem for pilgrims to the Holy Sepulchre. Their first rector, Gerard, formed them into a strictly constituted religious body subject to the jurisdiction of the Patriarch of Jerusalem. The Order soon became predominantly military and the Hospitallers were sworn to defend the Holy Sepulchre to the last drop of their blood, and to make war on infidels everywhere. In 1191, after Saladin had captured Jerusalem, they retired to Acre. Bitter rivalry arose between them and the Knights Templar (the first of the military-monastic orders, so named because of the location of their headquarters, on the Temple Mount, in Jerusalem), ending in hostilities in which the Templars got the upper hand. Clinging to Acre, the Hospitallers were driven out in 1291 after a terrible siege, and they sailed to Cyprus. In 1306 they fled from Cyprus to Rhodes. When refused control of the island, they took it by force.

Arms of the Order

Foulques de Villaret
1310-1319

Hélion de Villeneuve
1319-1346

Dieudonné de Gozon
1346-1353

Pierre de Corneillan
1354-1355

Roger de Pins
1355-1365

Raymond Béranger
1365-1374

Robert de Juilly
1374-1377

Ferdinand d'Hérédia
1377-1396

Philibert de Naillac
1396-1421

Antoine Fluvian
1421-1437

Jean de Lastic
1437-1454

Jacques de Milly
1454-1461

Raymond Zacosta
1461-1467

G. B. degl'Orsini
1467-1476

Pierre d'Aubusson
1476-1505

Aimerie d'Amboise
1505-1512

Guy de Blanchefort
1512-1513

Fabrizio del Carretto
1513-1521

Ph. Villiers de l'Isle Adam
1521-1522

The members of the Order were divided into three classes—knights, chaplains, and serving brothers or fighting squires who followed the knights into action. In the 12C the Order was divided into seven Tongues or Languages—Provence, Auvergne, France, Italy, Spain (later subdivided into Aragon and Castile), England and Germany. Each Tongue had a Bailiff, and the Bailiffs, under the presidency of the Grand Master, elected for life by the Knights, formed the Chapter of the Order. The modern British Order of St John of Jerusalem, founded in 1827, can be regarded as a revival of the Tongue of England.

The time of the Knights in the Dodecanese was marked by generally civilised relations with the local population. The Knights retained ultimate authority in all matters, including ecclesiastical, but seem not to have seriously interfered with traditional customs.

For much of the 14 and 15C the Knights were subjected to Ottoman pressure and physical attack. Rhodes twice (1444, 1480) suffered major sieges before finally capitulating to Suleiman I in 1522. Other islands too were besieged (Kos; 1457, 1477, fell 1522) in the course of the Ottoman expansion, and all were eventually subjected.

The Ottoman period 1523–1912

After the departure of the Knights (for Malta) in 1523, 400 years of Ottoman control began, most evident on Rhodes and Kos, where there were military garrisons. On Rhodes, also the seat of the local civil administration (ultimately subject to Khíos), many churches were converted into mosques. As indicated above in discussing the term 'Dodecanese', the smaller islands were largely left to their own devices, while the larger were more closely supervised. In general there was little interference with commercial, religious or social life.

The islanders, notably the sailors of Kásos and the shipbuilders of Sími, took part in the Greek Wars of Independence (1821). Although the 12 islands were originally included in the new Greek kingdom of 1832, they were later exchanged for Evvia (Euboea), which was initially agreed to be a Turkish possession. Although the later 19C was a time of prosperity, based on trade in agricultural products and sponges, there was increasing Turkish interference in local affairs. During the 19C considerable numbers of islanders emigrated, particularly to Egypt.

The Italian occupation 1912–1947

In 1912, during their war with Turkey, the Italians took all the islands in the Dodecanese (except Kastellórizo which was occupied by the French from 1915 to 1921, when it was ceded to Italy) and captured Rhodes after a short siege. By the First Treaty of Lausanne in 1912 it was agreed that the islands should revert to Turkey once she had left Libya, but this agreement was negated by Turkey's participation in the 1914–18 war. Subsequent complex negotiations over the fate of the islands finally culminated in the Second Treaty of Lausanne (1924) by which Italian possession was confirmed. Under the Italians, the Dodecanese were administered by a Governor in Rhodes, a Regent in Kos, and by Deputies in other larger islands.

In attempts to impose the Italian language and culture (mostly from 1937), there was substantial interference with local civil and religious autonomy and in the education system, which on occasion led to riots and bloodshed (on Kalímnos in 1935, and elsewhere). In the latter part of the Second World War the Germans took over from the Italians on Rhodes, with some violence. In 1944–45 the islands came, one by one, under British military administration. The German surrender of the Dodecanese was signed on Sími on the 8 May 1945. In 1947 the islands were officially incorporated in the Greek state.

The perennially uneasy state of Greek-Turkish relations in this area was exacerbated in early 1996 with a Turkish attempt to claim the tiny islet of Imia, northeast of Kálimnos.

Art and Architecture in The Dodecanese: An Introduction

Most topics treated below are more fully discussed, with reference to Greece as a whole, in *Blue Guide Greece*.

Dates

Neolithic (late phase) c 4500–3500 BC	Hellenistic 323–late 1C BC
Early Bronze Age 3500–2000	Roman Empire 27 BC–AD early 5C
Middle Bronze Age 2200–1600	Early Christian AD 4C–629
(Minoan Palaces c 2200–1400)	Early Byzantine 629–843
Late Bronze Age 1600–1075	Middle Byzantine 843–1204
(Mycenaean Palaces c 1600–1200)	Late Byzantine 1204–1453
SubMycenaean/Minoan 1075–1025	Post Byzantine 1453–1830
Protogeometric 1025–900	Knights of St. John 1309–1522
Geometric 900–725	Ottoman 1523–1912
Orientalising 725–625	Greek independence formally recognised 1830
Archaic 625–479	
Classical 479–323	Italian occupation 1912–1947

Antiquity to the end of the Roman period

Prehistory

In the **Neolithic** period most of the settlement sites were caves and the most common artefact pottery. In the Early Bronze Age stone-built houses are found and, at the end of the period, the pottery shows connections with that of Asia Minor. In the middle and earlier part of the Late Bronze Age, the influence of **Minoan Crete** is apparent in both imported and local pottery and in the use of fine ashlar masonry for building.

From about 1450 BC **Mycenaean** influence succeeds Minoan and finds of this period are more prolific. Again they consist of pottery in shapes typical of the period such as the kylix (tall-stemmed cup) and stirrup jar: the decoration, in dark paint on fine buff clay, often consists of more or less stylised plant or marine motifs. At the end of the period (12C), the octopus is common. Rock cut Mycenaean chamber tombs have been found on several islands: these sometimes contain other finds—bronze weapons, sealstones, jewellery of precious metals, objects of faience (glass paste).

Pottery

Dark Ages

In the Dark Ages (early 11C–early 8C BC) which followed the collapse of Mycenaean civilisation, virtually all of the sophisticated arts and crafts of the preceding period were lost and there was no monumental building. The first major pottery style of this period, **Protogeometric,** which shows a revival of technique (firm shapes and neat decoration with compass drawn circles etc.), was copied from Athens where it originated. The following 300 years saw the development of the **Geometric** style, again similar to that of Athens and Attica but with some local features. Well-made vases are increasingly covered with Geometric motifs, which eventually include schematic human figures. A derivative of this style, characteristic of the Dodecanese and 'East Greece' (the term includes Greek settlements on the coast of Asia Minor), is the 'bird bowl'.

From the 8C contacts with the eastern Mediterranean became frequent. The Dodecanese, and Rhodes in particular, were important stages on sea routes between the Aegean and the Levant and North Africa. Foreign objects and influences are common and the century from 725 is known as the **Orientalising period**. In Greece, Corinth was the most important centre of pottery manufacture at this time and her characteristic products (particularly the tiny *aryballos* shape—for perfumed oil) are found everywhere, including the Dodecanese. Again, however, some local preferences are evident in style or choice of motif.

The Corinthians soon developed the use of the **black-figure** technique (figures in black paint on the light surface of the vase, with details incised), but this was not adopted by other production centres (including those in the Dodecanese) until rather later.

Archaic, Classical, Hellenistic and Roman periods
From early in the Archaic period (625–479 BC) the Athenians adopted the black-figure technique and began to dominate the market with finely-drawn narrative mythological scenes. Imported examples are common all over the Aegean, and beyond.

In the later 7 and 6C—that is overlapping the late Orientalising and Archaic periods—some interesting local styles were current in east Greece, including the Dodecanese and Greek sites in Asia Minor. Although the precise centres of production are not yet securely identified, they must surely have included Rhodes.

These did not at first use the black-figure technique, but rather a combination of **silhouette and outline** with painted detail. They often make use of 'Orientalising' motifs such as the cable pattern and large lotus flowers and buds. Amongst them are the **Wild Goat style** (from c 650 BC), named after the characteristic, though not the only, motif, which is sometimes thought to have been derived from tapestry designs. The trefoil-mouthed jug is a common shape. There are also some plates, with figured scenes (e.g. the Euphorbos Plate in the British Museum: Menelaos and Hektor fight over the body of Euphorbos, in an episode from the Trojan war).

An ancient cemetery in Rhodes, near modern **Fikélloura**, has produced attractive vases (named after it) where isolated human and animal figures are set in empty space, or zones of purely ornamental motifs are balanced with the light background of the clay. The **Vrouliá** and **Siána** cemeteries (6C BC) on Rhodes have given us local variants on the more widespread black-figure style. Vrouliá cups have floral motifs incised into their dark surfaces and colours added; the Siána cup is an early version of the stemmed cup which was a common shape in the Athenian black-figure style, but it has a rather short stem and a distinctive offset lip. East Greek black-figure pottery, although not particularly associated with the Dodecanese, has some distinctive features of composition and shows the use of trailing vegetation.

Although the black-figure technique continued to be used in Greek towns until much later, from about 530 BC it was increasingly supplanted by **red-figure**, which involved painting the surface of the vessel black, leaving the figures 'reserved' in the natural colour of the clay. Details were then painted in. The technique allowed a more fluid and more naturalistic style, especially since the figure colour was now more realistic. Athens was again the leading sentre of production, although there were also local workshops. This technique survived until the 4C BC.

In Hellenistic period painted decoration on pottery was much less common and usually restricted to small zones of pattern. However, mould-made vases ('**Megarian**' bowls) carried figure-scenes in relief. The Roman period saw a continuation of this method, especially in the red-coloured *terra sigillata* or '**Samian**' pottery.

Sculpture

There was no large scale sculpture in the Geometric period (unless wooden figures existed but have not survived). **Figurines** of terracotta or bronze are found with schematic characteristics similar to those of the humans or animals depicted on vases.

The Orientalising and Archaic periods saw both a great increase in the numbers and range of figurines and (from about 650 BC) the development of monumental stone sculpture. The Dodecanese received quite a lot of imported objects (small-scale) from the Near East and Egypt, and there was a factory producing objects of faience (vases, seals, trinkets) on Rhodes in the 7C which sometimes kept very close to Egyptian models.

Large scale sculpture

Two types dominate the early (**Archaic**) history of **monumental sculpture** in Greece—the *kouros* and the *kore*, standing male and female figures. The former stand naked, one foot advanced; the latter are clothed, often holding offerings. They were dedicated as offering in sanctuaries, marked graves, and sometimes stood as cult statues in temples. Near Eastern and Egyptian influence is evident, especially in the earlier pieces, in the stance (Egyptian) and the hair style and facial form (Near Eastern). Regional characteristics can be defined in different parts of Greece. In the northeastern Aegean and Asia Minor the female figures have cylindrical lower bodies with lightly incised drapery lines; the males have rounded fleshy faces and are often clothed. Eyes too are distinctively oriental. Relatively few examples of these types (there are some pieces from Kameiros in Rhodes Museum) have so far been found in the Dodecanese (and some of those were imported), though it is hard to believe that they were not as popular here as in other parts of Greece.

Stylistic development

As time went on the treatment of anatomy (in vase painting as well as sculpture) became more naturalistic and poses relaxed and more varied. To the earlier part of the 5C (c 480–450) belongs the so-called **Severe Style**: figures have naturalistic but not over-detailed anatomy and faces the bland, expressionless gaze that seems most typical of **Classical sculpture**.

In the 4C the trend towards greater realism (including portraiture) and variety continued with, amongst other things, the adoption of a new canon of proportions (smaller heads and slimmer bodies) and an increasing interest in the third dimension. **Lysippos of Sikyon**, the sculptor attached to the court of Alexander the Great and one of the most influential artists of his time, worked in Rhodes, creating there a famous four-horse chariot with a figure of the Sun.

The **sculpture of the Hellenistic period** shows considerably greater variety in both subject matter and treatment. One of its most distinctive characteristics is the much more powerful expression of feeling and emotion, whose suppression had previously been a feature of Greek sculpture. Colossal figures and massively complex groups are also now found. Although literary sources and finds elsewhere suggest that these were a particular feature of Rhodian work, there are few actual finds from Rhodes itself which could have belonged to such monuments, nor is there much evidence for the 'baroque' style which may have been associated with them.

Rhodian sculpture tends to incorporate individual features of the work of other areas (and periods) rather than aligning itself directly with the styles of other centres. This is in accordance with the cosmopolitan character of the island derived from its wide contacts. A more delicate and decorative approach is evident in figures of Aphrodite and nymphs, where polishing of the 'flesh', the use of blurring ('sfumato') of the features, and elegant drapery effects, often produced by undercutting, are found. Much of this and other Rhodian sculpture is less than life size.

Rhodes was a major centre of artistic activity at this time, as is clear from the substantial part it plays in Pliny's discussion of Greek art (*Natural History*, parts of Books XXXIV–XXXVI) and the numerous literary references to Rhodian artists of the 4–1C BC. The works produced were mainly portrait statues and figures of deities for dedication in sanctuaries or public centres, and smaller scale works with a more decorative intent. Kos too is the source of a good deal of sculpture. The other islands were surely customers rather than producers.

The sculptural 'school' of Rhodes may initially have developed under the influence of Lysippos. Leading artists included Protogenes, a painter (and artist in other media) from Caunus in Caria who lived in poverty until he was brought to public attention by his better known contemporary Apelles: some of his works adorned the sanctuary of Dionysos in Rhodes. Chares of Lindos, creator of the Colossos of Rhodes (see main text), was a pupil of Lysippos and the author of many other works. Bryaxis was responsible for at least five other important statues, and is reported to have worked on the Mausoleum at Halikarnassos together with Lysippos and Scopas. These were followed by many others, both native and immigrant, of whom little is known. Names of artists appear freqently on statue bases found on the Acropolis of Lindos.

From Chares onwards, sculptors worked mainly in bronze. Philiskos was known for a group of the Muses, which was carried off to Rome, perhaps by Crassus, and placed in the Porticus of Octavia. Inspired by Lysippos, Philiskos was especially skilled in the treatment of drapery. Some of his muses may have been prototypes for the 'nymphs' seated on rocks of which there are several examples in the museums of Rhodes and Kos, and which represent a delicate strain in the sculpture of the period. The famous Nike (Victory) of the island of Samothrace (in the Louvre), shown winged and descending on to the prow of a ship, was almost certainly by the Rhodian sculptor Pythokritos. Rhodian sculptors may have worked on the 2C Great Altar of Zeus at Pergamon (in Asia Minor).

In the period of Roman control, a local sculptor made a Colossos 12m high, which was dedicated to the Roman people and placed in the Temple of Athena Polias and Zeus Polieus on the Acropolis of Rhodes. Other artists working on the island included Boethos of Chalcedon, and Apollonios and Tauriskos of Tralles (like Chalcedon, in Asia Minor). They made a group of Dirce, who was tied to the horns of a maddened bull by Zethos and Amphion, for her treatment of their mother Antiope. A poor Roman adaptation of this (the 'Farnese bull') was found in the Baths of Caracalla in Rome and is now in the museum of Naples. Pliny mentions Aristonidas, who made a statue of Atamos bewailing the death of his son Learchos.

A famous group of Menelaus and Patroclus (the Pasquino fragment, now in Rome, belongs) came from Rhodes. Another version of this was found in 1995 in excavations of the Villa of Herodes Atticus at Loukou in the Peloponnese.

Perhaps the best-known Rhodian work, and one which particularly exemplifies the emotionalism and scholasticism of the period, is the Laocoön, found in 1506 in the Golden House of Nero in Rome. This group, made (or copied?) in the late 1C BC by the Rhodian sculptors Agesander, Polydorus and Athenodorus (two of whose names appear in inscriptions in the sanctuary at Lindos), shows a priest of Apollo, together with his two sons, being strangled by snakes, because he had offended the god. The same sculptors were also responsible for the dramatic sculptural compositions found in the Cave of Tiberius at Sperlonga in Italy.

As will be clear from the above, many of the statues produced in the Roman period were by Greek artists and in a Hellenistic style. More distinctively **Roman** in character are portrait busts—early in a 'veristic' style which stresses the depiction of physical maturity and ageing, then borrowing features of Classical Greek sculpture and, in the late empire, often adopting forms of rather brutal realism. Massive armed imperial figures are also characteristic. Deities and other mythological figures continued to be produced in large numbers, in the Hellenistic tradition.

Relief sculpture

In Greece as a whole the most common forms of relief sculpture are from the decoration of buildings (the metopes, friezes and pediments of temples, see below) and votive (dedicatory) and funerary reliefs. There is a striking lack of such architectural sculpture from the Dodecanese, but small stone altars (cylindrical or square) and reliefs of other kinds are common. Stone slabs, or stelai (s. stele), were erected over graves or set up as offerings in sanctuaries. Early (Archaic, Early Classical) grave stelai were taller and often had only a single figure in fairly low relief. Later the relief became deeper, and an architectural frame was often used as a setting for the figures who increased in number.

A common motif is that of the handshake—the dead person bidding farewell to his/her family. Sometimes the dead are shown as athletes or warriors. Funerary banquets are depicted, often with heroes participating. Votive reliefs may show mythological or other scenes. Both types sometimes bear inscriptions. In the Hellenistic and Roman periods common finds are funerary altars, circular or square, often decorated with bucrania (bulls' heads) and linking garlands. The motifs are from the garlanding of animals in preparation for sacrifice. The stylistic development of reliefs is similar to that of freestanding sculpture, though there are problems of composition which are unique to this medium. In the late Roman period there is a noticeable tendency to frontality (reliefs from Nísiros in Rhodes Museum), which is then taken up in Byzantine art.

Figurines, in whatever material, were most commonly manufactured for offering in sanctuaries, sometimes for deposition in the grave. They too follow the stylistic features of larger scale sculptures. Deities are often represented, sometimes identifiable by their attributes (the thunderbolt of Zeus). Hellenistic figurines are notably more varied in subject, style and pose than their earlier counterparts.

Rhodes was also well known for **metal objects**, such as jewellery and vessels. An example of this, on a much larger scale, was the Rhodian dedication at Delphi of a golden chariot of the sun: the base survives.

Painting and mosaic

Only rarely does ancient painting survive to any degree but painted scenes were a common form of decoration in houses and public buildings in the Hellenistic and Roman periods. Apelles, one of the most famous painters of antiquity, was a native of Kos, and the work of Protogenes on Rhodes has already been mentioned. In the earlier period such paintings often represented architectural elements (blocks of marble, columns or pilasters); in the Roman period mythological and other scenes became prevalent, although still within an overall architectural design.

Mosaic, which lasts much better, was used mainly for floor decoration but also sometimes on walls. In the late Classical and early Hellenistic periods mosaics were often made of natural pebbles and the range of colours rather restricted; later on artificially made components (*tesserae*) of stone or glass allowed a greater range of colours and sizes, enabling much subtler effects of tone and shading. At all periods most designs were purely geometric, but mythological scenes, sometimes single and set within an ornamental border, sometimes a series set in panels or roundels incorporated into an overall decorative scheme, become increasingly common. Mosaics were popular for the decoration of dining rooms. Mosaics (and marble panelling, or *opus sectile*) were particularly suitable to Roman bath buildings where they could be used to cover large areas of walls and floors and were resistant to moisture.

Architecture

Greek monumental architecture begins in the Archaic period at the same time as large-scale sculpture, with which it shares many problems and techniques. By the late 7C the Doric order had been developed, to be followed by the Ionic. Corinthian, which was not common until Hellenistic and Roman times, was similar to Ionic though with a different type of capital.

The two most common building types are the **temple**, in various forms, and the **stoa** (colonnade). The more ambitious and formal architectural complexes of the Hellenistic and Roman periods are well illustrated in the Dodecanese by such sites as the sanctuary of Athena on the acropolis of **Lindos** and the **Asklepieion** on Kos. To these structures should be added **fortifications** which were often constructed in excellent masonry and of which there are many examples in the Dodecanese, some of them outstanding (Nísiros, Tílos).

Columns are characteristic of almost all ancient Greek public buildings, and most temples had colonnades. In the **Doric Order** the column had no base but rested directly on the floor of the building (stylobate). The capital consisted of two parts—a rounded *echinus* topped by a flat square *abacus*. The whole of the upper part of the building above is called the entablature. Of this the lowest section (immediately above the abacus) was the architrave, consisting of a course of plain masonry laid from column to column. Above this was the frieze—in the case of a Doric temple consisting of alternate metopes (square panels, which could be decorated with relief sculpture) and triglyphs (groups of three vertical bars). The pitched roofs were made of either terracotta or stone tiles on wooden rafters. The pediments were formed by the triangular space between the roof slopes and the frieze course at each end of the building. These could also be filled with sculpture, often but not always in some way related to the deity to whom the temple belonged or to the locality in which it was set. The **plan** of the standard Doric temple consisted of an entrance porch (*pronaos*), an inner room (*cella*), with a cult statue at the far end, and an *opisthodomos* (back room), not connected with the cella, which could be used as a storage place for equipment or offerings.

The **Ionic Order** was different in several respects. Columns had moulded bases, and capitals with spiral projections (volutes). In the entablature the architrave was usually divided into three by 'steps' and the frieze was a continuous course (no triglyphs or metopes) which might be decorated with sculpture or with dentils (tooth-like projections, much used in western neo-Classical interior decoration). A type of capital (**Aeolic**), which preceded the Ionic, bearing floral decoration and upright volutes, is sometimes found in East Greece and probably points to the place of origin of the decoration—in the Near East.

The term **Corinthian** refers to a type of capital, decorated with acanthus leaves, which is first found in the middle of the 5C BC.

Building types and organisation

Although monumental architecture in the orders described above was at first mainly confined to temples, it gradually spread to other building types. Greek towns usually developed around an **agora**—an open space surrounded by public buildings—which was the focus of communal life and accommodated administrative offices, council chambers, lawcourts, shops, fountain houses and so on, as well as religious buildings. With the increasing use of the grid-plan layout, the agora was often precisely square or rectangular, occupying a number of blocks of the town plan. In the Hellenistic period the practice of defining all the borders of the agora with **stoas** developed, so that it became in effect a monumental colonnaded courtyard. The same elaborate treatment was given to sanctuary sites.

Amongst the major public buildings which are commonly found in the Hellenistic period are those associated with athletics and drama, both of which had significance within religious festivals, as well as for recreation. The **gymnasium** was a common element in the ancient Greek city and had often acquired monumental form by the Hellenistic period. There is no standard layout but changing rooms, bathing facilities, a practice area and perhaps a covered running track might be found: the gymnasium is often closely associated with a **stadium** (Rhodes, acropolis; Kos town).

By the Hellenistic period the **theatre** (Lindos, Rhodes town) consisted of a semicircular auditorium with rising tiers of seats divided by vertical stairways and one or more horizontal passages. The elevated stage building closed the semicircle, with entrance passages between it and the auditorium. Raised on columns it was backed by a wall with three doors, behind which were the actors' changing rooms. Theatres were often decorated with statuary. The earlier Greek theatre had a fully circular **orchestra** (the area between the auditorium and stage building, where the chorus performed); in the Hellenistic period all the action took place on the stage. The **odeion** is simply a smaller version of the theatre, where recitals rather than plays were performed.

Large scale **bath buildings** are a feature of the Roman period (Kos town) at both town and sanctuary sites. Arrangements of hot and cold rooms and baths were combined in vaulted complexes (often vast), frequently containing elaborate marble and mosaic decoration and statuary. Brick-faced concrete is the Roman building material *par excellence*.

A form of **grid-planning** for Greek towns was used as early as the 7C BC for colonial foundations on virgin territory. In the Classical period it is particularly associated with Hippodamos of Miletus, planner of the new city of Rhodes (408 BC). This type of planning was especially applied in the Hellenistic period. In earlier times houses were quite modest but the habit of laying them out round a courtyard seems to have developed by the Classical period. Only in Hellenistic and Roman times however do **houses** (Kos town) become worthy of particular comment. They begin to make use of architectural elements (columns, etc.) formerly confined to public buildings and may be extensively decorated with mosaics, wall painting and sculpture.

The fundamental elements of the early Greek **sanctuary** were the boundary, separating it from the secular world outside, and the altar, where sacrifices, the central ritual acts of Greek religion, were performed. Temples came later, to house the cult statue of the deity. As time passed sanctuaries acquired a more and more monumental character, with secondary elements (such as the entrance) given elaborate architectural treatment, and a variety of buildings added, as well as innumerable sculptural dedications, themselves a form of architectural addition to the sanctuary. The formal layout of the Hellenistic agora (stoas defining the open space) is also found in Hellenistic sanctuaries: at the Asklepieion on Kos, both the upper and lower terraces were bounded by stoas.

Early Christian and Byzantine

Buildings

The most important and easily the best-known form of building type is the church. In the Early Christian period the more important churches adopted the **basilica** form which was closely based on a type of Roman public building. The most common form is rectangular and has three aisles, the central larger than the other two and divided from them by arched colonnades: it may be preceded by a colonnaded court (*atrium*) at the west and is entered through a forehall (*narthex*). Inside the church proper the three-aisled rectangle (*naos*) is separated from the sanctuary by a screen (*templon*). There was frequently rich sculptural decoration on the templon (often of marble) and column capitals; also on the lectern or pulpit (*ambo*), in addition to marble panelling and mosaic, though this is usually now to be seen in fragments in museums. Motifs are more often patterns or symbols than figures. Relatively little remains of most basilicas, though there are more substantial remains at sites such as Ayios Stéfanos on Kos and the church of Christ of Jerusalem at Dhámos on Kálimnos.

In the Middle Byzantine period (mid 9C–early 13C) this was superseded as the most common form in the rest of Greece and much of Asia Minor by a type usually referred to as the **domed inscribed cross**. These buildings are square with barrel vaults. The cross is formed by the vaults at roof level, with the dome set over the centre of the cross. The arrangement of narthex, naos and sanctuary is retained, the latter divided into the central apsed *bema* with the *prothesis* (for preparation of the sacrament) to the north and the *diaconicon* (sacristy) to the south. The *iconostasis*, usually of wood, gradually replaced the templon. Although some important churches in the Dodecanese (Panayía tou Kástrou, or St Mary's, in Rhodes town) are of this form, it is not common in the area.

The existence of a bishop's throne shows that the church in question is the metropolis of a see. Another feature which may be noted is the seating for clergy (*synthronon*) which may be in raised tiers and is to be found in the apse or to either side of the bema. **Baptisteries** (with sunken immersion fonts) may be either incorporated in a church or located in a separate building nearby. Of various forms, sometimes quatrefoil, they may be lined with marble.

There are numerous variations in detail on the types described and **other plans**, which are related to these only in the sense that they share basic architectural forms: the inscribed cross is only one of five types into which the churches of Rhodes town built under the Knights can be subdivided (A. Orlandos; I. Kollias).The other four are the simple aisleless barrel-vaulted form, the free (i.e. *un*inscribed) cross, the three-aisled and the quatrefoil—the latter three all domed.

The Dodecanese, because of their geographical position, were influenced by architectural developments both in Asia Minor and the Greek mainland. Most **chapels**, especially in the countryside, are very small and modest and consist of a single plain-vaulted space with a tiny apsed sanctuary at the east, closed off by a wooden iconostasis. They are always worth investigating, however, if open, since many contain carved iconostases, icons, and even frescoes.

There is little to see of **secular architecture**, although some has been revealed in recent excavations in Rhodes town. Houses were undistinguished and there seem to have been few public buildings. Of the many **castles** and fortifications, the vast majority were adapted and re-used by Latins, Venetians, Knights and Turks, so that it is difficult to point out specifically Byzantine features. An exception is Palaió Pilí on Kos where there are remains of a Byzantine village with two frescoed churches and, above, within concentric circuit walls, a well-sited castle with a single steep approach and the remains of what must have been a fine, ceremonial entrance.

Painting and mosaic

In the Early Christian phase mosaics often used birds, animals and vegetable motifs, but also adapted pagan iconography to Christian themes and made extensive use of the medium for church decoration, although this is not strongly evident in the Dodecanese. While mosaic floors are the most common surviving decoration of Early Christian basilicas, some Byzantine churches contain extensive painted decoration, not in fact true fresco, although often referred to as such. This is arranged according to a hierarchical system based on the idea that the architecture reflected the structure of the universe, with heaven in the dome and lesser regions below. Hence in the dome, apse and higher vaults are located the most important figures—Christ in the Dome, the Virgin in the apse. Further episodes in the life and passion of Christ occupy important positions, while other biblical stories and personalities have secondary status. Images of the original donor of the church are sometimes incorporated. Church paintings were often touched up or repainted and buildings may have several layers of decoration, as at Moní Thári on Rhodes which has four, from 11C–17C. Churches in the Dodecanese contain an interesting range of frescoes of different periods and styles. Material of the earliest Christian and Byzantine periods is all fragmentary. There are important paintings which antedate 1309 but, somewhat paradoxically, the arrival of the Knights was followed by a period of considerable activity in wall painting (see below)—some of it secular.

Small churches may have no decoration apart from that in the apse and on the iconostasis. The latter may be carved and will bear icons. The **position of the icons** in orthodox churches is more or less standard and worth knowing because it helps to identify the patron saint whose name is unlikely to be recorded anywhere. To the left and right (as viewed by the visitor) of the central door in the iconostasis are, respectively, the Virgin (Panayía) and Christ. Beyond the Virgin is the patron saint of the church; beyond Christ, St John the Baptist (Ayíos Ioánnis Pródhromos). If the church is dedicated, as many are, to the Virgin, she will be represented twice in the icons to the left: once in the specific form in which she is worshipped in the church concerned (e.g. as the Zoödhókhos Piyí, or lifegiving spring). Icons prominently displayed elsewhere in the church (often near the door) may represent the patron saint but are just as likely to show a saint whose festival is close at hand.

Minor objects of Byzantine art are not much in evidence in museums, but attractive bowls with a green or yellowish glaze and pictorial designs are characteristic. Examples of church plate and equipment may be seen, for example in the Treasury of the Monastery of St John on Pátmos, which is of course also notable for its fine monastic buildings.

The Knights

Domestic and public architecture

With the arrival of the Knights of St John the art and architecture of Rhodes, especially the town itself, which still today remains essentially a medieval construct of the period, was subjected to Western influences. The Grand Masters, most of whom came from France or from Spain, naturally favoured the style of their native countries, and French or Spanish Gothic predominated. The most obvious features are pointed arches of doors and windows and the decoration of their surrounds, the use of string courses to break up the exteriors and, in later buildings, a fondness for breaking the straight lines of these; ornamental bosses, gargoyles, etc. may be added, and finely carved coats of arms are frequent.

Two periods are sometimes distinguished. In the earlier (1309–1480), the use of local labour led to plainer and more traditional forms (e.g. the original Hospital of the Order in Plateía Aryirokástrou; the Inn of Spain). In the second period (1480–1522), which was inspired by d'Aubusson (1476–1503), one of the most eminent and influential of the Grand Masters, there is subtler work and stronger western influence, probably reinforced by the presence of foreign craftsmen. Towards the end of the period a few Renaissance motives were introduced, alleviating the severity of the monastic Gothic. These included a preference for horizontal rather than vertical emphasis on façades, marble cornices to doors and windows, new motifs, and inscriptions carved in fine Latin characters. Occasionally there are specific forms deriving from Sicily and southern Italy and Spain (the 'Aragonese' portal).

Buildings of the period are inward looking, the exterior giving little indication of the interior. Houses and some other buildings (the Hospital/Museum, Hospice of St Catherine) have a central coutryard. In houses the ground floor is occupied by store and utility rooms which open on to the court, reached by broad rather flat arches on the exterior. A separate door may give access to the court and stairway. Some buildings have an exterior stair, a local Aegean feature. The upper floor is similar but the rooms are differently disposed for domestic use. Decoration, apart from the features mentioned above, is provided by variations in openings into the façade and the quite extensive use of mouldings. The windows of the upper floors are rectangular, often partly framed by mouldings. Roofs are normally flat.

A distinctive feature of the interiors comes out in a comparison between the vaults of Byzantine buildings (especially churches) and those of the Knights. Byzantine vaults are plain and rounded, whereas those in buildings of the Knights are often higher and pointed, and decorated with cross-ribbing, which divides the vault into four triangular sections. This can be seen in the porticoes which surround the main courtyards in the Hospital, and in the Palace of the Grand Masters. Ribbing, in combination with high pointed arches, can be seen in the Panayía tou Kástrou in Rhodes, where it contrasts markedly with the simple Byzantine cross-vaults of the original inscribed-cross plan.

Churches
The Knights constructed relatively few churches of their own but took over some of those belonging to the local population (Panayía tou Kástrou in Rhodes town). The new Gothic elements are most clearly seen today in Our Lady of the Bourg, also in the old town of Rhodes, in engravings of the now lost St John of the Collachium, and in the modern (1925) cathedral which is a copy. However most of the churches built in the Dodecanese during the period of the Knights were for the indigenous population and in traditional Byzantine style.

Military architecture
By the time the Knights occupied Rhodes, all of the former Byzantine empire which had not already been taken over by the Turks was at risk of attack. Accordingly the Knights first restored the Byzantine walls of Rhodes, which in turn had been partly built on the ancient fortifications, and secured the rest of Rhodes and other islands in the Dodecanese (not Astipália, Kásos and Kárpathos which remained under Venetian control) by building castles. There were six others in Rhodes (Filérimos, Kritinía, Monólithos, Arkhángelos, Fáraklos and Líndos; possibly also a seventh, never located, at Kattavía); and further examples on most other islands, except Pátmos which had its own fortified monastery.

Both in Rhodes and on certain other islands, some castles were built from scratch on new sites (Monólithos on Rhodes, Antimákhia on Kos), but many were constructed on the site of an existing Byzantine fortification (Péra Kástro on Kálimnos; Léros). Others made use of an ancient acropolis (Líndos, Sími, Tílos). Such sites either provided sound bases for the Knights to build on, or else a ready source of cut stone for their own constructions. Most of these fortifications were on commanding heights, often on isolated, almost inaccessible rocks, and had high but comparatively thin walls, depending for their defence more on their position than the solidity of their construction. In most cases they were not adapted to cope with the more efficient artillery that came into use in the 15C. They vary considerably in size, and some are too small ever to have held a large garrison: these were perhaps well-defended signalling posts, always an important factor for a naval power such as the Knights had now become. One possible example is the castle on the little island of Alimniá, between Kritinía on Rhodes and the island of Khálki.

It is the two vital harbours of Kos and Rhodes that show the later style of the Knights' work: low but very thick walls, massive curved bastions, and elaborately defended gates that enabled them to make full use of the new, heavier, cannon, as well as to resist them. The catalyst for change was Mehmet II's attack in 1480. Rhodes and Kos both held out, but only just, and it was clear to the Grand Master, Pierre d'Aubusson, that drastic changes were needed.

There is an interesting intermediate example between the old and new styles in the castle of Antimákhia on Kos. This castle, in the centre of the island, was first built in the old style around the middle of the 14C. Later, almost certainly under d'Aubusson (whose arms, complete with the Cardinal's hat that he received in 1495, are carved over the only entrance), parts of the walls were thickened, battlements added and the vulnerable west side was strengthened by a noticeable batter. A semicircular bastion with an entrance at the side was built in front of the gate. This may well date from the time of the Grand Master del Carretto, as it recalls his work in Kos town and Rhodes.

Perhaps the best example of the differences between the old and new styles is to be seen in the harbour-side castle in Kos. This is easier to take in than the 4km circuit of the walls of Rhodes, though the latter do contain further refinements (below). The hurriedly built town walls of Kos are not particularly impressive in their ruined state, but the castle is a very clear indication of how the defensive skills of the Knights had been forced to develop in the 60 or so years that separate the inner part of the castle from its massive outer enceinte.

The original castle was a rectangle of some 45m by 35m with round towers at each corner and a keep in the middle, centrally placed on the spit of land that forms the east side of Mandráki harbour. Most of it is still intact except on the east side, facing the open sea, where its wall was incorporated in that of the new castle. Although this comparatively thin-walled edifice managed to withstand Mehmet's assault in 1480, it was badly damaged by an earthquake the following year, and the great builder d'Aubusson resolved to rebuild.

The new enceinte of about 100m by 60m occupies nearly all of the available land on the east side of Mandráki. The work was begun by d'Aubusson, carried on by d'Amboise, and completed by del Carretto in 1514. The walls were very thick and solid with a broad path along the top behind the massive battlements, to make it easier to move men and guns. They, and the corner towers, have a marked batter at the bottom. They are faced with carefully squared stones and incorporated a great deal of ancient and Early Christian material, and are decorated with the arms of the Order, the Grand Masters, and several governors. On the south side, which is not protected by sea or harbour, there was a moat, now a palm-fringed road (Od, Finíkon), across which a bridge led to the only gate.

The two towers overlooking the harbour, like the walls, had gun positions in deep embrasures on the top, but they also have more, half-way down, and at ground level, so that cannon could still be brought to bear even if an enemy penetrated right into the harbour. (A problem with early cannon was that, if the barrels were depressed too far, the balls were inclined to lose contact with the charge and just trickle out of the barrel.) This feature can also be seen in Rhodes at the del Carretto bastion and in the moat near the gate of St George.

In Rhodes the visitor can have difficulty distinguishing the original, medieval work, from the Italian reconstructions of the first half of the 20C, both in the fortifications and the Palace of the Grand Masters.

The most important additions to the defences after 1480 involved an enormous earth-moving operation to extend the moat, leaving a solid bulwark in the middle, and to thicken the main walls. The dry moat was to become a 'killing ground' enfiladed by gun-fire from the walls and towers and accessible through posterns for counter attacks, and to keep it clear. At the same time the number of gates was reduced by three, and the blocked-off gates became defensive towers. Further additions were machicolations on some of the gate-towers, e.g. at the Marine gate, and on the towers of the Palace. Machicolation is also found at the gate of castle of Líndos.

As can be seen the curtain wall descends vertically to the moat. It was topped by a wall-walk with deep embrasures for cannon, and smaller apertures for archers and small arms. Here and at many other points a smaller, advance wall was built at a lower level. This had crenellations and small towers at intervals. The moat had a high counterscarp and was sometimes doubled (as here) with a defensive bulwark in the middle.

Painting

Although the majority of the churches continued to be decorated according to traditional principles, three different stylistic trends can be identified (I. Kollias): traditional Byzantine, Western European and Eclectic. The first is self-explanatory, and common throughout the islands, often in modest buildings; the second parallels the Gothic architectural innovations and is perhaps best exemplified in the figure of St Lucia in the Panayía tou Kástrou, where the severity of the Byzantine figures and style is modified in ways which can be directly related to Italian painting. Some miniatures, now in Paris but probably painted in Rhodes and including scenes of the medieval town, fall into this group. It is also evident in what survives or is known of the painted decoration of some secular buildings of the time of the Knights (the Castle, the Castellania, etc.).

The third can be seen in other paintings of the Panayía tou Kástrou, churches in Rhodes town and elsewhere. As the term suggests, the painters in this style drew inspiration from a variety of different sources, both traditional and Western, and they developed orginal stylistic devices and approaches to iconography. A good example of the latter is the treatment of the mocking of Christ in the church of Ayy. Nikólaos and Aikateríni at Triánda on Rhodes.

Relatively little survives in the way of **other art** from the time of the Knights. Sculptural remains consist of escutcheons sometimes with associated reliefs, tombstones in a severe style which recall the medieval brasses in English churches, and some elegant inscriptions. In the later part of the period, Renaissance influences become evident (Castellania relief) in the use of new motifs and softer forms, sometimes derived from antiquity, and more fluid composition.

Ottomans

In the Ottoman period, relatively few new buildings were constructed. There are some large new **mosques** on Rhodes and Kos, but most mosques of the period were converted Byzantine churches, with frescoes whitewashed over, furniture removed and minarets added. Oriented towards Mecca, the genuine mosque is normally preceded by an arcade of elegant arches. The domed interior, spacious and largely devoid of furniture or figurative decoration, in the Islamic tradition, will contain a *mihrab* (niche indicating the direction of prayer) and a tall *minbar* (pulpit). In the court outside is often a domed and colonnaded structure with characteristically wide and pointed ('cusped') arches covering a fountain for ritual ablutions, the fountain itself regularly surrounded by trellis work. There are also **fountains** unassociated with mosques, much simpler in character. The *turbeh* (mausoleum) is rather similar in style to the fountain building just described. Rhodes has the greatest variety of Ottoman architecture, including a school, a fine hamam, a library and an imaret. **Houses** were often altered (floors added and spaces subdivided) rather than constructed from scratch. Other common changes were balconies overhanging the street and projecting window embrasures. These additions were frequently removed by the Italians. In original houses of the period the ground floor was devoted to storage and the domestic quarters were above. The latter had no direct contact with the street. The two most important rooms were the *harem* and the reception room (*selamlik*). Although containing little furniture they were often painted and had brightly coloured rugs and cushions.

The Ottoman period has left little in the way of distinctive objects, although the subject has never been studied. The plates of Líndos however (see below) belong to this period and betray influences from further East. They may indeed have been manufactured in Asia Minor.

Painting in the Byzantine style after the Knights falls into the category of Post-Byzantine art (from the fall of the empire in 1453 to c 1830). We do not know much about individual artists but one figure of the post-Byzantine stage whose work is represented more than once in the Dodecanese (Tílos, Sími, Rhodes (Líndos)) is Gregory of Simi. Working in the late 18C he may have been trained in a school at the Panormítis Monastery on Sími whose other painters included Neófitos.

Italians

The Italian occupation of the Dodecanese has left a strong mark on three of the islands—Kos, Léros and Rhodes. On Kos the town plan, with broad streets and open spaces, is due to the Italians since the city had to be largely rebuilt following the devastation of the 1933 earthquake, and public buildings were constructed at this time. At Lakkí on Léros the important naval base required facilities and administrative buildings, some of them subsequently re-used as technical schools and mental hospitals. The architecture of the civilian administration is most clearly reflected on Kos (Palace of the Regent, etc.) and Rhodes (Cathedral; Nomarkhía; Limenarkhíon, New Agora, etc). The following description (S. Kostof) may help to set it in context:

> More typical in Fascist buildings is a style that derives partly from a generalized Mediterranean vernacular, and partly from that Late Antique architecture ... whose plain, noncolumnar aesthetic was now becoming known through the excavations at Ostia and ancient Roman colonies in North Africa. The ingredients of this style are primary geometric shapes, largely unadorned, flat unfeatured walls into which are cut unmolded arches or semidomed niches, shallow running bands that are the simple straight-edged abstraction of proper classical string-courses, semicylindrical corner towers. With the temple-front motif relegated to doorways and niches only, and the almost total absence of the column or its derivatives either as load-bearing or modulating elements, this Fascist architecture has a very ambiguous scale. It deprives itself of the varied play of light available to most classical styles and stresses instead the stark drama of broad, straight-edged shadows.

Although the derogatory adjectives 'pompous' and 'bombastic' sometimes employed to describe these buildings may often be justified, they show at least considerable variety. The Governors' Palaces on Rhodes and Kos are relatively ornate: generally characteristic are low-columned arcades, crenellated roofs and towers or other projections at roof level. The New Agora and Theatre on Rhodes have much plainer surfaces. *Bauhaus* design appears too (as in the Police Station at Ayía Marína on Léros), a reminder of architectural developments elsewhere and the reasons for their appearance in the Dodecanese. These buildings do however offer a violent contrast both to the vernacular architecture and to that of the Knights and Ottomans.

Vernacular architecture and 'Folk Art'

Architecture

The vernacular architecture of the Dodecanese in general, and Rhodes especially, is a particularly attractive and interesting feature of the islands. Whether in simple country dwellings or more elaborate town houses, builders were adept at blending their structures with the landscape or with the immediate urban environment, and the variety of buildings (no one is exactly the same as another) is endlessly fascinating. Rural villages gain their charm from this lack of uniformity. The basic geometry of the house is always modified, the lines never straight, and hard edges usually softened. Extensive use of whitewash is attractive against the bright blue sky (and effective at repelling heat) but this too is relieved by coloured doors and shutters and occasional decorative devices. This variety is compounded by the appearance of external influences, especially in the decoration, which derive from the complex history and wide foreign contacts of the Dodecanese.

Many of the houses in the villages of the Dodecanese follow the common Aegean type of low flat-roofed buildings with plain white-washed exteriors. The simplest form has just a single room. Most buildings, particularly in country villages, have an exterior court of some kind, however small. An alternative arrangement, found in larger and more complex houses, is to have an interior courtyard, reached by a passage from the street and often approached through an imposing doorway. There are thus basic distinctions, not only in size, but also in orientation. Buildings with an exterior court are open and integrated into the community; those with the interior court, concealed from view, keep themselves apart.

While the simplest versions can be seen almost anywhere, the grander houses of flat-roofed type are most impressively exemplified in Líndos where they were built from the 16C by wealthy merchants and seamen who, in masonry style and some Gothic decorative features, copied the houses of the Knights in the town of Rhodes. Closed structures with interior courts, they have large and elaborately carved doorways and windows, whose designs mix Byzantine, Arabic, Gothic and native motifs, black and white pebbled courts and floors with figured and other motifs, and a richly appointed main room (called 'the good house').

The traditional contents and arrangement of the main room were essentially similar both in the fine mansions and in ordinary houses, although the multiplication of rooms in the former meant that some domestic functions (e.g. cooking), originally performed in part of the main room, were put elsewhere and the quality of furniture etc. varied according to the means of the inhabitants. The room is normally divided into two parts, often by a large arch which helps to support the wide ceiling. The further wall opposite the entrance is occupied by a raised wooden sleeping platform reached by steps. The marriage bed was part of this but divided off by a special and elaborately embroidered curtain (the *spervéri*) with a 'doorway'. Beneath the platform were cupboards and storage space. Wooden settles incorporating also storage chests, shelves, and stands for water jars are other items of furniture. They and the sleeping platform may carry carved decoration. Ceilings, and sometimes room partitions, may be painted with various motifs and the floors paved, like the courts, with pebble mosaics. Embroidered textiles add to the colourful appearance as do the rows of gaily decorated plates which are a distinctive feature of the decoration of Rhodian houses.

The most important subsequent development in more substantial housing was the spread of a taste for the neoclassical style in the 19 and earlier 20C. These houses were more regularly designed (usually square or rectangular) had pitched and tiled roofs and made use of classical decorative forms (pilasters, mouldings etc) in a distinctive, though usually quite restrained manner. The sober elegance of these buildings is evident in many of the houses of Sími (here the lower floors were often used as business premises, the upper for domestic; and wrought iron balconies are a regular feature), in the suburbs of Rhodes (not the old town) and in the public buildings of smaller communities.

Folk art

The presence of items of folk art (objects which have a practical function as well as being decorative) is evident from the above description of the contents of Rhodian houses. Embroideries are treated more fully below and other categories include metalwork, carved and/or painted wooden objects, and pottery.

Of Dodecanesian **pottery**, Lindos plates are particularly notable on Rhodes.

These colourful products were originally manufacture in the 16 and 17C and continued into the 18C. Some scholars suggest that they were made, not on Rhodes, but at a centre in Asia Minor. One story tells of a Grand Master of the 14C who captured a ship in which some Persian potters were travelling and forced them to work for him at Líndos. The early designs are often florals, carefully adapted to the circular field. Later humans, animals and ships become more prominent. The tradition continues today.

Wood-carving, often extremely detailed and elaborate, is frequently found on the iconostases of churches and on the structures of and wooden furnishings in the main rooms of richer houses. Other wooden objects (e.g. chests) could also have carved decoration.

Embroidery

Although the working of embroidery is no longer an integral part of women's domestic life in Greece, fine examples of this delicate and colourful craft can be seen in museums, including many of the smaller, local establishments, and sometimes in private houses. Pieces have also found their way abroad, originally via private collectors (Victoria and Albert Museum).

Embroidered decoration was applied to dresses, particularly those parts of the white underdress (sleeves, hem, etc.) which would have been still visible beneath the outer garment, and to some other personal items (kerchiefs). It was used too on a wide range of domestic items—cushion covers and pillow cases, bedspreads, curtains, etc., either as an edging or more widely spread. A particular feature of Dodecanesian embroidery is its association with the covering of the bed-platform (a characteristic element of traditional houses in this part of Greece), and the separate bed-tent (*spervéri*) which enclosed the marriage bed and separated it from the rest of the sleeping-platform.

The prevalence and high quality of the embroidered decoration of these items draws attention to the association of the craft with the constituents of a bride's dowry, for which many of the fine embroidered pieces were made. This also helps to explain the spread and exchange of motifs, when a bride from one area took embroidered objects to her new home elsewhere.

The craft was already largely defunct in the late 19C, discouraged by the import of mass produced silks. Its derivation is much more problematic. Though influences from Byzantine (double-headed eagle and other heraldic devices) and from medieval Italian textiles is certain, and connections can be seen with designs found in Turkey (the mosque and cypress pattern converted, in Greece, into a monastery and cypress design) and further east, it seems quite possible that some of the motifs, and perhaps the techniques, are of even older origin. One recalls that the suggestion that the 'Wild Goat style' of pottery decoration (6C BC) was based on tapestry designs.

The colours of Dodecanesian embroidery are predominantly, though not exclusively, red and green, and they are worked in two basically different styles— one very fine, and the other with a much thicker silk.

Particularly common motifs in the Dodecanese are a number of variants of a single, isolated, though often repeated element, sometimes called '*glastra*' ('flower-pots'), but known by different names on different islands and according to the tastes of different scholars. These appear in widely differing forms and are found in both the fine and the coarser styles.

Also widespread are motifs drawn from the natural world—birds, animals, flowers, leaves, trees—which are often reduced to highly stylised shapes, with mainly rectilinear elements. They are quite frequently found in a heraldic arrangement, where two identical forms are disposed to either side of a '*glastron*' or other central element. A greater variety of more 'realistic' motifs, including ships and human figures, closer in character to the embroidery of the Cycladic islands, is found in the northern Dodecanesian islands of Pátmos and Astipálaia, which are both closer to the Cyclades and shared with them in the medieval period a stronger strain of influence from Italy than from the Knights, whose monastic attitudes may have had a negative influence on the production of embroideries.

Particular motifs or versions of them (e.g. of the '*glastra*') can be attributed to specific islands, though the origin of many pieces now in central collections is often in doubt and the exchange of motifs by marriage has already been mentioned.

Museums and buildings to visit

Museums
The Archaeological Museum on Rhodes and the new exhibitions in the Castle of the Knights, between them covering the history of the island to 1522, have the most extensive and comprehensive collections of finds from the Dodecanese. The upper floors of the Castle of the Knights have excellent Roman and Early Christian mosaics. The Museum on Kos has a large and good collection of sculpture, with a strong emphasis on the Hellenistic and Roman periods; the pottery collection is not at present open to the public. There are mosaics in the museum and on some of the archaeological sites on Kos. The Museum of Decorative Arts on Rhodes has excellent Folk Art and the Municipal Gallery a fine collection of modern paintings. There are no other museums with large collections; on the other hand there are several minor archaeological collections, and good small local museums (the latter often in old houses, themselves excellent examples of vernacular architecture, and with contents to match) with interesting objects or collections relating to one or more of the categories described above.

Buildings
No island is without interest from the point of view of vernacular architecture. Olimbos on Kárpathos is a centre of great importance for the simpler traditional houses, Líndos on Rhodes is exceptional in the wealth of its grander housing from the 16C onwards. The suburbs of Rhodes town and the houses of Sími have good examples of imposing neoclassical buildings, which are to be found everywhere in the public sphere. Unexpected islands like Kastellórizo and Khálki have fine structures from periods of past prosperity, though not all have been restored to their former splendour. For the best examples of ancient architecture, you must look to sites like the Asklepieion on Kos and the sanctuary of Athena on the acropolis at Líndos (Rhodes); and in the military field, to the walls of ancient Nísyros or the ancient gateway built into the castle of the Knights on Tílos. Kos is particularly rich in remains of Early Christian churches. There is a good range of Byzantine churches in Rhodes town, the monastery on Pátmos should not be missed and other islands have their jewels (the monastery of Ayíos

Pandeleímon on Tílos, Moní Thári on Rhodes). For the time of the Knights, the old town of Rhodes is unparallelled, although almost all islands have their castles. Ottoman mosques, houses, tombs and fountains can be seen mainly on Rhodes and Kos. The public architecture of the Italian occupation is prominent on Léros, as well as Rhodes and Kos.

Flora and fauna

Flora

The flora of the islands is as varied as their landscape, which includes the bare, almost lunar, summit of Mt Atáviros on Rhodes, or the barren hills north of Khóra on Kálimnos, and the lush green of some of the valleys and coastal strips. Most common is the evergreen scrub and maquis that forms the background in so much of the Mediterranean area. Many of the islands were formerly much more tree-covered than today, but man, goats and fire have all taken their toll, so that anything approaching a forest is a rarity. The commonest trees are pines and cypresses, oaks—especially the evergreen varieties—and junipers. In the wetter areas the plane, *Platanus orientalis*, sometimes of considerable size, may be found—for example, the 'Plane tree of Hippocrates' in Kos town. Also found in Rhodes, alone in Greece, is the Anatolian species *Liquidambar orientalis*.

Naturally enought the *flora* are influenced by those of Anatolia and of the neighbouring islands, especially Crete. Crete itself has some 130 endemics and about 20 of these are also found on Kárpathos (e.g.in Spring: *Anemone heldreichii, Cyclamen creticum, Ophrys cretica, Paeonia clusii, Ranunculus creticus*) but not, so far, recorded elsewhere in the Dodecanese, though some of them are almost certainly to be found on Kásos too. There are also many other trees and shrubs which may be found in the wild, but which have been domesticated and are prized for their fruit, their flowers, for shade and for roadside planting. Apart from the ubiquitous olive and vine, these include fig, almond, orange, lemon, bay, pomegranate, carob, arbutus, Judas, storax, tamarisk, mulberry, oleander, myrtle and Spanish broom. And you must not be surprised to meet what we think of as a small household plant, the Rubber plant, *Ficus elastica,* as a full-grown tree towering above the Carretto bastion of the harbour-side castle of Kos.

There have also been many plants imported for commercial or garden use in recent centuries. The Asian hibiscus and the bougainvillea from Brazil decorate gardens and houses all over Greece, and it is hard to imagine a Greek meal without potatoes and tomatoes, but it is not generally known that the agave, *Agave americana*, and the prickly pear, *Opunta ficus-indica*, which now seem so much at home in the Mediterranean, are also American imports.

A word of warning to those looking for wild flowers in the islands, and indeed elsewhere in Greece: what may look a soft and gentle landscape will usually be packed with extremely spiny and prickly plants. The sandals and shorts or skirts that are fine on the beaches are not recommended for flower hunting. If your legs have been scratched to bits, you are not going to fuss over whether it was by *Silybum marianum* or *Onopardum acanthium,* or some other sort of thistle. Stout shoes or boots and long trousers are advisable, and a stick can be useful to clear a path. Beware, too, of snakes.

Plant lovers should be aware that the digging up of wild plants and their importation from Greece into Britain is forbidden under international laws. The only exceptions are, for UK residents, if you have a special permit from the Ministry of Agriculture, Fisheries and Food, or if you are part of an expedition organised by a national body such as the Royal Horticultural Society or the Alpine Garden Society.

The best time for wild flowers is undoubtedly between March and May, but the summer and autumn are far from colourless, and there is still some colour even in winter. Mentioned below are a very limited and personal selection. Anyone keen to know more should take a good reference book with plenty of colour pictures to help identification e.g. *Flowers of Greece and the Aegean* by A. Huxley and W. Taylor, or one of the many books by George Sfikas, readily available in Greece—*Wild Flowers of Greece*, *Trees and Shrubs of Greece* etc.

A good area for spring flowers is to be found on the moss-covered slopes under the trees on Mt Profitis Ilías on Rhodes. Here you may find many varieties of crocus, orchids and cyclamen including some of the Rhodian endemics such as *Crocus fleishceri* and the orchids *Ophrys bornmuelleri* and *O. fuciflora candica*, *Cyclamen repandum rhodense* and possibly another endemic, *Paeonia rhodia*. Lower down on rocky hillsides by roads, or wasteland and in fields you can expect to find marjoram, thyme, Jerusalem sage (*Phlomis fruticosa*), various other sages, cistuses (the cistus - rock rose is so common that it may be the source of Rhodes' name of the 'Island of Roses'), mulleins, spurges and campanulas, common asphodel and *Asphodeline lutea*, and fields full of various anemones, chrysanthemums and poppies, such as *Anemone coronaria*, *Ranunculus asiaticus*, *Chrysanthemum segetum*, and *C. coronoarium* and *Papaver rhoeas*. Many of these will carry on flowering into June and even July.

In later summer and autumn look out by the sea for the tall spikes of the giant squill, *Urginea maritima*, and the sweet-scented white flowers of the sea daffodil, *Pancratium maritimum*. Autumn also brings out the Autumn-flowering crocuses such as *Crocus tourefortii*, colchicums, sternbergias and **Cyclamen graecum* and *C. hederifolium* as well as the colourful fruits of the pistachio family *Pistacia lentiscus* and *P. terebinthus* and the arbutus, which often carries its red fruit and white heather-like flowers at the same time. (**Cyclamen coum* is not found on Kos nor elsewhere in the Dodecanese. The name perhaps derives not from Kos but from an area in southern Turkey. It may be a matter of season, but I have not seen the cos lettuce in Kos either.)

Fauna

The *fauna* include deer (reintroduced by the Italians), foxes, hares, badgers, martens and hedgehogs; partridges, vultures, jackdaws, and jays. In antiquity Rhodes was infested with snakes (its name may derive from 'erod' a Phoenician word for snake), and farmers still wear leather boots to the knee as protection against a small species which is poisonous. The larger snakes are harmless. Some of the lizards are large: the 'Rhodes dragon' (*Agama stellio*) grows to 35.5cm. There are so many butterflies that Rhodes has been called 'Butterfly Island'.

Sponge-fishing

The sponge industry, which now survives to a limited extent only on Kálimnos, was formerly the main source of livelihood both there and on Sími, and important too on Khálki, Kastellórizo, and Astipálaia. Sponges were fished and used continuously from ancient times, but demand increased dramatically from the Industrial Revolution. In the 19th and earlier 20C large numbers of people were occupied both in the fishing itself and in the subsequent processing and packing of the produce, which explains the very high population levels on those islands at the time. Reminders of this state of affairs can still be seen in the continued sale of sponges (now mostly imported) and the abandoned or converted warehouses where they were stored, treated and packed for export.

Although sponges were originally harvested in the Aegean, the supplies were eventually depleted and, in the mid 19C, the north African coast became the main source. During the Italian occupation, exploitation of that area was prohibited to the Dodecanesian islanders, the industry declined, and many emigrated, including the Kalimnian founders of the sponge-diving community at Tarpon Springs in Florida.

Expeditions to north Africa were long and dangerous. Contracts were agreed and crews assembled in the spring for an absence of 6–7 months. Songs and customs grew up around the departure (the week after Easter) and return of the fleets, which were attended with great festivities. The diving boats would be accompanied by a larger vessel with provisions, and a transport, for taking home the catch and returning with mail and replenishments.

There were several methods of getting sponges. Apart from the process of spotting and plucking or netting sponges in shallow water, the simplest involved a diver equipped only with a stone weight, a basket and a hand-line to the surface. Both the time spent below water (1–2 minutes) and the depth (20–30 fathoms) was severely restricted. A second method made use of a special suit with an air-line to the surface. The diver again carried a stone weight and a bag. He also took a special skin bag to provide air in case of interruption to the supply line. With this equipment divers could reach a greater depth (30–40 fathoms) and work for longer (1 hour).

The most elaborate system (introduced c 1880) was the *skáfandro*. This consisted of a metal helmet with large windows, bolted onto a corslet (also of metal) and worn over a rubber suit; additional weights were attached and a line allowed communication with the surface. Diving took place from a special boat, to a depth of 35-40 fathoms, where the diver could stay for 1–2 hours. An air-line to the helmet supplied air from the surface via a pump.

The deeper the diving the more dangerous it became and lives were frequently lost and injuries sustained, whether as the result of too rapid decompression, ruptures to the air-line, sharp rocks, poisonous plants or fierce marine creatures. The return of the fleet after so long was greeted with much celebration and rejoicing—at least by the families of those who had survived unscathed.

When first collected the sponges were raw and slimy. Some initial treatment—removal of natural juice, soaking, drying—was required if a good colour was to be maintained. Back on land they were trimmed, and further cleaned, with chemicals and washing in sea-water. After drying, they were graded according to quality and size, and packed for export.

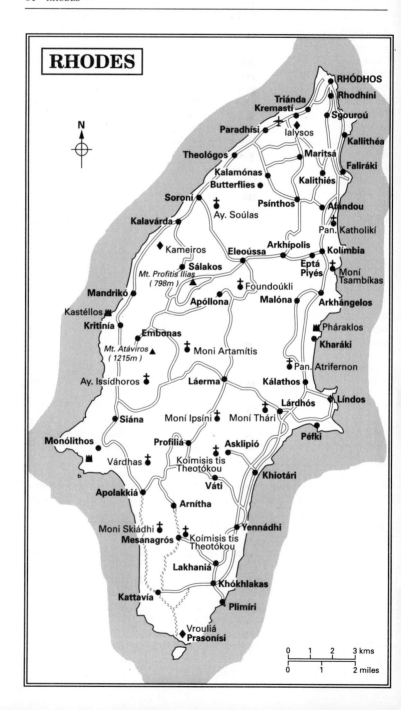

RHODES

Rhodes

Rhodes (Ρόδος; in Greek, Rhódhos, anc. *Rodos*) is the largest, richest and most varied of the islands of the Dodecanese. Its associations with the Sun God, Helios, on the one hand, and the rose, on the other, testify to its warm climate and fertility. Rhodes is well-equipped to cater for the sun and pleasure-seeker (unusually for Greece it boasts a golf-course and casino), while offering quiet spots and plenty of sights for other tastes. For a single-centre holiday it is ideal. Rich in both seaside and mountain scenery, the island is big enough to absorb the large numbers of tourists which it now attracts. The coasts to the (more sheltered) east and west of the main town have long expanses of fine sandy beaches and numerous hotels. Further south, although there are one or two busy resorts, like Faliráki, the coast is progressively less developed, even deserted, and it is not difficult to find unspoilt rural communities, either by the sea or further inland. In contrast to the areas of rich coastal plain are high mountains in the centre, much of them covered with unexpectedly luxuriant forests. The foothills have some wooded glens and shaded streams. Much of the island is good for walking—gentler rambles in the coasts and foothills, more strenuous on the mountain slopes. The remarkable walled medieval town of Rhodes itself, preserved almost intact, is an experience not to be missed and the island has other castles and some fine frescoed Byzantine churches, as well as ancient sites at Ialysos, Lindos and Kameiros, and fascinating museums in the main town. Spring and autumn are the best times to visit.

Rhodes has a population of 84,300. It is separated from the southwest coast of Turkey by the Strait of Marmara, about 11km wide. The island is diamond-shaped, with an area of 1398.5sq km, 77km long from north to south and with a maximum width of 35.5km. A range of hills runs from north to south rising from either end towards the west of the centre, where Mt Atáviros rises sharply to 1215m. The other summits do not exceed 823m. Much of the island is fertile, with a wide variety of plants and trees; vegetation grows to some of the mountain-tops. There are oranges, lemons, figs, pears, pistachio and olives. Amongst the flowering plants, oleanders, bougainvilleas and hibiscus are most striking, especially against the whitewashed background of country houses.

The climate of Rhodes resembles that of eastern Sicily. The temperature varies from 10° C in winter to 30°–32° C in summer. The winds are constant and occasionally violent, though the east side of the island is usually sheltered. Windmills are a feature of the landscape. The dry season lasts from April to the end of October, while the period from November to the end of March is relatively wet.

History

Note: since Rhodes has played such a dominant role in the Dodecanese, there is inevitably overlap between this description of the island's history and the overall picture provided in the introduction, The Dodecanese, above. In the section that follows attention is concentrated on details of specifically Rhodian history; art and architecture, in whose development also the island was of overriding importance, are covered only in the introductory article above.

In antiquity the island was called *Aithrea*, *Ophioussa* (from its snakes), *Telchinia*, and several other names. The name of *Rhodes* is of uncertain etymology, but is probably not derived (as so often thought) from the Greek word for rose, ρόδον. Pindar tells of the birth of Rhodes, offspring of the love of Helios, the Sun God, for the nymph Rhoda.

Neolithic remains have been found at various cave sites. In the Bronze Age the island was influenced first by Minoan and then by Mycenaean culture, Ialysos and Trianda, in particular, having produced important finds. Volcanic ash layers at Trianda show that Rhodes was affected by the volcanic catastrophe on the island of Thera which occurred in the middle of the second millennium BC.

Homer mentions three cities in Rhodes—*Lindos*, *Ialysos* and *Kameiros* (*Iliad*, II, 656), as contributors of ships to the fleet which sailed to Troy: in the Archaic period they were members of the Dorian *hexapolis*. These three Dorian cities of Rhodes were active and prosperous, trading widely in the Mediterranean and North Africa, and founding or sharing in the foundation of colonies from Sicily to the coast of Asia Minor. Mercenaries from the island fought for Egyptian pharaohs. In the 6C BC government by tyrants was the norm.

Having submitted to the Persians in 490, in 478 the Rhodians joined the Delian Confederacy as subject-allies of Athens, but in 411, late in the Peloponnesian War, they revolted in favour of Sparta. In 408 the three cities united to found a new capital city of Rhodes, which they populated with their own citizens. The overall layout, attributed to Hippodamos of Miletus, the most famous town-planner of antiquity, has been traced by archaeologists. This new city, whose planning was extravagantly praised by Strabo, immediately became prominent. At first it had an oligarchic government, and in 396 submitted to Sparta. Later a democratic constitution was adopted and its citizens joined the Athenians, whom they helped, in conjunction with the Persian fleet, to defeat the Spartans at the battle of Knidos (394).

In 378 Rhodes joined the Second Athenian Confederacy, but in 357 she revolted again, this time at the instigation of Mausolus, king of Caria, who placed a Carian garrison in the island. As allies of Persia the Rhodians helped the city of Tyre when it was besieged by Alexander the Great. In 332 a Macedonian garrison was installed but this was expelled after the death of Alexander. In the wars that followed, the Rhodians allied themselves with Ptolemy I, who assisted them in 305 when their city was besieged by Demetrios Poliorketes. When, after a year, Demetrios was compelled to raise the siege, he was so impressed by the defenders' valour that he left them his siege artillery. The proceeds from the sale of this were used to make the Colossos. The Rhodians awarded divine honours to Ptolemy as their saviour: hence his name Soter.

The following period saw the acme of Rhodes' prestige and prosperity— she became the first naval power in the Aegean. Her port became the centre of trade between Italy, Greece and Macedonia, and Asia and Africa; her currency was accepted everywhere. Rhodian law, the earliest code of marine law, was universally respected: Augustus took it as a model, an example followed by Justinian, and its provisions are still quoted today. With a population of 60,000–80,000, the city was lavishly adorned with works of art. Her school of sculpture was widely renowned and its products in demand. Devastation by the great earthquake of 222 BC inspired an international programme of aid in money and talent. Even as late as the 1C AD, when the city had been despoiled of most of its treasures, Pliny counted no fewer than 2000 statues, many of them colossal.

The Rhodians were enthusiastic admirers of athletics, music, and oratory. The orator Aeschines (389–314 BC), after his discomfiture at the hands of Demosthenes, founded at Rhodes a school of rhetoric, which was later to be attended by famous Romans, including Cato, Cicero, Julius Caesar, and Lucretius. Apollonius (fl. 222–181 BC), a native of Alexandria, taught rhetoric at Rhodes with so much success that the Rhodians awarded him the cognomen 'Rhodius'.

By the 2C BC the Rhodians were allies of Rome. Their help against Philip V of Macedon, which led to his defeat at Cynoscephalae in 197, gained them the Cyclades; the participation of their fleet in the war against Antiochus the Great, king of Syria, in 188 BC, the former Syrian possession of south Caria, where they were already established. Rhodian support for the cause of Perseus brought swift Roman retribution. After Pydna Rhodes had to surrender her possessions on the mainland of Asia Minor and, in 166, her trade was injured when the Romans declared Delos a free port.

In the Mithridatic wars Rhodes recovered the favour of Rome. Mithridates unsuccessfully besieged the city. Sulla restored to Rhodes her lost Asiatic possessions. In the civil war Rhodes sided with Julius Caesar and suffered in consequence at the hands of Cassius, who plundered the city in 43 BC and destroyed or captured the island's fleet. This was a fatal blow to the naval power of Rhodes.

Augustus accorded to Rhodes the title of Allied City. Vespasian (emperor AD 70–79) incorporated it in the empire. Reattached to the province of Asia, it became under Diocletian (284–305) capital of the province of the Islands. It was visited by St Paul during his second or third journey (*Acts*, xxi, 1) and had a bishop very early. In the 4C the bishops of Rhodes were granted the title of Metropolitan, with jurisdiction over 12 of the dioceses of the Archipelago.

After the division of the Empire in 395, Rhodes naturally became part of the Eastern Empire and followed its destiny. From 654 it was frequently pillaged and for a time occupied by the Saracens. In 1082 Alexander Comnenus gave the Venetians important privileges there. In the Crusades Christian ships used the ports of Rhodes as a convenient stopping-place. During the Fourth Crusade, which established the Latin empire of Constantinople, the Greek Governor of Rhodes, Leo Gavalas, declared the independence of the island. Although the Rhodians deserted the Roman church in the 9C, the Metropolitan of Rhodes attended the Council of Lyons in 1274 and was a signatory to the short-lived reunion of the Eastern and Latin churches. Later the Genoese obtained control of the island and in 1306 took in as refugees the Knights of St John of Jerusalem who had been expelled from the Levant by the Knights Templar. Refused possession of Rhodes by the Byzantines, the Knights of St John took it in 1309, after a siege lasting two years.

Having conquered Rhodes, the Knights established a powerful fleet which protected the island's trade. Pope Clement V assigned to them part of the property of the Templars who had been suppressed in 1312. For two centuries the Knights of St John defied the attacks of the Turks. For his assistance to the Knights during the siege of 1313, Amadeus V, count of Savoy, was rewarded by a grant of the arms of the Order with a collar bearing the letters F.E.R.T. (Fortitudo ejus Rhodum tenuit). The Knights took part in the capture and later in the defence of Smyrna, and withstood two great sieges—in 1444 by the Sultan of Egypt, and in 1480 by Mehmet II, at which time their infantry general ('turcopolier') was an Englishman, John Kendal.

At last, in June 1522, Suleiman I, after capturing Belgrade, attacked Rhodes with a force said to have numbered 100,000 men. The Knights mustered only 650, with the addition of 200 Genoese sailors, 50 Venetians, 400 Cretans and 600 of the inhabitants. Pope Adrian VI vainly implored the Christian princes to come to their aid. The Turks had the city blockaded by sea. They eventually secured the heights above it and from there shelled the fortifications. Several times the besieged repaired the breaches in the walls, but their numbers daily diminished. They had spent their strength and traitors had infiltrated into their ranks. In December the Turks made another and final breach in the walls. The Knights capitulated on honourable terms. On 1 January 1523, the Grand Master, Villiers de l'Isle Adam, with 180 surviving brethren, left the island. They first retired to Candia (Herakleion), Crete, and in 1530 to Malta.

The military architecture of this period has left a strong mark on the islands of the Dodecanese. The old town of Rhodes, the headquarters of the Knights, has fine examples of their public and domestic architecture in western European styles.

After the departure of the Knights at the beginning of 1523 began 400 years of Ottoman control, the most obvious consequence of which was the conversion of churches into mosques.

Not till 1660 were the Fathers of the Mission able to return to Rhodes and administer to the Christian slaves. In 1719 they were placed under the protection of the Apostolic Prefecture of Constantinople. In 1873 French Franciscan Sisters established schools and in 1889 the Brothers of the Christian Doctrine founded the College of St John. In 1877 the island was created an apostolic prefecture.

In 1912 the Italians captured Rhodes after a short siege and remained in possession for 35 years. It became the seat of the Governor of the Dodecanese. The Italian occupation has left its mark particularly in the massive public buildings of the main town. In the latter part of the Second World War the German takeover was initially resisted by the Italians. Its Jewish population were deported to concentration camps. In 1945 the island was freed by British and Greek commandos, and in 1947 it was officially returned to Greece.

Getting to Rhodes

■ **By air.** The airport is 16km southwest, near Paradhíssi. **International** services consist of weekly scheduled flights to Rome and Larnaka and, in season only, numerous charters to most European countries, including most British regional airports.

There are several **domestic** services (Olympic Airways and, once, by Air Greece which is over 10% cheaper) a day to Athens; also (Olympic) daily to Kárpathos; 4 weekly to Iráklion; less frequently to Thessaloníki, Míkonos, Thíra, Kos, Sitía (Crete), Kásos, Kastellórizo. SEEA (Southeast European Airlines) operates twice daily to Athens, and weekly to Thessaloníki.

■ **By sea**, some international services from Italian ports to Cyprus and the Near East call at Rhodes.

There are various routes from Piraeus to Rhodes: (1) direct in c 16 hours; (2) via Kos (sometimes also Kálimnos); (3) via the larger islands of the Dodecanese—Pátmos, Léros, Kálimnos, Kos; (4) as (3) but adding Nísiros, Tílos and Sími; (5) as (3) or (4) but calling at some of the Cyclades, plus Astipália; (6) via Mílos, Crete, Kárpathos and Kásos. (1)–(3) operate daily in season, less frequently at other times; (4)–(6) are never more than twice a week. There is a weekly service from Thessaloníki via northern Aegean islands (Límnos, Lésvos, Khíos, Sámos) and the larger of the Dodecanese.

Within the Dodecanese, the **Nísos Kálimnos** operates local services between Sámos and Kastellórizo, via Rhodes, twice weekly in each direction. There are services (daily or more in season) between Rhodes (Kámiros Skála) and Khálki, and Rhodes (Mandráki) and Sími. There are also excursions (e.g. to Líndos, Turkey) from Rhodes town.

Hydrofoils (seasonal) connect Rhodes with all islands as far north as Sámos.

Getting around Rhodes

■ **Local buses** from the sea front, opposite the Néa Agorá, frequently from c 06.00–21.00, including No. 3 to Rhodíni and No. 5 to the acropolis (Monte Smith) Buy tickets in advance from the kiosk by the stop.

Buses for the **west side** of the island, from Od. Avérof (west side of Néa Agorá/New Market) frequently to destinations as far as the airport (Paradhíssi), 24 daily; to Dhamátria (5), Embona (2), Kalavárdha (7), Kámiros (2), Kremastí (8), Maritsá (8), Monólithos (1), Petaloúdhes (2), Sálakos (4), Theológos (11); and to various hotels on the coast.

Buses for the **east side** of the island, from Od. Papágou/Plateía Rímini (Sound and Light Square), south of the Néa Agorá, Rhodes town: Afándou (13), Apolakiá (3 x week), Arkhángelos (13), Asklipió (3 x per week), Faliráki (21), Kalithiés (10), Kattavía (3 x per week), Kharáki (2), Kolímbia (10), Láerma (1), Lárdhos (3), Líndos (13), Malóna/Másari (4), Péfkos (2), Psínthos (3), Tsambíka (1), Yennádhi (3). Also from Kolímbia and Arkhángelos to Tsambíka Beach (1); from Líndos to Péfkos (2).

■ **Car hire** is readily available from **Avis** at the airport (tel. 92897) and Gallías 9 (tel. 24990); **Hertz** at the airport (tel. 92902) and Gríva 16 (tel. 21819);

Just, Orfanídhou 45 (tel. 31894). Others, mostly small companies, at the west end of A. Dhiákou (**Roderent, Thrifty**) and behind the Hotel des Roses (**Express, European, Auto-Europe**). You should be able to negotiate reductions at quieter times of year. **Motorcycles** and some bicycles are also available.

■ **Taxis**. There are taxi ranks in Sound and Light Square (list of fares displayed) and by Marine Gate, etc.

■ **Excursions boat**. From Mandráki, to Líndos and various beaches.

Rhodes town

The city of **Rhodes** (Rhódos; anc. *Rodos*) with a population of 42,400, is located at the northern tip of the island. Today it consists of two distinct parts. The OLD CITY, enclosed by walls built by the Knights, is immediately west of the central **Commercial Harbour**, used today for the larger vessels, and is itself divided into two. In the northwest is a walled enclosure, the **Castle of the Knights**, or Collachium. The rest of the city is the **Chora**. The NEW TOWN, built since the Italian occupation of 1912, and containing the public buildings of that period as well as numerous hotels, stretches north of the Old City as far as the north point of the island, and west to the foot of the acropolis of ancient Rhodes. It includes in the northwest the suburb of **Neokhóri** which was built and prospered during the 18C. There has also been modern development to the south of the Old City where, during the Turkish occupation, most of the communities of Greeks who were not permitted to reside within the walls were concentrated. The eastern border of the New Town is formed by **Mandráki**, the second and smaller harbour of Rhodes, now mainly used by yachts, caiques and smaller excursion boats. South of both Mandráki and the Commercial Harbour is a third anchorage, **Akándia**, protected since antiquity by a mole on the south, but it is not much used.

The city has suffered badly from earthquakes. In 225 BC the Colossos was overthrown; others occurred in AD 157, 515, 1364, 1481, 1851 and 1863. Rhodes town and its immediate vicinity have been subjected to massive tourist development in recent years. One side of this is represented by the existence of a golf course (at Afándou) and casino (in the Grand Hotel, Akti Miaoúli).

Historical topography of Rhodes town

Much of the **street plan** of the **ancient city** of 408 BC and after has been plotted by excavation in conjunction with aerial photography, largely under the present town. Except on the western acropolis and some sections of the wall, visible traces are not prominent. The town had a second (lower) acropolis in the area of the Palace of the Grand Masters, which was the location of other important buildings, including the Temple of Helios. The **agora** may have been to the south of this, in the vicinity of Od. Sokrátous. The **walls** of defence enclosed a large area, including the western acropolis and reaching almost to Sandy Point on the north, and the Rhodíni valley on the south—that is virtually the whole of the northern tip of the island.

The **medieval town** is clearly defined by its fortifications, within which the **Collachium** is a smaller walled area (castle) on the site of the ancient lower acropolis. The fortified area is considerably smaller than that of the ancient city.

In the Ottoman period, Turks and Jews occupied, respectively, the north-western and southeastern quarters of the fortified town, while the Greek population was obliged to live outside. Thus new quarters grew up, mainly to the south, beyond the Turkish cemeteries, and were named after their parish churches. Neokhóri (= New Town), to the northwest, developed rather later (?18C) and was mainly occupied by richer Greeks and foreign residents.

Visitors interested in the topography of the ancient town are strongly recommended to see the **exhibition** 'Ancient Rhodes: 2400 years', described below under the Palace of the Knights, which has an informative booklet available in English.

Two excellent studies, covering also some other sites on the island, are G. Konstantinopoulos, *Ancient Rhodes*, 1986, Cultural Foundation of the National Bank of Greece (in Greek only) and Chr. Karouzos, *Rhodes*, 1973 (also in English, though now difficult to find; especially for the town of Rhodes). Two outstanding works (available at museum desks and in local shops) on the remains of the period of the Knights are E. Kollias, *The city of Rhodes and the palace of the Grand Master*, 1988 and (by the same author) *The Knights of Rhodes: the Palace and the City*, 1991. Both have the same excellent plan of the old town but that in the latter is smaller and easier to manipulate when walking. The more peaceful atmosphere of former years in delightfully reflected in Lawrence Durrell's *Reflections on a Marine Venus*, 1960.

■ **Sources of information. NTOG/EOT/Tourist Police**, 5 Makaríou/Papágou; **Local Tourist Office** (seasonal), Plateía Rímini (Sound and Light Square). A tourist newspaper, *Rodos News*, is available free from the NTOG and other outlets. There are numerous **travel agents**, including **Gem Travel**, Papaloúka 31, tel. 0241 76206, 35348, fax 0241 37548; **Kariba Travel**, Ionos Dhragoúmi 18, tel./fax 0241 24650, 75391, 78170; **Kástro Travel**, Ameríkis 49, tel. 0241 21008, 31671, fax 0241 31778.

■ **Post office**, on Mandráki, opposite the cathedral (Mon–Sat 07.30–20.00 for most services; Sun 08.30–14.00). Mobile post office on Orféos.

■ **OTE**, 25 Martíou and Ameríkis.

■ **Limenarkhíon**, Makaríou and Pl. Elefthrías, next to the post office.

■ **Cash machines** (ATMs) taking Access/Visa, etc., at the bottom of the Street of the Knights (Commercial Bank of Greece) and (opposite) the National Bank of Greece. There are also some in the new town.

■ **Olympic Airways**, 9 Ieroú Lókhou (tel. 0241 24571); for **Air Greece** ask travel agents

■ **Bookshops**. **To Dhéntro**, Kheimarrás 14, is the only decent bookshop in Rhodes. The books occupy a spacious basement with a coffee and reading area. Above are stationery, childrens' games and pictures. English language material is restricted but not non-existent, and there are lots of beautifully produced and illustrated volumes to enjoy.

Tomarás, Sof. (not El.) Venizélou 5–7 has some English novels and guide books and **Papaioánnou** at Tarpon Springs 27 a few novels. Official guidebooks can also be got from the desks of major museums or the bookshop in the Street of the Knights.

■ **Supermarket**. **Páppou**, Od. 25 Martíou 7 (large food department in basement). Mon–Fri 08.30–13.15 and 17.00–20.30; Sat 08.30–14.00.

■ **Police**. Od. Eth. Dhodhekanísson (tel. 0241 27423).

■ **Consulates**. United Kingdom: Ameríkis 111 (tel. 0241 27247); USA: none.

■ **Excursions** to Líndos, Kámeiros, beaches, etc. Book at travel agents or (for boats) on the quay.

■ **Accommodation**. There are large numbers of hotels, both in Rhodes itself and down the coasts to the south (especially southwest, towards the airport, at Ixiá and Ialisós/Triánda). These are often mainly geared to the needs of visitors on package holidays. But there is also a wide range of other establishments and, in the Old Town, many pensions and rooms for rent. On the spot, the Municipal Information Office in Sound and Light Square (tel. 0241 35945) will help find accommodation in season. Representatives of rooming establishments meet boats and, increasingly, also flights.

Hotels in Rhodes town (area code 0241)

■ **New Town**

L Grand Hotel Astir Palace (378), Akti Miaoúli; pool, tennis etc.; 17,600–30,300 drs. Tel. 26284/9; fax 32217, 35589.

A Chevalier Palace (188), Stratigoú Gríva 3; pool; 14,300–26,590 drs. Tel. 22781; fax 21411.

A Iviskos (205), Nisírou 17; 12,500–20,500 drs. Tel. 24421/3; fax 27283. April–Oct.

B Cactus (177), Ko 14; 9380–15,800 drs. Tel. 26100, 26088, 26094, 22219.

B Plaza (132), Ieroú Lókhou 7; pool; 13,000–19,000 drs. Tel. 22501; fax 22544.

B Capitol (9) Dhilveráki 65–7; 8000–10,000 drs. Tel. 74154; fax 23991. March–Oct.

C Ambassadeur (50), Othonos 53 and Amalías; NPA. Tel. 24679, 30431. April–Oct.

C Filoxenía (22), Savá Dhiákou 28; 8000–10,000 drs. Tel. 37244. April–Oct.

C Tílos (21), Ethnárkhou Makaríou 46; 8000–11,500 drs. Tel. 24591, 24991.

C Victoría (35) 25 Martíou 22;
9700–13,500 drs. Tel. 24626.

■ **Old Town (Rooms and
Pensions**; 4000–8000 drs):
Andréas, Omírou 28. Tel. 34156.
La Luna, Ierokléous 21, off
Orféos.

Tel.25856, 25023.
Mínos, Omírou 5. Tel. 31813.
San Nikólis, Ippodhámou 61,
near the walls, with a wide range
of differently priced accommodation, some of which exceeds the
above prices. Tel. 34561, 36238;
fax 32034.

■ **Restaurants**. The food in Rhodes, and particularly in the Old Town, is
neither exciting, nor particularly cheap by Greek standards, though the
surroundings may sometimes compensate for this.

There are numerous eating-places in the **Old Town** and several rather
cheaper inside the **Néa Agorá**. In the **New Town**, the west end of A. Dhiákou
has several restaurants, and there are reasonable pizzerias in the area of Odd.
Ko and Papanikoláou, inland of the Hotel des Roses.

In the old town the **Poseidon** (Posidhón), seaward of the church of St. Mary
of the Bourg by the Gate of the Panayia, has a wide choice of good Greek dishes.
The service is pleasant and efficient and the atmosphere relaxing, if a little staid.
Unpretentious establishments include **Ta Astra** in Pithagóra, just off Plateía
Ippodhámou and the taverna **Nísyros** in Ayíou Fanouríou. Of the restaurants in
Od. Orféos, the **Cavo Doro** is tolerable, especially for lunch, and has a nice
garden. **Latíno** at Ippoddámou 11 is good for pizzas.

In the **New Town**, **Alatopípero** (M. Petrídhi 76; tel. 32421) and **Paliá
Istoría** (Mitropóleos 108; tel. 65494) are good.

In the **Néa Agorá** (mostly grilled food), look for places with old-fashioned
furniture and oil-cloth table-covers secured with elastic (often the outward
signs of a good meal) like **María's** or **Ikaros**.

The restaurant with the best reputation in Rhodes is the **Kioúpia** (tel.
91824) some distance away at Trís, inland from Ixiá, in the direction of the
airport.

The New Town

The public buildings of the new town, imposing and varied in style, are laid out
along the attractive waterfront of **Mandráki**, northern of the two natural
harbours. Comfortable cafés fill the arcades of the New Agora and gardens separate the street from the promenade. Excursion boats, hydrofoils and vessels for
Sími depart from here.

The word Mandráki, used elsewhere (cf. Kos) for small enclosed harbours,
means a sheepfold. An alternative name 'Harbour of the Galleys' is misleading,
since Mandráki was always secondary to the Commercial Harbour (the name
similarly misleading), and under the Knights was occupied by small boat builders.

The harbour entrance is guarded by two bronze deer, symbols of Rhodes:
during the Italian occupation a she-wolf, symbol of Rome (now in the Palace),
stood in the place of the figure nearer the sea. On the mole protecting the
eastern side of the basin stand three windmills and Fort St Nicholas, a cylindrical tower dating from 1464–67, topped by a lighthouse (view).

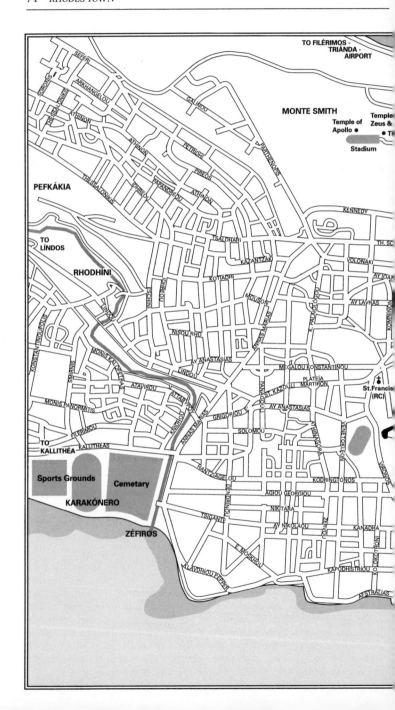

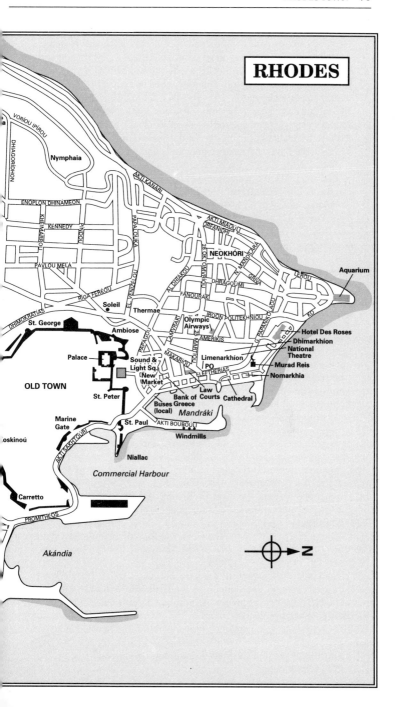

RHODES

Aquarium

VORÍOU IPÍROU

Nymphaia

DHAGORÍDHON

ENÓPLON DHINÁMEON

KENNEDY

AKTÍ KANÁRI

PAPALOÚKA

PÍNDOU

ELEVTHERÍOU VENIZÉLOU

AKTÍ MIAOÚLI

OREÁNICHI

NEOKHÓRI

ALEX. DHIÁKOU

KOLOKOTRÓNI

DHRAGOÚMI

GRÍVA

T. REOU

PAVLOU MELA

RIGA FEREOU

Soleil

Thermae

FANOURÁKI

ÍROON POLITEKHNÍOU

NIÓ

G. PAPANIKOLÁOU

KO

DHIMOKRATÍAS

St. George

Ambiose

Olympic
Airways

AMERIKÍS

PÁPADHÍAMÁNTÍ

MAKARÍOU

Hotel Des Roses

Dhimarkhíon

National
Theatre

Palace

Sound &
Light Sq.
(New
Market)

Limenarkhíon
PO

Murad Reis

OLD TOWN

ELEFTHERÍAS

Nomarkhía

St. Peter

Law
Courts

Cathedral

Bank of
Greece

Marine
Gate

Buses
(local)

Mandráki

oskinoú

St. Paul

AKTÍ BOUBOÚLI

AKTÍ SAKHTOÚRI

Windmills

Niallac

Commercial Harbour

Carretto

PROMITHÉOS

Akándia

N

The Colossos of Rhodes

Here, according to one theory, stood the Colossos of Rhodes, a bronze statue of Helios, the Sun-god, set up by Chares of Lindos c 290 BC and one of the Seven Wonders of the World. Its erection was financed by the sale of the siege artillery that Demetrios Poliorketes had presented to the city at the end of his unsuccessful siege (305–304 BC). It was 60 cubits (c 27m) high. Helios, the protector of the city of Rhodes, was represented with his head framed in sunrays and dressed in a *chlamys* (cloak); in his right hand he held a torch, which acted as a beacon for mariners. The tradition that the statue bestrode the harbour entrance and that ships passed beneath is not based on fact.

The statue fell in the earthquakes of 225 BC, and for 800 years its huge fragments lay undisturbed, respected by the superstitious reverence of the Rhodians. At last, in 653, Saracen corsairs collected them and took them to Tyre. There they were sold to Jewish merchants of Emesa, who carried them away on 900 camels to be melted down and resold. Reports of the discovery of a piece of the figure in 1987 proved groundless.

The public buildings lining the waterfront all date from the Italian occupation and were designed in various monumental styles by Florestano di Fausto. If it is hot or you are feeling lazy, the easiest way of getting an overall picture is to take the no. 3 bus (see excusion to Rhodíni, below). At the north end of Mandráki and dominating its mouth is the square campanile of the **Cathedral church of the Evangelismós** (Annunciation), built in 1925 on the model of the church of St John in the Old City (see below), which was destroyed in 1856. The fountain outside the west end is a copy of the 13C Fontana Grande at Viterbo. Joined to the cathedral is the bishop's residence and the former governor's palace, now the **Nomarkhía** (Prefecture). This is the most substantial monument of the Italian period, built in a Venetian Gothic style. The upper floor of the seaward side is decorated with varicoloured brickwork. Its arcaded inland façade, with marble decoration, closes the seaward side of Plateía Vas. Yioryíou, and contrasts with the severity of the **Dhimarkhíon** (opposite) and the **theatre** (north side of the square). To the north is a popular public beach (fee).

Beyond the theatre rises the elegant minaret of the **Mosque of Murad Reis**. In front stands a circular *turbeh* enclosing the tomb of Murad Reis, admiral of the Turkish fleet during the siege of Rhodes. In the shady cemetery by the mosque are the tombs (*turbehs* and sarcophagi, with tombstones) of many noble Turks who died in exile in Rhodes, including a Shah of Persia and a prince of the Crimea. Here, on the edge of the cemetery, was the **Villa Cleobolus**, featured in Lawrence Durrell's *Reflections on a Marine Venus* and, beyond, the former Hotel des Roses (1927).

The road follows the shore to the bare Akrotíri Ammou (Sandy Point), the most northerly point of the island. Here the **Hydrobiological Institute** houses a remarkable collection of preserved marine creatures caught in local waters (including sharks, sun-fish, manta and sword-fish) and an aquarium (09.00–16.30 daily; fee) which is unusually rich in octopods, molluscs, crustacea, etc.

The shore to the west of the Institute, although overlooked by many hotels, is accessible for swimming.

Returning to the cathedral and heading south along Mandráki, past the gardens, you pass in succession various **public buildings**: the main post office, moderately ornate, the Limenarkhíon then, on the other side of the narrow Od. Makaríou, the plain but forceful law courts, popular cafés under a neo-Gothic loggia, and the Bank of Greece. (Some features of the town further inland are mentioned with the visit to the akropolis, below.)

Contrasting with the golden stone of these buildings is the flat whiteness of the **Néa Agorá** (New Market), a huge polygonal precinct of the Italian period but in a Turkish style, with shops and restaurants. On the far side, Od. Avérof (parallel with the seafront), has the station for west coast bus services. Beyond the far end of the market is **Plateía Rímini**, more often known as Sound and Light Square (Πλατεία Ηχως και Φως), off which is access to the Son et Lumière auditorium beneath the north wall of the medieval city.

Outside the walls stretches the shady Garden of the Deer, ablaze with sub-tropical flowers. The bus station for the east coast is in Od. Papágou, which leaves the square heading inland.

The Old City

To enter the Old City, you continue parallel with the waterfront, here on a pleasant shaded footpath, and turn right under the massive Gate of Liberty (Píli Eleftherías) which was opened in 1924.

The Old City is described under two walks which can be combined, if you have enough energy. Apart from the main buildings where access is possible only at specified hours, the area is best seen in random wanderings and at quiet times of the day. The area continues to house a living community and, especially on its periphery, you will find the bustle of ordinary domestic life under the shadow of the medieval walls. Early morning is a good time to walk, especially in the summer when you avoid both heat and crowds, which can be oppressive. Odd. Ay. Fanouríou and Omírou are attractive streets, narrow and arched.

Walk 1   The Collachium and east to St Catherine's Gate

Note. In the case of the Old City asterisks (*) are given to buildings (not museums) on the grounds of particular interest and/or accessibility. Many churches are locked and access has to be specially arranged with the archaeological service. These are not normally asterisked, nor the contents described in detail.

Through Píli Eleftherías you enter the pleasant Plateía Símis, which is within the boundaries of the Collachium or Castle of the Knights proper. This, as the exclusive preserve of the Knights of St John, is divided from the remainder of the city by an inner wall (see plan). It includes the Palace of the Grand Masters and the 'Inns' or residences of the 'Tongues' (see The Dodecanese, above).

The centre of **Plateía Símis**, which communicates with the commercial harbour by the **Arsenal Gate** (Píli Navárkhou), is occupied by the picturesque if dismembered remains (discovered in 1922) of a 3C BC **Temple of Aphrodite**. These include foundations, bases and shafts of columns, and fragments of the entablature.

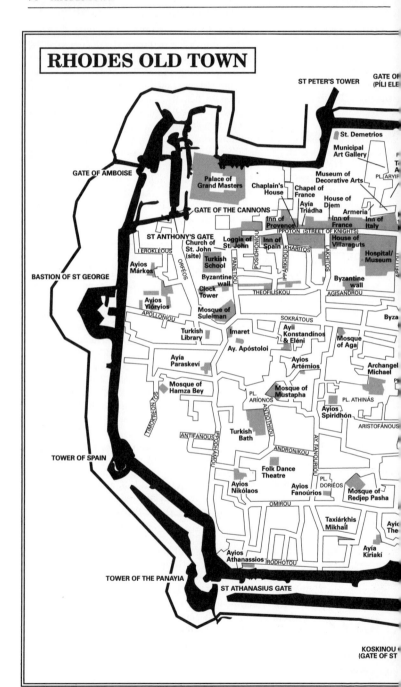

RHODES OLD TOWN

ST PETER'S TOWER

GATE OF (PÍLI ELE

St. Demetrios

Municipal Art Gallery

PL. ARYIF

GATE OF AMBOISE

Museum of Decorative Arts

Palace of Grand Masters

Chaplain's House

Chapel of France

House of Djem

Ayía Triádha

Armeria

GATE OF THE CANNONS

Inn of Provence

Inn of France

Inn of Italy

IPPOTON (STREET OF KNIGHTS)

ST ANTHONY'S GATE

Loggia of St. John

Inn of Spain

House of Villaraguts

Church of St. John (site)

KHARITOS

I EROKLÉOUS

ONFÉOS

Turkish School

POSIDHONIO

PPÁRKHOU

LAKHITOS

Hospital/ Museum

Ayios Márkos

PANETIOU

Byzantine wall

APERTOU

Byzantine wall

BASTION OF ST GEORGE

Clock Tower

THEOFILISKOU

AGISANDROU

Ayios Yióryios

APOLLONÍOU

Mosque of Suleiman

SOKRÁTOUS

Byza

Turkish Library

Imaret

Ayii Konstandínos & Eléni

Mosque of Aga

Ay. Apóstoloi

Ayía Paraskeví

Ayios Artémios

Archangel Michael

PI

Mosque of Hamza Bey

PL. ARÍONOS

Mosque of Mustapha

PL. ATHINÁS

Ayios Spiridhón

ARISTOFÁNOUS

TIMOTHEON OS

ANTIFÁNOUS

IPODHÁMOU

ANTIOHÍOU

Turkish Bath

ANDRONIKOU

AY. FANOURIOU

TOWER OF SPAIN

Folk Dance Theatre

PL. DORIÉOS

Ayios Nikólaos

Ayios Fanoúrios

Mosque of Redjep Pasha

OMÍROU

Taxiárkhis Mikhaíl

Ayic The

Ayía Kiriakí

Ayios Athanassios

IRODHÓTOU

TOWER OF THE PANAYIA

ST ATHANASIUS GATE

KOSKINOU (GATE OF ST

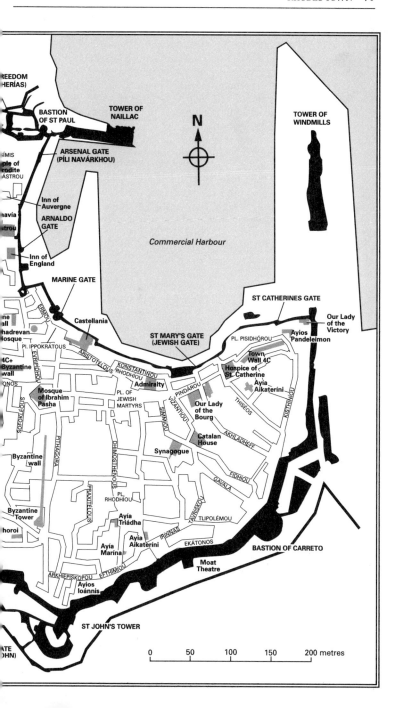

FREEDOM
(HERÍAS)

BASTION
OF ST PAUL

TOWER OF
NAILLAC

TOWER OF
WINDMILLS

N

SÍMIS
ple of
rodite
ÁSTROU

ARSENAL GATE
(PÍLI NAVÁRKHOU)

Inn of
Auvergne

navía
strou

ARNALDO
GATE

Inn of
England

Commercial Harbour

MARINE GATE

ne
all

Castellania

hadrevan
Mosque

ST CATHERINES GATE

Our Lady
of the
Victory

ERNOU

ST MARY'S GATE
(JEWISH GATE)

PL. PISIDHÓROU

Ayios
Pandeleimon

PL. IPPOKRÁTOUS

EVRIPIDHOU

ARISTOTÉLOUS

KONSTANTÍNOU
RHODHÍOU

Town
Wall 4C

4C+
Byzantine
wall

Admiralty

Hospice of
St. Catherine

PINDÁROU

Ayía
Aikateríni

ONOS

Mosque
of Ibrahim
Pasha

PL. OF
JEWISH
MARTYRS

SIMMÍOU

VIZANTÍOU

Our Lady
of the
Bourg

THISÉOS

KISTHINÍOU

SOKRÁTOUS

Byzantine
wall

PITHÁGORA

DHIMOSTHÉNOUS

Catalan
House

AKHLADHÉEF

Synagogue

PRAXITÉLOUS

FIDHÍOU

GAVALÁ

Byzantine
Tower

PL.
RHODHÍOU

AGÍSSKOU

horoi

Ayía
Triádha

TLIPOLÉMOU

Ayía
Marína

Ayía
Aikateríni

PÍNNAS

EKÁTONOS

BASTION OF CARRETO

ARKHIEPISKÓPOU

ETHIMÍOU

Moat
Theatre

Ayios
Ioánnis

ST JOHN'S TOWER

ATE
OHN)

0   50   100   150   200 metres

On the right of the square, is the **Municipal Art Gallery** (Mon–Sat 08.00–14.00; Wed 17.00–20.00; closed Sun), whose airy rooms contain an excellent collection representing numerous important Greek artists (including Theófilos, Ghíkas, Bouziánis, Kóntoglou, Tsaroúkhis, Lítras and Fasianós).

On the upper side of the square, above the temple, is the back of the **Inn of the Tongue of Auvergne**, a 15C building restored in 1919. On the ground floor, storerooms are reached through arches in the façade while, above, an arcaded passage fronts the domestic quarters. There is an external staircase. Opposite the side of this building you enter the lovely **Plateía Aryirokástrou**. The fountain in the centre is made out of a Byzantine font; the heaps of cannon-balls were amassed during the siege of 1522.

On the far side the **Institute of History and Archaeology** (with the Ephorate of Antiquities) occupies the *Armeria, used as an armoury by the Turks, perhaps also by the Knights. Built in the 14C under Roger de Pins (his arms and those of the Order are on the main façade), its original function was as the first hospital of the Order. It was altered in the early 15C under Del Carretto when the main entrance, which bears his arms, was formed in the place of the apse of the hospital chapel: the arcade beyond is modern. The arrangement of the windows and the lines of the roof reinforce the tripartite division of the façade and give the building a strong vertical emphasis.

At right angles to the Armeria is the fascinating **Museum of Decorative Arts and Folklore** (daily 08.00–15.00), definitely worth a visit. The contents are from Rhodes and other islands, especially Sími; also Asia Minor. They include carved and painted woodwork, costumes, embriodery, curtains, bed-hangings and some household equipment. It is particularly rich in the gaily decorated pottery and tiles for which the island was well known (see Líndos).

You pass through an archway between the side of the museum and the Inn of Auvergne, whose main entrance has fine decoration, and the arms of the Order and de Blanchefort. On the left is the 13C Byzantine church of the *Panayía tou Kástrou which, as St Mary's, became the first Cathedral of the Knights. After 1522 the Turks converted it into a mosque called Enderoum. Its form, essentially the original one, is an inscribed cross. The building was either unfinished at the time of the arrival of the Knights or needed repair after earthquake damage. In any case some Gothic features (a higher roof and pointed vaults and windows) were incorporated in the 15C; a colonnade later by the Turks. It now houses a fine **Byzantine Museum** (08.30–15.00; closed Monday). The frescoes which survive *in situ* are few but important: those on the pillars of the eastern arch are 13–14C Byzantine work (various saints and martyrs, in poor condition). The rest, including St Lucia in the north west, are Frankish. The richness, soft modelling and colouring of St Lucia show Italian Renaissance influence which contrasts sharply with the earlier figures. Also shown, imaginatively hung to reflect their original positions, are some of the frescoes (12 and 17C) from the church of the Archangel Michael, at the monastery of Thári in the south of Rhodes; also from Ay. Zakharías at Finíki on the island of Khálki (late 14C). There is a display of icons. Off the church opens a court with architectural fragments and marble and mosaic floors.

In the courtyard of the Commercial Bank opposite is an amusing modern mosaic of black and white pebbles (*khokhlákia*) in a style that has survived unchanged in Rhodes from Byzantine times.

With the Street of the Knights (Odhós Ippotón; see below) to the right, you now enter **Museum** (or Hospital) **Square**. Here on the left is the **Inn of the Tongue of England**, built in 1482, despoiled and almost destroyed in 1850, rebuilt on the original plan by Colonel Sir Vivian Gabriel, and repaired by the British in 1949. Opposite stands the imposing *__Hospital of the Knights__, begun in 1440 over the remains of a Roman building (some of which survives in one of the inner courts) and completed in 1481–89. During the War of Greek Independence the Turks used it for their sick and wounded, but later degraded it into barracks. It was skilfully restored under Amedeo Maiuri in 1913–18. The south side was damaged by bombing during the Second World War but has been repaired.

The façade, projecting from the plain east wall above, consists of eight deep arches with no decoration. Seven of them, topped by a wall relieved by two string courses, lead into open magazines, occupied by shops; the eighth, to the right of centre, forms the main gateway, and supports a projecting apsidal chapel on the upper floor (see below). The vertical mouldings lend this combination the appearance of a gate-tower. The pointed portal is decorated with a rope design. The original door of cypress was presented by Sultan Mahmoud to Louis-Philippe in 1836 and is now at Versailles. The relief above the arch shows the flag of the order, angels holding the arms of Fluvian, and an inscription recording his donation for the building of the Hospital.

Since 1916 the building has housed the **Archaeological Museum** (08.00–15.00; closed Mondays). With its open central court and appealing mixture of colonnades, spacious galleries and smaller court and rooms, it is an intriguing building and a fine setting for an archaeological collection. Since the opening of exhibitions in the Palace of the Grand Masters (see below), where more recently excavated material is displayed, the museum now contains finds excavated up to the Second World War.

Inside, a **Great Court** is surrounded by a two-storeyed portico; the lower is vaulted. In the ground-floor colonnade are various fragments of sculpture; in the centre of the court crouches a marble lion (1C BC); in the corners are cannon balls and catapult shot. An outside stair leads to the **upper gallery**, which contains funerary stelae and altar-bases. Many of the latter are circular and decorated with bucrania linked by garlands, in a manner particularly popular in the island.

The entire east wing is occupied by the **Infirmary Ward**, a rectangular hall divided lengthways by an arcade carried on seven columns; its ogee arches support a ceiling of cypress-wood. The ward held 32 beds with brocaded canopies, and the patients ate from silver plate. Two surgeons were permanently on duty. The dark cubicles that open from the hall have been variously explained as confessionals, isolation wards and wardrobes. In the long wall a flamboyant arch opens into the vaulted exedra, with three Gothic windows, that projects above the main gate. This held an altar where mass was said daily.

Round the walls of the ward are displayed Memorials of the Knights from the destroyed church of St John. Note a Classical marble sarcophagus used in 1355 as the tomb of Grand Master Pierre de Corneillan (lid in the Cluny Museum, Paris; copy here) and tomb-slabs of Thomas Newport (1502), of Nicholas de

Montmirel (1511), commandant of the Hospital, of Tomaso Provena (1499), and of Fernando de Heredia (1493). Heraldic devices include the royal arms of England.

Off the ward opens the former staff refectory with reliefs (several from Nísiros) on the walls—those in a frontal, simplified Late Roman style are particularly striking. Off this are reached the three (two of them small) rooms of sculpture. Although the display is rather cramped, the works give a good idea of the variety of subject and treatment, and often the delicacy, of Rhodian Hellenistic sculpture.

There are several examples of the **Nymph** seated on a rock (**Room 1** etc.). In **Room 2**, other works of note are a 1C **Crouching Aphrodite**, after the famous work of Doidalsas, a '**Marine Venus**' (which provided the title for Lawrence Durrell's book), a **torso of Artemis**, a copy of the **Tyche** (Fortune) of Antioch, an example of the **Artemis Hekate** type, an **Asklepios**, a **Hygieia**, a **Zeus**, a bearded **Bacchus**, a **Satyr reclining on a wineskin**, several elegant female statues (note the drapery). In **Room 3** are included an **Aphrodite Pudica**, a three-sided **Hekataion** in Archaising style, and a fine **Nymph** (or Aphrodite), with her arm resting on the knee.

At this point you can enter a pleasant garden overlooking the **Little Court**, excavated in 1907, and now holding a 6C mosaic pavement from Arkassa in Karpathos. In an alcove to the left a funerary naḯskos (frame in the form of a miniature temple façade) contains memorial sculpture; a mosaic is laid in front. Amongst the sculpture in the garden is a fine Hellenistic dolphin.

Off the corner of the garden opposite the sculpture galleries, two further inter-connected rooms include a famous **funerary stele of young Timarista** taking a last farewell of her mother Crito, a delicate work of the 5C BC; Crito's hair was recut after damage in antiquity; two headless **kouroi** (6C BC) found at Kameiros, but apparently made on Paros and Naxos; two fragmentary heads; a sculptured perirrhanterion (bowl for ritual ablutions) stand of the 7C BC.

From here you return to the gallery overlooking the main central court to visit its surrounding rooms, some of which are likely to be closed. The first three contain Geometric-Archaic **pottery** mainly from tombs in the territory of ancient Ialysos. On the west side three rooms have prehistoric (mainly Mycenaean) pottery and other finds, while six more rooms (on the north) have a large selection of mainly Archaic pottery (and some other material). There are good examples of both Rhodian and Attic black-figure, fine Rhodian amphorae and oinochoai, including examples decorated in the **Wild Goat style**, also some Corinthian imports. Other Archaic pottery particularly characteristic of Rhodes (see Art and Architecture) is Fikelloura ware, and Siana and Vroulia cups.

Leaving the building you turn left and out of Museum Square to ascend the cobbled **Street of the Knights** (Odhós Ippotón), the main street of the Collachium, which it crosses from east to west, rising towards the Palace. Finding yourself for the first time in a street rather than an open square the sober formality of the architecture, so alien to its Greek environment, forces itself upon you. The impressive buildings, frequently adorned with coats of arms, were carefully and accurately restored in 1913–16, so that the street provides a faithful picture of late medieval architecture, though the overall effect is perhaps too tidy to evoke the full spirit of the Middle Ages. In the course of restoration, the projecting balconies and embrasures added by the Turkish occupants were removed. On the right hand side various offices of the Archaeological Service have been installed and there is a bookshop.

The houses and inns of the Knights follow the same basic design of two storeys with a flat façade, varying degrees of ornament, and a terrace roof. Vaulted store-houses or stables (?) occupied the lower floor; the upper was reached by an open staircase and gallery from a central court. Rounded arches, the horizontal emphasis given by string-courses, and the large square windows suggest that the Renaissance was already affecting even a military order of medieval chivalry.

To the left at first is the plain north façade of the Hospital, with a decorated Gothic portal at the far end. Arms and an inscription refer to P. Clouet who was in charge of its construction. Opposite are plainer houses, then the **Inn of the Tongue of Italy**, rebuilt in 1519 when Del Carretto (his arms at first floor level) was Grand Master.

Beyond a house bearing various arms, including those of de l'Isle Adam quartered with those of his mother (died 1462), is the **Inn of the Tongue of France**, architecturally one of the most attractive buildings of the period. Built in 1492–1509, it was disfigured by the Turks, and carefully restored at the expense of Maurice Bompard, French ambassador to the Porte. The escutcheons include that of Pierre d'Aubusson (Grand Master 1476–1503). Noteworthy are the fine ornate doorway, the horizontal mouldings which 'step' as the street ascends, the mouldings which frame the upper parts of the windows and main door and, at roof level, the crenellations and little semicircular projecting 'towers'. The crocodile gargoyles recall the legend of Gozon (see below). The details are Gothic but their synthesis and the horizontal rather than vertical emphasis betray the influence of the Renaissance (Karouzou, see bibliography).

The building opposite, with an Aragonese portal and an attractive garden court, bears the Spanish arms of Villaraguts. Next to it is a charming building; its upper floor in Turkish style.

In a side street (right, opposite Od. Lákhitos, and passing beneath the Inn of France) is the so-called **House of Djem** (or Zizim), pretender brother of Bayezid II, who was given asylum here for a short time in 1482 before being taken to France. There is a fine *marble doorway in Renaissance style. Beyond (now inaccessible), a Gothic church of St Dhimítrios (1499) overlies remains of an ancient temple, apparently that of Dionysos, famed in antiquity for its works of art. In this area, which is in the grounds of the Ephoreia of Antiquities, have been found remains of ancient shipyards and of a Roman *tetrapylon* (ceremonial gateway with four arches over a right-angle crossroads).

Houses line each side of the street. Further on (right) are the 15C Byzantine church of **Ayía Triádha** and the small **chapel of the Tongue of France** (various arms), with a statue of the Virgin and Child and the lilies of France. The adjacent **Chaplain's House** dated by the arms of Beranger (Grand Master 1365–74) on the façade, now houses the Italian consulate.

An arch spans the road immediately before the enticing Od. Ippárkhon. Two buildings, to the left of the street before and beyond the arch, constitute the **Inn of the Tongue of Spain**; the first (Aragon and Castile) dates from the mid 15C and has decoration applied both vertically and horizontally; the second is c 50 years later and has a gateway of Aragonese type, that is with a rounded arch composed of large wedge-shaped blocks. The **Inn of the Tongue of Provence** of 1518, to the right, has an elegant decorated portal surmounted by four coats of arms (of the Order, France, Del Carretto and Flotta; 1518) set in a cross-shaped niche.

At the top of the street you pass beneath the lofty arches of the **Loggia of St John** with the entrance to the square in front of the Palace to your right. The Loggia is a modern reconstruction of a 15C portico (some bases and column fragments survive) whose original purpose is unknown. Already in ruins before the explosion of 1856 (see below), it used to join the entrance-court of the Palace to the Conventual **church of St John**, which lay parallel to the palace. A fragment of wall remains of the church, and a Turkish school now occupies the remainder of the site.

> The church (its character is well known from engravings) was built in a plain 14C style, which has been more or less faithfully copied in the cathedral church on Mandráki. It had three aisles, divided by antique columns, and contained the tombs of the Knights. Turned into a mosque after 1522, it was destroyed in 1856 when lightning struck the minaret and exploded beneath it a forgotten underground cache of gunpowder, killing c 800 people.

In Panetíou, in front of the school, and further east, part of the Byzantine fortifications and other medieval buildings are being excavated. The fortifications are on the line of the south wall of the Knights' Collachium, but slightly to the north.

Palace of the Grand Masters

On the north side of the square in the highest part of the Collachium stands the Palace of the Grand Masters, rebuilt in 1939–43 from old drawings of the original 14C building.

■ Open 08.00–15.00; closed Mon. There is a café off the inner courtyard. Son et Lumière in English, French, German and Swedish (entrance from Plateía Rímini (Sound and Light Square; see above)). The tour of the walls (see below) begins from the far end of the outer court of the Palace.

History
The Palace stands on the site of the lower acropolis of the ancient city and probably that of the temple of Helios, where stood Lysippos' famous four-horse chariot and, most likely, also the Colossos (described above with Mandráki). The Palace, a massively impressive rectangular structure 79 x 75m, was begun soon after the arrival of the Knights in Rhodes, and completed at the end of the 14C. In effect it was an independent fortress, and was designed with underground store-rooms to withstand a siege. In peacetime it was the residence of the Grand Master and the place of assembly of the Order. Repaired after the earthquake of 1481, it suffered little damage in the siege of 1522. The Turks turned it into a prison.

Badly damaged by the earthquake of 1851, the structure was further shattered by the explosion of 1856. Some of the material was used by the Turks to build a military hospital (since razed) in the grounds. The Italians, intending it as a summer residence for Victor Emmanuel III and Mussolini, rebuilt the exterior as far as possible in the old style, but redesigned the interior for modern occupation, including central heating, disguised lifts, and electric chandeliers. The refurbishment had hardly been completed when Italy relinquished Rhodes.

In the high and spacious entrance hall is the ticket office. To the left you can climb a vast staircase to the **first floor**. At the foot of the staircase is the **Chapel** with a copy of Donatellos's St Nicholas and a modern relief of the Annunciation. The **upper floor** is grand, though sometimes rather tasteless. The spacious halls have timber ceilings supported on Roman and Byzantine columns and are paved with coloured marbles or vast Roman and Early Christian **mosaics** brought from Kos. Although the removal of these was an archaeologically criminal act, they illustrate excellent work in the medium from the 4C BC to the 5–6C AD. The Early Christian mosaics use subtle patterns and colours and limited figure decoration, often of birds and animals, perhaps intended to provide intimations of paradise. The Hellenistic and Roman floors mostly have figured scenes but do not fully represent the overall geometric designs which formed a high proportion in antiquity. Both the *emblema* type of composition (single figured panel within a patterned surround: e.g. Nymph on sea-horse) and more complex designs (e.g. multiple figures in linked roundels, as the nine Muses) can be seen. Of the mythological scenes that of Poseidon defeating the giant Polybotes is of particular interest to visitors to the Dodecanese in view of its connection with the island of Nisyros. Some rooms are lit by alabaster windows.

The furniture, of many styles and periods, includes good Renaissance woodwork from Italian churches. Painted and gilded figures support lamps. There are several ancient sculptures, both originals and copies (including one of the Laocoön). From the windows there are good views of the city and sea. The garden contains sarcophagi of Masters, and the bronze she-wolf of Rome that once adorned the east mole of Mandráki.

The wide **central courtyard**, with interesting façades, contains Roman sculpture, and elements from a Byzantine church at Arnitha. To the east, now marked by marble well-heads, are the remaining grain storage silos from the time of the Knights.

Some of the **ground floor** and **basement rooms** of the Palace now house two outstanding permanent **exhibitions**, installed to commemorate the 2400th anniversary of the City of Rhodes in 1993 and drawing mainly on archaeological discoveries since the Second World War (earlier material is in the Archaeological Museum). The first, **Ancient Rhodes: 2400 years**, illustrates the earlier history of the island; the second covers **Rhodes from the 4C AD to the Turkish conquest (1522)**. The material is beautifully displayed, without crowding, and treats the past of the island mainly according to themes, which are illustrated by the objects shown. Excellent illustrated booklets are available.

In the earlier display, the first two rooms show the history of Rhodes from the Neolithic period until the synoikism, and the foundation and organisation of the town thereafter. There follow galleries which present public buildings and sanctuaries (**3**), the Rhodian house (**4**), implements of domestic use (**5**), cosmetics and daily life (**6**), artistic and spiritual life (**7**), Rhodian ceramic workshops (**8**), the manufacture of bronze, glass and terracotta sculpture (**9**), trade, the economy, coinage (**10**), the cemetery (**11**), burial customs (**12**).

The displays in the second exhibition are of crafts and trades (including the refining of sugar), fine pottery (local and imported), table ware, military equipment and organisation, intellectual life (including books), ritual (including icons), wall paintings, the Early Christian basilicas and their art.

Leaving the Palace again via the Loggia, you turn right into the empty **Plateía Kleovoúlou** (parking for permanent residents only) and cross the line of the Collachium wall through two wide arches into **Od. Orféos**, a long and attractive tree-lined 'piazza' with small shops, cafes and restaurants. To the right is a sheltered corner with seats. Beside this the **Gate of St Anthony**, set in a cross wall linking the palace with the outer fortifications, opens onto the shaded *terre-plein* (see below under Tour of the Walls), giving access to the **Amboise Gate** and, over the moats, to the new town.

You turn left. Off Od. Ierokléous, opposite, by the La Luna hotel, is a small 14C church of *****Ayios Márkos** (closed), later used as a mosque. The attractive building has been restored but the interior is bare. Further on, beyond public lavatories, is the ugly **Clock Tower** (ascent (fee) permitted for views over the town), which replaced a 15C tower (destroyed in 1851) on the site of the southwest tower of the Collachium defences, whose southern line is followed by Odd. Theofilískou and Agisándrou, parallel to the Street of the Knights. Down Agisándrou a recently excavated section of the Byzantine wall incorporates the remains of a small Byzantine chapel with some traces of fresco. A few yards farther on Odhós Apolloníou leads (right) to the 15C church of *****Ay. Yeóryios** (closed for restoration) and associated buildings. It was adapted by the Turks into the **Kurmale Medresses** (College of the Date-Palm). The church has a quatrefoil (tetraconch) plan, unique in the Old Town. The unusual and lovely dome, set on a drum of 21 blind arches, preserves its ancient tiles. The narthex and colonnade are Frankish additions. Od. Apolloníou ends at St. George's Tower.

The impressive **Mosque of Suleiman** (closed), erected soon after 1522, perhaps on the site of a church, and rebuilt in 1808, is fronted by the usual court with a fountain. It has a double portico, a *portal in a Venetian Renaissance style with rich sculptural decoration, originally part of a funerary monument, and an elegant minaret with a double balcony. Opposite is the fine *****Turkish Library** (open; 1793) set in a pleasant courtyard (seats), with bookcases and an illuminated 15–16C Koran.

Passing Od. Ippodhámou on the right, the road winds and a gateway (also right) opens onto the compound of a **Turkish imaret** (hospice or public kitchen). A small Gothic church of the Apostles with ribbed vaulting has re-emerged from the oven of the later building and excavations now in progress will further clarify the history of this area.

You are now in Od. Sokrátous, the former **bazaar** and heart of the Turkish quarter. Its balconied houses and open shops, shuttered at night, still preserve something of the atmosphere of the period. Early in the morning or out of season you can easily feel part of the past; later on and in high summer, the place is thronged with visitors unmistakeably of the 20C. To the right now is the **Mosque of Aga** (closed), oddly raised on wooden pillars. A short distance up Od. Apéllou (left) a section of the Byzantine city wall and some bits of a Turkish bath-house are visible in a small pleasant square (cafés). In the next street to the left is the **Chadrevan Mosque** (closed). You are now close to the Marine Gate, in Od. Ermoú, beyond.

In Plateía Ippokrátous (cafés), with a Turkish fountain and Italianate arcades, is the Municipal Library and Archives of the island of Rhodes occupying the so-called **Palace of the Castellan**, or Castellania (closed to visitors), a square building of 1507 (only part survives) with the arms of Amboise. It was probably the commercial court of the Knights and was restored by the Italians after use as a mosque (above) and a fish-market (below). The upper hall, over an arcaded loggia, is reached by an external staircase and has early 16C paintings in the eclectic style. The Renaissance style of the marble *doorway (fine relief above) to the upper hall at the top of the stairs contrasts with the elaborate Gothic frame surrounding the arms of D'Amboise on the west wall nearby. Next to that a window retains its sculptured marble insert. From the landing there is a good view back up Sokrátous and to the palace, with the Chadrevan mosque in the foreground. The **Library** (Mon–Fri 09.00–14.00, 17.00–19.30) is delightfully located in the cloisters of a lovely court.

East of Od. Pithagóra, the long street which runs south from the Plateía towards the **Koskinoú** (or St. John) **Gate**, lies the former Jewish quarter (now called Ovriakí), which was known for its liveliness in contrast to the Turkish streets.

Odhós Aristotélous continues southeast from the Plateía, past houses with Turkish wooden balconies, to the large **Square of the Jewish Martyrs** (seats, cafés, restaurants, public lavatories), possibly on the site of the medieval square of St Sebastian, damaged in the Second World War, after which it acquired its present name. A fountain decorated with bronze sea-horses, stands in front of a building quite wrongly called the Admiralty (closed), whose inscriptions in Latin and Greek suggest that it was an *archiepiscopal palace*, either of the Orthodox metropolitan or of the Latin archbishop. It is an excellent example of a high class house of the 15C, with arched openings to the ground-floor store-rooms and an imposing doorway, with pointed arch and sculptural decoration, leading to the interior court. A projecting moulding marks the division between the storeys. The first floor, with the domestic quarters, has rectangular windows, framed with mouldings and relief courses.

In Od. Simíou, reached via Od. Dhosiádhou (right), east out of the square, is the well-maintained **synagogue** (open) and, further, the medieval **Catalan house**, a grand residence with an Aragonese portal and some good carved ornament. Continuing by Odhós Pindárou you pass (right) the impressive high ribbed Gothic arches of the east end of the three-aisled 14C church of *Our Lady of the Bourg*. Od. Akhladhéf, which until recently cut through the remains of the church, runs northeast to an arched exit (the Gate of the Panayía) to the water-front; southeast, through gardens, to the **Akándia Gate**. Through this a modern gate (right) and path lead past the Carretto bastion to the modern **Moat Theatre**, where summer performances and concerts take place against a splendid backdrop of the medieval walls.

Od. Pindárou ends in front of the **Hospice of St. Catherine** (closed; restoration in progress), built round a central court. It was founded by Fra Domenico d'Alemagna in 1392 to shelter and care for Italian pilgrims travelling to the Holy Land; and enlarged in 1516. In a frame, at first floor level, are the arms of Del Carretto, St. Catherine and C. Operti. In Thiséos, next to the hospice, are foundations and fragments of mosaic floors of a 14–15C cruciform church of **Ayía Aikateríni**.

A large excavation in Plateía Pisidhórou beside the hospice has revealed a long section of the 4C **town wall**. At the most easterly corner of the town is the small late 15C church of **Ayios Pandeleímon** (open), built to a modified cruciform plan, with modern frescoes but a carved and gilded templon and some older icons. Beyond this, through a gateway (seats), on the ramparts to your left, are the ruins of the Gothic church of Our Lady of Victory. It was built to commemorate the heroic defence of this rampart in 1480 inspired by the appearance of the Virgin Mary, and destroyed c 1522. Off the open Plateía Pisidhórou, you can pass through **St Catherine's Gate** to the **Commercial Harbour**, the larger of the two harbours of Rhodes.

In the time of the Knights, this 'Grand Harbour', was protected by two moles, defended with artillery. Between them was stretched a chain. On the north mole was the **Tower of Naillac**, a key-point during the siege, but destroyed in 1863. The east mole, which separated the harbour from the Bay of Akandia and was once adorned with 15 windmills, has been enlarged to form the modern quay where all large vessels dock. The defences of the town, on the harbour side, consist of a high curtain-wall with a *Marine Gate (1478; sometimes by confusion called St Catherine's Gate, see above) that recalls the Fort St Andre at Villeneuve-les-Avignon in Provence; it figured prominently in the film *Guns of Navarone*. If you follow the outside of the wall, which towers forbiddingly above, you can re-enter the old city by the Píli Navárkhou, or reach Mandráki by crossing the northeast salient by the **Bastion of St Paul**.

Walk 2   The southern sector of the Old Town

Begin in the southeast, near the walls towards the bottom of Od. Perikléous which starts at the Plateía of the Jewish Martyrs. Here are two churches which were later converted into mosques. The Turkish name (Ilk Mihrab Cami) of the 14C irregular three-aisled *Ayía Aikateríni marks it as the first shrine at which Allah was worshipped in 1522. The church has extensive and interesting frescoes (14 and late 15C) in the Byzantine tradition but is not usually open. Close by in the quiet Plateía Rhodíou, is the15C *Ayía Triádha (custodian at the house on the west side), the Dolapli Mescidi or Oratory of the Well. The cruciform church has vaulted arms and a central dome raised on a drum with windows. The room added to the north may be a baptistery: it is clearly Gothic in character with prominent ribbing. The main (west) door too is decorated in a Gothic style. Above and to both sides of the north door were Latin crosses of ceramic tiles (the settings of these are still visible). Part of the minaret is standing. The floor is patterned in varicoloured marble; the settings for the columns of the templon can be seen. The fresco decoration is not very well preserved but some scenes can be made out and the work is subtle, showing some western influence. In the central apse is a Deisis with, below, the Communion of the Apostles (neither scene in good condition). In the south arm are good figures of Hierarchs in a blind arch which were revealed behind a covering wall in 1979. In the southeast corner the Abbot Zosimos offers communion to St Mary of Egypt. Most interesting are the scenes (in panels) in the north part of the vault of the west arm with episodes from the stories of Cain and Abel and, graphically depicted, Noah's Ark.

Between the two churches just described and a little to the south, in narrow Od. Dhimosthénous, is a chapel of Ayía Marína (in use but normally closed).

You go west along Arkhiepiskópou Efthimíou, through an area richer in local than tourist life, leaving to your left, by the Koskinoú Gate, a 14–15C chapel of Ay. Ioánnis Pródhromos (closed; some frescoes), after whom the gate is also sometimes named. You turn right into Pithagóra. Past the junction with Omírou (a Turkish fountain on the corner) is a tower of the Byzantine wall with a medieval windmill then, in Plateía Aristoménous, a section of the **Byzantine wall** which incorporates drums from a Classical temple or other public building. Between Omírou and the wall of the medieval city are four churches. Ay. Theódhoroi (14–15C), hidden behind a doorway at right angles to the entrance of the Pension Minos near the beginning of Omírou, was 'borrowed' for domestic occupation some years ago but is soon to be restored as a church.

Ay. Kiriakí (14-15C), further west in a street south of Omírou, is in a nice garden but protected by a forbidding if sleepy alsatian. The church retains a minaret. The Catholic **Taxiárkhis Mikhaïl** (sometimes open) has been restored (no frescoes) and is in use. For Ayios Athanássios, see below. Three of the four were at one time mosques. In the pleasant Plateía Doriéos (cafés—perhaps time for a rest), off Omírou, is the **Redjeb Pasha Cami** (1588), the most impressive mosque built by the Turks on Rhodes, with Persian faience decoration and using columns from earlier churches. In front is a fountain and behind a *turbeh* with the tomb of Redjep Pasha. The building is being conserved.

The 13C ***Ayios Fanoúrios** (open; entrance in Od. Fanouríou) nearby became a mosque, the Peial ad Din Mescid. Of modified cruciform plan (?13C), it was extended to the west in the 14C. There is an unappealing modern forehall. The frescoes (traditional Byzantine), some of which were restored by the Italians in 1938 and seem to repeat the compositions of an earlier layer beneath, are important but not easy to see. In the north arm you need to be told that the Feast of Herod, with Salome and the head of John the Baptist, have been depicted on the east part of the arch. Likewise the seated figure of the Panayia below is indistinct. She holds Christ who unusually has his arm on the mother's knee rather than raised in blessing. The large figure occupying the central space is the Archangel Gabriel. In the west arm there are various saints on the south wall. In the southern of the blind arches in the extension towards the door (restored), beneath a protome of Christ, is a figure offering a model of the church, with his brother (?). The main figure may be the founder of the church or the restorer, or the benefactor who paid for the extension (dated by inscription to c 1335/6).

Further west, the first of two alleys off a sharp bend of Omírou takes you to the monastic church of **Ayios Nikólaos** (at present closed for restoration and excavations; some frescoes). This was later the Abdul Djelil Mescid. The simple early 16C Ay Athanássios (closed), a little out of your way in the opposite direction, is up against the tower and gate of the same name.

From Plateía Doriéos, you can climb Od. Ay. Fanouríou and turn left for Plateía Aríonos. Here are the **Mustapha Cami** (1765), with a fountain whose arcaded dome has not survived, and the remarkable *Turkish baths (1765, later rebuilt, and, in the last couple of years, restored for continued public use): the building has a large domed hall and its floor incorporates antique marbles. Nearby to the northeast are the three-aisled **Ayy. Konstandínos and Eleni** (12–13C; some frescoes in Byzantine style) later the Kadi Mestid and, in Od. Ergíou, the attractive 14–15C Ay. Artémios (restored; some fresco remains).

Off the square to the southwest down Od Antithéou is a **Folk Dance Theatre**. Further in the same direction, beyond Ippodhámou, is the 15C cruciform church of **Ayía Paraskeví** (access from both Ippodhámou and a park off Timokréontos), once the Takkeci Cami. Both entrances have 15C Gothic portals, the west a descending stairway. Along (Timokréontos) is the small Mosque of Hamza Bey, intriguing but inaccessible.

Past Ayios Artémios (above) you reach Plateía Athinás, more or less in the centre of the Old Town. Here is the charming three-aisled *Ayios Spiridhón (closed), converted into a mosque (the Kavakli Mescidi) after 1523. The church (recently restored) has a complex architectural history back to at least the 6C. Frescoes in the apse are 6–7C and 13C. There is a fine 16C Crucifixion in the eclectic style where Byzantine tradition is modified by western influence. The minaret is intact.

On the other side of the square are the remains of a 15C church in the form of an inscribed cross, which later became the Demirli Cami. Although it is now roofless (it was badly damaged in the war), the east and west sides survive to a substantial height and there are a few traces of fresco in the central apse. Excavations have shown that it overlies both a Middle Byzantine predecessor and the important Early Christian **basilica of the Archangel Michael**. The 15C church may have been the Orthodox cathedral in the time of the Knights.

A short distance further east, along Od. Plátonos (to the left, parts of the ancient fortifications, both Classical and Byzantine), is the well-kept *Ibrahim Pasha Cami** (open), a spacious mosque of 1531 with fine painted woodwork. In front is the attractive Plateía Dhamagítou, and a fountain. The plane-tree is said to have been a place of execution under the Turks. You are now close to Plateía Ippokrátous and the Plateía of the Jewish Martyrs.

Walk 3   A tour of the walls

■ A tour of part of the walls, normally inaccessible, is allowed on Tuesdays and Saturdays at 14.45 (tickets from Palace desk), starting from the Gate of the Cannons at the west side of the forecourt of the Palace (see below). From here you walk over the crosswall (see above) to the outer circuit. The tour (c 30mins) ends at the Koskinoú Gate but should in future be extended (Italian Tower). From the top a good defender's view is obtained; for an attacker's perspective you can return (mostly by shaded walks) along the outside of the same section. This experience is a must if you want to get a proper feeling of the scale, complexity and atmosphere of these extraordinary fortifications.

A full circuit on your own takes about one and a half hours (for description, see below).

The walls of Rhodes, a masterpiece of 15–16C military architecture, are well preserved for their full extent of 4km. They successfully withstood the siege of 1480 and, for a long time, that of 1522. On them can be seen 151 escutcheons of Grand Masters and Knights.

The post-Classical city of Rhodes, with the area of the Collachium as its acropolis, may have been fortified as early as the 6 or 7C AD. In places the medieval walls have ancient or Byzantine foundation blocks. The **Byzantine enceinte** is known to have resisted the Knights for three years. Its inner circuit followed very roughly the line of the walls of the Collachium. Several towers of the southern limit have been traced in excavations just north of the line of streets Theofilískou–Agisándrou–Protoyénous. The section of wall mentioned above near Plateía Ippokrátous must belong to the fortifications of the lower town, whose limits have not been determined.

The **towers** which survive today probably date in part from before 1330, as does the **moat**. Reconstruction began under Grand Masters Heredia (1377–96) and de Naillac (1396–1421), who built a massive tower on the north mole of the main harbour. In 1437–71 the walls were rebuilt to incorporate a number of detached towers. After the siege of 1480 and the earthquake of 1481, Pierre d'Aubusson (1476–1503) began a systematic and thorough reconstruction; the curtain-walls were thickened, parapets widened, the number of gates reduced from five to three and access to them made more difficult. The ditches were doubled in width. The work was completed by del Carretto (1513–21), with the technical help of Italian architects. In 1522 Villiers de l'Isle Adam, again with Italian help, organised the final defences. In 1465 the enceinte had been divided into eight sectors, each allotted to one of the Tongues, and this arrangement was in force at the time of the final siege.

The fortifications, strongest on the landward side, consist of a continuous vertical or scarped **wall**, on which is a **walkway**, 13.7m wide and also continuous, protected by **battlements** and embrasures sited for firing in any direction. In many sectors there is also a **lower walk**. This circumvallation is surrounded by an external **fosse**, 32–46m wide and 15–20m deep, provided with scarp and counterscarp.

The walls can be approached from various viewpoints (inside the Old City, the moats, modern roads round the exterior or, in the case of the official tour between the Cannon and Koskinoú Gates, the top of the fortifications).

You can begin your tour either from the palace or from outside the fortifications in the modern town opposite. From the palace you proceed as in the tour of the old town (Walk 1) but, at Od. Orféos, turn right, through St Anthony's Gate (on the north side is a relief showing St Anthony, and the arms of the Order and de Lastic) in a cross-wall. The top of the cross-wall, which provides a bridge giving direct access to the outer fortifications, is reached via the **Gate of the Cannons** (closed except for the official tour) in the southwest corner of the palace forecourt. Guarded by two semicircular towers, this carries the arms of de Lastic and the Order.

Beyond St Antony's Gate you proceed along the **terreplein**, now a shaded avenue (seats), separated from the Collachium wall by a dry moat (right). By turning left you approach the Amboise Gate. At the far end of the terreplein is the polygonal **Battery of the Olives** (Arms of de Lastic), and a minor gate into the Collachium. Now you can cross the moats (bridged) for a view of the *****Gate of Amboise** (1512). The main gate, which bears the arms of the Order and of Amboise, opens below between massive cylindrical towers. Returning to the interior of the fortress the vaulted road makes an S-bend within the thickness of the wall, then passes beneath a second gate, over an inner moat, and through a third gate to the terreplein.

South of here is the short sector of the **Tongue of Germany** the smallest defensive group. On your left are the Clock Tower, the mosque of Suleiman and Ayios Yióryios. The **Bastion of St George** has a relief of St George on the original square tower, with the arms of Pope Martin V, of the Order, and of Grand Master Antonio Fluvian (1421–37). A polygonal bulwark was added later, and in 1496 the roadway through it was closed when the final bastion was erected. The next sector is that of the **Tongue of Auvergne**, ending at the circular **Tower of Spain**.

Beyond the tower is the sector of the **Tongue of Aragon**, one of the most picturesque, which runs first southeast, then south. From it there is a comprehensive view, taking in the mosques of Suleiman, Mustapha, Ibrahim Pasha, and Redjeb Pasha, the Tower of the Windmills, the Commercial Harbour, the Tower of St Nicholas, the port of Mandráki, the New Town and the coast of Anatolia. The ravelin was completed in 1522 but here, in December of that year, the Turks made the breach that enabled them to capture the city.

The **Tower of St Mary** (or of the Panayía) has a relief of the Virgin and Child and an inscription dated 1441. In 1487 a great polygonal bastion was added by d'Aubusson round the tower to protect the **Gate of St Athanasius**; later he closed the gate. Reopened for a sortie in 1522, it was closed again by Suleiman in 1531 and remained so until 1922.

Koskinoú Gate

The wall turns east to one of its most striking sectors, that of the **Tongue of England**. Along it are numerous windmills. The **Gate of Koskinoú** (or St John), shows clearly the difference between early and later military architecture. The earlier wall has a square **Tower** (**of St John**) with small embrasures and battlements, while the additions of c 1480 are in the form of a huge bastion of horseshoe plan with ravelins and embrasures for larger artillery. A bilingual inscription attests to the contribution of a local technician in the rebuilding. Its defence was shared between the Tongue of England and the Tongue of Provence. This sector follows a zigzag line marked by three towers.

The large ***Bastion del Carretto** (or of Italy) is a blend of an older tower and a semicircular bastion of 1515, 50m in diameter and three-storeyed. The sector which skirts the Bay of Akandia, fronted by a ravelin, was defended by the Tongue of Italy. Near the mole which separates the Commercial Harbour from Akandia, with the Tower of the Windmills, the wall makes a right-angled turn to the left. Just beyond the tower is the **Gate of St Catherine**. The new sector of the **Tongue of Castile** skirts the Commercial Harbour (described above). Halfway along is the picturesque ***Marine Gate**, with large guardrooms.

Beyond it the wall coincides for a time with the east wall of the Collachium. Beyond a square tower of Byzantine origin, with a chapel of the Knights (frescoes), the **Arnaldo Gate** leads into Museum Square. After the **Gate** into Plateía Símis (Píli Navárkhou) are the **Gate** and **Tower of St Paul**, where the wall turns west, but also projects east along the mole with the tower of Naillac (see above). The gate is protected by a low triangular curtain with a parapet. At a late period the defence of the Naillac mole was allotted to the Captain of the Port.

From the Gate of St Paul to the Gate of Amboise (where you began) is the sector of the **Tongue of France**. This runs in a general east-west direction, passing above the **Gate of Liberty** (Píli Eleftherías). At the circular **Tower of St Peter**, which has a figure of St Peter and the arms of Pope Pius II, the wall turns abruptly south and then again west. Skirting the Palace of the Grand Master, you reach the original starting point in the square in front.

To Monte Smith (or Ay Stéfanos) and the acropolis

20 minutes' walk, or bus no. 5 from the Néa Agorá (New Market).

Odhós Arkhiepiskópou Makaríou runs inland from Mandráki, near the post office. You pass the Soleil Hotel, now a training centre for tour guides, in whose grounds excavations (1960) revealed a cellar containing more than 100 intact amphorae, possibly buried in the earthquake of 227–226 BC.

Along Od. A. Dhiákou (right at roundabout) is the **Cultural Centre of Rhodes** (exhibitions; teaching in music and the arts; café) in an attractive house with large gardens.

Beyond the roundabout Leofóros Dhimokratías follows the line of the medieval walls: pleasant streets climb to the right. Up one of these (Kheimarrás), at the junction with P. Melá, the remains of one of the most important Early Christian basilicas discovered in Rhodes have been preserved (visible from the street) in the basements of blocks of flats.

Further along P. Melá, you turn right into Od. Dhiagorídhon which rises towards **Mt Ayios Stéfanos** (111m), a ridge called also **Monte Smith** after Admiral Sir Sidney Smith (1764–1840), who lived in a house here in 1802 while keeping watch on the French fleet. The **acropolis**, identified in 1916 and partly excavated in 1924–29, occupies its gentle east slope. Attractively situated among olive groves (left) are a **stadium** (restored) and a small **theatre**, of unusual square plan (only the orchestra and three seats are original work). A massive retaining wall supports a higher terrace where the stylobate of a **temple of Pythian Apollo** bears three corner columns tastelessly fabricated from fragments. A small **fountain-house** (below) has a plaster-lined cistern and feed channel with draw-basin behind. At the north end of the ridge is the site of a **temple of Zeus Polieus and Athena Polias**, marked now only by some foundations and a few column drums, the latter lying close to the main road.

Odhós Voríou Ipírou winds back down into the town. Subterranean chambers to either side of the main road round the first bend are thought to belong to **Nymphaia** (on the left is a plastered cistern).

The acropolis, Rhodes (restored)

Excursions in the island

■ **Road conditions**. The coastal circuit is almost entirely surfaced, though sections are still being improved in the soutwest. The main roads crossing the island from west to east are adequate, but in less good condition.

■ **Buses**. See Getting around Rhodes.

To Rhodhíni

3km south on the Líndos road (frequent buses, town service no. 3 from the seafront opposite the entrance to Néa Agorá, in 15 minutes. Buy tickets before boarding from kiosk by the bus stop).

The bus goes north up the sea front, passing all the public buildings described above, the Murad Reis mosque and the Hotel des Roses, before turning inland through the town centre. The road then follows most of the fortifications which you can walk on the official tour, but turns inland by the prominent Catholic church of St Francis of Assisi. Further on (Megálou Konstantínou/P. Rhoḯdhou) part of the wall of the ancient city is visible below to the left. Much of the building in these suburbs is modern but there are some pleasant older houses.

There is a stop immediately outside the entrance to **Rhodíni**, a delightful ancient **park** (restaurant), said to have been the site of the School of Rhetoric of Aeschines. Shaded by plane-trees, it occupies a natural glen with a stream and ponds. Peacocks strut and call, and there are some mountain goats. Below the restaurant and a little to the right, a section of a Roman aqueduct, crossing the glen, would have made a good illustration for Rose Macaulay's *Pleasure of Ruins*. If you turn left through the restaurant, walk up the path for 15–20 minutes, and cross to the far bank where there is a rough football pitch on the flatter ground above, you can find several rock-cut tombs (alternative access from the main road (sign) further on from park entrance). The most impressive of these is the so-called **Tomb of the Ptolemies**. To form this Hellenistic monument, the rock was shaped into a 28m square, and the interior was excavated to contain two chambers, the outer wide and narrow, the inner narrow and deep, both with niches for the deposition of the dead. The walls were plastered and painted. The exterior was decorated with 21 Doric half-columns in relief on each façade (restored 1924). The north side is well preserved, and something of the east: but the other two have disintegrated. There are niches below door level. It is not certain how the upper part of the monument was treated.

The bus back to town (stop opposite entrance to park) follows a different route, reaching the sea on the bay of Akándia and following the line of the walls to the terminus.

To Triánda and Mt Filérimos (ancient *Ialysos*)

15km southwest (buses, for Paradhísi etc., but only taking you as far as Triánda, then 6km hard walk up steep winding road; taxi or tour bus).

Hotels in Ixiá, Kritiká and Triánda (area code 0241)

■ **Ixiá**
L Grecotel Rhódos Imperial (402), pool, tennis, etc; 22,300–37,500 drs. Tel. 75000; fax 76690. April–Oct. Also F/As 32,000–144,000 drs.
L Olympic Palace (333), pool, tennis, etc; 11,500–24,000 drs. Tel. 77444, 28775; fax 30434. March–Oct. Also F/As 24,500–96,000 drs.
A Bel Air (158), pool, tennis, etc; 9000–13,500 drs. Tel. 23731/4; fax 33625. April–Oct. Also F/As 14,500–23,000 drs.
A Golden Beach (266), pool, tennis, etc; 10,050–19,600 drs. Tel. 92411; fax 92416. April–Oct. Also F/As 16,000–36,000.
B Argo Sea (F/As) (26);

9000–15,000 drs. Tel. 36163.
B Leto (102), pool; 12,400–14,000 drs. Tel. 23511/2. April–Oct.
C Róma (43); 7000–10,000 drs. Tel. 96447, 96821, 96358; fax 96358. April–Oct.
C Blue Eyes (F/As) (30); 9000–14,500 drs. Tel. 36797, 73689.
D Ippókambos (18); 7500–8500 drs. Tel. 36206, 90206.

■ **Kritiká**
A Siríni Beach (108), pool, tennis etc.; 17,800–22,000 drs. Tel. 34592, 30650; fax 26531. March–Nov. Also F/As, same price.

■ **Triánda (Ialisós)**
L Rhódos Palace (788), pool, tennis etc.; 23,000–56,000 drs. Tel. 25222/15; fax 25350. March–Oct. Also bungalows 29,900–204,300 drs.
A Ialisós Bay (232), pool, tennis etc.; 9190–16,760 drs. Tel. 91841/5; fax 93420. April–Oct.
A Sun Beach (F/As) (157), pool, tennis etc.; 18,500–36,000. Tel. 93821/5; fax 95688. April–Oct.

B Edhém (21), pool; 8000–15,000 drs. Tel. 94284, 94044, 94432; fax 30530. April–Oct.
B Summer Land (45); 10,300–14,000 drs. Tel. 94941. Also F/As 16,400–21,250 drs.
C Lísa (34); 7250–8700 drs. Tel. 93557, 93181. Also F/As 10,000–12,000 drs.
C Triáta (30); 8000–15,000 drs. Tel. 94525. Also F/As , same price.

From the Néa Agorá you can take any road leading west. When you reach the sea, turn left and follow Leofóros Triándon, the coast road, past the huge Rhodos Palace (left) and a succession of other hotels.

Leaving Rhodes town, you pass through **Kritiká**, an unexpectedly attractive suburb of identical single-storey houses. The name is derived from the Turkish refugees from Crete who first settled this township in 1898.

In 3km turning (left) to **Malpasós**. On the right of this road is the **Cave of the Dragon** with a cypress in front. The legend of the dragon, said to have been killed here by Dieudonné de Gozon, a Provencal knight who later became Grand Master (1346–53), is an interesting example of the association of a historical character with a legendary event. The name Malpasós signifies a place 'difficult to pass' (i.e. for the dragon!). 5km **Ixiá**.

9km **Triánda** (or Ialisós; pop. 7193). Inland, the older part of the town is quiet and pleasant. In Od. Ayías Aikaterínis is the neat church of Ayios Nikólaos and Ayía Aikateríni. The frescoes here, although limited in extent, are excellent. Dating to c 1500, the lovely subtle colouring and modification of the severity of earlier Byzantine work make these outstanding examples of the eclectic style and there are original features, especially in the Mocking of Christ where the crowd lower their garments and make obscene gestures. Not much survives in the sanctuary apart from a fine group of angels in a niche on the north. Of the panels in the vault those on the north are the best preserved. These (including the mocking) are all associated with the Passion and Crucifixion. Also in Triánda, the Koímisis tis Theotókou (Frankish style, rebuilt 1756) has a fine carved templon.

Within the area of Triánda village, excavations (earlier 20C; and from 1982) have revealed a major **prehistoric settlement**, within the area of Triánda village. Parts of this can be seen in various open spaces. Ashlar buildings, and the tombs, suggest that it was an important centre. A thick (30cm) layer of ash from the Thera volcano (visible) was found in strata at one site.

Ancient Ialysos

Off to the left, a good road climbs to (15km) Mt Filerimos (*Phileremos*), an isolated wooded hill (267m) whose level summit (magnificent views) was the site of *Ialysos*.

■ Open 08.00–15.00; closed Mon; car park; useful guidebook, G. Konstantinopoulos, *Ialysos-Kamiros*, 1971, Apollo Editions.

History

Ialysos was one of the three ancient cities of Rhodes. The strategic value of this hill, dominating the plain, has been recognised from Phoenician times; John Cantacuzene was besieged here by the Genoese in 1248. It was the first place fortified by the Knights in 1306 and from here Suleiman directed the siege of Rhodes in 1522. In 1943 it was disputed between the Germans and Italians.

Of the Classical acropolis there remain (just east—that is left, on arrival—of the car park) the foundations of a 3C **Temple of Athena Ialysia** scattered with column drums, and fragments of entablature. A three-aisled Christian basilica was built over the temple in the 5–6C AD. The southernmost apse, visible to the south east of the temple, houses a distinctive cross-shaped baptistery with two steps in its eastern arm. The northern side of the basilica later became a single-aisled chapel in the Byzantine or early medieval period.

The sanctuary of this church was subsequently adapted as the entrance to a medieval successor, of Our Lady of Phileremos, built to house an icon of the Virgin believed to have been painted by St Luke. In the mid 15C this gave access to two h e x a g o n a l chapels, with distinctive tall Gothic w i n d o w s.

Our Lady of Phileremos

Towards the end of the 15C two further chapels were added to the east and a bell-tower built over the site of the central apse of the Early Christian basilica. This was replaced in 1931. The church is imposing, if slightly over restored. Set high on the external wall (east) of the church is a pulpit looking onto the courtyard of the monastery beyond.

This **monastery**, built by the Knights during the 15C, was later ruined by the Turks who used it as a stable. The buildings were restored by the Italians, and then occupied by Capuchin monks until the Second World War. Despite its turbulent history the place has a serene and tranquil atmosphere. And although the monastery has now been closed for 50 years, visitors' tones are still hushed.

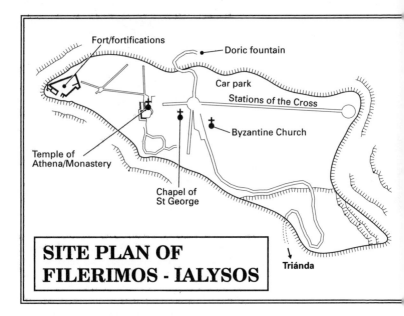

Fort/fortifications

Doric fountain

Car park

Stations of the Cross

Byzantine Church

Temple of
Athena/Monastery

Chapel of
St George

SITE PLAN OF
FILERIMOS - IALYSOS

Triánda

A low colonnade runs around a courtyard off which are the monks' cells. To the
south, a two-storey building has a refectory on the ground floor, and steps
leading up to the abbot's quarters and a reception room.

A path leads east to a ruined **fort**, c 35m x 25m, with a Byzantine, medieval
and more recent history. The Byzantine elements (lower sections of the walls
and tower) include reused pieces of ancient structures. From the east end of the
fort there are spectacular views as far as the distant slopes of Mt Profítis Ilías and
the summit of Mt Atáviros: its strategic situation is clear.

To the west, below the temple, is a small underground **Chapel of St George**.
The barrel vaulted interior is decorated with 14–15C frescoes. Although badly
damaged much can still be identified. The vault has scenes from the Life of the
Virgin and the Passion of Christ. The side walls have been painted as tapestries
with loops attaching them to painted rails. These show kneeling knights in a
western style accompanied by saints. The chancel is decorated with paintings of
Christ and the Apostles and to the right (below) St George slaying the dragon.

Returning to the car park, an easy pebbled path (west) is lined with 14 copper
reliefs of the Stations of the Cross erected by the Italians. It leads to a large cross
(under construction), at a belvedere. To the right of the path are the remains of
a small 10C Byzantine **church**, three-aisled, with a narthex. It was of domed
inscribed cross type; the bases for columns supporting the dome survive.
Unusually, there was a screen only in front of the central aisle. The church was
the katholikon of a monastery, although many of the ancillary buildings are
unexcavated.

Downhill to the south is a **Doric fountain** of the 4C BC, reconstructed in 1926
but now too unstable to allow public access. Behind a Doric façade, water flowed
from lions' head spouts set in a low parapet between pillars, with cisterns behind.

On the northern slope of the hill and towards the coast c 500 tombs have been excavated in Late Mycenaean, Geometric, Archaic and Classical cemeteries.

To Kallithéa

10.5km, by bus.

Hotels in Rení Koskinoú (area code 0241)	
■ **Rení Koskinoú** **A Paradise** (615), pool, tennis etc.; 17,500–23,000 drs. Tel. 66060; fax 66066. April–Oct. Also F/As 32,500–50,000 drs. **B Virginia** (95), pool;	9190–13,515 drs. Tel. 62041, 61103, 61125; fax 63420. April–Oct. **C Kallithéa** (15); 6900–10,400 drs. Tel. 82498, 62498. April–Nov.

From the St Paul's Gate you follow the shore road, then, by a large cemetery (left), turn left over a bridge. Soon after (right) are a British War Cemetery (1943–45) and the caves of the Hellenistic and Roman necropolis (1C BC–AD 1C). 6.5km **Rení Koskinoú**.

10.5km **Kallithéa** is an enchanting but decaying hydropathic establishment, built by the Italians in the 1920s. It has mock-Moorish buildings, gardens and grottoes linked by winding paths, all set among the natural shore rocks. During its heyday this was a fashionable spa, the waters recommended for various internal ailments. The treatment often involved drinking large quantities of water first thing in the morning. The large number of lavatories (over 200) therefore comes as no surprise. More recently the spa was converted into a German prisoner of war camp for the film *Escape to Athena*. Although sadly neglected, Kallithéa provides a unique glimpse of Italianate architecture of the period at its most opulent. The sheltered coves are ideal for swimming and snorkelling and a snackbar is available during summer.

To Líndos, Lakhaniá and Kattavía

95.5km (59 miles); regular bus service to Líndos, also excursion coaches daily; 3 times weekly to Kattavía; daily as far as Yennádhi. The old road is described, ignoring newer bypasses.

Hotels in Afándou, Arkhángelos, Asklipió, Faliráki, Kálathos, Khiotári, Kolímbia, Lárdhos, Líndos, Péfki, Pilónas and Yennádhi	
■ **Afándou** (area code 0241) **A Oasis Holidays** (37), pool; NPA. Tel. 51771/5, 51359. April–Oct. **B Afándou Sky** (34), pool;	8500–16,500 drs. Tel. 52347, 52325; fax 52303. April–Oct. **B Xenia Golf** (26), pool; NPA. Tel. 51121/12, 51128, 51129. March–Nov.

C Skála (F/As) (10);
9000–16,000. Tel. 51788, 52400;
fax 51788. March–Oct.
D Saint Nicholas (14), pool;
7000–10,000. Tel. 51171.
May–Oct.

■ **Arkhángelos** (area code 0244)
C Káravos (F/As) (37), pool;
6400–13,000 drs. Tel. 22961; fax
23263. April–Oct.
C Méandros (20), pool;
6500–9000 drs. Tel. 22896; fax
23896. April–Oct.
C Nárkissos (20); 6500–9500
drs. Tel. 22436, 23089; fax
23089.

■ **Asklipió** (area code 0244)
Rooms in village: **Agapitós** (5);
5000–8000 drs. Tel. 47255.

■ **Faliráki** (area code 0241)
L Esperos Village (Bungalows)
(209), pool, tennis etc.;
11,400–42,400. Tel. 86046; fax
85741. April–Oct.
A Olympos Beach (162), pool,
tennis etc.; 9600–22,800 drs. Tel.
87510/15; fax 86551. April–Oct.
A Epsilon (F/As) (63), pool;
21,000–29,000 drs. Tel. 85912;
fax 85990. March–Nov.
B Atalándi (52); 11,000–14,
000 drs. Tel. 85255. April–Oct.
C Ideál (55); 8050–10,640 drs.
Tel. 85518, 85867.
C Telkhínis (51);
10,000–13,000 drs. Tel. 85015,
85003. April–Oct.

■ **Kálathos** (area code 0241)
L Atrium Palace (171), pool,
tennis, etc.; 18,000–32,000 drs.
Tel. 31601; fax 31600. April–Oct.
Also F/As 22,000–72,000 drs.
C Kalligá (F/A) (16); NPA. Tel.
21969, 42350. May–Oct.
D Xéni (16); 9000–13,000 drs.

Tel. 31171, 31505. May–Oct.

■ **Khiotári** (area code 0244)
A Rhódhos Máris (317), pool,
tennis etc; 19,000–30,000 drs. Tel.
47000, 43333; fax 47051.
April–Oct.
C Kabanáris Bay (56); NPA. Tel.
43279. May–Oct.
C Vílla Sylvána (F/As) (14); NPA.
Tel. 44116. April–Oct.

■ **Kolímbia** (area code 0241)
A Kolímbia Beach (122), pool,
tennis etc.; 12,100–23–800 drs.
Tel. 56311, 56225; fax 56203.
March–Oct.
A Niríides Beach (96), pool,
tennis etc.; 12,000–23,900 drs. Tel.
56210; fax 56461. March–Oct.
B Allegro (32), pool;
9000–14,000 drs. Tel. 56286.
April–Oct.
B Aquarius (F/As) (18);
9500–16,000 drs. Tel. 27608,
28107.
B Tína-Flóra (30);
10,000–12,000 drs. Tel. 56431.
C Kolímbia Sun (64);
9000–12,000 drs. Tel. 51420,
56213. March–Oct.

■ **Lárdhos** (area code 0244)
B Lydian Village Hotel
(Bungalows) (97), pool, water-
sports; 12,400–26,500 drs. Tel.
44161/3, 44165. Jan–Oct.
D Phaedra (11); NPA. Tel. 44218.
Campsite at Ayios Yióryios. Tel.
44203; fax 44249. April–Oct.

■ **Líndos** (area code 0244)
A Lindos Bay (192), pool, tennis
etc.; 16,800–24,000 drs. Tel.
31501; fax 31500. April–Oct. Also
F/As 26,500–39,000 drs. The
hotel is at Vlíkha, outside Líndos
village.
B Amphithéatro (F/A) (8); NPA.

C **Avra tis Líndhou** (F/A) (31);
NPA.
Hunting for accommodation on
the spot in season is not recommended but, if necessary, is best
done through a local travel agent.
**Travel Agents, Líndos Sun
Tours**. Tel. 31333, 31345, 31453;
fax 31353. **Pallas Travel**. Tel.
0244 31494; fax 31495.

■ **Péfki** (area code 0244)
B **Péfki Líndou** (57), pool, tennis;
14,500–20,400 drs. Tel. 48259; fax
48259. April–Oct.
C **Péfkos Beach** (50);
9730–11,900 drs. Tel. 44018,48008.

C **Thália** (30); NPA. Tel. 44458.
April–Oct.

■ **Pilónas** (area code 0244)
D **Pilóna** (11); NPA. Tel. 42247, 42207.

■ **Yennádhi** (area code 0244)
B **Ampélia Beach** (38), pool;
9000–12,000 drs. Tel. 43184.
April–Oct.
C **Christiána** (F/As) (31);
7500–15,000. Tel. 43228.
C **Tina's** (16); 4800–6200 drs.
Tel. 43204.
C **Yennádhi Bay** (37);
8000–10,000. Tel. 43311.

3km Rhodhíni (see above). The road passes through varied scenery of hills interspersed with fertile plains and orange groves. White cubic houses and date
palms give the villages a Saharan appearance. 7km **Sgouroú** (properly
Asgoúrou) has a Hellenistic cemetery site to the east of the road. Near (8km)
Koskinoú (pop. 1691) Late Helladic vases and Roman tombs have been discovered and, at the eastern edge of the village, an Early Christian cemetery. The
countryside begins to unfold before you and there is a good beach 500m left of
the main road. 13km **Faliráki** (pop. 702;) has become a noisy modern resort.
Several roads lead down to beaches and there is an official campsite (Apr–Oct;
tel. 0241 85358, 85516).

3km inland is **Kalithiés** (pop. 2532), where Neolithic to Late Helladic
remains have been discovered in the nearby cave of Ayios Yióryios.

21km **Afándou** (golf course), is the first 'Saharan' village (pop. 5317).

To the southeast, near the coast, is **Katholikí**, where the 16C church of
Panayía Katholikí, built over the central aisle of an Early Christian basilica,
includes inscribed capitals of the 6 or 5C AD, and has 16C and 18C frescoes.

26km **Kolímbia**. The beach is 3km left. Immediately after a river bridge, a
short detour (right) takes you to (3km) **Eptá Piyés** (restaurant in summer), a
cool sheltered gorge where the Seven Springs of its name well up to form a
stream, running through a 186m long tunnel to a small reservoir. Although
dark and narrow, you can walk through the tunnel and get your feet wet, otherwise go by a path over the top. The collected water is used to irrigate the Kolímbia
plain. This is a lovely place to take a break on the east coast journey, quiet but for
the rustling trees, and the peacocks. The road continues to Arkhípoli.

Returning to the main road you pass through a narrow gap with Mt Tsambíka
(326m) to the left.

The tiny **Moní Tsambíkas** (signposted), restored in 1760, is prominently situated on the summit. The road leads three-quarters of the way up then there is a
15 minute walk. An ancient tree stands in the courtyard and there are splendid
views both inland and along the coast, where the long sandy beaches and vivid

blue sea look especially inviting after the steep ascent. The small chapel of the Panayía has an ornately carved screen to the left of which is a section of fresco.

This chapel is the focal point of a local superstition. It is said that a woman who fails to conceive should come to the chapel on 8 September (by foot), eat a small piece of the candlewick and pray to the Virgin Mary. If she subsequently has a baby it should be called either Tsambíkos (boy) or Tsambíka (girl). The interior of the chapel is full of old and new representations of the Panayía as well as photographs of proud mothers holding their babies.

Some 300m after the monastery turning there is a road leading down to a long sandy beach. You cross a ridge (233m) and descend to **Arkhángelos**, another African-looking village (pop. 5781), where carpets and footwear are made, dominated by a spectacular **castle** built in 1467 by Grand Master Orsini. Nearby the **church** of Ayioi Theódhoroi (1377) has wall paintings.

On the northern outskirts of the village is the hill of **Anagros**. The discovery of pottery dating from the Neolithic to Early Bronze Age suggests that a site here was occupied from the prehistoric period. Medieval or later circuit walls are visible. Southwest of Arkhángelos, two Mycenaean chamber tombs were discovered at Mála and Petrokopió.

The road turns inland, then drops steeply to a fertile valley with nut and orange groves. From (38.5km) **Malóna**, a road descends in 5km to the coast and the pleasant resort of **Kharáki** (Rooms). On the limestone promontory above stands the **castle of Pharaklos**, one of the strongest built by the Knights and thus one of the last to fall to the Turks. Under the Knights it was used as a detention centre for prisoners of war and errant knights. The enclosed area is over 200m in diameter but the site is now overgrown and there are few discernible remains. The climb (20 minutes) is steep and precarious and only advisable for those with sturdy footwear and a keen interest in castles.

At the northeast end of the bay (10 minutes from the foot of the castle hill) are the remains of two Early Christian basilicas. The smallest (5C) incorporates earlier architectural fragments and traces of ancillary buildings.

4km beyond the second turn to Kháraki is a tiny whitewashed chapel of Ayios Yióryios, with a Pantokrator surviving in the dome. In the hills behind is the tiny church of **Panayía Atrifférnon** (or Trifaínou as she is named on the icon, and often called by the locals) which could be the objective of a pleasant diversion. To reach it, take the (unsigned) road (right) *before* Ayios Yióryios. After 2km you cross a bridge and immediately diverge sharp left along a riverside track. After 100m you must leave your car and use the stepping-stones across the river. Walk along the broad track, taking the left (uphill) branch after c 7 minutes. After another 7 minutes, beyond an S-bend, a broad but unpromising track rises to the left. Climb this for 5 minutes to the church. Not much of the fresco decoration is visible but much is still concealed beneath the whitewash. There are fragments in the apse and on the north wall, but best preserved is the decoration of a blind apse on the south, where two layers can be seen, the lower defaced by hammer marks. The upper shows the Panayía and her Child.

50km **Kálathos** (pop. 526).

At **Palaioekklesiá**, 1.5km northeast and about 500m from the sea, is a 5–6C three-aisled Early Christian basilica with a double narthex. Excavations revealed mosaic floors and marble flooring slabs. Beyond Kálathos the road divides, the right branch continuing to the south of the island.

You turn left. From the top of a low but rocky pass you get a sudden view of Líndos on the descent to the village.

Líndos

Líndos, now a village of 724 inhabitants, was the most important of the three cities in the island before the foundation of Rhodes and, in the Middle Ages, was second only to Rhodes itself. The delightful situation, with a beautiful beach, the old houses and streets free of traffic, and the superb acropolis give the village a unique charm. But take precautions! This is the most popular excursion in Rhodes and can be unpleasant in high season. Much of the accommodation is pre-booked. It is better to go early in the day when you can both avoid the midday sun on the exposed acropolis and wander through quiet streets before the throngs arrive. And, if necessary, check the time of the last bus; taxis back to Rhodes are not cheap.

History

Finds of obsidian show that the site was occupied in the 3rd millennium BC. A temple of Athena existed from at least the 10C BC. Although the surrounding land has little agricultural potential, the geographical position between two good harbours, with access to eastern trade routes, and a prosperous shipbuilding industry, led to *Líndos* becoming the most important of the three ancient cities of Rhodes. Colonists from Líndos founded *Parthenopea* (ancient predecessor of Naples) and *Gela*, in Sicily, during the 7C. In the 6C Lindos was governed by tyrants, the best known of whom was Kleoboulos (fl. 580 BC), one of the 'Seven Sages', who had a weakness for setting and solving riddles.

After the foundation of the city of Rhodes, Líndos remained the religious centre of the island. St Paul is said to have landed at Líndos on his way to Rome. In the Byzantine period the acropolis was turned into a fortress, which the Knights of St John later made into the headquarters of a castellany, with twelve knights and a Greek garrison. In 1317 Grand Master Foulques de Villaret took refuge in the castle after the Knights had deposed him. The Turks seized the fort in 1522 and continued to use the acropolis as a fortress. In 1902–14 and in 1952 Danish archaeological teams excavated the acropolis. The restorations were done mainly by the Italians before 1938. New restoration of the stoa, temple of Athena, and chapel of St John is now in progress.

For **Domestic Architecture and Líndos pottery**, see introduction to Art and Architecture.

At the west entrance to the village is a small bustling plateía (no parking), shaded by mulberry trees, with an old fountain and two restaurants. Near the plateía donkeys can be hired for the acropolis. Most of the streets in the village are only just wide enough to take a donkey with panniers.

Following the arrows for the **acropolis**, to the left is the church of the Panayía (see below). The path climbs steeply.

■ Open Tues–Sun 08.30–14.30; refreshments and public toilet to the left of the entrance).

The acropolis, towering above the huddled village, occupies a triangular outcrop of rock (116m) accessible only from the north side. From below it seems to be simply a huge medieval **castle**, remodelled and enlarged by the Knights on an earlier stronghold. Passing through the outer gate you reach a terrace with cisterns and Byzantine storage bins, where a rock-cut exedra carries a **relief**, 4.6m long and 5.5m high, of the stern of a ship, with lateral rudder and the helmsman's seat. The deck acted as the base of a statue of a priest of Poseidon called *Hagesandros* (inscription). To the right of the relief are the remains of the ancient **sacred way**.

A long staircase leads to the main gate. There are remains of another stairway to the left which approached a higher gate, now walled up. The staircase gives

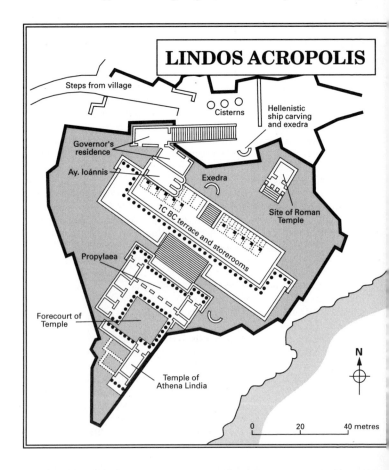

LINDOS ACROPOLIS

Steps from village

Cisterns

Hellenistic ship carving and exedra

Governor's residence

Ay. Ioánnis

Exedra

1C BC terrace and storerooms

Site of Roman Temple

Propylaea

Forecourt of Temple

Temple of Athena Lindia

N

0   20   40 metres

onto the vaulted lower floor of the Governor's Residence of the time of the Knights, lined with column capitals and monument bases. Above (spiral stair) is another room. Adjacent to that, on the same higher level, is the ruined 13C Byzantine **chapel of Ay. Ioánnis**. Turning left through a second room you emerge in front of a series of open storerooms. These support a terrace (that on which the Ayíos Ioánnis church was later built), which is reached by a stairway. During the 3C a statue of the priest of Athena Pamphilidas stood on the **exedra** to the left before the stairs. Further left is the site of a small Roman temple (no longer visible). The terrace was constructed in the 1C BC in front of the huge double winged **stoa** which now rises above. The stoa (added in 208 BC) is 87m long and has a total of 42 Doric columns, some of which have been restored with entablature.

A monumental staircase (21m wide) leads to a higher terrace with foundations of the **propylaea**, built after 407 BC. Its façade was Doric, with projecting wings at either end. Within, five doors lead into a colonnaded court, off which three rooms (for ritual dining?) open to the right. The stoa on the south side, added in the 1C AD, was Ionic. The small **temple of Lindian Athena** (23m × 7.5m; Doric, amphiprostyle and tetrastyle) beyond, stands at the edge of the cliff near the south point of the acropolis. The remains, including the west wall of the cella, date from a rebuilding after a fire in 348 BC.

To the south of the acropolis is the small rocky **harbour** associated by tradition with the supposed visit of St Paul. The story has it that the sea was too rough for his boat to land. As he prayed for guidance, two arms of rock rose from the sea to create a sheltered harbour. Mt Kraná is visible to the west above the village. Rock-cut tombs have been discovered here dating from the 2C BC and later. The most prominent (visible from the acropolis but inaccesible) is the **tomb of Arkhokrates**, which consisted of a central chamber (collapsed) with tombs cut into the rock, and an ornamental two-storey façade, with Doric columns and entablature below, and four altars above.

The southeast end of the stoa gives a splendid view of the **Great Harbour**, with the two islets at its entrance and the promontory beyond. The slope to the west of the propylaea is covered with bases of statues inscribed with the names of local artists. Below the acropolis to the northeast are the foundations of the **Boukopeion**, in use from the 10C BC. It is thought that this small sanctuary was the centre for cattle sacrifice.

The Village

Plunging into the maze of narrow streets, you are bound to get lost. But this is part of the attraction for, round every corner, waits a little chapel or a fine old house. As you descend from the acropolis and enter the village, to the right is the **House of Faídhra Moskhorídhis**, with a doorway of 1642. Off the main road you can explore the maze of unspoilt streets to the south, with their many old houses, courtyards, and staircases. Individual houses are not necessarily marked or easily identified, but worth looking for are the **House of Ioánnis Krékas**, for its wooden ceiling, and the **House of Papás Konstandínos**, the most elaborately decorated of the Líndos houses. Here and elsewhere, the stone carving reflects a variety of influences. Its gatehouse has an ogival doorway and

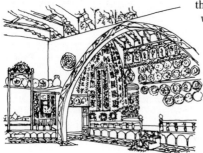

Líndos interior, with bed tent (sperveri), *etc.*

the courtyard an elegant staircase, while the main façade is pierced by ogival and rectangular windows.

At the south end of the village is an ancient wall of well-made limestone blocks, part of the peribolos of a temple of 2–1C BC. Alongside, set in the hill, is the **theatre**, of the 4C BC. Its cavea is divided into two by a landing and into five cunei by four staircases; 27 steps remain. Near the theatre is a large quadrilateral building of the 3–2C BC with an internal colonnade. The function of this building is not yet known: it may have been a gymnasium or had some religious purpose.

Returning towards the Plateía you find the **church of the Panayía**, bearing the dates 1484–90 but probably earlier; also the arms of d'Aubusson. It is in the form of a Latin cross, with an octagonal drum and cupola. The interior has **frescoes** executed in 1779 by Gregory of Syme (restored 1927) and a 17C wooden screen and bishop's throne (1620 by Ignatius of Lesbos). The floor is made of black and white sea pebbles.

Earlier frescoes (1637+) decorated a commemorative or burial chamber (inaccessible) attached to the north arm of the cross, where figures of Christ, the Panayía and other scenes accompany images of the deceased. The frescoes in the main church include a complex Holy Trinity in the apse (the Holy Spirit shown as a dove in a frame with rays) and (vault before the apse) the Ascension with, lower, scenes of Abraham. In the dome is a Pantokrator accompanied by the Panayía, Archangels, Prophets; then the Evangelists in the pendentives.

The north and south arms contain (a) major episodes from the gospels and (b) scenes from the life and apotheosis of the Panayía. The vault of the west arm is divided into zones in each of which the panels (on both sides) have scenes belonging to a single cycle: the Creation and Adam and Eve (top), scenes from the gospels (those on the south better preserved) (middle), the Panayía (lower). Below these are full-length saints.

Above the west door is a very striking representation of the Second Coming, with the Panayía and John the Baptist interceding for men. Below is the preparation of the throne and the choirs of the just. At the bottom left saints are being conducted to the door of Paradise, which is shown on the adjacent wall, with the Panayía, the Just Robber carrying his cross, etc. Below and to the right of the Preparation are realistic depictions of the weighing of souls (an angel pierces a devil with a spear) and the tortures of hell. A fiery stream issues from the mouth of Hades (shown as a sea monster) in which sinners burn and Beelzebub tortures. In an arched building, female sinners hang in chains.

On the adjacent wall is another dramatic scene of the Raising of the Dead. Although the composition as a whole is closely integrated, there is considerable variation in style. The subtle naturalism of the Holy Trinity and Second Coming contrast with the austere figures of saints (west) and the crudely powerful scenes of Hell (Orlandos). The large icon (Jesse) which forms the door into the sanctuary is inscribed as a dedication of Konstantios, Bishop of Rhodes from 1691–1702.

On the promontory of Ayios Aimilianós, near the northeast end of the Great Harbour, is the so-called **Tomb of Kleoboulos**, a Classical cylindrical structure of square blocks of masonry. The burial chamber is approached by a dromos. In the Middle Ages the tomb was converted into the church of Ay. Aimilianós.

Beyond Líndos village a road follows the coast via the resort of **Péfki**, then turns inland. Returning to the main road and turning south, you pass the village of **Pilónas**. At c 62km (left) excavations of the church of **Panayía Katholikí** (13–14C; some 17C frescoes) have revealed the remains of two Early Christian basilicas, the oldest of which is three-aisled and of Syrian type,

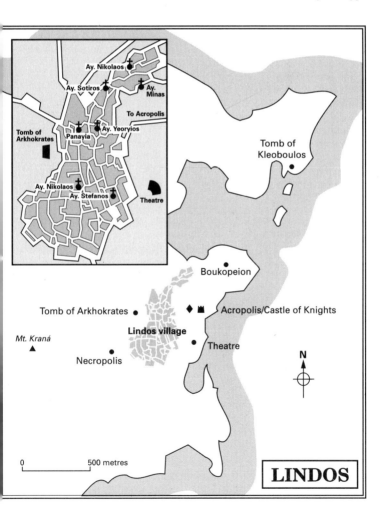

perhaps dating from the 4C AD. 63km **Lárdhos** (pop. 912). The coastal area is highly developed but the village has retained a warm atmosphere: there is a small **museum**. A large Mycenaean cemetery has been found to the north of the village.

A good road runs west to **Láerma** (pop. 646) where in the late 1970s a cemetery of the early 4C AD was found, some graves containing iron tools. Nearby were the remains of a building, probably contemporary. The church of Ayios Yióryios has a splendid gold **painted screen** decorated with fantastic flora and fauna.

From Láerma there is an unsurfaced road (4km, signed Profiliá) to the 12C **Moní Thári** (open all day), now revived and lending its name to a Rhodian ecclesiastical broadcasting station, a lovely cruciform building in a beautiful situation. The dome is particularly fine. Once your eyes have become accustomed to the dim light, you can make out excellent frescoes in four layers, dating from 11–18C. Some of the later ones have been removed to the Byzantine Museum in Rhodes, making it possible to see several different stages of painting. In the apse is a Deisis with, at the bottom, hierarchs to either side of the Holy Table. Below this is an earlier layer of painting; the upper is dated (1506) by an inscription in the conch of the prothesis. At window level, a scene of Abraham's welcoming the angels is unusual in showing Abraham and Sarah seated with their guests. In the east vault is the Ascension. Below the Pantokrator in the dome (13C, the later 17C paintings are those in Rhodes) are the Panayía and John the Baptist with angels. Between the windows, 16 prophets and, in the pendentives, the Evangelists. The north and south arms are very shallow. To the south are pictures of the Archangels: Michael in the centre is concealed but his local epithet (Tharinos) can be read. Scenes on the inside of the arch include the Repentance of David. The north arm includes the mounted saints, Yióryios and Dhimítrios. The west arm (18C) has scenes from the life of Christ, in panels, and numerous saints.

Returning to Lárdhos, you can get to the **Moní Ipsíni** (3km; signposted), in idyllic countryside. The monastery is set around a courtyard with an orange tree: off it are the cells. The church has a fine olive-wood screen, surmounted by dragons.

At 71.5km **Khiotári** (pop. 106) has a monastery of the Metamórfosis. Soon a turn leads inland to (3km) the friendly hill village of **Asklipió** (nice café with rooms, above the church; pop. 544), with a small but worthwhile castle above and a prominent **11C church** of the Koímisis tis Theotókou (open Mon–Fri 09.00–18.00; Sat 10.00–15.00). By the church is a well set out **ecclesiastical museum**: among the contents some architectural fragments suggest the existence of an Early Christian basilica nearby. There are some good icons and a fine 18C marble candlestick. Adjacent is an equally good **folk museum**. The church was originally a free cross but was altered, not for the better, in the 18C when side-aisles were added at northwest and southwest. The frescoes (mostly 17C) are impressive. In the apse of the sanctuary is the Panayía and, in the east vault, a Revelation. The dome and pendentives have a Pantokrator and standard imagery. In the north arm, at the end is a large figure of Ay. Mámas mounted on a lion; to the east a massive Archangel Michael and (west), various scenes including a Crucifixion, with frequent use of background architecture. In the south vault is Christ in Judgement. The west arm is divided into numerous panels. In the upper zone are scenes of the Creation and Adam and Eve (the garden is positively depicted). Below are episodes from the lives of Christ and the Panayía including a fine Raising of Lazarus and Presentation. The lower level on the south is dominated by the Trial, Passion, Crucifixion and Resurrection. Other frescoes have been removed to the Byzantine Museum in Rhodes town.

At 75km **Yennádhi** (pop. 542) is an attractive little town with good beaches. Váti (7km inland, the road continuing to Apolakiá and the west coast) has (1.5km to the east) the site of a Mycenaean and later necropolis, now largely overgrown.

At 77km you can follow the coast or turn inland to (84km) **Lakhaniá** (pop. 346), rejoining the shore road at (88km) **Khókhlakhas**, 2km to the south of which is the good beach of **Plimíri** (tavernas), with a church of Zoödhókhos Piyí and some ancient remains, including tombs and parts of a circuit wall, on the landward side of the promontory above the church.

The main road continues east via Ayios Pávlos to (95.5km) the sleepy village of **Kattavía** (pop. 550) where Mycenaean tombs were discovered on the slopes between the chapel of Ayios Mínas and the village. There was probably a Mycenaean settlement on the spur of Ayios Mínas. Subsequent occupation of this area is attested by the discovery of later Greek and Roman pottery.

From Ayios Pávlos or Kattavía it is possible, by poorer roads (better suited to 'off-road' vehicles), to reach the extreme south of Rhodes off which is the promontory/islet of Prasonísi (taverna; lighthouse; good beach). Here are scanty remains (houses, temples) of the Late Geometric–Early Archaic settlement of *Vrouliá*, excavated at the beginning of the century, which gave its name to a distinctive style of Archaic pottery.

To Kámiros, Monólithos and Kattavía

To **Kámiros** *(36km; 5 buses daily),* **Monólithos** *(73.5km; 1 bus daily), and* **Kattavía** *(see east coast route; 101.5km, 63 miles; 3 buses weekly). This excursion can be combined with that to Ialysos (see above).*

Hotels in Apolakiá, Kalavárdha, Kremastí, Monólithos, Paradhíssi, Profítis Ilías, Sálakos and Soroní

■ **Apolakiá** (area code 0246)
C **Amalía** (18); NPA.
E **Skoutas** (8); NPA.

■ **Kalavárdha** (area code 0241)
D **Voúras** (12); NPA; Tel. 40003.

■ **Kremastí** (area code 0241)
A **Kremastí Village Apartments** (F/As) (20); pool; NPA. Tel. 92424, 47159, 47856. April–Oct.
B **Iliotrópio** (84); 9000–13,500 drs. Tel. 93893, 93514.

March–Oct.
C **Anséli** (24); 8000–9000 drs. Tel. 92013.
C **Maritime** (F/As) (50); pool; 12,000–24,000 drs. Tel. 92232, 94455. April–Oct.

■ **Monólithos** (area code 0246)
D **Thomás** (9); 8000 drs. Tel. 61291, 61264; fax 28834.

■ **Paradhísi** (area code 0241)
B **Vallian Village** (58);

13,000–15,000 drs. Tel. 81127.
C **Savelén** (32); NPA. Tel. 81855.
C **Villa Hélena** (F/As);
8000–12,000. Tel. 81175, 92915.

■ **Profitis Ilías** (area code 0246)
A **Elafos-Elafina** (68), tennis; NPA.
Tel. 22225, 21221/3.

■ **Sálakos** (area code 0241)
B **Nímfi** (4); NPA; Tel. 22206.

■ **Soroní** (area code 0241)
C **Sílvia Soronís** (14); NPA; Tel.
41025.

Beyond (9km) Triánda, you continue along the shore, with views across the sea to the coast of Turkey. 12km **Kremastí** (3604 inhab.) is noted for its annual festival, held 14–23 August, which like those of antiquity combines religious ceremonies (in this case centered on a miraculous icon of the Virgin) with athletic games, music and dancing.

Inland, near **Maritsá** (5.5km; the road continuing beyond Maritsá down the centre of the island to meet other east-west routes, at Psínthos and Arkhípoli) is a church of Ayios Yióryios with 14C frescoes.

At **Paradhísi** (16km), at one time called Villanova, the **airport** is to the north of the road; the old airport was to the south in the direction of Maritsá. The church of Ayios Ioánnis Theológos (refurbished 1886) has a good icon of its patron saint. From a site close to the shore in this area came a collection of amphorae of the 2C BC, nearly all with the craftman's name and mark, stacked and awaiting shipment.

At 18km, a turning (left) leads to the wooded area of **Kalamónas** with a cattle breeding station and an agricultural school. Beyond a boy scout village stretches the **Valley of Butterflies** (Petaloúdhes). The myriad moths (rather than butterflies) are best seen July–August. They are attracted to the valley to mate by the thick growth of storax with its pungent scent. The population has decreased drastically over the past few years, with visitors disturbing them into flight. A path leads (2km) to the **monastery of Kalópetra**, built in 1784 by the exiled Prince of Wallachia, Alexander Ipsilántis.

Back on the main road, at 20km (right) the quiet village of **Theológos** (pop. 580) had a shrine of Apollo Erithimios and there are Early Christian remains. Around the ruined chapel of Ayios Ioánnis Theológos were found ancient architectural fragments, including column drums. Archaic tombs were discovered in the area as well as a Mycenaean chamber tomb. The main road continues through fig orchards and past numerous wind pumps. 24km **Soroní** (pop. 1232). Mycenaean cist graves were discovered here at the beginning of the century, and an Early Christian cemetery has been found at nearby Dhipótamos.

3km inland (on the Eleoússa road) through pinewoods is the little **Church of Ayios Soúlas**. Normally a quiet spot, ideal for a shady picnic or a quiet stroll, once a year it becomes the focus of local attention with its festival on 29–30 July. During the afternoon a clearing which forms a simple 'stadium' is the site for a series of athletic competitions and donkey and horse races, which culminate in an evening of dancing. This festival is the subject of one of the chapters of Lawrence Durrell's *Reflections on a Marine Venus*. Above the village of (26km)

Fánes a long plateau stretches to the southeast: on this were identified scattered remains of Helladic and later settlements.

At (30km) **Kalavárdha** (pop. 488), eight Mycenaean chamber tombs were discovered on the nearby hill of Aníforo (500m south), and prehistoric and later pottery. On the outskirts of the village the coast road bears right.

From Kalavárda it is possible to turn inland, either **A** to make for the east coast at **Kolímbia** (41km from Kalavárdha) or **B** to rejoin the coast road 31km further south in the region of Amartos. From the Kalavárdha fork you ascend the lower slopes of Mt Profítis Ilías via **Sálakos** (8km; pop. 580) where the remains of a medieval fortress stand on a hill (180m) and, after 13.5km, reach the turn for Kolímbia.

A. This well-engineered but steep and winding road climbs continually, with fine retrospective views of the sea. It soon enters the **Wood of the Prophet**, luxuriant—mainly pines including umbrella pines and cypresses—thanks to a local superstition that the Prophet will slay anyone cutting down a tree. At 20km, and 701m above the sea, are two hotels suitably called Elafos and Elafína (Stag and Doe), from of the number of deer in the neighbourhood. Rather whimsical buildings, which resemble alpine lodges, they fit the high altitude and forested setting and are a good example of the unpredictable pleasures which a closer acquaintance with the island provides.

The road passes north of the summit (799m; path) of **Mt Profítis Ilías** and continues (gravel section of 7km) via (25km) the attractive church of **Ayios Nikólaos Foundoúkli**, in a lovely setting among the pines (picnic area; water fountain). The small chapel has a quatrefoil (tetraconch) plan. It is entirely covered with wonderful, lively frescoes, of the 14–15C though in some cases modified by Italian restoration. In the apse of the sanctuary is a Deisis and Communion of the Apostles; in the vault the Ascension. Among the figures on the wall (right) is Ayios Nikólaos. His figure, together with those of the Panayía and John the Baptist shown (with others) in the narrow L-shaped angles formed at the junction of the eastern apse with the central area below the dome, replace the scenes normally shown in the icons. In the dome (the Pantokrator has not survived), groups of prophets alternate with the windows; Evangelists below in the squinches. In the north, south and west apses, the semicircular zones at the top show, respectively, the Crucifixion, the Birth of Christ and the Dormition. The scenes below these include—north: Simon of Cyrene carrying the Cross, and the Descent into Hell; south: the Flight into Egypt, the Presentation, the Baptism with, in the bottom zone, a winged Taxiárkhis Mikhaíl carrying a large sword, a hierarch and (right) Ayios Yióryios on a horse; west: the Transfiguration, Raising of Lazarus, Entry into Jerusalem with (below) the donors of the church (shown as a model), and their family.

Eleoússa (28.5km) surprises you with a now derelict Italian governors' palace but the setting is lovely, with a fountain and large pool and a small white monastery.

At **Arkhípolis** (35km) there is a turning to **Psínthos** (10km, left), site of the Turkish garrison's last stand against the Italians in 1912. 41km **Kolímbia** (pop. 317).

B. Ignore the Kolímbia turn and 1.5km further on you can make a detour to **Apóllona** (9km, left; pop. 1038) which has a delightful and well-arranged **museum** in a renovated mill, exhibiting folk art and agricultural tools as well as a few ancient artefacts from local sites.

Embona (435m), 22.5km from Kalavárdha, a village growing vines and tobacco, is the starting point for the ascent of **Mt Atáviros**, the highest mountain on the island. The ascent and descent each takes about two hours. The mountain is bare of vegetation and has no springs. If you make the steep climb to the summit, you will be rewarded with a spectacular, panoramic view of the whole island of Rhodes. Here are the scanty remains of the **Temple of Zeus Atabyros**, said to have been built by Althaemenes, founder of *Kretinae* (see below). It is certainly one of the oldest temples on Rhodes, adapted in Byzantine times into a church of Ayios Ioánnis Pródhromos. The site was excavated in 1927 but the cella of the temple could not be found. About 100m northeast are the remains of a stoa or propylaea. Votive offerings found on the site and now in the Rhodes Archaeological Museum include bronze, lead and terracotta statuettes of oxen, goats and other domestic animals.

East of Embona is the monastery of Artamíti (380m). At 57.5km, in the area called Amartos, the inland road meets the coastal route.

Ancient Kameiros

After leaving Kalavárda on the coastal route, at 34km there is a turning (left, signposted) to ancient *Kameiros* (1km; 08.30–15.00; closed Mon).

History

The third of the ancient cities of Rhodes, called 'chalky' by Homer. *Kameiros* flourished between the Archaic and Hellenistic periods. Most of the extant buildings date from the Hellenistic period when extensive rebuilding became necessary after a severe earthquake in 226 BC. The site was probably destroyed by yet another disastrous earthquake in 142 BC although occupation appears to have continued on a much reduced scale until the Early Christian period. It was rediscovered in 1852 after centuries of oblivion and the acropolis area was excavated between 1852 and 1864 by Biliotti and Salzmann. In 1929 the Italian School began excavation of the rest of the site.

The **site**, undisturbed in the Middle Ages, occupies a gentle slope overlooking the sea. The city had no fortifications and can be divided into three sections: the lower terrace with the public buildings, the residential area rising up the slopes to the south and east, and the acropolis above to the south.

You enter the site at the lower terrace, excavated during the Hellenistic period to accommodate a new scheme of public buildings. To the left are the remains of the **retaining wall** (1). South and southwest of the wall are remains of post-Hellenistic buildings, probably houses (2). To your right are further buildings of a later date. East of these is the base of a Hellenistic **shrine** (3), 5.50 × 4.20m, dating from the late 3–2C. Inside there is a statue base, and traces of plaster were discovered on the outside of the building. The proximity of this shrine to the temple in an area dominated by votive monuments suggests that it might have been an offering, but a very substantial one.

To the southeast is the **temple** (4), approximately 8 × 19m and orientated north–south. The dedication is uncertain, although a likely candidate is Pythian Apollo. Because of the slope of the terrain, the stylobate is reached by four steps at the back (north), although there are none at the front. The temple was not

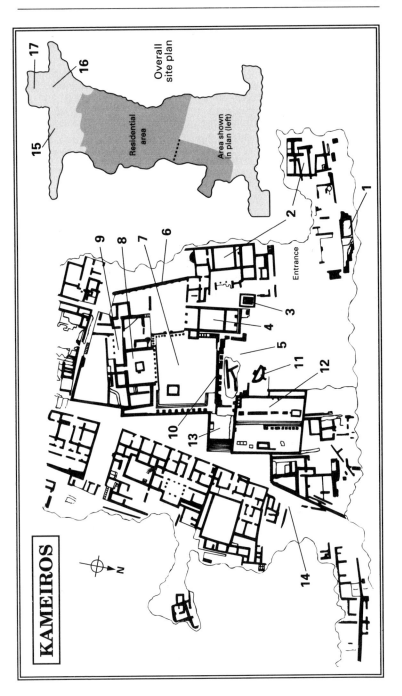

peripteral, but both front and back porches had two columns (still standing) *in antis*. Entering through the front porch (pronaos) you find, in the corners of the cella to either side of the door, bases for votive offerings. Facing the door is the base of the cult statue, behind which is the sunken treasury of the temple (c 2m deep). In the area (5) to the north and east of the temple (see below) were displayed large scale **dedicatory offerings**, mainly of the late 2C BC.

If you leave the temple through the front (south) porch, you can see to the right the Hellenistic retaining wall (6; restored) of the upper level. The blocks here are smaller and better finished than those used in the construction of the lower wall. To the left is the restored **Fountain House Square** or temenos (3C; (7)) around whose walls can be seen the bases for dedicatory offerings; those now on the steps would have been originally distributed around the area. A flight of three steps framing the east end of the square was probably used by

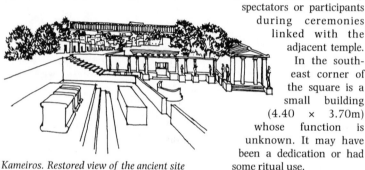

spectators or participants during ceremonies linked with the adjacent temple. In the south-east corner of the square is a small building (4.40 × 3.70m) whose function is unknown. It may have been a dedication or had some ritual use.

Kameiros. Restored view of the ancient site

Off the south side is the **Fountain House** (8), with a façade consisting of Doric half-columns. At the east corner two columns have been restored with entablature. A low parapet ran between these columns in front of a trough which was filled with water from the walled reservoir behind (now open). During the early 3C the reservoir and low wall were removed and the fountain was replaced by a well. In the centre of the reservoir area a statue was erected (the base still visible). Behind is a series of small buildings including a narrow stepped passage to the east and a small stoa (9) reached by steps from the back of the Fountain House. To the west is a large threshold of the stoa, and the remains of a pebble mosaic in the southwest corner.

On the north side of the temenos, a wall with engaged columns and a central door (10) was built during the Middle Hellenistic period. Leaving the area through the north wall entrance, you see in front again the lower level (5) of excavation with poros walls dating from the Classical period. Beyond this, standing at an angle to the temenos is an **exedra** (11).

You cross this area to gain access to the **precinct of the gods** (12) behind the exedra, and enter it through the west door. The precinct contains altars dedicated to a variety of gods, and is divided into two levels. On the lower level is a large **altar** dedicated to Helios, with steps added at a later date. To the left are four smaller altars and to the right a statue base. The front row of the upper level consists of nine poros altars with the names of the divinities to whom they are dedicated inscribed on the front. Behind these are more altars, the most prominent of which is the large altar dedicated to Agathos Daimon.

Returning to the path in front of the exedra you ascend a broad **staircase** (13) to the predominantly residential area. This has not been fully excavated and the buildings probably continue some distance to the north, east and west. At the top of the stairs the **main street** runs north–south. At the north end are large **public baths** (14). In the corner is a big triangular cistern and, next to it, the rooms of the complex, some with basins and hypocausts. To the north and northeast are remains of earlier buildings (unidentified).

As you walk up the road (south) it is difficult to make out where one house ends and another begins. At various points you can enter the warren of paths and corridors and wander up through the buildings. Set in many of the paths are remains of the Hellenistic stone conduits and the Roman clay pipes, reminders of the advanced water distribution network that existed at this site. Despite the confusion, several particular elements of this area can be distinguished. Set back from the left of the road, southeast of the staircase, is the central atrium of a house, clearly visible due to the restoration of the **peristyle court**. Slightly further up on the left can be seen the restored columns of another peristyle court.

If you continue to the end of the road, steps lead up to the rather disappointing **acropolis**. The remains in this area are meagre, movable objects having been taken to the Rhodes Archaeological Museum. The front of the plateau is dominated by the 200m long **stoa** (15) of the late 3–2C. It was fronted by two rows of Doric columns behind which were set small rooms, probably shops. The stoa was built over an earlier **cistern** (16) now visible towards the west end. This huge tank has a capacity of 600 cubic meters. It was constructed during the 6–5C to collect rainwater from the roofs of the acropolis buildings for distribution to the settlement below through a series of conduits and, later, clay pipes. The flow could be regulated by moving large stone lids over the two exit holes in the bottom. Traces of the waterproofing plaster are still visible and steps giving access for cleaning can be seen against the north wall. When the stoa was built the cistern was replaced by 16 wells set in the rooms of the stoa and connected by underground pipes.

In front of the cistern stands a small poros altar. Above are the barely discernible remains of the Doric Temple (17) and **Sanctuary of Athena Polias**, of the late 3–2C. The temple had a Classical predecessor. From the acropolis there are splendid views of the coast, and of the summit of Mt Profítis Ilías. Taking the path to the west back down to the entrance, you get a good overall view of the site. On the surrounding slopes are the remains of ancient cemeteries.

Leaving Kameiros along the coast road you pass through the ruins of *Kretinae*, a city said to have been founded by Althaemenes from Crete. At 43km is **Mandrikó** (pop. 239) with, to the northeast on the hill of Melissáki, a Mycenaean chamber tomb with dromos. On a hillock to the northeast of Melissáki are signs of Hellenistic and Late Roman occupation. **Skála Kamírou** (50.5km) has a daily boat to Khálki. About 6.5km out to sea is a group of islets, of which the largest is Alimniá (8q km; see Khálki).

At 53km is a sign (right) for 'Kamiros Castle' (road in 2km, rough but passable), leading to **Kastéllos**, an important **castle** of the Knights, perched on a rock (130m) and dominating the sea. Probably built in 1480, it is on three levels, each assigned to a different Grand Master. High on the southwest outer wall are the arms of Grand Masters Aimerie d'Amboise and Fabrizio del Carretto. It is dilapidated on the precipitous northeast side.

At 55km **Kritinía** (pop. 661) has a small **Folk Art Museum** (10.00–18.00; closed Mon). To the north the rocky hillock of Kastráki has a section of Hellenistic polygonal wall on the north side, with inscriptions. A small fort was also erected on a nearby hill by the Knights. The village of **Fikélloura** (inland) has given its name to an important style of Archaic pottery found in graves there.

At 60km you meet the inland road (see above). At 68km it is possible to make a detour to the **Monastery of Zoodhókhos Piyís** situated 1km off the road (left) to Ayios Issidhóros. The chapel contains sections of frescoes including a Virgin and Child in an arched niche to the left. Continue along the main road, through sparsely inhabited hills, to (69km) **Siána** (443m; pop. 280) about 3km northwest of which is the site of Ayios Fokás, the centre of an important settlement during the Classical and Hellenistic periods. To the west, on the plain of Vasiliká, are extensive ancient building remains including sections of a perimeter wall and tower. The discovery of Late Neolithic and Early Bronze Age pottery indicates also earlier occupation. To the south are extensive cemeteries, with tombs dating mainly from the Archaic to Roman periods. Siána has given its name to a distinctive type of cup made in the 6C BC.

73.5km **Monólithos** (pop. 515) has a daily bus from Rhodes. In the 1940s a mid 6C BC cremation pyre was excavated near the school, containing over 40 vases. A steep and winding road leads to the **castle of Monólithos**, widely

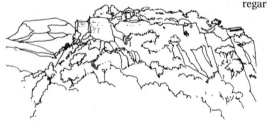

Monólithos

regarded as the most spectacular in Rhodes. It is situated on the top of a precipitous rock called Monópetra (236m) and accessible only by a single short path. The site is breathtaking. But take care, especially on the coastal side, where the wall has fallen away leaving an unprotected drop of over 200m. Inside are two cisterns and the modernised church of Ayios Pantaléonos, with another structure beside it. There are magnificent views over the sea towards Khálki, and inland of Mt Akramítis. From the castle (car park) a rough track runs down to the coast. After 1km it forks, right for the monastery of Ayios Yióryios; left for the long beach of Foúrni which, although picturesque and quiet, is often buffeted by strong winds.

At 83.5km there is a turn inland for **Apolakiá** (2km; pop. 647) where in 1993 fossilised elephant bones were discovered.

If you like small and isolated churches (and frescoes) the chapel of **Ayios Ioánnis Várdhas** is well worth seeing. To find it, take the road signed 'Dam 2' on the further outskirts of Apolakía. In fact it is nearer 4km to reach the dam (and its lake behind). Just before the dam, a rough track (left) leads to a pumping station. The church is a five-minute scramble up the hillside behind the building, or the road will take you there by a more roundabout route. There are frescoes of the 13–14C which follow Constantinopolitan prototypes rather than those of the eastern Empire. This trend is represented not only by some splendidly imposing and ornate figures (the saints in the northwest corner, especially Ayios Trífon), but also by the appearance of the Panayía (rather than the Deisis) in the apse of the sanctuary. Within the iconostasis (north), immediately above the spring of the vault, is a fine figure of the Panayía. Of major episodes represented in the main vault the Raising of Lazarus (north) is indicated by an inscription. On the south and better preserved are an Entry into Jerusalem and a Presentation. The lower walls are occupied by busts and full-length figures of saints. A large figure of Ayios Yióryios spreads over two layers on the south while opposite, in smaller scale, the Panayía holds her child. Pottery vessels built into the structure were to help amplify sound.

3km to the south of Apolakiá is the picturesque village of **Arnítha** (pop. 302). To reach the Early Christian complex of Ayía Irini, take the narrow Istros road on the north side of the bridge at the crossroads below Arnítha and, after 1.5km the site is visible near the road to the left. There are the remains of a large basilica 6C with ancillary buildings and a second smaller three-aisled church. The apse of the basilica retains its synthronon, the base of the altar and some marble columns.

A rough but spectacular mountain road continues south from Arnítha towards Kattavía (25km). A poor by-road (to the west) approaches the 14C **Moní Skiádhi** (3km; best to walk), more easily reached from the coast road. Although the monastery is no longer in use there are resident caretakers who run the monastery as a hostel for up to 30 visitors. There is no formal charge, but visitors are expected to make a contribution to the monastery's upkeep.

At **Mesanagrós** (12km; Rooms) two Early Christian basilicas and other buildings dating from 5–6C underlie a 13C church of the Dormition (Koímisis tis Theotókou). The church is reached by a small wooden bridge over the earlier remains of the two three-aisled basilicas including lower sections of the walls and fragments of mosaics. Above the door is set a marble column from one of the earlier churches (three similar columns are visible inside). The screen, surmounted with dragons, is set with painted panels and to the side there is a 15C painting of St George. There is a pebbled mosaic floor. The key is available from the taverna, whose owner is an entertaining guide. The road continues to Kattavía.

Beyond the Apolakiá turn the coast road (being improved) continues south and (97.5km) swings east for Kattavía (101.5km; see west coast route, above).

Kárpathos

Kárpathos (Κάρπαθος; anc. *Karpathos* or *Carpathos*; also known by its medieval name *Scarpanto*), most important of the islands between Crete and Rhodes, is another place of contrasts. From Pigádhia, well supplied with tourist facilities, to the south, the land is soft and there are several good beaches, with hotels and watersports. The centre of the island has attractive mountain villages and is interesting to walk. In the rugged and isolated north, the striking village of Olimbos is known for its traditional customs. Because of the diversity of Kárpathos, its largely mountainous character and the limited public transport, you need more time here than other islands; many visitors return year after year.

Long and narrow, Kárpathos is 48km from north to south with a maximum width of 11km and about the same area as Kos. The coastline is steep but not much indented: there are bays, but only the Bay of Trístomo at the north end gives much protection from the prevailing winds. A mountain range runs from north to south, rising to Mt Kalolímni (Lástros; 1215km). The twin peaks in the centre virtually divide the island in two.

The long north section, covered with stunted pine trees on the east and bare on the west with few springs, is sparsely populated. Here the traditional way of life is better preserved. The more populous, better watered and more productive southern section is known as 'European' Kárpathos. Farming is the mainstay of the 5323 inhabitants. There are said to be more Karpathiots in Piraeus than on the island itself. In 1966 a great gathering of emigré islanders was held to discuss the island's future economy.

The small airport is 10km southwest of Pigádhia.

History

In antiquity, as officially today, the island was called *Karpathos*, though Homer has it as *Krapathos*. It was supposed to have belonged to the Minoans in the Bronze Age and later to have been colonised by Argives. Minoan and Mycenaean remains have been found at various sites in the Pigádhia area, including cemeteries and possibly settlements. Over 90 Bronze Age vases have been recovered from tombs, reinforcing the evidence for occupation during this period. There are few signs of earlier occupation although in 1886 the British Museum was presented with a Neolithic limestone figure (65cm) found in or near Pigádhia. The island appears in the Athenian tribute lists but later was incorporated into the Rhodian state.

In antiquity three or four independent cities can be associated with the island—*Karpathos*, *Arkaseia*, *Brykous* and *Nisyros* (this possibly an older centre which was defunct by the Classical period), as well as *Potidaion* which was the port of Karpathos and a community of aboriginal inhabitants, the *Eteokarpathioi*. There is some disagreement about the locations of the sites of these settlements (see main text): *Arkaseia* and *Brykous* are known; it is likely that the site at Pigádhia is *Potidaion*; and there is a suggestion (disputed) that *Nisyros* was on the small island of Sariá (q.v.). But this means that *Karpathos*, the ancient capital, has not yet been identified.

In the Early Byzantine period Kárpathos was under the archdiocese of

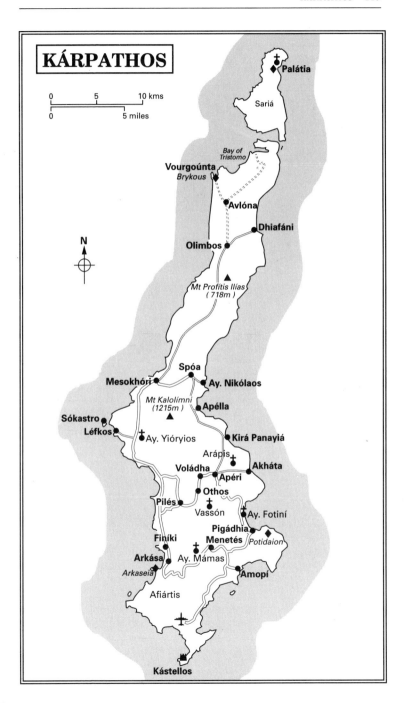

KÁRPATHOS

0   5   10 kms
0   5 miles

Palátia

Sariá

Bay of Tristomo

Vourgoúnta
Brykous

Avlóna

Dhiafáni

Olimbos

N

▲
*Mt Profítis Ilías
(718m)*

Spóa

Mesokhóri

Ay. Nikólaos

*Mt Kalolímni
(1215m)* ▲

Apélla

Sókastro

Léfkos

Ay. Yióryios

Kirá Panayiá

Arápis

Akháta

Voládha

Apéri

Othos

Pilés

Vassón

Ay. Fotiní

Pigádhia
Potidaion

Finíki

Menetés

Arkása

Ay. Mámas

Arkaseía

Amopí

Afiártis

Kástellos

Rhodes. In the 7–10C it was raided by Arab pirates who may have established bases on the island.

The medieval name of *Scarpanto* was revived by the Italians and is still sometimes used; the Turks called it *Kerpe*. Despite its size, Kárpathos has had a relatively uneventful existence. The Latin Empire gave it in fief to the Genoese Andrea and Lodovico Moresco. In 1306 it was acquired by the Venetian family of Cornaro. The Knights took over the island in 1315 but held it for only two years before returning it to Andrea Cornaro. The family eventually gave it up to the Turks in 1538. In 1835 Sultan Mahmoud II gave it the privilege of self-assessment.

The most useful historical guide to Kárpathos (also with plenty of other helpful information) is by Y. von Bolzano in German (Salzburg, 1994; available locally). The most comprehensive study of the island, by N. Moutsopoulos, in Greek with a substantial French summary, would be very difficult to obtain outside specialist libraries in Greece.

Getting to Kárpathos

■ **By air**. There is a small airport 10km southwest of Pighádia with flights to and from Rhodes (daily), Athens (3 times weekly), Kásos (3 times weekly) and Crete (once a week).

■ **By boat**. Ferries (3–4 times weekly) link Kárpathos with Athens, Crete and some other islands in the Cyclades and southern Dodecanese.

Getting around Kárpathos

■ **By bus**. The central bus station is just off the waterfront in Pigádhia. Although the services are increased in summer to accommodate visitors, many villages are still only served by one bus a day. In the north there is an irregular service between Dhiafáni and Olimbos. **Tours** of the island are organised by private operators (book at travel agents).

■ **By car**. Cars and motorbikes (expensive) can be hired from several outlets in Pigádhia (during season only). The major agencies are not represented. The service provided by **Wheels** (tel. 0245 23330) is good; or contact a travel agent. If you hire transport, bear in mind that the only petrol stations in the island are on the two main roads out of Pigádhia.

The **road network** is very variable in quality. Asphalt roads link Pigádhia, the airport and the main villages (from Apéri to Pilés) and the west coast route has a surface of gradually deteriorating quality to about 4kms south of the turn for Lefkó. Otherwise the roads (including the east coast route from Apéri to Spóa) are quite rough, though mostly passable. The road from Spóa to Olimbos (21km) is passable, in over an hour of careful driving.

Taxis are available (rank near the waterfront in Pigádhia).

■ **By boat**. In summer there is a daily boat running between Pigádhia and Dhiafáni and, once a week, an excursion to Kásos. There are also sporadic trips down the east coast to the beaches of Akháta, Kirá Panayiá and Apélla and sometimes excursions to the island of Sariá in the north.

■ **Travel agents. Possí**, Pigádhia; tel. 0245 22235, 22627; fax 22252. **Kárpathos Express**, Pigádhia; tel. 0245 22578, 22579; fax 0245 22173. See also Dhiafáni.

Pigádhia

Hotels and restaurants in Pigádhia (area code 0245)

A Possiráma Bay (F/A) (10); NPA. Tel. 22916; fax 22919. April–Oct.	**C Panórama** (30); 6500–8500 drs. Tel. 22739.
B Miramáre Bay (43), pool; 13,200–17,000 drs. Tel. 22345; fax 22631. April–Oct.	**D Anessis** (12); 3000–7000 drs. Tel. 22100.
B Seven Stars (57), pool; 10,500–13,500 drs. Tel. 22101, 22750, 22751; fax 22753. April–Oct. Also F/As 12,000–13,500.	**Restaurants** As so often, the crowded restaurants on the main harbour do not offer very good value, although the ouzeri **To Periyiáli** is worth a visit. Try also **Kalí Kardhiá**, **Romiós**, **To Kíma** or **Zórbas**. A short distance back from the seafront **Byzantion** has a nice atmosphere and reasonable fare.
C Amaryllis (F/A) (22); 7000–15,000 drs. Tel. 22375, 22530.	
C Ilios (56); 8670–10,300 drs. Tel. 22448. May–Oct.	

The capital (since 1894) and main port is Pigádhia, or Kárpathos, set at the end of the wide sandy bay of Vrónti in the southeast of the island and fringed by gardens and olive-groves on the northwest. A modern town of 1692 inhabitants, it has a wide selection of accommodation. Restaurants, tavernas and bars are concentrated around the waterfront—the centre of activity, especially during the evenings.

In Od. Dhimokratías, the broader of the streets leading inland behind the harbour, are the **taxi rank** and **bus station**. The north end of the harbour is marked by a promontory which forms the apex of a triangle of streets containing other main facilities: the **police station, OTE, post office** and **Olympic Airways**.

Northwest along Vrónti bay are 4km of sandy beach. There are several bars and places renting watersport equipment at the Pigádhia end, while it becomes quieter further along.

In town, in a playground near the Hotel Atlantis on the promontory, are various Early Christian architectural fragments from a basilica which once stood on the acropolis (at Paliá Pigádhia).

The rocky citadel to the east, locally known as Possí or 'the **acropolis**', is thought to be the site of Classical *Potidaion* and, earlier, of a Minoan and

Mycenaean settlement (tombs nearby). There is not much of archaeological interest to be seen but it makes a pleasant walk and there are good views of the town and beach.

The south of the island

34.5km by road; buses to all villages.

Hotels in Afiártos, Amopí and Arkássa (area code 0245)	
■ **Afiártos**	**C Poseidon** (38); 9000–11,000
C Sea View Studios (8); 10,000	drs. Tel. 22020. April–Oct.
drs. Tel. 23116; fax 23116.	
	■ **Arkássa**
■ **Amopí**	**B Dhimítrios** (33); NPA. Tel.
B Helios; NPA. Tel. 22448,	81256. May–Oct.
22877; fax 22171.	**C Heléni** (F/As); NPA. Tel. 61248;
C Amopí's Bay (65); NPA. Tel.	fax 61248.
22184. April–Oct.	

Leaving Pigádhia to the north, the road runs flat behind the beach while the mountains rise dramatically behind, white clusters of village houses clinging to the slopes. At 1.5km (right) are the remains of **Ayía Fotiní**, a 4C Early Christian **basilica**, surrounded by auxiliary buildings. The lower marble section of the iconostasis has been restored as well as several columns. The capitals are carved with floral and faunal designs typical of the period. Part of the synthronon survives. At Míli, not far away, is a large rock-cut Mycenaean tomb.

The road continues upwards through countryside laid bare by a fire in 1983. At (7km) **Apéri** (149m; pop. 407), the former capital, is divided into two by a stream. It is the seat of the Metropolitan of Kárpathos and Kásos. In the Middle Ages it was called *Corachi*, the name perpetuated in that of the suburb of Korakiá. The streets are steep and narrow, many of them stepped. The church of the Panayía (mid 19C, but on the site of an earlier building; the campanile more recent) contains a beautifully carved screen of gilded flora and fauna set against a deep red and blue background. The mid 19C paintings include the expulsion of Adam and Eve and Jacob's ladder. The frescoes in the main body of the church are more recent.

There is an interesting story about the founding of this church. A local man noticed a large piece of wood on the beach and decided to split it for the fire. With the first blow of his axe, the timber began to bleed. On turning it over he discovered it was an icon of the Virgin Mary. He took it home and set it in his house. The next day he awoke to discover it missing. After searching the village he found it in a small chapel. Again he took it home, only to find it in the chapel the following morning. The locals decided to build a large church on the site of the chapel to house the icon, now encased in silver. The split caused by the axe is still visible.

Above Apéri rises its **kastro** (more easily reached by a track from Voládha) with ancient and medieval (?14C) remains and three churches on its flanks. It has been suggested that the kastro of Apéri may have been one of the centres of the shadowy Eteokarpathian community of antiquity.

By following signs to Akháta out of (or just before) Apéri for c 1.5km, you can visit the interesting small church of **Ayios Yióryios Arápis**, the middle of three on the slope which rises beyond the football and basketball pitches. The lintel block is ancient and the double interior arch makes use of an Early Christian column and impost blocks. There are a few traces of fresco decoration. Also accessible from Apéri (signs, 3km) is the pleasantly situated inland monastery of **Ayios Yióryios Vassón**, burial place of two metropolitans of Kárpathos and Kásos. The complex (mostly modern, but with a history going back at least to the 17C), which is under the direct authority of the Ecumenical Patriarchate ('stavropegial'), is not permanently occupied.

The road up the east coast to Spóa is described below.

The main road ascends southwest to (9km) **Voládha** (450m) with a castle on a prominent hill. This small **medieval fort** was probably used by the locals as a refuge during piratical raids. There are now only scanty ruins, although on the lower slopes 5–4C graves have been discovered as well as Archaic and later pottery. As you reach the top of the village there is a football pitch—unexpected at this altitude—where ransacked Geometric tombs were discovered. From this high road there are panoramic views across the bay to Pigádhia and the south of the island.

1km northwest of Voládha lies **Píni**, where in the 1960s an inscription was recovered recording a gift of cypress wood by the people of Kárpathos for the rebuilding of the Temple of Athena in Athens. There is a turn (right) for the heights of Lástros/Kalolímni.

At 11km is the charming village of **Othos** (399m). As you enter the village, on the right of the road is a small **Folk Art Museum** (ask in taverna if closed). This two-roomed house belonged to a childless couple (photos hang in the main room). After their deaths, the family decided not to sell the house and divide the proceeds, but to preserve and restore it as a museum. The main room is dominated by a two level platform bed with storage space beneath. The central column, as tradition dictates, is used to display the finest fabrics of the household. Other items on display include ceramics and tapestries. There are also several interesting photographs including one of 117-year-old Father Sakéllis and his 60-year-old son, Father Yiórgos. The second smaller room served as both the kitchen and the grand-parents' room.

On the right of the road, towards the end of the village is the church of the Panayía. By the side steps lead down to a spring issuing from beneath the church. Thirty metres before the church is the small workshop of a local artist who paints delightful scenes of village life and Karpathian festivals on ceramic tiles. The medieval fortresses of Othos are at Kástellos and Palaiókastro. From here you can detour inland (1.5km) to the hamlet of **Stes**.

At 14km pretty **Pilés** (399m), with pleasant gardens, looks towards the west coast with splendid views out to the island of Kásos. You descend to the west coast and turn south to (19km) **Finíki**, a small fishing harbour, under development but still peaceful. On the harbour there is a monument to commemorate the seven men who sailed from here in 1944 to seek help against the occupying forces.

Close by at the south end of the same bay is (22km; pop. 394) **Arkássa**, a picturesque village, with fruit orchards.

On entering the village a road to the right leads to the **museum** (the local priest holds the key). Outside are architectural fragments and sections of mosaic floor from the nearby Byzantine chapel of Ayía Anastasía. In the first room there is a platform bed and a collection of icons. The second room is laid out like a flea market with everything from an old sewing machine to a couple of dolphin skeletons. Among this array of objects there is an interesting collection of old agricultural tools and a small model of a church, a ciborium taken by the priest to parishioners too sick to attend services. At the church of **Panayía Marmariní** (?18C) a number of ancient marbles can be seen re-used in the structure.

At the bottom of the village is a road leading to **Ayía Sofía** (0.5km). A section of the mosaic pavement of this 5C Early Christian basilica is in Rhodes Museum but there is still a lot to be seen *in situ*. The later chapel on the site houses the font from the earlier basilica. It was thrown into the sea three times by the Turks and three times it washed up on the shore. The locals took this as a good omen and still say that children baptised in this font grow up to be exceptionally strong. The road continues to the promontory, with good beaches on either side.

The spectacular acropolis with precipitous slopes, which looms towards the sea, was the site of the **ancient city** of *Arkaseia*. The presence of Mycenaean sherds and possible Cyclopean masonry suggest that the site was occupied as early as the Bronze Age. The upper 'Cyclopean' wall, about 2m thick, appears to have formed a complete circuit. It is best preserved to the southeast of the summit. Lower down to the northeast there is a section of, presumably later, polygonal masonry; but too little survives to determine whether this was part of a lower circuit wall, a building, or terracing. On the summit the remains of a small cist grave were discovered.

South of Arkássa at Voniés a Mycenaean chamber tomb was discovered in 1978 containing four burials, possible evidence of cremation and 60 Late Mycenaean vases.

The road now climbs inland. After about 6.5km (the place is called Exíles) there is a sign (left) to the tiny white church of **Ayios Mámas**, a short distance down the track. Its unusual conical superstructure has been thought to derive from Arab influence. It may even have been constructed as a shrine by raiders in the 9 or 10C and later converted to Christian use. There are interesting frescoes of the 11–14C, including an Ascension with angels in the dome; Apostles below; and the Panayía, with angels, in the conch.

At 28km is **Menetés**, a sleepy village which can be reached in 20 minutes by bus from Pigádhia. To the left of the road is a small **museum** (key held by taverna owner, ask in village) while, to the right, narrow traffic-free streets wind up the hillside. Slightly further on is the 19C **church of the Koímisis tis Theotókou** (Dormition) with a splendid screen decorated with fantastic creatures and hovering birds carrying incense burners, attached to the front of the screen by thin rods.

From Menetés you reach (30km) the east coast and can make straight for (34.5km) Pigádhia. On the outskirts of the town, about 2km beyond the petrol station and 300m up a narrow road (right; there is a sign to 'Taverna Poseidon View') immediately before a prominent round concrete water cistern, is an interesting Geometric **Sanctuary of Demeter**, with rock-cut niches for votive offerings. It is visible from the track, c 50m above to the right.

Alternatively you can turn right then left (1km) to the touristy villages of Lakkí and **Amopí** which seem to consist entirely of hotels, bars and tavernas, though it has two pleasant beaches, one pebbled, one sandy. Beyond the turn to Amopí, you can continue south into the area called Afiártos. Remains of a prehistoric settlement have been discovered near the Poseidon Hotel. There are ancient tombs (some visible) in the vicinity of the airport (10km from Pigádhia). This part of the island is flat, rather dull and relatively deserted. At the southern tip of the island, the obvious promontory of Kástellos had a medieval settlement and Second World War military installations.

The centre of the island

This area can be reached either by (**1**) a **west coast route** via Arkássa or Pilés (20km, see above) to **Mesokhóri** (39km) or (**2**) by the **east coast road** from Apéri to **Spóa** (23km). Mesokhóri and Spóa are 6km apart.

1. Northwest of Pilés the road winds high above the coast with sweeping views. 33.5km from Pigádhia via Arkássa, in the hamlet of upper **Lefkó**, is a byroad (5km) to the pleasant seaside resort of the same name (Krínos Hotel (C), tel. 0245 71222, and others). Just before the turn, 100m to the right of the road, is the architecturally interesting five-domed **church of Ayios Yióryios tou Notará** (12C), with some poorly preserved frescoes of the 12–13C. On the hillside above the church are medieval fortifications.

Opposite seaside Lefkó, the islet of **Sókastro** has a medieval **fort**: one theory ascribes the remains here to a pirate base built by raiders rather than locals. The fertile coastal plain backing the sea here is known as Yialoú Khoráfi. The church of Panayía Yialoukhorafítissa is constructed on the site of an Early Christian basilica and incorporates masonry from it. Behind the northern bay of Frangolimiónas are remains of another basilica.

In between upper and lower Lefkó (ask directions using the toponyms 'Pelekitó' and 'Riá') are ancient (including Mycenaean) tombs and buildings which have not been throughly investigated. The most interesting (at Riá) is a structure (granary?) cut into the rock with pillars to support a raised floor.

The village of **Mesokhóri** (39km; a few Rooms; tel, 0245 71341) is built on a steep slope overlooking the west coast, surrounded by rich orchards. The church of Panayía Vrisianí (originally 16C?, but much altered) is built over perpetually flowing springs which give the village its fertility. The little plateia at the seaward edge of the village was used in ancient and medieval times as a vantage point. It has three little churches, Ayía Triádha, and the twins Stavrós and Ayios Nikólaos. The churches of Mesokhóri often have attractively painted iconostases. In a bay to the north, visible in the distance, a church of Ayía Iríni (festival on the 8 May) has Byzantine frescoes.

From Mesokhóri the now uninteresting road leads across the island to (45km) Spóa.

2. Beyond Apéri is a turn (9km) for Spóa. From this road, which runs among trees high above the coast and with good views to the mountains of the north, are roads down to various beaches and coastal settlements betwen 3 and 5km below. The first is **Kirá Panayiá**. Next (17km) is **Apélla** (rough track) with a lovely beach (no facilities) and, to the left of the road just before you reach the sea (marked by a large dead branch) the intriguing tiny semi-subterranean chapel of Ayios Loukás. In spite of the dank atmosphere and mess some of the frescoes are surprisingly well preserved.

Just before (23km; 351m) Spóa is a road down (5km) to the tiny harbour of **Ayios Nikólaos** (Taverna; Rooms). On the other side of the small bay are remains of a substantial but rather overgrown Early Christian complex with a **basilica**, part of whose apse stands to 5m and which had mosaic floors, and a bath building. High above Ayios Nikólaos, a prominent hill with excellent visibility has slight remains of a medieval fort, presumably belonging to Spóa.

From Spóa, Mesokhóri is 6km to the west, Olimbos 21km north.

Olimbos and the north

Hotels in Dhiafáni and Olimbos (area code 0245)

■ **Dhiafáni**
E Khrissí Akti (11); NPA; Tel. 51215.
Níkos (16). NPA. Contact travel agent.
  Also **rooms**. Several **restaurants** on the short seafront.
  Travel agent. Orfanós, tel. 0245 51410; fax 51316.

■ **Olimbos**
Hotel Aphrodite, tel. 51307.
Hotel Poseidon, tel. 51264.
Olimbos Pension, tel. 51252.
  Restaurants at the entrance to the village; **cafés** in or near the central plateia.

Olimbos can be reached in about an hour and a quarter by car (poor road—taxi from Pigádhia 19,000 drs) from Spóa. The trip is not particularly interesting but the forbidding landscape emphasises the isolation of this part of the island which is approached more easily (in 2 hours) by boat from Pigádhia.

You land at **Dhiafáni** on the northeast coast. This isolated harbour village nestles between the hills. During the late 19C seven Mycenaean vases and a bronze sword were discovered in tombs on the slopes above Dhiafáni. Less than 1km south is Kámbi, a broad promontory with evidence of occupation dating from at least the Classical period. On the southwest flank there are the remains of a small Byzantine chapel. To the north is a beach at Vanánda.

A road ascends (9km) to Olimbos, perched on the flank of Profitis Ilías, overlooking the west coast. At 4km is a turn (right; rough track but just motorable) for the depopulated village of Avlóna (3.5km), in a broad, sloping valley, from where a path leads (left; 1 hour) to **Vourgoúnda**, a promontory on the south side of the bay of Limiónas on which is the ancient site of *Brykous*. There are extensive remains of city walls, also interesting rock cut tombs, probably dating from the late Classical/Hellenistic, and later periods—also an Early Christian basilica. An ancient rock-cut stairway leads down to the shore. Pottery sherds of possibly Mycenaean date have also been discovered on the site. A cave-chapel of **Ayios Ioánnis** becomes, on 19 August, the focal point of the festival of St John the Headless. The islanders make their way along the rough track to this remote headland. Feasting and dancing continues throughout the night and often carries on for several days.

Also accessible from Avlóna (path over the bare hillside to the right; c 3 hours) is **Trístoma**, with a landing place in a deep and relatively sheltered bay. Inscriptions found here suggest that this may be the location of a **temple of Poseidon Porthmios** ('of the strait'): the archaeologist R.M. Dawkins thought that it might lie beneath the church of Ayios Nikólaos, near the harbour entrance.

The road reaches a plateia (restaurants) at the edge of **Olimbos** (pop. 331). On the hillside immediately above is the delapidated 12C church of Ayios Onoúfrios, one of the oldest in the vicinity. On the steep slopes round the village are more than 40 windmills. Olimbos is supposed to be the oldest settlement in Kárpathos (it is first mentioned in literature in the early 15C but the churches suggest earlier occupation) and keeps alive many customs that have died out elsewhere. Most obvious is the unselfconscious wearing of traditional dress by the women, including brightly embroidered skirts, waistcoats, headscarfs and goatskin boots. The society is matrilineal, property being passed from mother to eldest daughter. The local dialect retains ancient Doric words.

The cubic houses, tumbling down the hillside, give the place its character. They are in three sections and have fine doors, with wooden locks and keys said to be of a form dating back to Homeric times. Inside many have traditional wooden furniture, notably the communal bed, and are decorated with embroideries, rugs and plates. The **church of the Panayía** in the small central plateia (cafes) has frescoes and an iconostasis of 1742.

Olimbos is no longer an undiscovered haven: in season there are daily trips from Pigádhia. Gift shops and tourist amenities have now appeared, but the village remains unique and is certainly one of the highlights of a visit to Kárpathos.

Below the village, in the bottom of the valley and best reached from the opposite side off the road to Dhiafáni beyond the turn for Spóa, are two small restored churches. Ayioi Saránda, the smaller, has a trace of 12C painting in the conch. **Ayía Anna**, the larger has very interesting decoration for its frescoes are entirely aniconic and stand in the tradition of iconoclast art, also found in some other local churches.

Islet of Sariá

Immediately north of Kárpathos and separated by a channel only 27m wide is the islet of Sariá (10.5 sq. km), inhabited in summer only by shepherds. There is a good beach and anchorage (occasional boat trips from Dhiafáni). The earliest finds date from the Bronze Age and include a dagger blade and bronze chisel.

The main site of **Palátia** is situated in the only bay on the east coast. The scanty remains include marble architectural fragments and pottery; some Classical inscriptions were found here and the site is sometimes suggested as that of the elusive ancient *Nisyros*, though there were people called *Sarioi* who seem more likely to have been the inhabitants of this site. Most of the extant remains are of medieval vaulted houses and watchtowers (on the cliffs). The style of architecture, some of which has parallels in Syria, has led to the suggestion that the settlement (like Sókastro) was built as a base by Arab raiders. Before this there was Early Christian occupation. The **chapel of Ayía Sofía** stands on the ruins of a larger, older church (5C AD) with a synthronon in the apse.

Kásos

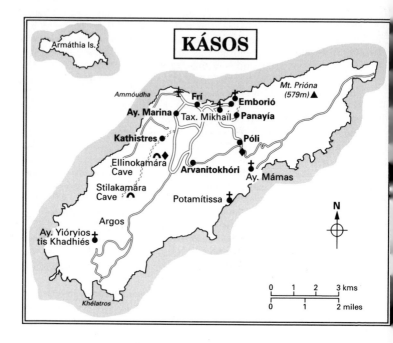

K ásos (Κάσος; anc. *Kasos* or *Casos*) captivates the visitor without apparent effort. Small, remote and not much visited, it offers the charm of rural communities not seriously touched by the depredations of tourism, and people whose welcome is both genuine and generous. The plain where the villages are concentrated is relatively fertile and attractive. Walking is pleasant and, round the villages and in the western part of the island, not too strenuous. There are some interesting caves and the scenery is spectacular. Its modest beaches are augmented by trips to neighbouring Armáthia.

Kásos is the most southerly of the Dodecanese, a fact which is emphasised by the presence of occasional palm trees. It lies 48km east of Zákro in Crete and is separated from Kárpathos by a channel of 11km. The island, elliptical in shape and 49 sq. km in area, has an overall length of 18km. The coast is precipitous and inaccessible, except on the northwest where the few villages lie. The sea is often rough. The hilly interior rises at Mt Prióna to 549m. The population (1088) has been greatly reduced by past emigration, particularly to Egypt where more than 5000 Kassiots are said to have worked on the Suez Canal. Some of the houses are quite elaborate, with fine portals and neo-classical elements. Each of the settlements has a large church. All these are relatively modern, built in the mid 19C, often of fine cut masonry. Spacious and airy, with elaborate Italianate campaniles, they usually have a separate gallery for women.

Characteristic of Kásos are 'mitáta', buildings for the production of cheese and butter, with special interior arrangement and equipment.

History

Evidence of four Minoan settlements has been discovered in the southwest of the island. During the Mycenaean period these sites seem to have been abandoned in favour of the northern area. This was probably because the north offers a naturally defensible citadel, good agricultural land and easy access to the southeastern trade routes. *Kasos* is mentioned in the Homeric catalogue of ships (*Il.* 2. 676). It appeared in the Athenian tribute lists but probably remained independent into the 2C BC when it was incorporated as a Rhodian deme.

The island was made subject to the Venetian family of Cornaro in 1306, when they acquired Kárpathos, and was lost to the Turks only in 1537. By 1820 the island had a population of approximately 11,000 and a large mercantile fleet. Its sailors were prominent in the War of Independence but it was ravaged by the Egyptians in 1824, an event remembered as 'the Holocaust' by Kasiots. It has been estimated that about 7000 islanders were killed or sold into slavery. For several years afterwards the island was deserted and, although in time people began to return, the economy never fully recovered. The Italians occupied Kásos from 1912 until the Second World War, after which it became a part of Greece. Émigré Kasiots from other parts of Greece and all over the world retain their connections with the island both by visits and substantial benefactions.

Getting to Kásos

■ **By air.** There is a small airport, 2km west of Frí, with flights to and from Athens (1 weekly, in c 2 hours), Kárpathos (3 times weekly in 15 mins), Crete (Sitía; weekly in 30 mins), and Rhodes (daily in 40–75 mins).

■ **By boat.** Twice a week a boat from Rhodes to Piraeus calls at Kásos. The route may be either through the Cyclades or the Dodecanese. There are sometimes additional services. During summer day **excursions** to Kásos are organised from Kárpathos.

Getting around Kásos

■ In summer a **bus** does a circuit around the villages. **Taxis** are available. There are a few scooters for hire in Frí. All the trips described below are within walking distance and there are routes to suit all levels of stamina and enthusiasm.

■ **Travel agent. Kásos Maritime**, in Frí; tel. 0245 41323; fax 0245 41036.

■ **Police.** Tel. 0245 41222.

■ **First aid.** Tel. 0245 41333.

Frí

Hotels and restaurants in Frí (area code 0245)

C Anayénnisis (10); 3930–8813 drs. Tel. 41323, 41495, 41305. April–Dec.
C Anesis (7); 5000–7000 drs. Tel. 41201, 41234.
   Some **rooms** are also available.

Restaurants. The range is limited and some are seasonal only. Frí has various establishments including the **Kásos** and an attractive small ouzerí, the **Meltémi**. Emborió has two or three places to eat: **Kiría Kalliópi**, at the furthest, will give you a warm welcome, some reasonably-priced fish and show you the church. On the road to Ayía Marína is the ambitiously named **Cásos Tropicána**.

Frí, an abbreviated form of Othrys, is the island's capital. Somewhat rundown but nonetheless attractive, it was built in the 1830s to house Kasiots returning after the destruction of 1824: ruined and empty houses are a poignant reminder of the large scale emigration that has taken place during the last century.

Overlooking the harbour is the prominent **church of Ay. Spiridhon**, patron of the island. There is a modest archaeological collection (no sign or regular hours; ask for custodian) with some antiquities and more modern 'folk' material. Interesting are the circular inscribed gravestones dating from 4–3C BC, discovered at Póli (see below).

On the outskirts of the village (road to Ayía Marína) the house of D.I. Antoníou, a sea-captain and poet who died in 1994, is marked by a plaque. The house is a good example of one of the finer Kasiot residences.

Frí to Emborió, Panayía, Póli and Ayios Mámas

East of the capital is the small port of Emborió (10 minutes). Between Frí and Emborió, to the right of the road, is the modern **chapel of Archangel Michael**, which stands on the remains of an Early Christian **basilica**. A patchwork of rectangular areas of mosaic, each containing a different pattern, can be seen in the courtyard to the front of the chapel. The interior is modern but contains an unusual crypt (modern) with the tomb of Nikólaos Makrís (d 1978), a Kasiot doctor who became governor of the Dodecanese.

The island's yacht and commercial harbour is situated at **Emborió** (tavernas); this was also the site of the ancient harbour. There were important shipyards here in the 19C. In a field 200m to the southwest traces of Late Roman occupation were discovered. Emborió is dominated by the church of the **Eisódhia tis Panayías** (Presentation of the Virgin Mary) behind which is a small chapel where an icon of the virgin is said to have miraculously appeared in 1843. Close to the church (southwest of the enclosure wall; access easiest via the adjacent cafeneion) are the as yet unexcavated remains of an Early Christian **basilica**: some foundations and members are visible. To the south of the basilica was a two-roomed **baptistery** (5–6C AD), probably contemporary with the church. The most important surviving element of this is the cylindrical immersion font, which formed the centre of an isosceles cross, two of whose arms had steps for access. It was treated with hydraulic plaster and partly faced in marble. Architectural fragments litter the area; others have been transferred to the island's archaeological collection.

Above Emborió is the small almost deserted hamlet of **Panayía** (1km). The large houses were built by wealthy sea captains and, although some have been restored as summer residences, Panayía has few permanent inhabitants, though the festival of the Assumption (15 August) is enthusiastically celebrated. In the courtyard of the large church at the end of the village is an ancient undecorated sarcophagus set in a niche, supposedly that of Ayios Kasianós. At the top of the village there is an unusual terrace of six small identical chapels, each surmounted by a small plaster cross—an incongruous arrangement which seems better suited to a film set than a Greek island village.

From here you can rejoin the main road to **Póli** (2km), situated on the slopes of the acropolis of the ancient capital: tombs of the 4C BC were excavated in the vicinity. In the village is the 12C Byzantine **church** of Ayios Onoúfrios which is apparently built on the site of an Early Christian basilica, reusing some its material. Rising above is the acropolis of the **ancient city** with a central ridge measuring 60 × 40m; the lower courses of a **fortification wall** of roughly squared blocks are still visible on the east side. Tombs dating from the 4–3C were discovered on the slopes along with unusual circular grave markers (in the Frí archaeological collection).

From Póli you can follow a steep road (6km) to the deserted **monastery of Ayios Mámas**, with splendid views down to the sea. 1km before the monastery turn, a road continues to the east end of the island.

Frí to Arvanitokhóri

Arvanitokhóri (Rooms, tel. 41432), reached by road, 4km southwest of Frí, is a charming village set in a green and fertile plain. The name means 'village of the Albanians' which according to the locals refers to a one-time resident sea captain who took to dressing in Albanian costume—a more likely explanation is that the village was established by Albanian settlers, who migrated south in large numbers during the 16C. The village consists of a combination of old and new architectural styles with large older houses fronted by walled gardens— reminders of former prosperity—predominant towards the top of the village. From there a broad path leads (4km) to the unusual **chapel of Potamítissa**, built into a cave to the left of the path some distance past a concrete dam. One of the houses in Arvanitokhóri, equipped and decorated in traditional style, is open to the public (the so-called 'Kasiótiko spíti' = Kasiot House).

Frí to Ayios Yióryios tis Khadhiés

A longer but rewarding **walk** takes you to the monastery of Ayios Yióryios tis Khadhiés (15 km, 4 hours from Frí). The road at the west end of the harbour leads to the junction with the road to the airport. At the corner there is a walled enclosure containing a sarcophagus on a raised platform. This tomb dating from the end of the 19C is of a sea captain's daughter; her father had it set in this prominent position so that he could see it from his ship whenever he sailed past the island.

The road continues up to the village of **Ayía Marína** (1.5km), where on 17 July the islanders celebrate the festival of their patron. This is a picturesque village with blue and white church towers set against a rich landscape of pomegranate and palm trees. At the end of the village, past two disused windmills, the road divides. The left fork runs down to Arvanitokhóri, while a rougher track continues up through the valley towards the monastery.

Through the plain of Argos, at 9km, the track divides. The left fork continues downhill to **Khélatros beach** (no amenities) a secluded sheltered harbour, backed by fertile land and streams. Four Minoan settlements were identified in this region but there are no visible remains. The beach can also be reached by a path from the monastery. The right fork continues up to the **monastery of Ayios Yióryios tis Khadhiés**. Although it is no longer in use, there is a resident caretaker who provides up to ten beds for visitors (free, but donations are appreciated). The church is quite recent but is on the site of an earlier structure. During Easter many islanders make the journey up to Ayios Yióryios where a feast is held.

The caves of Ellinokamára and Stilokamára

There are two **caves** of note: Ellinokamára (1 hour from Frí) and Stilokamára, or Sélai (2 hours from Frí). To reach these, take the road to Ayía Marína (see above). Shortly after the two disused windmills follow a road up to the right to the small village of **Kathístres**. Follow this road through the village until it veers sharply right. Here take the rough path which continues straight ahead. After c 300m, take steep path to the left—it has distinctive modern walling (unfinished) and is visible from a distance as a deep red gash in the hillside. Three quarters of the way up is a gate (right). Through this you can climb up to the **Ellinokamára cave**, close by but not immediately visible.

The cave has been in use since the Prehistoric period; Linear A and B inscriptions have been identified. The walling at the entrance probably dates from the 3–2C and consists of massively impressive isodomic blocks about 1.5m thick. Two entrances are reached by steps down, the main one leading into a walled porch. The interior is divided by a wall to the left, which is of later date. The ancient function of this cave is unclear; indeed it may not have remained constant. Possible explanations are that it was a tomb or a cult centre. During more recent times of trouble it was used as a place of refuge, as it commands spectacular views of the surrounding area but is invisible until you are almost on top of it.

Further west, across rugged landscape, high on the western slope of the gorge of Karavásaras is the **cave of Stilokamára** (or Sélai). Neither path nor cave are marked, so be prepared for a long search or take a guide. A low and narrow entrance leads to a tunnel about 15m long, towards the end of which is a stalagmite. The passage terminates in a long oval chamber with a group of six stalagmites towards the centre.

Beaches on the island

Along the northwest coast of the island, past the airport, are a series of small coves where swimming is possible; however, as this is the exposed side of the island, the winds can be quite strong and the sea rough.

More appealing beaches can be found on the nearby **islands of Armáthia** and **Makrá**, both reached by caique from Frí (during summer). They belong to a group which includes several other smaller islets to the north of Kásos.

Khálki

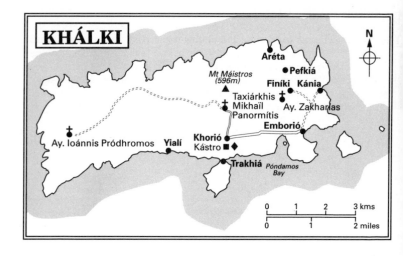

Khálki (Χάλκθ; anc. *Chalce*; the medieval name Charki is still sometimes used by sailors). For a small, rugged island, Khálki has attractive features. Fine buildings on the town's waterfront have been well restored to provide good accommodation. Tourism is important to the economy but even the new hotels have been designed to blend with the distinctive architectural style of the village. Apart from the main beach, there are other attractive places to swim, though reaching them may involve walking or a boat-trip. The interior of the island has good scenery and several churches and monasteries to aim for on foot. The island is an ideal place to relax and it is not surprising that people return year after year.

16km west of Rhodes, Khálki is roughly rectangular, c 10 km long, 3 km wide and 28 sq km in area. The bare and hilly interior peaks in Mt Máistros (596m). There are no springs and few wells. Water used to be collected and stored in cisterns but much is now brought in by sea. The land is stony and rough but there is some agriculture inland, although the quality of the land was seriously affected in 1965 when a cloud burst washed away tons of soil and destroyed terracing. Sponge fishing used to play a prominent role in the island's economy but this has now ceased and the islanders rely mainly on herding and fishing. Wax and award winning honey are also produced. The population (281) has been greatly reduced by emigration, especially to America and Australia. These emigrants have funded several large scale building projects on the island. Many Khalkians now live and work on Rhodes.

The local festival of Ay. Sotíris is held on 6 August and is celebrated in a most unusual manner. The men spend the morning ambushing each other with flour, yoghurt and eggs. This is a relic from earlier times when the community was divided into two distinct camps and fights were frequent.

History

The earliest evidence of occupation is provided by obsidian tools of the Neolithic period found at Kefáli. Nothing is known of *Chalce* before the 5C BC, when it appears in the Athenian tax records, and an inscription dating from the 4C found at Knidos describes the Chalcians as autonomous up until this time. It seems to have been incorporated in the Rhodian state quite early, as a deme of Kameiros. This state of affairs is verified by Theophrastos (372–287 BC) who describes it as a Rhodian island. Its prosperity in the 4C is demonstrated by the contents of ancient tombs. The most outstanding of these finds is a gold amphora (60 cm high) decorated with scenes of the Trojan War and now in the Louvre, Paris. A temple of Apollo is mentioned by Strabo (X. 488) and in inscriptions. Various possibilities are proposed locally but the site is unknown.

The Middle Ages saw a succession of piratical raids which led to the abandonment of many of the settlements. When the Venetians and Genoese arrived in 1204 they set about repairing the Hellenistic acropolis which was subsequently replaced by the Knights. In 1366 Khálki was granted to the Assanti family. Seized by the Turks in 1522, it was controlled by them until 1912 when the Italians took possession. Many older people still speak Italian as this was the language taught in school, a situation which resulted in the locals setting up a secret school in a cave where the children were taught Greek. In 1943 the Italians surrendered to the Germans who occupied the island for a short period. It was returned to Greece in 1947.

Recent years have seen rapid depopulation of the island. Until the Second World War the population was as high as 2000 but the decline in sponge diving and agriculture has led to a large scale exodus. A UNESCO youth scheme in the 1980s resulted in a number of new and refurbished buildings which have helped to encourage the growth of some tourism.

Getting to Khálki

■ **By boat.** A ferry from Athens to Rhodes, via Crete and/or the Cyclades, calls once a week at Khálki, and there are one or two additional services to Rhodes. There is a daily boat between Khálki and Kámiros Skála on Rhodes; and some **hydrofoils** in summer.

Getting around Khálki

■ There is no public transport. All the places described below can be reached **on foot**. In summer there are **boat trips** to beaches, and occasional excursions in season to the neighbouring islet of Alimniá.

■ **Travel agent. Zífos Travel**; tel. 0241 45241/45218 (one line can also be used for fax). A sketch map of walks is offered.

■ **Police.** Tel. 0241 45213.

■ **First aid.** Tel. 0241 45206.

Emborió

Hotels and restaurants in Emborió (area code 0241)

Accommodation is very difficult to find in season without prior booking.

B Kleánthi (7), NPA. Tel. 57334. April–Oct.
B Roúla (3), NPA.
C Chálki (25), NPA. Tel. 45208, 45390
C Márkos (F/A), NPA. Tel. 45347. May–Oct.

Recommended is the **Captain's House** (tel. 45201), a beautiful restored mansion. There are rooms at **Póndamos Beach** (tel. 57295).

Restaurants are to be found on the waterfront at Emborió and there is a taverna at Póndamos.

Huddled around its bay, the small town of Emborió (or Skála), now the capital—and also the port—of the island has a distinctly north Aegean appearance, the grand houses with orange tiled roofs, large windows and balconies, providing a reminder of days of greater prosperity. The waterfront is the centre of village life and it is here that the few tavernas and bars are situated.

Set above the harbour is the Dhimarkhíon, next to which stands a clock tower built with funds donated by emigrant Khalkians. Propped up behind the Dhimarkhíon is a triangular Hellenistic relief with a head of Medusa: its find-place is unknown.

Near the waterfront to the east of the jetty is the 16C church of **Ayios Nikólaos** with a large pebbled mosaic in the surrounding courtyard (1867) and an impressive bell-tower, said to be the tallest in the Dodecanese. Built in 1894, it is the work of the Rhodian architect, Leftéris Sellás, who incorporated marble taken from an ancient temple in the construction of the arch. The church itself contains an impressive screen set with icons.

Continuing east to the end of the harbour, take a rough path through a gate and walk up to a large enclosure set on a terrace with a shepherd's house. Here are the remains of a building, locally believed to be a church or monastery.

Emborió to Khorió

Khorió can be reached in 40 minutes from Emborió. Leave the port by the only road, leading up from the quay. The road, surprisingly called Tarpon Springs Boulevard, was built in the 1960s with money donated by the Khalkians of Tarpon Springs, Florida, who have established a prosperous community based on sponge diving. Their emigration was the result of the decline of the sponge industry on Khálki itself.

After 10 minutes you reach **Póndamos beach**, a small sandy bay, ideal for swimming and backed by a taverna. Rich tombs of the Classical period have been excavated to either side of the road at this point and, in the 1930s, Classical buildings were also investigated.

Continuing up the winding road you pass through fields scattered with derelict buildings, terracing and modern bee hives. In the cemetery, the **church of Sotíris** (or Metamórfosis) contains marble elements of a predecessor. Round the final bend **Khorió** comes into view, sprawling over the steep hillside. During the Middle Ages this was the main town of the island, built inland near the castle to protect the people from piratical raids. Most of the properties are now derelict and the remainder are occupied only seasonally. Here too was the site of the ancient town which probably extended further to the east than the present village.

You follow the steps to the prominent **church of the Panayía**, with a long history and, in post-Byzantine times, the cathedral of Khálki. This building incorporates some Hellenistic material, including part of a dentil frieze built into the wall to the left of the door, and a section of architrave in a post at the north-east corner of the courtyard. The church contains a good carved screen (1889) and mid 17C frescoes: these include Hierarchs (in the apse). Both north and south sides of the vault are divided into four horizontal bands. On the south, these contain 22 saints, scenes from the Akathist Hymn, scenes from the life of Christ, miracles. On the north are 22 saints, further scenes from the Akathist Hymn, the passion and Resurrection, miracles.

Leaving the church through the gate at the west end of the courtyard, you follow the path (marked by occasional blobs of red paint). A short distance up, just off the path to the right, is a small chapel (patron unknown) with badly damaged 15C wall paintings. On the wall to the right is a row of saints, one set in a separate arch. Above these are a series of scenes similar to those in the vault of the church of Panayía.

In the south part of Khorió the church of **Ayía Triádha** is largely constructed of blocks from the Hellenistic fortification wall and its altar consists of an ancient predecessor. Other churches in Khório incorporate Classical or Early Christian masonry.

Returning to the path—increasingly steep and rugged—you continue up the hillside, littered with blocks of ancient masonry. Prominent among these is a section of architrave to the left of the path, with an inscription. Sections of the **Hellenistic wall** of the ancient **acropolis**, several courses high, can be identified on the slopes. The entrance to the **Castle of the Knights** (at the east end) incorporates large ancient dressed stones, many more of which can be seen in the castle walls, especially in the lower courses. Above and to the right of the entrance is a coat of arms (d'Aubusson). When you enter the castle the good state of preservation of the north wall becomes immediately apparent. All along is a high rampart with parapets. Beneath this are rooms built into the wall for use by the inhabitants of the town below during periods of siege. To the south side the walls have largely fallen away although the lower courses of two towers can be seen. From here there are splendid views out towards Rhodes and down to the fine beach of **Trakhiá** below (accessible only by boat).

In the enclosed area is the Byzantine **church of Ayios Nikólaos**. You enter through the south-facing door of the vestibule into the single aisled chapel. Despite the fact that the chapel is roofless and there is no protection from the elements, several areas of Byzantine fresco (two layers, probably 15C and 17C) remain intact. Figures on the right wall include the Taxiárkhis Mikhaíl, Ay.

Nikólaos, Ay. Ioánnis Pródhromos, and Ayy. Konstandínos and Eléni. Above are smaller rectangular panels, with scenes from the life of Ayios Nikólaos.

Returning now to the bottom of **Khorió**, a rough track to the left (in front of the school) leads in 30 minutes to the secluded pebbled cove of **Yialí**.

Monasteries

Two hours' hilly walk from Emborió, through spectacular countryside (the track is steep and rough, and there is no shelter from the sun) is the **monastery of Ayios Ioánnis**. Take the route described above as far as the turning on the left for **Khorió**, continue up the concrete road (right). The next feature of interest is the chapel of Ayía Varvára, built into the rock face (right). Shortly after this a path (right) crosses to a modern chapel with, behind, a smaller disused chapel of earlier date. It has low benches on either side and fragments of frescoes. Some poorly preserved figures can be made out on the side wall.

Shortly above this you round a bend and see, to the east, the **monastery of Taxiárkhis Mikhaḯl Panormítis**, an oasis of greenery and trees against the barren slope. Shortly (20m) after the bend in the road, steps (right) descend to the path (marked with red paint; 15 minutes) which leads across the slope to the now disused monastery. The main church (locked) contains interesting icons and frescoes of the 10–12C (the earlier aniconic; the later including fragmentary scenes of the Ascension). A small disused chapel behind has fine frescoes, with some good human figures and horses. There is a badly damaged pebble mosaic and, in the centre of the apse, an ancient statue base. To the left is the inverted base of an ancient column.

Returning to the main road you continue over the central ridge of the island, with splendid **views** down to inaccessible bays. The road turns to the left and continues across the plateau—a sea of poppies during spring. In the distance is the **monastery of Ayios Ioánnis Pródhromos**, where on 29 August the islanders celebrate his feast. For most of the year it is uninhabited but, in summer, a local shepherd and his wife are in residence (beds available for visitors). The courtyard is surrounded by cells. In the centre of this is the chapel, and a large pine tree said to be 350 years old. About 150m to the northwest is the **church of the Panayía Enniamerítissa** which incorporates material probably from an Early Christian basilica and has extensive frescoes and a founder's inscription dated 6875 (= 1367). In the area of the monastery is a deserted **medieval settlement** with several **churches**, including one of Ayios Nikítas with frescoes of the 10–15C.

Emborió to the north coast

A 40 minute walk to the northeast of Emborió will take you to the sea at Kánia, and allow a detour to Finíki. Just as you leave Emborió via Tarpon Springs Boulevard, a concrete road off to the right winds upwards, soon becoming a dirt track. A branch to the left leads to **Finíki** and the (ruined) **church of Ay. Zakharías**, whose frescoes were removed for conservation in 1984: they are now part of the Byzantine display in the church of the Panayía tou Kástrou, in

Rhodes. The church itself had a predecessor, some of whose architectural members are reused.

The main road continues down to the tiny pebbled cove of **Kánia**, backed by olive trees. Also from this cross-roads you can reach **Pefkiá**, supposed site of the Temple of Apollo.

Another attractive cove is that of **Aréta** which, with others on the north coast, can only be reached by boat.

Island of Alimniá

The small island of Alimniá lies about half way between Khálki and Rhodes, a little to the north of the direct line. It was inhabited until the 1960s, since when it has been used only for summer grazing by the people from Khálki. There are some excursions for swimming, from Khálki. The large deep bay was used as a submarine base during the Second World War, first by the Italians, then by the Germans: the Italian barracks are still visible. Part of a Final Neolithic settlement has been excavated on a hill in the middle, and there is a ruined medieval castle on the east side of the central Mt Voúni. The castle is said to have a Classical predecessor. Between Alimniá and Rhodes are other islets, including Makrí and Strongilí.

Kastellórizo

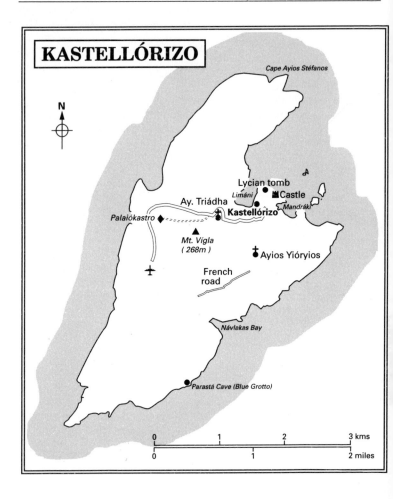

KASTELLÓRIZO

Cape Ayios Stéfanos

N

Lycian tomb

Limáni ● Castle

Ay. Triádha ● ■Castle

Palaiókastro ◆ **Kastellórizo** Mandráki

▲

Mt. Vígla
(268m)

✝ Ayios Yióryios

French
road

Návlakas Bay

● *Parastá Cave (Blue Grotto)*

0		1		2		3 kms

0			1			2 miles

Kastellórizo (officially Megísti) (Καστελλόριζο/Μεγίστη; anc. *Megiste*) is unique. At the extreme edge of Aegean Greece, rocky and nowadays unfertile, the island makes up for its lack of obvious tourist appeal with the warmth and directness of the welcome given to visitors, and a highly distinctive character. The architecture of the town is striking with grand sea-captains' houses, well maintained, on the waterfront, even if some of those further inland are now deserted and photographs of its former prosperity make for nostalgia. Interesting excursions include the Blue Grotto and neighbouring islets by sea, a

Lycian tomb near the harbour, and the ancient acropolis and various churches a steep climb inland.

The name is derived from the Italian Castelrosso, after its medieval castle. 133km east of Rhodes, Kastellórizo is really in the East Mediterranean rather than the Aegean, but is linked to the Dodecanese by its Greek culture and tradition. Largest of a miniature archipelago lying close to the coast of Lycia, Asia Minor, it is a small triangular island 6km long by 3km wide, with an area of 9 sq. km and thus the smallest of the 14 major islands of the Dodecanese. Of its 11 dependent islets none is now inhabited.

The coastline is precipitous and mostly inaccessible except on the northeast, where two bays are the only focus of population. The interior is hilly. Cape Ayios Stéfanos, at the north end of the island, is only 2.5km from the Anatolian coast. A desalination plant augments tanks of rainwater collected during the winter rains. The chalky soil yields only olives, grapes, and vegetables in insignificant quantities.

The 275 inhabitants are now entirely concentrated in the little port and village of Kastellórizo, or Megísti, on the northeast coast. Many thousands of Kastellorizians, however, live abroad, and the island is largely supported by summer tourism and the remittances of its emigrants who may retire here when their fortunes have been made, or pay visits. The port of Kastellórizo provides the only safe shelter on or near the Asiatic coast between Mákri (opposite Rhodes) and Beirut, and the island is well placed for transit trade, though both this and the formerly close relationships with the Anatolian mainland are now non-existent. The island was the setting for the Oscar-winning film *Mediterraneo*.

History

In antiquity the island was called *Megiste*, the largest, that is, of the small archipelago; the Turks called it *Meis*. Although lacking natural resources its strategically valuable location and natural harbour have resulted in a turbulent history. Stone tools discovered round the island indicate Neolithic occupation and Mycenaean material suggests that this may have been continuous throughout the Bronze Age. Dorian settlers built a fortified acropolis at Palaiókastro. Apart from a short period of autonomy, abolished by the tyrant of Halikarnassos, the island was under the administration of Rhodes from the early 4C BC until the Roman period. Some 4C tombs were found early this century, one containing a gold diadem. A recent archaeological survey (N.G. Ashton, University of Western Australia) has shown, amongst other things, that the island produced and traded widely in wine in antiquity. Numerous grape-treading establishments and fragments of transport amphorae bear witness to this.

Occupied by Cilician and Carian pirates, it was subjected to frequent raids during the Byzantine period. In 1306 it was occupied by the Knights of St John, who strengthened the existing castle and used it as a place of detention for recalcitrant knights. The island was captured from the Knights in 1440 by Djemal ed Din, Sultan of Egypt, who destroyed the castle. In 1450 Alfonso I of Aragon, king of Naples, reconquered the island and rebuilt the castle. Kastellórizo remained in possession of Naples, except for short intervals, until it was captured in 1522 by the Turks. It was temporarily occupied by the Venetians in 1570 and again in 1659, when the castle was again destroyed.

From 1828 to 1832 it was held by the Greeks. In 1913 the islanders, inspired by the Italian occupation of the other islands of the Dodecanese, overthrew the Turkish authorities but failed to win the support of the Greek government and remained almost autonomous under a Greek governor from Samos until late 1915. From December 1915 to March 1921 it was occupied by the French, after which, ceded to Italy, it shared the fortunes of the other islands of the Dodecanese. The main reminder of the French occupation is a series of substantial roads.

Up until the early 20C Kastellórizo had a prosperous merchant fleet, with a population as high as 9000 in 1910. As late as 1939 up to eight seaplanes a day called at the island. It suffered rapid depopulation as a result of the severing of its Anatolian connections after 1913 and because of a series of natural and manmade disasters. During the First World War it was bombarded from the Anatolian coast and in 1926 there was a severe earthquake. A British commando raid in February 1941 failed to wrest the island from Italian control and it was not until September 1943 that it was liberated with the Italian surrender. The island then suffered from heavy German bombing and in July 1944 fire destroyed a large part of the capital. The inhabitants were evacuated and returned in 1945 to find houses that had not been destroyed by bombs and fire ransacked by the occupying British troops. Most of the remaining Kastellorizians emigrated, particularly to Australia, leaving only the present population of under 300. The island's isolation was lessened by the opening of the airport in 1986, and its adoption as an official port of transit between Greece and Turkey (Kas).

Further information can be found in two recent monographs, both published in Australia: N.G. Ashton, *Ancient Megiste: The Forgotten Kastellórizo*, Perth, 1995; N.G. Pappas, *Castellorizo: An Illustrated History of the Island and its Conquerors*, Sydney, 1994.

Getting to Kastellórizo

■ **By air**. Three or four times a week, in 45 mins, from Rhodes (and Crete); minibus to/from the airport.

■ **By sea**. Twice weekly to and from Rhodes in 6–8 hours.

Getting around Kastellórizo

■ **Walking** is the way to get around, as there is no public transport. For **excursions by boat**, see below.

■ **Travel agent. Dízi Tours**; tel. 0241 29239; fax 37153

■ **Police**. Tel. 0241 49330, 49333.

■ **First aid**. Tel. 0241 49267.

Kastellórizo town

Hotels and restaurants in Kastellórizo town (area code 0241)

C Megísti (17). 6000–9500 drs.   **Restaurants** are around the
Tel. 49272, 49219/20; fax 49221.   harbour.
Also **rooms** (owners meet boats),
or ask at the travel agent.

Boats dock at the capital Kastellórizo, in the larger of the two bays (Limáni). From the sea the village is exceptionally picturesque, against a spectacular mountain backdrop. Off the long curved waterfront—the focus of the island's life, with all the shops, tavernas and bars—open several squares including the central Plateía Ethelónton Kastellorizíon, and Australia Square, one of the many indications of close ties maintained between emigrants and their homeland. The squares are connected by narrow streets, winding between two and three-storeyed houses with wooden balconies, Anatolian-style windows and walled gardens. Although some, especially on the waterfront, have been restored, the majority are uninhabited and have fallen into disrepair.

The Italian-built seafront agora (1934) is a poignant reminder of how times have changed on Kastellórizo. This once-busy fish and meat **market**, complete with a large marble-topped fish stall, and meat hooks set in the walls, is no longer used. Fishermen now sell their catches direct from the boat as there are insufficient customers to warrant a market.

From the far (west) side of the bay a well-defined path leads along the promontory of Ayios Stéfanos, with good swimming at the tip (1 hour).

A path climbs up from the waterfront on the south, across the promontory which divides the two bays, to Plateía Louká Santrapé in the area known as Khoráfia. Santrapé was a local benefactor. Here is situated the **cathedral of Ayy. Konstandínos and Eléni**. Built in 1835, the interior is divided into nave and aisles by monolithic granite columns from the Temple of Apollo at Patara in Lycia; the columns support ogival arches. The groin vaults are characteristic of later Dodecanesian church architecture. The apse contains a stepped synthronon and the bishop's throne.

In a square to the southwest is the more modern **church of Ayios Yióryios** (1903), built over 17C and Early Christian predecessors, with mosaics. Some of the architectural members of the basilica are in the island's archaeological collection.

Returning to Plateía Santrapé, take Od. Ayíou Nikoláou up to the **Castle of the Knights**. To the sides of this street are the remains of houses: until the Second World War the capital reached up to the ridge where the castle now stands in isolation. It was built between 1379 and 1383 by Juan Fernando Heredia, 8th Grand Master of the Knights of St John. The Knights renamed the island Kastellórizo because of the deep red colour of the earth and rocks that formed the foundations of the castle. Its vicissitudes up to the time of its second destruction have been noted above. Parts of the curtain wall, and of three partially restored towers survive. These imposing remains were used as part of a backdrop in the film *The Guns of Navarone*. A Doric inscription found on the site suggests that a fort existed here in Classical times.

The castle has splendid views of Kastellórizo's major harbour, the Limáni, to the west, and the smaller Mandráki, to the east. The latter is a quiet pebbled bay used only by a few fishing boats. In recent years a government-backed building project has been launched in this area in the hope that, if modern housing is provided, young people will be persuaded to stay. The east arm of Mandráki bay is now the site of the modern cemetery. A few prehistoric potsherds have been found in this area but their significance is uncertain.

Towards the Anatolian coast a small group of 'stepping-stone' islands can be seen. At the eastern edge of this group is the island of **Ayios Yióryios**, with a chapel of the saint. On the mainland opposite is the town of Kas (anc. *Antiphellos*), with a Hellenistic theatre, numerous Lycian tombs, and other ancient remains. An ancient shipwreck has been excavated here by Professor G. Bass and colleagues.

On the east side of the main harbour, in the square known as Kávos, which also contains the mayor's office and the Limenarkhíon, is a memorial to a local hero of the Second World War, dedicated and erected by the Kastellorizians of Sydney, Australia, in 1983. From here both the museum and the Lycian tomb can be visited. A delightfully restored 17C building houses the **museum** (sign; 08.00–14.00, closed Mon) with Hellenistic and Roman inscriptions, a Lycian relief from Antiphellos, and pottery from wrecks of the 9–13C. There are also fine examples of more recent folk art, including a range of fabrics and costumes.

A good path leads round the end of the harbour to rough stone steps which ascend to the **Lycian tomb**. Such tombs consist of rockcut chambers with the façade sculpted in relief, often in the style of a Greek temple (Doric or Ionic columns with a gabled pediment). Here there is an Ionic façade (stepped architrave topped by a frieze of dentils, below the pediment; pilasters flank the doorway). A 5–4C BC date is suggested for the tomb. There is a groove for the door and a shallow recess on the inside to the left which tapers towards the bottom. This would have provided support for a heavy door, when pulled back. To either side of the entrance are niches for a door bar. There are no ancient parallels for these from similar tombs, which suggests that they might have been added here at a later date. The rectangular interior, c 2.5 x 3m, has lower and upper shelves on the back and side walls, with a pillar of rock in the right corner rising between the two levels. Many similar but less elaborate tombs are to be found on the Anatolian coast opposite.

A concrete road to the west of the harbour takes you to a paved path (left), which passes the monasteries of Profítis Ilías and Ayía Triádha to join an asphalt road (turn left). After 150m steps (left) ascend via a steep path (1 hour) to the Palaiókastro (270m). The path meanders through dense scrub inhabited by small orange geckos, camouflaged to blend in with the deep reds and oranges of the surrounding rocks and soil.

Palaiókastro was an ancient Greek stronghold, fortified in the 9C and strengthened in the 5–4C. It was built on a rectangular plan (81 × 61m). The partially restored walls are well preserved at several points and there was clearly an inner and outer enceinte with evidence of at least three towers. The massive tower of the inner wall has drafted corners and uses headers and stretchers. This is the best preserved example as only a few courses of the other towers remain. The style of construction of the two walls is different, the outer being earlier in date. The inner fortifications probably belong to the Late Classical period. Most of the earlier remains were covered by medieval and later structures. A wall of one of these is complete with its fireplace. This structure was probably the upper storey of the medieval Monastery of the Panayía.

Between the Panayía and Ayios Stéfanos (to the north) is a pebble mosaic. The churches are in a poor state. There are numerous cisterns and, in the southeast, the remains of propylaea, with a Doric inscription of the 3C or 2C BC on which is recorded the name *Megiste* and its dependence on Rhodes. Of the **churches** outside the circuit, that of Ayios Yióryios to Ftokhouláki has some interesting work, including paintings of the apostles Peter and Paul on the bema door (inscriptions).

The interior of Kastellórizo is not much visited. To the east of the Palaiókastro is **Mt Vígla** where 'Cyclopean' **walls**, visible for c 50m, were located in 1910 and thought to date from the Mycenaean period: more likely they belong to the 9C. About 1.2km southeast of Ay. Yióryios to Ftokhouláki, the church of Ay. Ioánnis Pródhromos incorporates ancient blocks. Close to the church are two ancient **grape-treading areas**, with channels cut into the rock. Further east is the fortified monstery (abandoned) of **Ay. Yióryios tou Vounioú**. Its courtyard is surrounded by cells. An inscription shows that it was refurbished in 1759. There are slight remains of late 18C frescoes. 30m to the south is another grape-treading installation. The latter church (Ay. Yióryios) may also be reached (in 1 hour) by a stepped pathway up the cliff from south of Plateía Santrapé in the Khoráfia. The view from the top of this pathway of the town, the Limáni and Mandráki, the numerous islets and the Turkish coastline, is well worth the climb. Beyond Ayios Yióryios, about half an hour southwest along one of the French roads, is the picturesque bay of **Návlaka** (swimming).

Excursions by boat

Although lacking in sandy beaches, Kastellórizo has inlets ideal for swimming and, in summer, boats offer excursions to these as well as some of the small islets including **Rho**, to the west. This was the home of Kiría Dhéspina, locally known as the 'Lady of Rho', who died in 1982. She was the last inhabitant of the island, remaining after her husband's death, defiantly hoisting the Greek flag every morning within view of the Turkish coast. She is commemorated by a bust in the Khoráfia.

There are occasional day trips to Kas in Turkey.

The visit to the **Blue Grotto** (an hour and a half by boat) is probably the most attractive excursion on the island. Leaving the harbour and heading southeast, you follow the inaccessible east coast to a slight curve of the coastline in which is the narrow mouth of the Grotto, at the Cave of Parastá. The Blue Grotto, also known locally as Fokiáli (Refuge of Seals), recalls the Blue Grotto of Capri, but is larger. It is 40–46m long, 24–30m wide, and 20–24m high. As at Capri, the gorgeous colouring is said to be caused by the reflection and refraction of the sun's rays through the water. The roof on the left side has collapsed, the debris forming a little island. At the end of the cave, on the right, is another grotto.

Sími

Sími (Σύμη; anc. *Syme*) is a revelation. Sailing into the harbour, you get a sudden view of the houses of the port and village, with its castle high above, crowding steeply down the slopes, unexpectedly grand and numerous, their lines picked out in light as sharp and clear as that of Attica. The neo-classical mansions seem quite out of character with the island's size and rugged topography, and contrast strikingly with other neighbouring islands of similar size. They recall rather the architecture of Ithaka or Síros and testify to a past prosperity, now to some extent returning through the island's popularity as a holiday centre, and bolstered by fast and easy connections with Rhodes.

Sími has managed to absorb the tourist influx (a good deal of it transitory, on day trips from Rhodes and elsewhere) without losing its charm and friendliness. Nearly all the accommodation is in the port or the upper village, some in renovated traditional houses, and there is a good variety of restaurants. Several beaches are easily accessible but others, more remote, are better and can be reached on foot or by boat. Walking (there are organised rambles) is good but, unless you stick to the high central plateau, involves a good deal of climbing. There are plenty of churches and monasteries to search for (map available), indeed the number of frescoed churches is unusually large for such a small island and its important early 18C school of painting is strongly represented, as well as earlier work (a visit to the Museum will give a guide as to what is to be seen). There is rural scenery to enjoy and the interior still has some woods.

With a population of 2332, Sími lies c 60km east of Nísiros in a gulf of the Anatolian mainland, which is about 7km away to the north (Cape Krio) and 6.5km to the east. Rhodes town is 35km southeast. The island is a mass of hard limestone, with an irregular coastline and relatively little flat land. There are several small islets off its shores: the larger of these are Nímos to the north and Sésklia to the south. The Dhiavátes islets are off the west coast. The highest point, Mt Vígla, is in the centre. Until relatively recent times Sími was richly forested, but the tree cover was largely exhausted in building ships during the Wars of Independence. This put an end to one of the main sources of the island's prosperity, the other being sponge-fishing, now also virtually defunct, but which used to occupy most of the island's population. Agricultural production is limited. The population are almost all in the linked villages (collectively known as Sími) of Yialós, the port, and Khorió, on the hillside above.

History

In mythology *Syme* was the daughter of Ialysos of Rhodes and mother of the first inhabitants of the island to which she gave her name. Her husband Glaukos sailed with the Argonauts. In the Trojan War the island sent three ships, a large contingent for such a small community, under Nereus. He died at Troy and, according to one tradition, was buried on *Syme*. Later colonists are said to have been Lakonians, Argives, Rhodians and Knidians.

For much of the island's history it was under the influence of Rhodes. Independent for at least part of the 5C BC, it featured in the Athenian tribute lists of 434/3 but was probably incorporated in the Rhodian state

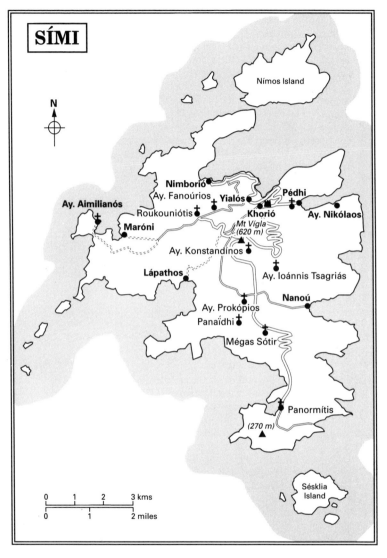

SÍMI

Nímos Island

N

Nimborió
Ay. Fanoúrios   Yialós
Ay. Aimilianós   Pédhi
Roukouniótis   Khorió
Maróni   Ay. Nikólaos
Mt Vígla
(620 m)
Ay. Konstandínos
Lápathos   Ay. Ioánnis Tsagriás
Nanoú
Ay. Prokópios
Panaïdhi
Mégas Sótir
Panormítis
(270 m)

0   1   2   3 kms
0   1   2 miles

Sésklia
Island

about 400 BC. In 411 BC the Lakedaimonians defeated the Athenians in a naval engagement off Knidos and subsequently set up a trophy on Syme. This event led to the revolt of Rhodes from the Athenian confederacy. Syme was often closely associated with the settlements on the mainland opposite, for instance in the assessment of tax.

From 1309 it was held by the Knights of St John who built the castle. The islanders provided ships for the Knights. The garrison repelled an Ottoman attack in 1456 before succumbing, with Rhodes, in 1522. The island was important in the Ottoman period, in commerce, shipbuilding and sponge-fishing: at this time islanders also cultivated land on the mainland. This prosperity is reflected in the fine neoclassical mansions of the late 18 and early 19C which provide the island with its unique character. In the later 18C an important school of fresco painters seems to have been established on Sími, presumably at the Panormítis Monastery. Its main exponent was Gregory of Sími, who decorated churches here, on Tílos and on Rhodes.

Sími was taken by the Italians in 1912, at which point it had a population of over 22,000. In the Second World War it changed hands several times. The German surrender of the Dodecanese was signed here in 1945.

A useful guidebook in English by K. Farmakídhis and A. Karakatsáni can be got from the museum. Another, by Ewen Clarke, is more difficult to find.

Getting to Sími

■ **By boat.** Although there are one or two **ferries** calling weekly at Sími en route between Piraeus and Rhodes, via other islands in the Cyclades and Dodecanese, the most frequent and reliable connection (twice daily in summer) is with Rhodes. The *Nísos Kálimnos* also links the island (twice a week in either direction) with Tílos, Nísiros, Kos and Kálimnos to the north; and Rhodes and Kastellórizo to the south.

There are also **excursion boats**, from Rhodes and other neighbouring islands, some of which call first at the monastery of Ay. Mikhaíl Panormítis.

Getting around Sími

■ **By bus.** There is a limited bus service between Yialós, Khorió and Pédhi; and **excursions** (summer only, most days) to the Panormítis Monastery. **Taxis** are available and **scooters** can be hired through travel agents.

■ **By boat.** Boats operate a taxi-service and run excursions to beaches, including the islet of Sésklia.

■ **On foot.** There are guided **walks** in season (ask at travel agents), and a **map** of the island is widely available on which are marked some of the footpaths and many of the island's churches. A map is essential to give you some idea of the relationship of the road system to the footpaths, though it is a mistake to expect absolute clarity when mapping of the latter is so difficult.

■ **Travel agent. Sími Tours,** tel. 0241 71689, 71307; fax 0241 72292.

■ **Police.** Tel. 0241 7111.

■ **First aid.** Tel. 0241 71290.

Yialós

Hotels and restaurants in Yialós (area code 0241)

A **Alki** (15); 10,500–16,500 drs. Tel. 71665; fax 71665. April–Oct.

A **Dorian** (9); 12,000–14,000 drs. Tel. 71181/2; fax 72292. April–Oct.

A **Opera's House** (F/A) (29); NPA. Tel. 71856; fax 72034.

B **Khorió** (17); 7000–13,000 drs. Tel. 71800. April–Oct.

B **Metapóntis** (11); NPA. Tel. 71491, 71077. April–Oct.

B **Nirūdhes** (8); 9700–17,300 drs. Tel. 71784. April–Oct.

C **Albatross** (5); 7500–10,000 drs. Tel. 71707, 71829. April–Oct.

C **Fiona** (11); 7800–9500. Tel. 72088.

C **Nírefs** (40); 11,000–16,000 drs. Tel. 72400.

C **Taxiárkhis** (F/A) (20); 6300–13,650 drs. Tel. 72012, 72013. April–Oct.

Others include the cheap and quaintly antiquated **Hotel Gláfkos** and the clean **Heléni**, usefully close to the departure quay. Also **rooms** (from travel agents).

Restaurants. The places lining the waterfront are best avoided. There is much better food at **O Meraklís**, in the port a little inland, and **Yiórgos**, in the upper village; with alternatives **Neraídha**, and **Dalláras** (nice terrace, below Yiórgos). The new **Kalí Stráta** café, near the top of the climb to Khorió, has friendly service and a lovely view.

The harbour village, Yialós encloses a narrow oblong inlet off the much larger Bay of Sími. The water is deep and boats dock at the quay on the north.

The village is well supplied with accommodation and restaurants, but advance booking is essential in season. Shops, hotels and restaurants line the waterfront. Sponges are sold, now imported, in homage to the island's former speciality. At the head of the inlet is a 'square' with imposing **Dhimarkhíon** in an area previously occupied by ship building and the sponge industry. Here (boat in concrete and stone, with quotation from Palamás) and at the other end of the quay (bronze, boy fishing) are sculptures by C. Valsámis who comes from Sími. Near the Dhimarkhíon is a small **Nautical Museum** (open 10.30–15.00 daily). The **church of Ay. Ioánnis** incorporates some ancient material and may be on the site of an earlier building.

At the foot of the stairway which ascends to Khorió, is a sign for the **Archaeological Museum** (10.00–14.00, closed Mon) but do not be misled— the museum is up the hill. From the port you can either take the bus or (more interesting) climb, with stops to admire the views and architecture, up the 500 steps beyond the museum to **Khorió**, the upper town.

Its focus, for the visitor at least, is the **castle**, at the west edge, clearly visible from below. Substantial sections of the fortifications can be seen on all sides of the castle, some within the village. Originally an ancient acropolis, it was converted into a medieval castle by the Knights after 1407. Both ancient and medieval construction can be seen well, in sequence, in the tower and walls by the gate on the south side, just beyond steps leading up to the church. The lowest courses are of polygonal masonry; above these are coursed ashlar, then the construction of the Knights. Over the gate, the arms of d'Aubusson are quartered with those of the Order. The present church, originally Ay. Yióryios, was renamed Megáli Panayía after a building to the west which, together with much of the surrounding structures and munitions, was blown up by the Germans in their retreat from the island in 1944. The earlier church (now being reconstructed) seems to have stood on the site of a Temple of Athena.

Looking east from the kástro, on the other side of a saddle, you see a line of windmills rising beyond the end of the houses: the area is called Pondikókastro. If you walk over in this direction and ascend the path beyond the windmills, you find two courses of a large circular structure in good ashlar masonry, probably the *tropaion* (victory monument with spoils of battle) erected by the Spartans and their allies after the victory over the Athenians in 411 BC.

The area round the castle is particularly attractive. Near the centre of the village is a 19C **pharmacy**, still used for consulting by local doctors. The well laid-out and labelled **museum** (signs) is in an old house with an attractively pebbled courtyard, shaded by a vine. It contains, apart from very useful background information, some pieces of Classical sculpture and pottery; Early Christian architectural sculpture; Byzantine pottery; photographs of Byzantine and post-Byzantine frescoes in the island's churches; some good icons, a carved and painted *epitafios*, copies of early maps of the island, carved furniture, costumes, paintings and ship models. Close by, the **Khatziagapitós house**, an impressive early 19C fortified mansion of a prominent local, is being restored as a monument to that period of the island's history.

Yialós to Nimborió and the west of the island

At the seaward end of the quay, a road passes hotels, shipyards and a beach backed by a large building, formerly a private nautical club (NOS) but now open to the public.

You can continue round the coast to the larger bay of **Nimborió** (beach, taverna). Here the church of Ay. Iríni is built on the site of an Early Christian **basilica** and incorporates some decorated blocks from it. A section of mosaic is also visible.

If you leave Yialós from near the Dhimarkhíon, you can take an alternative route to Nimborió, which cuts across the promontory rather than following the coast. This also gives access to a track up into the hills, leading first (in 45 minutes) to the pleasant **church of Ay. Fanoúrios**, built on the remains of an earlier predecessor, visible high on the hillside to the west of the harbour.

Beyond the church you join a road which comes from the centre of the island and Khorió and continue west for another 10 minutes to one of the most attractive places on Sími, the **monastery of Taxiárkhis Mikhaïl Roukouniótis**, no longer functioning, but beautifully cared for by a local shepherd (resident) and his wife. The church is in the centre of a walled complex with a pebble-paved interior; outside there are seats under a big oak tree. The church itself, originally an Early Christian foundation, is double, on two storeys. The lower has some traces of 15C paintings; the upper, built in the 14C following destruction of the monastery by fire, has a full cycle of interesting frescoes, the work (1738) of

Gregory of Sími; a carved and painted wooden ambo with a rampant lion as its base and a fine carved templon. The silver icon of the patron is set in a carved porch. Originally the monastery had a library and special privileges; later it was under Russian protection. A 12C gospel which was saved from the fire is now in Rhodes.

A short distance further on is another church, of Ay. Anáryiroi; below is an army camp. West of the church you can continue on paths, right for the bay of Maróni, left for Skoúmisa where the attractive **monastery of Ay. Emilianós** (about an hour and a quarter on from Roukouniótis) occupies a little islet off a pretty beach: you can swim at either. These excursions can equally well be started from Khorió via the road to the monastery of Panormítis (see below).

Yiálos to Pédhi

On the other side of Yiálos, the **bay of Pédhi (B Hotel Akti Pédhi** (54). 6000–10,400 drs. Tel. 71981; beach, tavernas) has a bus service. Near the sea are remains of Early Christian buildings (mosaic in Archaeological Museum), including a **basilica**, over the north aisle of which is the later church of Ayía Marína Avlakiótis. If you choose to walk, it is better to climb up to Khorió and continue from there, rather than following the long detour taken by the road.

Off the south side of the bay of Pédhi is the good small beach of Ayíos Nikólaos (taverna), also with some ancient remains near the church.

The centre and south of the island

On foot from Khorió it is best *not* to make for the motor road at the east side of the village which ascends in endless steep zigzags (also branch for Pédhi) but to leave from the edge of the settlement at the southwest (upper right as you look inland from the kastro) by an older track, which soon joins the main road. Here there are three possibilities. (**1**) Going right along the road takes you to **Roukouniótis** (see above). (**2**) If you cross the road and follow paths on the far side you can get down to the sea in about an hour at **Lápathos** on the bay of Ay. Vasilíou. (**3**) Turning left along the road you soon come to a junction. Here you can bear left to head back to Khorió or turn right for the interior and the Panormítis monastery at the south end of the island. After a couple of sweeping zigzags, which can be avoided by taking older tracks to the right, you pass the **monastery of Ay. Konstandínos** up on the left. A little further is an army camp.

Beyond the camp a rough track (left) takes you in 20 minutes to the early chapel (?12C) of **Ayíos Ioánnis Sangriá**. Just past this, to the right, ancient masonry in walls on a hillock to the right mark the site of a Classical ?**fort**. There are other churches in the Kokkinídhis area further east.

Off the main road to the right (no. 35 on the local map), the **church of Ayios Prokópios** has 14–15C frescoes and, beyond it (no. 34), that of **Panaïdhi** (or Koímisis tis Theotókou; 1728) a carved templon and 18C frescoes.

Further on, a path (left; by the church of Panayía Stratéri) descends eventually to **Nanoú Bay** (an hour and a half; swimming; taverna). Right of the main road, in a wooded setting, is the **church of Ayía Marína** with paintings of the 15–16C. Further on, also on the right, is the attractive early 18C **church of Mégas Sótir** (or Metamórfosis tou Khristoú) with a pebbled court, a carved templon and good early 18C frescoes.

Just after Mégas Sótir you come to the edge of the central plateau with a panoramic view of the south of the island, and the 18C monastery of **Taxiárkhis Mikhaïl Panormítis** on its bay far below. The descent, at first in zigzags, takes about 50 minutes. The monastic complex is large (restaurant; shop; beach) and busy in summer (the festival is on 7–9 November). There are hostels for pilgrims with plenty of rooms. In 1945 it was used as a staging camp for refugees returning from Turkey. The centre is supposed to have an ancient and Early Christian history.

The church (1783) has **frescoes** by the Karakostides brothers, artists of the Simian school, and a massively intricate carved wooden iconostasis by Maestro Diaco Tagliaduro of Kos, whose two other known works are in Russia and Jerusalem. The enormous 18C icon is sheathed in silver, set in a complex carved and gilded frame, and swathed in ex-votos. There is a carved and painted ambo. The state of the frescoes is variable. Best preserved are saints on the north wall, near the iconostasis. By the ambo, St Catherine is graphically portrayed, tied to the wheel. Over the west door is the weighing of souls. The church contains a rich profusion of offerings (especially lamps) from Simians all over the world. Many of these are associated with St Michael in his role as protector of seamen.

The grand **campanile**, with elaborate terracotta antefixes, is relatively modern (1905) and copies that of Ay. Fotiní in Smyrna. There are two **museums** (one ticket admits). The first is a folk collection with a wide variety of domestic and agricultural items. A room of *pithoi* (storage jars), in their original settings, is particularly interesting. Some have their capacities marked (up to 300kg). There is also a room dedicated to the memory of Abbot Khrísanthos, executed by the Italians. The Ecclesiastical Museum has a collection of icons, vestments and church plate. There are also books, furniture (including an *epitafios*), elaborately carved ivories offered by Simians from Africa, and furniture. Striking are votive ship models and plaques.

Tílos

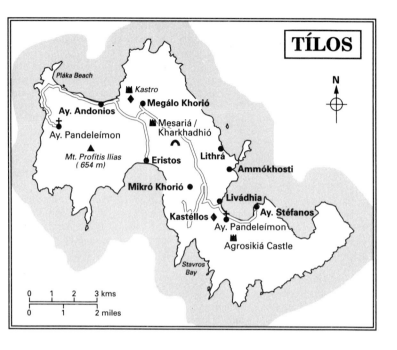

Tílos (Τήλος; anc. *Telos*) is a pleasant and friendly island, off the beaten track and not yet disfigured by mass tourism, though it is on the books of one British travel operator and has a devoted band of regular visitors. Too quiet for some; for others it represents a haven of relatively undisturbed tranquillity, even if quite small numbers of people can fill up the port in summer. The countryside is attractive and there are some good beaches. The tiny monastery of Ayios Pandeleímon is a gem. The castle above Megálo Khorió incorporates a spectacular Classical gateway, while the lovely traditional village on its slopes occupies part of the site of the ancient settlement. Medieval forts and forgotten chapels wait to be discovered by walkers.

Tílos lies 15km southeast of Nísiros, and to the west of Sími, about half way between Kos and Rhodes. Shaped like an inverted 'S', it is some 14.5km long from northeast to southwest, has a maximum width of 8km and an area of about 63 sq.km. In antiquity an alternative name was *Agathousa* (beneficent), perhaps from its agricultural produce, and Pliny mentions it as a source of perfume. But, in the Middle Ages, it was known as *Episkopí* ('lookout') from its high mountains, often crowned with castles, which give good views of the surrounding seas. *Telos* was the name of an early colonist. The highest point is Mt Profítis Ilías in the northwest at 654m.

Although the island is hilly, there is a narrow coastal plain behind the port, Livádhia, and another larger and more fertile below the main village of Megálo Khorió, stretching from the sea at Ayios Andónios to Eristos beach. The elevated plateau along which the road runs from above Livádhia to Megálo Khorió also has agricultural potential. Although the population (172) has declined, the people are proud of their ability to supply neighbouring Sími with tomatoes, oranges and olives, and there is some fishing.

There are beaches on the broad sweep of Livádhia Bay, further north at Ammókhosti and Lithrá (paths from Livádhia, or boat) and on the opposite side of the island at Stavrós (remote). Eristos has the best reputation and there are beaches too on the broad bay of Playió near Megálo Khorió, from Ayios Andónios (east) to Plaka (west). There are occasional summer excursions by boat to some of these.

History

Telos does not figure in mythology or tales of the Trojan War. The island has produced evidence for the earliest animal life in the Dodecanese (Upper Pleistocene, c 45,000 years ago) in the Kharkadhió cave, and human existence from the Neolithic period. At some point it was colonised by Dorians. In the 7C the islanders took part with the Rhodians in the foundation of Sicilian Gela. It seems to have been an independent state until about 200 BC, in spite of appearing in the lists of the mid 5C BC as paying tribute to Athens.

In the 4C it issued its own bronze coinage and various strands of evidence suggest closer legal and artistic connections with Kos rather than Rhodes. It was the birthplace of the lyric poetess Irinna (4C BC). During the 3C Telos was allied with Rhodes and, by about 200, had become incorporated into the Rhodian state as a deme of Kameiros, subsequently following the fortunes of that island.

After 1204 it was taken by the Venetians, and in 1366 given in fee to Barrello Assanti of Ischia. In 1373 the Knights of St John assumed control and in 1479 defended Telos from attack by Manuel Palaiologos. Plagued by pirate raids it became subject to the Turks after the fall of Rhodes in 1522 and was on occasion attacked by them.

Getting to Tílos

■ **By sea**. The island has similar communications to those of Nísiros, on a twice weekly **ferry** route between the Greek mainland and Rhodes via the Cyclades. These are supplemented by the *Nísos Kálimnos* which calls here (twice weekly in either direction) en route from Kálimnos to Kastellórizo via the intervening islands.

There are some seasonal **hydrofoils** to both Kos and Rhodes. Winter services are much restricted and a matter of constant complaint from the community to central government.

Getting around Tílos

■ **By bus**. There is a basic **minibus** service (twice daily in winter, about five times in summer) linking the two villages of Livádhia and Megálo Khorió, sometimes continuing to Ayios Andónios and Eristos beach and, once a week on Sundays, to the monastery of Ay. Pandeleímon. Some **scooters** can be hired in Livádhia.

■ **On foot.** The best way of exploring Tílos is undoubtedly on foot. The distances are not great, although some climbing is always involved, and the landscape quiet and pleasant, especially in spring.

■ **Travel agent. Stefanákis Travel Service**, tel. 0241 44310, 44360, 44384; fax 44315 A useful map, published by the Friends of Tílos Association (FOTA), a group of foreign visitors devoted to the welfare of the island, is available from here and other outlets.

■ **Police**. Tel. 0241 44222.

■ **First aid**. Tel. 0241 44210.

Livádhia

Hotels and restaurants in Livádhia (area code 0241)

C **Eléni** (20), 7000–10,000 drs. Tel. 44062; fax 44063.	Also **rooms**, including those above Stefanákis Travel (tel./fax, see above).
C **Iríni** (23). NPA. Tel. 53293. April–Oct.	
E **Livádhia** (15). 5000–6800 drs. Tel. 44266, 44032. May–Oct.	**Restaurants. Sofía's, Kóstas'** and **Blue Sky** (fish) are all good.

Boats dock at the pleasant port of Livádhia which has a fair amount of accommodation and restaurants.

The small village lies at the northern end of a broad bay backed by a narrow plain, with jagged-topped hills rising sharply behind. From the sea their outline is sharply dramatic.

Near the shore, to the south of the village, the small church of Ay. Pandeleímon is built over the remains of an Early Christian **basilica**, the source of architectural and mosaic fragments. Nearby, on a long low hill projecting into the plain is Kástellos, the site of a **fort** of the Classical period, with some walling and traces of a round tower near the highest point. In the hills above to the southeast (track, then path) is the medieval **castle** of Agrosikiá.

You can walk south behind the long beach, past Ayios Stéfanos with a little harbour, and climb up to the chapel of Ay. Ioánnis on the promontory at the far end, with a view back to the port: from there paths go on to the deserted south of the island.

To the northeast of Livádhia are paths to the **beaches** of Ammókhosti and Lithrá.

The island

Climbing out of Livádhia on the main road, you pass several interesting but dilapidated olive pressing mechanisms. It is about 20 minutes' walk to the top of the hill where you turn off to the left, either on an old paved trackway or, a short distance further on, beyond an OTE relay building, onto a narrow metalled road. These take you in the direction of **Mikró Khorió**, an abandoned village soon visible on the hillside (20 minutes' wander). The village and its situation are picturesque, if you can put aside regret at its desertion. In spring the fields around are idyllic. The main church and one or two other buildings are white-washed and maintained: in summer, a café operates in the evenings. At the highest point of the village are the remains of a medieval **watchtower**: nearby the cemetery **church** of the Dormition (Koímisis tis Theotókou; locked) has 18C paintings by Neófitos of Sími. In the village the small church of Sotíra also has frescoes (?14C).

In the hills behind, to the southwest, in the direction of Stavrós, is a medieval **watchtower** known as To kástro tou Lámbrou.

You can descend from Mikró Khorió by a rather overgrown track to join (25 minutes) the main road further on. There is a chapel of Ay. Anáryiroi on a hillock to the right, and behind it a track to the beach at **Lithrá**. The road continues across a level plain, then drops into a broad defile where the main settlement of Megálo Khorió comes into view, the castle and ancient acropolis dramatically towering above it. Perched on the hill above you to the left is the medieval **fort** of Mesariá. This can be reached by a track (left) opposite the helicopter pad as you emerge from the defile.

Also reached by this track and in fact nestling below the fort on the far side of the hill from the road, is the **Kharkadhió Cave**, closed except when excavations are in progress but partially visible from outside. The cave was discovered in 1971 and excavated subsequently by a team from the Department of Palaeontology and Geology of Athens University. As well as traces of human occupation from the Neolithic to medieval periods, it has produced important fossilised remains of small (1.20–1.50m tall) elephants from the Upper Pleistocene age (c 45,000 years ago) and of deer of an even earlier period; also other material. An explanatory display with some finds is in a small museum in Megálo Khorió but most are in the Museum of the Department in Athens. In the vicinity of the fort are several small churches; one, Ayios Nikólaos has a domed narthex appended, and two conches.

Continuing across the plain you pass a road to the left (see below), on the outskirts of the village. This soon divides, the left branch for Eristos (4km, beach, tavernas, some rooms); right for Ayios Andónios (2km, beach, small hotel), Pláka (5km, beach) and the monastery of Ayios Pandeleímon (9km).

Ignoring the turn you enter **Megálo Khorió**, a delightful village which nestles on the lower slopes of the castle rock and partly occupies the site of the Classical town. (**Rooms**, belonging to the **Kástro** restaurant, tel. 0241 53236; **Milíou**, tel. 0241 44204; **Yiannourákis**, tel. 0241 44213, 44242. **Restaurant. To Kástro**, unpretentious but good.)

At the entrance to the village, in a narrow square opposite the school, is a small museum with a **display** related to Kharkadhió (opened on request;

enquire at Dhimarkhíon). The Dhimarkhíon is on the upper floor of the building in which the museum is housed, but is entered from the opposite side.

Also in the village is a **church** of the Taxiárkhis Mikhaïl, with a patterned pebble court and a campanile (1827). An inscription on the latter says that it belongs to a church of the Metamórfosis, suggesting that the functions of the church of Taxiárkhis Mikhaïl on the kastro (see below) were transferred to the village below at some point after 1827 and displaced another dedicated to the Metamórfosis (Transfiguration).

Immediately above the church is a well-preserved section of the southern wall of the ancient city, which runs through the village.

Kástro above Megálo Khorió

Megálo Khorió huddles in the shadow of the ancient and medieval **kastro**. To reach this, leave the village by a road at the southeast (the right hand side as viewed from your original line of approach), which skirts the houses and climbs to some modern cisterns. Beyond these you enter the precinct through a gate in the wire fence and follow a rough path diagonally across the face of the hill. Its slopes are covered with remains of terraces which supported the buildings of the ancient **settlement**, whose circuit wall can be traced from below the acropolis rock to the modern village. The climb is steep and takes the best part of an hour: the path can be lost during the last part of the ascent but the final stretch consists of a stairway cut across the rock face from left to right, up to the clearly visible entrance.

Although the fortress is not large, parts of it are very well preserved. Much fine **Classical masonry** is visible in the lower courses (some is polygonal and may be Archaic) and especially in the **gate** (Classical) and corner towers. Above, the construction is medieval. Immediately inside the gate, flights of marble steps ascend ahead and to the left. Those on the left have slots, probably for the erection of stelai. These steps may have formed part of the entrance to a sanctuary of Athena Polias or Zeus Polieus whose existence is known from an inscription. Ahead is a **church** of the Taxiárkhis Mikhaïl (Archangel Michael), largely constructed of ancient blocks and with some fragments of frescoes still *in situ*. Some of the blocks bear inscriptions, as do some of those in the gate. Most of the house remains within the fortifications are medieval. There are splendid **views**, back across the broad tree-studded plain towards Míkro Khorió in the south and Eristos in the west; north across the sea where Nísiros looms, with the village of Nikiá perched high on its southern rim. From the far side (precipitous drop) you see the hamlet of Ayios Andónios on the sweep of the bay of Playió. The descent takes only about 20 minutes!

In the hills to the southeast of the village are several small churches, which are not well known and mostly in bad condition. Of these, Ayios Nikólaos sta Kheíli has some interesting fresco remains (15C).

Below the village, near the turn to Eristos, an army post stands by a church of the Panayía, which includes ancient blocks. The church itself, a dependency of the monastery (below) has not much of interest, but the wooden templon (1743) is good work. Beyond is the modern cemetery, with a plethora of Hellenistic and Roman altars and column drums built into the circuit wall, also early Christian material. The cemetery church, of **Ayios Konstandínos**, and the paving in front of it, incorporate architectural members and sculptural fragments in their construction: there are also sections of mosaic. This material shows that, on this site, were an **ancient cemetery** and, later, an **Early Christian basilica**.

Taking the by-road, you turn right to reach (about a 30 minute walk) the sea near **Ayios Andónios** (hotel/restaurant). Some burials of c AD 800 (?) made in the sand have solidified (as so-called 'beach rocks') and given rise to various curious explanations. People will point them out to you. They are probably late antique burials which have petrified.

Heading left along the quiet rolling coastal road you pass an abandoned windmill with an ancient inscribed altar built in over its door and, further on, on a rise to the left, the modern chapel of Panayía Kamarianí. At the end of the bay a track leads down to the sandy beach at **Pláka**. The road heads inland and climbs quite steeply in a barer landscape; in places the surface is poor.

The **monastery of Ayios Pandeleímon**, under 2 hours walk (9km; bus on Sun; patronal festival 27 July) from Megálo Khorió, is well worth the effort. Beautifully situated among trees with abundant running water, it is a small fortified monastery (wall and tower), with a tiny attractive church. This has good frescoes (18C) by Gregory of Sími, recently restored, with earlier layers beneath. An inscription refers to the building of the monastery in 1703, but it is not clear whether this was the date of the original construction or a rebuilding. Probably it is considerably older (?15C). Its former importance is reflected in local songs and traditions, and the fact that it once issued a local currency. The monastery is normally closed and in order to make sure of access you must contact the guardian (Pandelís Yiannourákis, in Megáló Khorió, tel. 0241 44213, 44242) in advance.

The other branch road below Megáló Khorió takes you to **Eristos** beach (5km; some rooms, tel. 0241 44213, 44242; small restaurant).

Kos

Kos (Κῶς; acc. Ko; anc. *Cos*). From the the pretty villages of Asfendioú on the green and tree-clad slopes of Mt Dhíkaios, to the flat and fertile central plain, the broad sandy bays of Kamári and the southeast, and the deserted peninsula of Kéfalos, the island seems spacious like no other of the Dodecanese apart from Rhodes. Its 'European' aspect, which derives partly from the presence of large numbers of visitors, is reinforced by the flat rural countryside of the centre and the noticeable presence of cattle and horses (there is a riding school), but counteracted by more eastern elements—the mosques and small Muslim communities, the palm trees. Rich in antiquities, Kos has the memorable Asklepieion and a fine collection of ancient sculpture in the town museum, the most important castle of the Knights after that in Rhodes, and impressive mosques. The main town and resorts, especially Kardhámaina, can become very busy in season and will not be to everybody's taste, but there is good swimming, sailing and watersports, and plenty of night-life.

One-fifth the size of Rhodes and smaller than Kárpathos, with a population of 26,379, Kos is second only to Rhodes in the scale of its tourist trade. Long and narrow, it stretches 45km from northeast to southwest. The narrowest point is at the isthmus leading to the peninsula of Kéfalos in the southwest; elsewhere the width varies from 1.5 to 11km; the length of the coastline is 112km. The island lies at the entrance to the deeply indented Gulf of Kos, the 'Ceramic Gulf' of antiquity, between the Turkish peninsulas of Bodrum (*Halikarnassos*), only 5km away to the north, and Knidos (*Knidos*) to the south (16km).

A long mountain chain in the south of the island runs from Cape Fokás, at the east, to the area of Pilí in the centre. The highest point is Mt Dhíkaios, perhaps the ancient *Oromedon* (847m), gently sloping to the north, precipitous on the south. The higher slopes are fairly barren, the lower well-wooded with pine. In the northwest there is an uncultivated plateau, from which the ground slopes towards the sea. Between the Dhíkaios range and the sea to the north is a low flat coastal plain, highly fertile and the agricultural centre of Kos.

The peninsula of Kéfalos, in the southwest, is relatively undeveloped and quite hilly, with Mt Látra rising to 428m: the hills sloping down to Cape Kríkelos, the southernmost point of the island. The coast, windier in the north than in the south, has few bays and inlets and there is only one real harbour, Mandráki, in Kos town at the northeast end of the island.

The island produces large quantities of juicy grapes (and wines), as well as fine water melons, olive oil, cereals, vegetables, honey, and tobacco; and has given its name to a variety of lettuce. The port has some trade.

Of all the Dodecanese, Kos has the most water. Its abundant warm ferruginous springs were famous even before the time of Hippokrates, the greatest physician of antiquity, who was born at Kos c 460 BC and is said to have died in 357 at the age of 104. Another native was the poet Philetas, a contemporary of Ptolemy II Philadelphos (285–247 BC). The bucolic poet Theokritos, born at Syracuse c 310 BC, lived for a time at Kos as a disciple of Philetas; his 7th idyll has a Koan setting. The painter Apelles, whose Aphrodite Anadyomene adorned the Asklepieion, was claimed as a native of Kos, though he may have been born

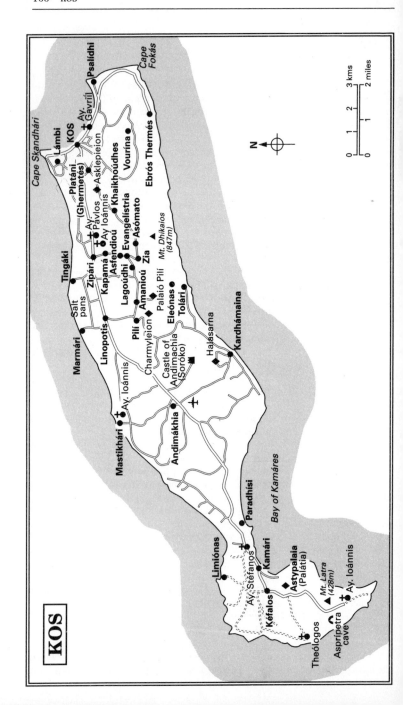

in Ionia at Kolophon or Ephesos. He flourished in the time of Alexander the Great (336–323 BC).

An excellent guidebook (still available) is C. and C. Mee, *Kos*, Athens, 1979 (Lycabettus Press).

History

The island has had several names. Thucydides, Diodorus, and Strabo called it *Kos Meropis* (also used as the name of its second main settlement, after *Astypalaia*), Pliny *Nymphaea*, and Stephanos of Byzantium *Karis*. In the Middle Ages it was known as *Lango*, perhaps because of its length, and later as *Stanchio*, a corruption of 'stin Ko'. From this name was derived the Turkish *Istanko*. Its mythical founder was Merops and the indigenous population were later referred to as Meropes. Finds in the Cave of Asprípetra, near Kéfalos, show that Kos was inhabited in the Neolithic period. It was colonised by Carians and, in Homeric times, by Dorians from Epidauros. According to the Homeric Catalogue of Ships, Koan forces in the Trojan War were led by the Herakleidai Pheidippos and Antiphos. They were said to have succeeded the first (Thessalian) dynasty of the island.

Later Kos was a member of the Dorian hexapolis and of little importance. The island lost its independence after the Persian victory over the Lydians in 546 BC. During the Persian Wars it was under the control of Artemisia, queen of Caria, and so fought on the losing side, but defected after the Greek victory at Cape Mykale in 478 BC. In 477 it joined the Delian League, and during the Peloponnesian War participated in the expedition to Sicily as an ally of Athens. In 412 BC the island was hit by a serious earthquake, and in the aftermath was sacked by the Spartans. The old town (*Astypalaia*) in the southwest of the island was not subsequently rebuilt or re-occupied. In 410 BC Alkibiades fortified and garrisoned the island, but it was subsequently occupied by Lysander for the Spartans.

Following the example of Knidos, Kos became re-allied with Athens in 394 BC, and was also a member of the 2nd Maritime League. Following a *synoikism* (union of the towns of the island), a new city of Kos was founded in 366 BC on the site of the earlier Kos-Meropis, in the area now occupied by the modern capital. This soon prospered and became one of the greatest maritime centres of the Aegean. In the Social War of 357 BC the island fought against Athens and came under the control of Mausolos, King of Caria. After Alexander the Great's victory at Halikarnassos in 334 BC, Kos was in the Macedonian sphere. It was known all over the ancient world for the sanctuary of Asklepios and its school of medicine.

Kos produced purple dye, and its wines and silks had a great reputation; the light silk dresses called *Coae vestes* were well known in Roman times for their transparency. The city was adorned with numerous artistic monuments, but not Praxiteles' famous Aphrodite of Knidos; that statue was acquired by the people of Knidos after the Koans had rejected it in favour of a draped representation of the goddess which never won the reputation of its naked counterpart.

On Alexander's death in 323 BC, Kos passed to the Ptolemies. Ptolemy II Philadelphos was born on the island in 309. Cleopatra is said to have stored some of her treasures here. It was held by the Ptolemies until their navy was defeated by Antigonos Gonatas of Macedon in the vicinity in c 256 BC, who then gained control of the seas. Later Rhodes and then (early 2C BC) Rome influenced the island's affairs. Kos was made a *civitas libera* of the proconsular province of Asia. In 88 BC it was occupied and sacked by Mithridates. The apostle Paul visited the island. The Emperor Claudius patronised Kos and declared the island *immunus* in AD 53. Antoninus Pius contributed to reconstruction after the devastating earthquake of AD 142. In the reign of Diocletian the island was part of the *Provincia insularum* (in the administrative region of Samos). Later it was annexed to the Eastern Empire.

In the Byzantine period Kos was the seat of a bishop and many impressive Early Christian basilicas (5–6C AD) have been found. In the 11C Byzantine Kos was ravaged by Saracens. From 1204 it was controlled by the Venetians and, in 1304, passed to the Genoese, becoming a fief of the Zaccharia family. Two years later it was ceded to the Knights of St John, who did not take possession till 1315, but then made it into a stronghold. It was attacked by the Turks in 1457 and 1477, and fell to them, with Rhodes, in 1522. Hadji Ali Haseki, voivode and tyrant of Athens, was finally exiled to Kos, and beheaded there on 23 December 1795.

In 1912, after nearly 400 years of Turkish occupation, it was occupied by the Italians in the course of their war with Turkey. In the Second World War British forces temporarily held the island until driven out by the Germans. Kos was reunited with Greece in 1948.

The best study of the ancient history of Kos is S. M. Sherwin White, *Ancient Cos: an historical study from the Dorian settlement to the imperial period*, Göttingen, 1978.

Getting to Kos

■ **By air**. Kos is linked by air with Athens (daily); also, less frequently, with Rhodes, Sámos, and Thessaloníki within Greece; and directly, by charter flight, with many other European countries. There are Olympic Airways offices in Kos town (Leof. Vas. Pávlou 22, tel. 0242 28331) and at the airport at Andimákhia, 26km to the west (tel. 0242 51229). Buses from the town offices connect with the Athens flights.

■ **By sea**. There are ferry connections with Rhodes to the southeast, with the larger of the Dodecanese to the north and the Piraeus; every day in high season, at least four times weekly in low season. In addition **smaller boats** provide daily services to Kálimnos from Mastikhári, and to Nísiros from Kardhámaina. Excursion boats (below) can also be used for normal travel, though they may be relatively expensive. Note that in Kos town only small vessels use the old port; the larger ferries dock at a new quay to the east of the castle.

Getting around Kos

■ **By bus**. KTEL buses serve the island as a whole, the DEAS (Dhimotikí Epikhírisi Astikís Sinkinonías tis Ko) only the city and its environs. The KTEL station in Kos town is at 7 Kleopátras, near the junction with Pisándrou (tel. 22292). There are services to Zía and Asfendioú (3), Tingáki and Marmári (10), Pilí (4), Mastikhári (4), Andimákhia (3), Kardhámaina (6), and Kéfalos (passing the airport) (6). Services are reduced on Sundays. The DEAS, based at 7 Aktí Kondouriótou on the waterfront, has three services, one southeast along the coast to Ay. Fokás (useful for the campsite), one northwest along the coast to Lámbi, and another inland to Platáni and the Asklepieíon, with buses running from early morning through to roughly midnight.

In addition, **bus tours** of the island (full day), the town (half day), and the Asklepieíon are widely advertised in Kos town and in Tingáki. **Taxis** are readily available, and there is a rank on the waterfront in Kos town, below Pl. Platánou.

■ **By road.** Car hire is easily arranged in Kos and several of the major international companies have local agents. **Bicycles** are particularly popular in Kos town and the flat northeast coastal strip. Elsewhere, and for longer journeys, **scooters** or **cars** are understandably more common, and are readily available from travel agents.

■ There are excursions by **boat** to the nearby islands (Kálimnos, Psérimos, Nísiros, Sími) and to Turkey (Bodrum); also to some **beaches**. In Kos town, these start from Mandráki and can be booked either on the quay or through travel agents.

Kos town

Hotels and restaurants in Kos and Lámbi (area code 0242)

■ **Kos town**
A Continental Palace (210); pool, tennis; 12,500–22,000 drs. Tel. 22737, 22915, 28239; fax 23727. April–Oct.
B Aigaíon (41); 10,000–12,000 drs. Tel. 24701/2. April–Oct).
B Ayios Konstandínos (San Constantin) (128), Kanári; pool; 5850–12,740 drs. Tel. 23301, 23501; fax 23502. April–Oct.
C Ekateríni (Catherine) (28), P. Tsaldhári 6; 8000–13,000 drs. Tel. 28285.
C Eftikhía(F/A), Ambavrís suburb; 12,000–18,000 drs. Tel. 23212, 22350. April–Oct.
C Veroníki, P. Tsaldhári 2; 10,250–13,950 drs. Tel. 28122/3.

D Dhodekánissos (19), Ipsilántou 2; 4200–7700 drs. Tel. 28460, 22860.
  Rooms. Owners meet the boats, or the information office will help.

Restaurants on the waterfront are best avoided, although the traditional style **Límnos**, at the castle end, is reasonable and has a good bottled local retsina. Better fare is to be found inland at restaurants in Plateía Konítsis or near the junction of Alikarnassoú and Pindárou. Plateía Dhiagóra is attractive but gets very busy, although the **Anatolia Hamam**, just off the square, is delightful, relatively quiet, and has good food. A few minutes' walk from the south side of town (see below) takes you to the suburb of Ambavris and the good and friendly taverna (open both lunchtime and evenings) of the same name. A pleasant jaunt could be made by bus or taxi to Zía or one of the hill villages which have plenty of restaurants in a cool and attractive setting.

■ **Lámbi**
A Atlantis (356); pool, tennis; NPA. Tel. 28731/4, 24683, 28261;

fax 22852. April–Oct.
B Apéllis (33); pool;
9730–11,890 drs. Tel. 24629, 24831. April–Oct.
B Cosmopolitan (81);
6000–15,000 drs. Tel. 23411/5, 23698. April–Oct.
C Athiná (103); pool.
11,840–14,700 drs. Tel. 25044/5, 25647/8. April–Oct.
C Laura (28); 7500–9000 drs. Tel. 28981. April–Oct.
E Pasparás (12); NPA.

The town of Kos occupies a plain at the northeast end of the island, just south of the Kos channel (here at its narrowest: 5km), which separates it from the Anatolian coast. Despite undistinguished modern buildings (many resulting from the devastating earthquake of 1933) and some rather tasteless expansion, often the result of tourism, it is a pleasant town with tidy open streets, luxuriant gardens and orchards, and extensive Classical, Roman and medieval remains. The town can be extremely busy in season and booking of accommodation is essential. The nightlife is very active and geared to the needs of younger visitors. Roads radiate from the old harbour with cross streets reflecting its curve. Particularly attractive are the streets round the agora and near the western excavations, and Plateía Dhiagóra in the Seraglio. Of the 14,714 inhabitants, there is a substantial Muslim minority.

History

There is a prehistoric (Early Bronze Age onwards) settlement beneath the older part (Seraglio) of the modern town of Kos and a number of Mycenaean tombs have been discovered to the southwest, as well as Protogeometric and Geometric graves within its walls. Recent finds of Archaic and Classical material here, and in graves further away at Marmarotó, have shown that a settlement, presumably that of Kos-Meropis, continued to grow.

The new city, founded here in 366 BC, had a perimeter of c 4km and was laid out on a Hippodamian grid plan, although the grid was differently aligned in the eastern and western parts of the town. Sections of the city wall have been traced and dated to the 2C BC. Further walls running north from the main circuit to the sea, protected the harbour. Devastated by earthquakes c 5 BC, in AD 142, and again in 469, the town was virtually destroyed in 554. Materials from earlier structures were reused in each new rebuilding and later pillaged for the medieval defences.

■ **Police.** Akti Kondouriótou/Plateía Platánou, in the former Governor's Mansion, near the castle. Tel. 22222.

- **Tourist office**. In the Albergo Calsomino, Vasiléos Yioryíou B', opposite the end of Ippokrátous, Mon–Fri 07.30–20.30, Sat–Sun 07.30–15.00. Tel. 28724, 24460; fax 21111.

- **Travel agent. Aiolos**, Artemisías 17 (also branches in Kardhámaina and Kéfalos); tel. 26203–5; and others.

- **Olympic Airways**. Vas. Pávlou 22. Tel. 28331/2; Airport 51567. Bus to airport from office for each of the two daily flights (Drs. 1000).

- **Limenarkhíon**. At foot of P. Tsaldhári, close to Mandráki harbour.

- **Post office**. 16 El. Venizélou, Mon–Fri 07.30–14.00, Sat 08.00–14.30, Sun 09.00–13.30.

- **OTE**. 8 Víronos/Xánthou, Mon–Sat 07.30–21.45.

- **First aid**. Tel. 22330, 22539.

- **Cinema** (mainly summer). *Orféas*, Ipsilántou/31 Martíou (Plateía Eleftherías).

- **Bookshop. Thalassinós**, P. Tsaldhári 5–7.

- **Car hire. Avis**, P. Tsaldhári 3. Tel. 24272, 24489; **Hertz**, Ant. Ioannídhi 12 (Plateía Ayías Paraskevís). Tel. 28002, 23743; **J&K**, Navarínou 4. Tel. 25333, 27808. **Rent a Moto Serníkos** (for scooters, cycles etc.), Irodhótou 19. Tel. 23670.

- **Admission** to museum, castle, and Roman house at standard site and museum hours. Access to the main town sites is unrestricted.

The picturesque **harbour of Mandrakí**, with good yacht facilities, has the same name as its counterpart in Rhodes. It is used now by smaller craft, the large ferries docking at new facilities, east of the castle, whose walls present an imposing façade to the sea.

Opposite the quay the former **Palace of the Regent**, by F. di Fausto (1928), houses the town hall, customs house, and local bus station. At the left hand (east) end of the waterfront is a taxi stand with, beyond, a Turkish hamam now restored as a club. By the taxis you can climb, through the remains of a Turkish cemetery, to the terreplein of the castle, now Plateía Platánou (cafés). In the centre grows the so-called **plane-tree of Hippocrates**, a gigantic tree with a trunk 14m in diameter and branches propped up by ancient marble fragments. Inevitably tradition insists that Hippocrates taught under its shade, though it is not more than 500 years old.

To the right stands the attractive **Mosque of Gazi Hassan Pasha** (or the Loggia), a three-storeyed building of 1786, entered on the first floor by a graceful external marble staircase with a double portico or loggia. Damaged by

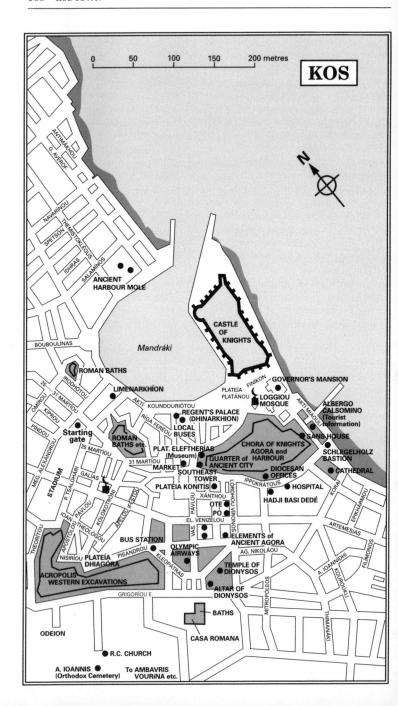

KOS

0   50   100   150   200 metres

ANTIMAKHOU
G. AVEROF

NAVARINOU
THEMISTOKLEOUS
SPETSON
IDHRAS
SALAMÍNOS

ANCIENT
HARBOUR MOLE

BOUBOULÍNAS

Mandráki

CASTLE
OF
KNIGHTS

ROMAN BATHS

IRODHÓTOU
25
31 MARTIOU
OMIROU
KIPROU
PINDOU

LIMENARKHÍON

AKTÍ
KOUNDOURIÓTOU

RÍGA FEREOU

Starting
gate
MEG. ALEXANDROU

ROMAN
BATHS etc.

25 MARTIOU

31 MARTIOU

STADIUM

P. TSALDHARI
GALIAS

PAVLOU
IOAN.
APOSTOLOU THEOLOGOU
KOLOKOTRONI
APELOU IFESTIOU

THEORÍTOU
NISIRÍOU
PISANDROU

ACROPOLIS
WESTERN EXCAVATIONS

PLATEÍA
DHIAGORA

KLEOPATRAS

GRIGORÍOU E.

ODEION

R.C. CHURCH

A. IOANNIS
(Orthodox Cemetery)

To AMBAVRIS
VOURÍNA etc.

PLATEÍA
PLATÁNOU

FINÍKON

GOVERNOR'S MANSION

LOGGIOU
MOSQUE

REGENT'S PALACE
(DHINARKHION)

LOCAL
BUSES

PLAT. ELEFTHERÍAS
(Museum)

MARKET

QUARTER of
ANCIENT CITY

SOUTHEAST
TOWER

PLATEÍA KONÍTIS

XÁNTHOU
PAVLOU
LORDHOU VIRONOS

OTE
PO
EL. VENIZELOU

VAS.

BUS STATION

OLYMPIC
AIRWAYS

ELEMENTS of
ANCIENT AGORA

AG. NIKOLÁOU

TEMPLE OF
DIONYSOS

ALTAR OF
DIONYSOS

BATHS

CASA ROMANA

CHORA OF KNIGHTS
AGORA and
QUARTER of HARBOUR
ANCIENT CITY

DIOCESAN
OFFICES

IPPOKRÁTOUS

HOSPITAL

HADJI BASI DEDÉ

LORDHOU VIRONOS

ALBERGO
CALSOMINO
(Tourist
Information)

SANS HOUSE

SCHLEGELHOLZ
BASTION

CATHEDRAL

KORAÍ

EPIKHÁRMOU

ARTEMESÍAS

FILIMONOS

MITROPÓLEOS

A. IOANNIDHI
KOUROUKLI

THIMANÁKI

bombing during the Second World War, it is still closed. An elegant minaret stands at the corner; arched and fretted windows look down on the square. Beneath a tree a Turkish **fountain**, no longer running, has an ancient sarcophagus as its basin.

The important **antiquities** in this part of town are (I) the Castle of the Knights, (II) the City of the Knights (or Chora) and (III) the agora and harbour quarter of the Hellenistic and Roman town (with some earlier remains). They are described in that order, and (II) and (III) separately, in spite of the fact that they occupy higher and lower levels, respectively, of the same site. After visiting the castle (I), it is suggested that you make a preliminary circuit of the excavated area to inspect (II), stop to view the remains of (III) from a vantage point by the mosque, and then enter the main excavations.

> Archaeological explorations, begun in 1900 by Rudolf Herzog, were continued after 1928 by Luciano Lorenzi of the Italian School, and given impetus by the severe earthquake of 23 April 1933. Extensive excavations took place in 1935–43. The same applies to the Western Excavations (see below). Many of the mosaics recovered were removed to adorn the castle in Rhodes.
>
> Recent work, both on these sites and extensively throughout the town, has been undertaken by the Greek Archaeological Service. Readers anxious to be thoroughly informed about recent work are advised to consult Archaeological Reports (see bibliography) and references supplied therein, since full information about the results of excavations takes a long time to become widely accessible.

I Castle of the Knights

From the terreplein in Plateía Platánou (see above) a stone bridge leads across the outer moat (now a palm-shaded avenue) to the Castle of the Knights, the town's principal monument. The fortress had two enceintes, one within the other. You enter via a drawbridge and a gateway in the south curtain wall of the outer enceinte. Above the **gate** are a Hellenic frieze and the quartered arms of Amboise and the Order.

The **original castle**, roughly rectangular in plan, was begun in 1450 by the Venetian Fantino Guerini, governor of Kos (1436–53), and completed in 1478 by the Genoese Edoardo de Carmadino (governor 1471–95). After the unsuccessful Turkish assault of 1480, an **outer enceinte** was begun in 1495 by Grand Master Pierre d'Aubusson and completed in 1514 by G.M. Fabrizio Del Carretto. Italian architects and craftsmen were employed in its construction. Both enceintes incorporate masonry from the Asklepieion and other ancient Greek buildings. There is a deep fosse between the two lines of walls.

A passageway leads to the south terrace, then a flight of steps to the **Antiquarium**. This is normally closed, but contains Koan marbles, inscriptions, sculptural fragments, sepulchral monuments, and a number of fine knightly escutcheons carved in marble. One of the inscriptions commemorates the physician Xenophon, who helped to poison the Emperor Claudius (Tacitus, *Annals*, xii, 67, 2).

The heavy cylindrical **Bastion Del Carretto**, at the southwest angle of the outer enceinte, resembles the bastion of the same name in the walls of Rhodes.

The corresponding northeast tower gives a good view over the sea towards Anatolia. The northwest tower, or Tower of Aubusson, overlooking the harbour, is polygonal. It bears the arms of Aubusson quartered with those of the Order, and an Italian inscription of 1503.

From the terrace a staircase descends to the left of the Antiquarium to a horseshoe ravelin in front of the inner enceinte. On its right is the entrance. All four angles of the **inner enceinte** have cylindrical towers, with battlements and embrasures, and appropriate escutcheons. The inner curtain wall is similarly adorned. On the inner south-west tower are the fleurs-de-lis of France.

On leaving the castle you descend to the palm-lined avenue below the bridge. Past the ornate Governor's Mansion, which backs on to Plateía Platánou, a restored gateway, in the middle of a row of shady cafés, gives access to the partially walled area of the City of the Knights (or Chora), excavated since the earthquake of 1933 down to the levels which represent the Agora and Harbour Quarter of the Hellenistic and Roman city.

II City of the Knights

The Chora, or City of the Knights, bounded by an enceinte erected in 1391–96 against the threatened attack of Bayezid, occupied only the agora and harbour area of the older city. Parts of the City of the Knights remain opposite the castle, from where the course of its **wall** can be traced to the **Pórta tou Fórou** and the **southwest tower** (see below). By the gateway (and entrance to the excavations to which you can return later) just mentioned is a **house** with the worn arms of Bailiff Francesco Sans (1514), and variegated masonry. Through the gate is a 15C chapel of Ayios Ioánnis (right) which makes use of earlier material and shows some western influence, and a modern one of Ayios Yióryios (left); further left is a third chapel dedicated to the Panayía (incoporating ancient inscriptions). This is close to the **Schlegelholz bastion**, at the southeast corner of the Knights' circuit. It is decorated with arms of Schlegelholz, governor from 1391–1412, and of Grand Master Heredia.

You are now on the corner of Od. Ippokrátous, a pleasant street with local colour which follows the course of the walls. Towards the sea the Italian **Albergo Calsomino** houses the **tourist information office** and broadcasting and municipal organisations. As you proceed along Ippokrátous, over to the left is the cathedral of Kos. To the right is a well preserved segment of the wall; left again, the hospital. On the right the ecclesiastical offices of the Diocese of Kos occupy a nice house which overlooks the excavations. Opposite this, on the corner of Mitropóleos, is a small domed Turkish shrine to Hadji Bashi Dedé, on the site of a former mosque and below the present offices of the Muslim community. Continuing along Ippokrátous, with frequent views of the excavations, you reach Plateía Eleftherías (see below) and the impressive west gate, the so-called **Pórta tou Fórou**. Passing through this you follow a raised path (cafés) along the other side of the site and return to the Mosque of the Loggia where you can transfer your attention to (III) the Classical site.

III The agora and harbour quarter

From the southeast corner of the mosque you can orientate yourself to the plan by the six re-erected columns of the stoa which are easily picked out nearby. The lines of the massive harbour basilica can be traced, and the baptistery, raised above its surroundings. Beyond you can make out part of the marble wall of the Temple of Herakles (also raised) within its precinct; a corner of the Sanctuary of Aphrodite and two columns of one of its temples. On the far side of the site (right) rise two re-erected columns of the agora.

The part of the excavations towards the sea (north) lay outside the walls of the Hellenistic town proper, although the harbour area was enclosed by walls which ran from the main circuit to the shore. You can now return to the entrance (1) by the Sans House (above). Through this and beyond the chapels can be seen, from left to right, some courses of the marble superstructure of a rectangular Hellenistic **sanctuary of Herakles** (2) can be made out. The temple belongs to

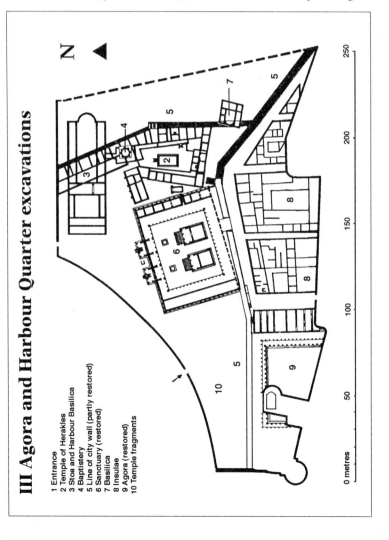

III Agora and Harbour Quarter excavations

1 Entrance
2 Temple of Herakles
3 Stoa and Harbour Basilica
4 Baptistery
5 Line of city wall (partly restored)
6 Sanctuary (restored)
7 Basilica
8 Insulae
9 Agora (restored)
10 Temple fragments

the 2C BC; the surrounding elements are 3C AD, with a series of rooms on four sides. Then you see a travertine **stoa** (4–3C BC, remodelled in the 3C AD), six of whose columns with acanthus capitals have been re-erected. These were recovered from the foundations of the **harbour basilica** (3), which was built over the stoa in the 5C AD. The basilica had three aisles preceded by an atrium and a narthex. To the south is a square **baptistery** (4) with a cruciform font. The back wall of the sanctuary and stoa was formed from the eastern arm of the Hellenistic **harbour defences** (5). The remains just described lie immediately south of the Mosque of the Loggia (see above).

Further west (right) are substantial parts of the **Sanctuary of the Port Quarter** (6), probably dedicated to Aphrodite in the 2C BC. The foundations which remain are of an enclosure on a podium with two propylaea in front. The complex has rooms to the west and an internal colonnaded court with two matching tetrastyle temples in the centre. Its south side backs onto the Hellenistic **city wall**, which is followed by a path and can be traced to some extent in both directions, although since it is does not everywhere survive above ground level, it can be difficult to relate to the plan. At the east side of the site the plan of another **basilica** (7) can be easily traced which helps you to locate yourself in relation to the town wall (5). The south (inland of the main east-west town wall) sector of the excavated area represents the north extremity of the ancient city proper: it is divided by **roads** running north–south.

To the east are insulae of **houses and shops** (8). To the west lies the agora (close to the Pórta tou Fórou); a fine stretch of rusticated ashlar masonry marks its eastern boundary, and some columns have been re-erected. The chapel of Ayios Konstandínos stands on an unexcavated tongue of land. The north side of the **agora** (9), c 82m wide, was built against the south side of the city wall. Part of its west side (4–3C) can be seen by a north–south road. The interior colonnades were reconstructed in marble in the 2C BC, with Doric columns fluted for two-thirds of their height. At that time the pavement was also made of marble, in regular slabs. The southern limit of the agora has been found much further south, near the altar of Dionysos in Od. Vas. Pávlou (see below).

The agora suffered in the earthquake during the reign of Antoninus Pius, after which the northern part was rebuilt with a monumental entrance. The three huge arches, parts of which can be seen, corresponded to vaulted rooms in the interior. These were barrel vaulted and plastered. In front of the arches, a fine marble staircase (a section survives) descended to the port.

North of the agora and the town wall drums and Corinthian capitals (10) are from a 1C AD **temple**.

You leave the site towards the Knights' west gate, which in the Middle Ages was called Pórta tou Fórou. Through this is **Plateía Eleftherías**, the main square of the town. Here the **museum**, built by the Italians during the excavations of the 1930s, contains an interesting and extensive collection of Hellenistic and Roman sculpture. An illustrated handlist is available in English. The upper galleries (pottery) are not accessible.

In the entrance hall are some colossal heads, funerary altars and a waterspout in the form of a frog. In the centre of the building, an attractive reconstruction gives a good idea of the peristyle of a Hellenistic or Roman house and has a mosaic of the arrival of Asklepios on Kos (2–3C AD). Around are figures of deities, etc. (Artemis, Dionysos, Asklepios, Hygiaea) of the 2C AD found in the House of the Europa Mosaic. Outside the peristyle are various Hellenistic and Roman statues, reliefs and table supports.

The room at the left of the building has some Archaic and Classical, but mainly Hellenistic, sculpture of the 3–1C BC from various places on Kos, but particularly from the excavations of the odeion.

At the far end of the gallery is a Hellenistic portrait statue, sometimes thought to represent Hippokrates. The far side gallery has small scale sculpture, dating from the late Classical period to the 1C AD, and including statuettes from the Sanctuary of Demeter at Amaniou. Several pieces come from the Casa Romana. The right hand gallery has Roman sculpture. Deities, emperors, private individuals and animals are all represented.

Across the square is the 18C **Defterdar Mosque**, partly converted to other uses, with a fountain. On the corner of 31 Martíou is a fine **theatre** (worth looking inside) built by the Italians and now sometimes used as the Cinema Orféas. On the outside an inscription commemorates the return of Kos to Greece in 1948 in the reign of King Paul I. The south of the square is bounded by an arcaded market (active), the other side of which opens another plateía (of Ayía Paraskeví, after its church), with pleasant cafés. Off the square, by the pathway which approaches the south side of the church, are some remains of Roman houses, apparently including a nymphaion.

You should now take Odhós Vas. Pávlou which leads south. At Kleopátras and Pisándrou are some **houses** of the Minoan and Mycenaean periods. Towards the top of the street, in the area bounded by V. Pávlou, Víronos, El. Venizélou and Grigoríou, are four important areas of excavation. In the two to the west you can see parts of the foundations of the stoa of the **agora**, including its return to the west. To the east are substantial remains of the **Hellenistic temple** and (further south) the **altar of Dionysos** referred to above as close to the southern limit of the agora.

Continuing to the top of Vas. Pávlou and crossing the main road (Od. Grigoríou E') you find, immediately opposite, the 3C AD **central baths**, parts of whose hypocaust are quite well preserved. Next to them is a large **Roman house**, often referred to as the Casa Romana and rebuilt, above its original lower courses, by the Italians to protect the many mosaics, some of which were removed to Rhodes. The house was built on the foundations of a Hellenistic predecessor. It has three courts, colonnades (one Ionic particularly attractive), frescoes, mosaics and marble paving and wall decoration. The mosaics include a seascape with fishes. In general it gives a good idea of a high class residence of the period.

Past the Roman house a road (left; unsigned) leads in c 600m, past remains of an Ottoman aqueduct (from Vourína), to the pleasant suburb of **Ambavrís** (taverna). This is a different world from the busy town. Just before the taverna, rising among trees to the left, can be seen the upper parts of a large Hellenistic **theatre**, restored in the 3C AD. It had a semi-circular orchestra and cavea with marble tiers built against a hillside, but has not yet been cleared or fully investigated. The southern line of the town wall has been found at various points nearby. On the other side of the road from the taverna is a fine gateway and interesting remains of a substantial Ottoman house, with swimming pool.

Beyond Ambavrís, the road continues, past two army camps, to a junction (c

2km). The left branch (tarmac) leads through quiet and lovely tree-clad slopes to the modern chapel of the **Panayía Tsoukalariá**. The right (roughish) leads up onto the montainside, through forests, to (c 4km further) the ancient spring-house of *Vourína* (or Vorína), the **sacred spring** of Theokritos. It is enclosed in a domed building, 7m high and approached by a corridor 35m long. It supplies the town of Kos. The place however is very difficult to find, even with directions, and it is preferable to have a guide. The wooded landscape is lovely and the views fine: in general it is a good place for walks.

The next turning (Od. Anapáfseos) off Grigoríou takes you first to the large Catholic church, then to the orthodox cemetery and church of **Ayios Ioánnis Pródhromos**, built in the baptistery of the largest Early Christian church of Kos; the rest of the original structure is now covered, though bits can be seen atttached to Ayios Ioánnis which is only opened for memorial services (held in the early morning from c 07.00). The interior is circular with a fine original colonnade (Ionic capitals and imposts) and marble floor in which the original position of the font can be made out.

By a final turning off Grigoríou the **odeion** is approached (left) by an avenue of cypresses. The semicircular auditorium (cavea) is enclosed by a rectangular structure and supported on two vaulted galleries: there are four stairways. There was probably a gallery at the top. Five of the 14 rows of marble seats are the original ones. The orchestra had *opus sectile* decoration; three doorways in the back wall of the stage leading to a room behind.

Opposite the Odeion avenue, on the other side of Grigoríou, are the **Western Excavations** (IV), occupying a huge L-shaped area below the ancient acropolis (see below), a low hill crowned by a minaret (in the Seraglio). It may be helpful first to return to the end of Anapáfseos and cross the excavations by a bridge (1) opposite, to ascend the acropolis. The path climbs to Plateía Dhiagóra but, for the moment, you should turn left onto a shaded path which gives a good overall view of the site.

Parallel with the main road a well-preserved section of **roadway** (2), often given its Latin title of *decumanus maximus*, is exposed with the **houses** in blocks (3-5) to the north: those to the south are now under or on the other side of the modern road. 150m of the street has been cleared to its junction further west with another street (the *cardo*). It is c 10.5m wide, including the sidewalks, had porticoes on both sides, and dates from the 3C AD. Several of the houses have mosaics (3C AD) and frescoes. That in the large **House of the Europa Mosaic** (*in situ*) is the best preserved. The house (5) is trapezoidal in shape, with rooms round a porticoed courtyard. It produced many complete statues (see museum). Behind is the Hellenistic **retaining wall** of the acropolis.

To the west you reach the junction with the *cardo* (6) which, beautifully paved with large irregular slabs (3C AD) and recalling the streets of Pompeii, heads north. To the right (east) were tavernas (7). To the left (west) are extensive **Roman baths** (8) which occupy most of the excavated area. Parts were later converted into Christian churches. In the southern part of the site is the recon-structed **marble door** (9) of the baptistery (with immersion font) belonging to an Early Christian **basilica** of the 5–6C AD, little else of which is visible.

Further north (standing vault) was the furnace room and caldarium (elevated floors). Beyond was the frigidarium which, with other rooms, was transformed into a Christian **basilica** (10) after the earthquake of AD 469, which destroyed

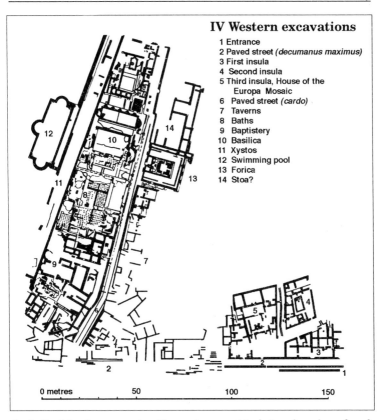

IV Western excavations

1 Entrance
2 Paved street *(decumanus maximus)*
3 First insula
4 Second insula
5 Third insula, House of the
   Europa Mosaic
6 Paved street *(cardo)*
7 Taverns
8 Baths
9 Baptistery
10 Basilica
11 Xystos
12 Swimming pool
13 Forica
14 Stoa?

0 metres   50   100   150

the baths. Mosaic pavements with ornate geometric designs have been found. This stands between the restored forica (see below) and a large **swimming pool** (12) of the 3C AD. This side of the swimming pool are the remains of the colonnade (partly restored) of the **xystos** (covered running track; 11) of a 2C BC Hellenistic **gymnasium**, most of which still lies hidden to north and west of the excavated area. Excavations elsewhere suggest that its dimensions were c 200m by 100m.

To the right of the road, beyond a row of taverns, stands the restored **forica** (latrine; 13) of the baths, an elaborate structure round a peristyle court. Although normally closed, the interior is partly visible through a window at the side. It is square in plan with an interior gallery on three sides; the sewer ran along the back wall. The gallery has Ionic columns surmounted by brick arches with vaults. On the fourth side of the latrine is a fountain with three niches and basins and, behind that, an access corridor with the entrance to the *cardo*. At the limit of the excavations, in the direction of the stadium (see below), a shelter protects a large mosaic with gladiatorial scenes.

A flight of steps by the forica leads up to the **acropolis**. At the top you pass the Anatolia hamam, now a delighful café/restaurant, which was the 16C residence of Mehmet Pasha. Rebuilt with great care, it has painted ceilings and a fine domed hamam with its own furnace. The servants' quarters were separate and the owner had a private mosque of which the minaret survives in **Plateía Dhiagóra** (restaurants). From there the picturesque Odhós Apéllou, an old street of the Turkish quarter, returns northeast. The area is still known as the **Seraglio**. There is an early 19C mosque, the Atik Cami, at the corner of Kolokótroni and Venizélou. Excavations have shown that prehistoric settlement in the Seraglio spans the Bronze Age and was probably the main centre of early Kos. It was fortified and was devastated by earthquakes at least twice. Recent work has shown that there was a settlement here in the Archaic and Classical periods and that this part of the town retained its older layout when Kos was rebuilt in 366 BC. Some traces, perhaps of the fortifications built by Alkibiades in 411/10 BC, have been found on the west side of the hill.

Further northwest, below the church of Ayía Anna on Od. 25 Martíou are some remains of the **stadium,** built against the slope. In antiquity it was connected directly to the gymnasium to the south (see above, Western Excavations). Some travertine seats (at P. Tsaldhári and El. Venizélou) belong to an early phase. Part of its unusual marble *aphesis* (**starting gate**; 2C BC), with pilasters and half-columns have been found at the corner of 31 Martíou and Megálou Alexándrou. The west tribune is Roman, 3C AD.

East of the stadium, there are remains of Roman houses at Galías/Makaríou and, at Kolokotróni and 31 Martíou, stretching right through to P. Tsaldhári, of 3–4C AD baths, probably belonging to the gymnasium. Bits of the town wall (west side) have been found in this area.

West of the stadium, in the area bounded by 25 Martíou, Kíprou, Omírou and Meg. Aléxandrou the remains of a sanctuary of Demeter (part of temple, terracotta figurines) have been located. The temple seems to have had a Mycenaean predecessor, and the sanctuary continued in use until the Roman period.

Other excavations have taken place in the western sector of the ancient settlement. In a plot at the junction of Irodhótou and Omírou, a segment (visible in the north-west part of the excavation) of the western leg of the Hellenistic walls protecting the port is overlain by the substantial 3C AD **harbour baths**. At the corner of Veriopoúlou and Alikarnassoú an Ottoman structure (well-house?) with a fine arch has been turned into an attractive little park. The walls incorporate masonry from a Classical building, including a Doric capital.

On the west side of the port, including between Themistokléous and G. Avérof, sections of the **ancient harbour** mole have been found.

Leaving the town by Od. Kanári, to the west, you can reach (3km) **Lámbi** on the exposed Skandhári promontory. There are some remains (near the Hotel Atlantis) of an Early Christian basilica, on an earlier site. From here it is possible to join the main road south of the Asklepieion turn.

Kos town to Ebrós Thermés

By road, 13km

Hotels and restaurants in Cape Fokás and Psalídhi *(area code 0242)*

■ **Cape Fokás**
A Dhímitra Beach (134), pool,
tennis. 21,000–31,000 drs. Tel.
28581/2; fax 28495.

■ **Psalídhi**
A Arkhipélagos (110), pool
tennis; 11,550–17,300 drs. Tel.
23408; fax 26287. April–Oct.
A Platanísta (148), pool, tennis;

19,000–27,000 drs. Tel. 27551; fax
25029. April–Oct.
B Theodhórou Beach (56);
11,000–15,000 drs. Tel. 22280,
23363, 23364. April–Oct.
C Entmark (63); 7800–14,500
drs. Tel. 25952. April–Oct.
C Fenix Beach (78);
10,000–15,600 drs. Tel. 21771.

You leave Kos town by the coast road and head east. Just outside the town proper, at the start of the long and continuous belt of hotels which stretches east along the coast to Cape Psalídhi, are (1km) the little-visited remains of the Early Christian basilica of **Ay. Gavriíl**, in a field to the right (south) of the road. The basilica was originally uncovered by the Italians, but excavations were only completed in the 1970s. The field is fenced off, but there is free access. The foundations and parts of the walls of the basilica proper, with triple-conched apse at the east end and narthex and exonarthex at the west, survive, covering an area of roughly 35 by 14m. Inside the church, but not in their original positions, various columns stand up to 3m high. One is diagonally fluted, the others unfluted; some have carved Turkish graffiti.

Adjoining the south wall of the basilica to the west is a rather confusing complex of smaller rooms. One, just to the southeast of the narthex, contains the sunken baptistery. The walls of the rooms to the west stand up to 2.5m high, and have clay and marble tiles. Originally the apse stood alone, built in the 4C over a 2–3C AD grave. It probably functioned as a martyrion until being enlarged to its final form in the 5C.

You continue along the coast road, passing (3km) the island's only **camping site** (April–Sept; tel. 0242 23275, 23910) and a succession of hotels, tavernas, busy sandy beaches, and a few quieter pebble beaches. A separate tarred path for cyclists runs alongside the tree-lined main road.

Heading inland for a short distance, as the shoreline stretches out to **Cape Psalídhi**, you rejoin the coast before reaching (9km) **Cape Fokás**, the eastern extremity of the island.

The road continues to (13km) **Ebrós Thérmes**. From the end of the road, a track leads down to, and then along the rocky coast, to a beach and taverna, and finally the hot sulphurous springs which empty into the sea and give the place its name.

Kos town to the *Asklepieion*, the villages of the interior and Kardhámaina

28km by road. Kardhámaina can be reached more quickly via Antimákhia, though the distance is about the same. From 2km beyond the Asklepieion to Zía the roads are poor.

Hotels and restaurants in Kardhámaina and Platáni (area code 0242)	
■ Kardhámaina **A Langas Aegean Village** (328); pool, tennis etc.; 22, 800–36,000 drs. Tel. 91401/2; fax 91635. April –Oct. Also F/As 33,600–52,800 drs. **A Norída Beach** (527); pool, tennis etc.; 14,000–20,000 drs. Tel. 91230/1, 91220; fax 91580. April–Oct. Also F/As 45, 000drs. **B Cárda Beach** (bungalows) (69), tennis; 14,000–20,000 drs. Tel. 91332, 91221/3. April–Oct. **B Río** (18); 8000–10,000 drs. Tel. 91627. April–Oct.	**C Angelikí** (F/A) (17); 10,000–22,000 drs. Tel. 91354, 91358. April–Oct. **C Kardhámaina** (16); 7000–8000 drs. Tel. 91252. **C Valinákis Beach** (73); 10,000–13,000 drs. Tel. 91354, 91358, 91205. April–Oct. **D Paralía** (11); NPA. Tel. 51205. April–Oct. **E Olimpía** (11); NPA. **■ Platáni** **C Alkíou**, 8000 drs. Tel. 23739. April–Oct.

The main archaeological excursion is to the Asklepieion (4km by road) which covers a large area on the secluded wooded slopes of Mt Dhíkaios, with views over the northeast part of the island. Take the Kéfalos road and, on the outskirts of the town fork left at a large roundabout. At 3km is Khermetés, or Ghermetés, a Muslim village, officially **Platáni**. In the plateia are cafeneions, shops, and restaurants: a right turn off the plateia leads to a nearby Muslim cemetery, with graves far simpler than their typical Greek Orthodox counterparts.

Continuing straight on through the plateia, you pass the International Hippocratic Institute and, along an avenue of cypresses, approach (4km) the **ASKLEPIEION**, or Sanctuary of Asklepios (open 08.30–19.00, closed Mon). The sanctuary occupies the site of a grove sacred to Apollo Kyparessios, mentioned in the 4C, but was not built until after the death of Hippocrates (357 BC) and dates from the Hellenistic period. The upper terrace and its temple are an addition of the 2C BC, when the sanctuary was enlarged.

The sanctuary was one of the main seats of the *Asklepiadai*, supposed descendants of Asklepios, who were a hereditary closed order of priests, jealous guardians of the secrets of medicine. The technique of healing differed from that at Epidauros and elsewhere, where cures were effected mainly by suggestion. At Kos, as demonstrated by inscriptions, patients underwent positive treatment at the hands of physicians on lines laid down by Hippocrates. Herondas in his fourth mime describes a sacrifice at the Asklepieion.

The **sanctuary** had the right of asylum. It flourished in the time of the Ptolemies and later under Nero. The rich court physician Xenophon (see Kos, Antiquarium), on his return to Kos, lavished on the sanctuary the statues he

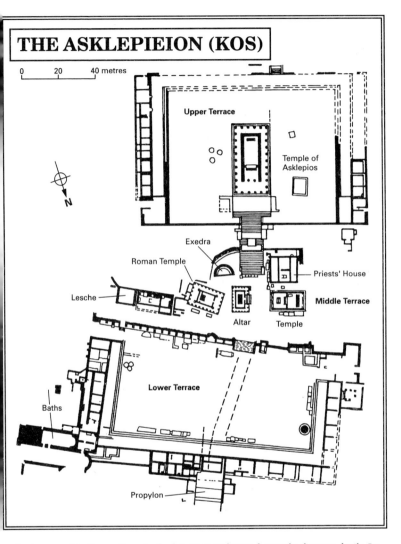

THE ASKLEPIEION (KOS)

0   20   40 metres

Upper Terrace

Temple of
Asklepios

Exedra

Roman Temple

Lesche

Priests' House

Middle Terrace

Altar

Temple

Lower Terrace

Baths

Propylon

N

had amassed in Rome. Even in the late Imperial period great baths were built. In the 6C AD the site was devastated, either by an earthquake or by Anatolian hordes who ravaged the island in 554. The Knights of St John used the ruins as a quarry. A local antiquary, G.E. Zaraphtis, identified the site; in 1902 the German archaeologist R. Herzog began systematic excavation, and the work was completed by the Italians who made extensive restorations.

Passing (left) remains of **Roman baths** (1C AD), whose hypocaust and plunge bath are well preserved, you climb through the main entrance to the lower terrace of the sanctuary. The **entrance** was by a Doric propylon; its foundations and the stairway are preserved. The terrace was surrounded on three sides by **porticoes**, from three of which opened various rooms for the sick. On the far side was a massive **retaining wall** which partly survives. Near the middle of the wall are a **fountain**, the **staircase** leading to the middle terrace, and several reservoirs fed by conduits from ferruginous and sulphurous springs and drawn from by invalids taking the cure.

Between the reservoirs and the staircase are the remains of a small **temple**, with the pedestal of a statue of Nero as Asklepios (the inscription records its dedication by the physician Xenophon). The Asklepian festivals which, on the evidence of inscriptions, included athletic games and other contests, were probably held on this terrace. The east (left) side was converted into a large **bath** complex in the 3C AD.

Steps lead to the middle terrace. On the right is an Ionic **temple** *in antis*, dating from the late 4C or early 3C BC, and so the oldest temple in the sanctuary. The capitals, of painted marble, are fine; the rest of the building was in white or black marble. In the floor of the cella was a coffer of marble slabs for votive offerings. The temple was adorned with paintings by Apelles, including the celebrated Aphrodite Anadyomene, removed by Augustus to Rome. Behind the temple is a Roman house on a Greek foundation, probably the **priests' residence**.

In front of the temple, to the left, are the remains of an elaborate **altar**, similar in shape to the altar of Zeus at Pergamon; it is in the form of the Greek letter Π, with a central staircase. Its ceiling (some components survive) was coffered; between the columns of the portico were statues of Asklepios, Hygieia, and members of their family, attributed to the sons of Praxiteles.

To the left of the altar is a Roman **temple**, orientated obliquely. It is a

peripteral Ionic building, with half-fluted columns and a magnificent entablature with floral decoration, part of which remains.

Nearby are the remains of a porticoed **lesche** (club house). In the centre of the south side of the terrace is a monumental **staircase**, and to its left, an **exedra**, with niches for statues.

Roman temple on the middle terrace

The upper terrace occupies the site of the sacred wood. On it stood the great Doric **Temple of Asklepios** (2C BC), now reduced to its foundations. It was peripteral, with six columns by eleven, and a base of three carved steps, the lowest of black marble. The well-preserved pronaos is *in antis*; its threshold a black limestone monolith. In Christian times a chapel of the Panayía tou Társou was installed here: its altar survives. Three sides of the terrace were lined with porticoes, over which houses were later built.

From the upper terrace there is a magnificent **view**. Below is the town of Kos, with its harbour, surrounded by gardens and orchards. In the distance, across the sea, are the Peninsula of Knidos to the southeast, the deeply indented Gulf of Kos to the east, the Promontory of Bodrum (Halikarnassos) to the northeast, and the islands of Psérimos and Kálimnos to the northwest. Behind the temple, steps lead higher up the hill.

The Asklepieion is situated near the foot of **Mt Dhíkaios** (847m). The mountain has many springs the **sacred spring** of Theokritos, including *Vourína* (see p 172).

Leaving the Asklepieion, you continue on the metalled road. After a large army base, take (6km) the signposted right turning for Zía. The rough but motorable track leads across the slopes of **Dhíkaios**, with views down to the green plain below. At (9km) a fork in the road by a small church you branch left and soon, following a cardboard sign, skirt above the largely deserted village (worth some exploration) of **Khaïkhoúdhes** (or Ayios Dhimítrios) where only the church and one farmstead are maintained: the rest of the houses rather dilapidated.

You continue along the rough track through pine trees to (12km) Asómato, one of a cluster of neighbouring hamlets which are situated on the line of transition from the lower agricultural zone to the upper pine-clad slopes of Mt Dhíkaios. Together with Zipári on the main Kos–Kéfalos road below, and Tingáki on the coast below that, they are known collectively as **Asfendioú**. The term denotes the whole of this part of the island, not simply a single settlement, and includes the farming hamlets of Asómato, Zía, Evangelístria, and Lagoúdhi. This cluster of hamlets, however, do have something of a collective identity, removed from the more commercial Zipári and the tourist resort of Tingáki. They have preserved their rural agricultural identity because of the fertility of the soil, the abundant water supply from fresh springs in the area, and their relative isolation from the main roads and the coast. Only Zía has subsidiary attractions, but the area as a whole makes for an interesting afternoon's visit and provides a peaceful break from the busier resorts on the coast.

Asfendioú

Asómato is the least developed of the hamlets, with no tavernas or shops, but a modest kafeneíon. The **church**, large and impressive for the size of the community, is dedicated to the Archangel Michael; its courtyard has linear designs in black and white pebbles.

Broad tracks continue across the hillside to **Zía** which, like Asómato, lies higher up the mountainside than most hamlets in the area. However, adopted as the 'unspoilt Greek village' of daily bus tours, Zía is the most tourist-orientated of all, with tavernas, cafés, and shops selling honey, herbs, rugs and lacework. The village has an annual wine festival, and its working **water mill** can also be visited. The upper reaches of Zía remain quiet and unaffected, and there is an interesting **church of the Theotókos** with three doors on one of the lateral sides, rather than the more conventional entrance. There are spectacular views to the north coast, the islands of Psérimos, Kálimnos, etc.

From both Asómato and Zía tracks lead up through the pine trees to the steep upper slopes of Mt Dhíkaios (which can be climbed in one hour), or on west across the hillside to the plateía of (14km) **Evangelístria**, with kafeneíons and tavernas. Three roads lead off from the far (west) end of the plateía—to Zía (uphill), Lagoúdhi (straight on), and winding down to Zipári. **Lagoúdhi** (15km; refreshments), is the last of the hamlets. 500m beyond Lagoúdhi you leave the metalled road, which descends to the coast, and take the signposted turning (left) for (18km) **Amanioú**, along an unmetalled track. This is another small, quiet, farming settlement; again no accommodation is available, only refreshments. In the area (at Kiparíssi) a Byzantine basilica and a small temple of Demeter and Kore were explored by the Italians, though no remains are now visible.

Entering the village you meet a T-junction, just downhill from (north of) a large whitewashed church with details in blue (and an ancient column drum at the back of the courtyard). The right turn will take you through to modern Pilí, but first you should turn left uphill and make the 2km detour to the castle and deserted village at **Palaió Pilí.**

You follow the road, through farmland, to the end of the metalled surface, where three troughs collect the outflow from a spring, home to a thriving community of frogs and tadpoles. From here a path leads up to the castle on the isolated height (343m) above (to the east).

On the saddle connecting the height with the castle to the main body of Mt Dhíkaios, which rises steeply to the south, are the remains of a ruined **medieval village**. Many of the house walls are still almost complete, and the ruins are interesting, if not spectacular. More noteworthy is the **church of the Ipapantís** (Presentation of Christ) which stands intact amongst the ruined houses, not far from the castle. The church, which has 14C or later frescoes is built over the east part of the central aisle of an Early Christian **basilica**. The foundations of the east side survive in front of the church, where an archway still stands, with two ancient inscribed bases in the foundations. There is a stepped synthronon. Built into the front wall of the church is an earlier doorway with marble lintel. The building incorporates other pieces of ancient masonry. A second church (Ayios Nikólaos; frescoes) lies within the lowest enceinte of the castle, on the low ground southeast of the castle hill.

A section of Cyclopean walling, visible as you approach the site, on the slopes just below (northwest of) the castle, and the discovery here of Mycenaean pottery fragments, suggest that the hill was a defensive acropolis as long ago as the Bronze Age. The concentric **castle**, originally Byzantine, was also used by the Knights. A path leads up the west side of the hill to the entrance to the kastro, through a fallen archway. Inside the castle, the path continues to rise, with traces of rock-cut and cobbled steps. Where the path first turns to the left, there is a squared block on the ground, with the arms of the order beside those of a knight. Little remains of the interior of the castle but there is room to walk around and a good view down to the coast.

Returning to Amanioú, you continue on the metalled road to (19km) **Pilí** (tavernas, kafeneíons), another farming community which owes its livelihood to the abundance of spring water on the slopes of Mt Dhíkaios. You turn left (south) onto the main road running through the town, and proceed straight uphill. As the main road starts to bend to the right, a track leads off to the left and skirts the southwest edge of Pilí. You take this track, and continue until it re-enters the town further uphill (south).

The first right turn then leads down to the *Charmyleion* (modern **Kharmíli**), nestling unfenced among the houses. This is a Hellenistic vaulted hypogeum thought to be the remains of the heroön of Kharmyleos, a local mythological figure said to have made the four fountains (springs) of Pilí. Another tradition maintains that Herakles, after an argument with the Koan king Khalkon, removed himself here and married a local woman. The hypogeum, and the small church of the Cross built on top of it, incorporate many ancient blocks from an earlier Ionic structure. One of the blocks in the front wall of the church has an inscribed Byzantine cross, while another has an ancient inscription which mentions the hero by name. Along the lateral sides of the dark, damp vault beneath are 12 deep coffin-sized recesses.

You return to the main road and pass through Pilí, heading roughly south. The winding road, with good views across Kos and over to the neighbouring islands, crosses the Dhíkaios range and descends to (27km) **Kardhámaina**, ancient *Halasarna*, on the south coast.

The busy town, formerly a fishing village, has lost its character to extensive tourist development, with hotels spreading along the coast to exploit the long sandy beaches which stretch northeast and (especially) southwest, continuing intermittently to Kamári in the Gulf of Kéfalos. Quieter beaches can be found wherever there are breaks of any size between the hotels lining the coast. All forms of watersports, including skiing and parascending, are available and there is an energetic nightlife. Kardhámaina has a caique service to Nísiros, with excursions in season. There is a notable festival of the Panayía on 7 September.

About 100m inland from the main square behind the harbour mole, you can turn right at a roundabout (past the Memories Bar) to see the remains of a three-aisled Early Christian basilica.

Starting from the same point and following the main shopping street behind the sea front, you cross a large bridge. Immediately before (right; 500m from the harbour) the Christópoulos Family Restaurant, hotel construction (now aban-doned) brought to light important ancient remains, now being excavated by the University of Athens (G. Alevras). An Early Christian **basilica**, probably destroyed in the earthquake of AD 554, overlies remains of the Hellenistic **Temple of Apollo Halasarnas** (impressive architectural fragments) and asso-ciated structures. On the far side of the hill of Tholós (perhaps the acropolis of *Halasarna*) which rises immediately behind this site, there are slight traces of a Hellenistic **theatre** which was built into the hillside. Three rows of seats in the cavea were found. In the fields between the Tholós hill and the Apollon Hotel (on the 'bridge' road into Kardhámaina) and best reached from there though access is not easy, are remains of the apse of an Early Christian **basilica** (Ayía Theótis, 5C), on the site of earlier structures.

Kos town to the northern coastal strip and Kéfalos

43.5km by road.

Hotels and restaurants in Andimákhia, Kéfalos, Marmári, Mastikhári, and Tingáki (area code 0242)

■ **Andimákhia**
C **Thalássia Avra** (18);
8000–13,000 drs. Tel. 51501.
D **Fainarétti** (12); 6000–7000
drs. Tel. 51395.

■ **Kéfalos/Kamári**
A **Kárlos Village** (392), pool,
tennis etc.; NPA. Tel. 71213,
71313. April –Oct.
C **Kokalákis Beach** (23); NPA.
Tel. 71466, 71496. April–Oct.
C **Kórdhistos** (38); NPA. Tel.
71251. May–Oct.
E **María** (8); 7000–9000 drs. Tel.
71308. April–Oct.

■ **Marmári**
A **Angel Mare** (196); pool, tennis;
16,500–19,500 drs. Tel. 41622/5;
fax 41663. April–Oct.
B **Yialákis** (F/As) (73);
9500–19,500 drs. Tel. 41586,
41686.
C **Blue Jay** (56); 8950–10,650
drs. Tel. 41533. April–Oct.

■ **Mastikhári**
A **Kanári Beach** (108); pool,
tennis etc.; 9000–14,000 drs. Tel.
51099, 51698; fax 51099.
May–Oct.
A **Neptune Village** (F/As) (124);
pool; 24,900–43,600 drs. Tel.
41785; fax 41646.
C **Artemis 2** (F/As) (13);
6430–12,280 drs. Tel. 51161/2.
April–Oct.
C **Kíma** (Wave) (13); 5000–7000
drs. Tel. 52545. May–Oct.

■ **Tingáki**
A **Tingáki Beach** (169); pool;
14,000–19,000 drs. Tel. 69446/7;
fax 69251. April–Oct.
B **Tingáki's Star** (73); pool;
9800–14,100 drs. Tel. 69541/2;
fax 29047
C **Aspro Spíti** (F/As) (26); pool;
8700–11,600 drs. Tel. 29296,
29189. April–Oct.
C **Méni Beach** (37);
9500–11,000 drs. Tel. 29217.
C **Villa Andréas** (31);
9000–11,000 drs. Tel. 29221; fax
29358.

On the outskirts of Kos town, you leave on the left the turning for the Asklepieion, which is visible from the road 1km further on, with Mt Dhíkaios behind. Spring water from the upper slopes of the mountain irrigates the long and fertile agricultural plain which runs down to the sea along the north coast, to the right.

At **Zipári** (9km) which had an early **basilica** of Ayios Pávlos (three-aisled with narthex; mosaics and baptistery with font) a winding road leads left (south). In the nearby hamlet of **Kapamá** is another **basilica** (of Ayios Ioánnis) three-aisled and with a reasonably well-preserved baptistery. The by-road makes for the upper hamlets of Asfendioú (3km; 244m, see above), on the slopes of Dhíkaios.

To the left is the mountain ridge which forms the backbone of the island; to the right, over the sea, are the islands of Psérimos and Kálimnos. Beyond Zipári is the turning (right) for **Tingáki** (3km), a busy holiday resort on the north coast, with full tourist facilities and a wide sandy beach stretching westwards unbroken to **Marmári** (watersports, particularly windsurfing), a smaller holiday resort with a larger indigenous population.

The lush fields around Marmári, watered from an aqueduct which runs along the roadside from the mountain slopes above all the way down to the sea, supports sheep, goats, and even cows. There is also a horse-riding school, on the east side of Marmári. Between Tingáki and Marmári, just behind the beach, is a large salt flat which, with the scrubland surrounding it, has been designated a nature reserve. This forms a 'break' between the developed tourist centres to either side. The area is home mostly to birds (marsh harriers, kingfishers, flamingo and many other waders) but is also an important sanctuary for turtles. The stretch of beach below the nature reserve, away from the bars and hotels, is considerably quieter than those by the resorts to either side.

Near the dispersed town of (15km) **Linópotis**, there is a ruined Roman **aqueduct**. Turnings lead (right) to Marmári and (left), past a large pool with fish and eels, to Pilí and Kardhámaina (3km and 11km respectively; see above).

Further on (right) is a road for the holiday resort of **Mastikhári** (6km; good beach with watersports; scooter hire; ferry service (daily) to Psérimos and Kálimnos), at the western end of the coastal plain. Before you enter Mastikhári, 1km off to the right are remains of the three-aisled 5C AD Early Christian **basilica of Ayios Ioánnis**, with a baptistery: its mosaics are covered.

Beyond the Mastikhári turn and a large windmill, the main road rises to a plateau at the southwest end of the Dhíkaios range. On the plateau are the extensive remains of the large **castle of Andimákhia** (144m), otherwise known as Soróko. A rough but motorable track (3km) leads from a signposted turning left (southeast) off the main road to the high and impressive outer walls of the castle on an elevated plateau at the west end of the Dhíkaios range. The site is undeservedly neglected by visitors, perhaps because of its isolation.

Built by the Knights in a position which commands the otherwise deserted scrubby plateau, the castle has a good view southwards over the coast around Kardhámaina and the seas beyond. The crenellated walls, principally of rubble and mortar, tower up to 12m above the land around. Inside the castle, the ground level rises to only 2m below the height of the walls. The castle is triangular in plan and originally had a drawbridge in front of its only entrance and corner towers. You enter by steps through the outer gate into a semicircular enceinte, and proceed through the inner gate into the castle proper. Above the inner gate are the quartered arms of Aubusson and of the Order.

Inside the castle walls are the tumbled ruins of numerous houses and cisterns, and two churches. The church nearest the gate, which has been restored, preserves one patch of fresco inside, and its walls incorporate a marble block with the date 1520 and three coats of arms, one of which (top left) belongs to Fabrizio del Carretto, Grand Master of the Order from 1513 to 1521. The second church also has decaying and fragmentary frescoes. A ruined wall to the right of the door of the church has an inverted block bearing the arms of the Order quartered with those of Aubusson. The remains of a tower at the southwest corner include steps and a part of the pavement, otherwise few details of the castle's structure are preserved.

You return to the main road, now descending, and soon reach (25km) **Andimákhia** (128m), a straggling village of 2089 inhabitants, an important centre of communications in this part of the island: roads lead to Mastikhári to the northwest, Kardhámaina to the southeast, and south to Kéfalos.

The island's **airport** is 2km outside Andimákhia, on the Kardhámaina road (but served by the Kéfalos bus from Kos town, as well as special buses of Olympic Airways). You continue on the Kéfalos road and, roughly 2km further on, pass an unsignposted fork to the right onto a rough road, immediately before a plain whitewashed church. That road leads westwards a few kilometres into an attractive area known as **Pláka**, with a recreation park set in a pine forest. Tracks through the forest extend for a fair distance. Though the scenery changes little, it makes a refreshing contrast to the seaside or more exposed landscape. Vehicles can be parked by the picnic area, which is provided with tables and benches, barbecue pits, and fresh water from a nearby spring. Here also is a colony of peacocks, whose calls provide a good homing signal for wanderers in the woods.

The main road continues, with views to the end of the island, dominated by **Mt Látra** (428m) and known as the Peninsula of Kéfalos. The road gradually descends to cross a stream and then rises quickly to a bare plain, where the island contracts into an isthmus only 1.5km across. The road approaches the north coast and then descends to (34km) the shore of the Bay of Kamáres, on the south (fine beaches, quieter away from the hotels): the area has considerable tourist facilities. In the bay is the picturesque St Nicholas Rock, with a small chapel. At **Ayios Stéfanos**, opposite the rock, are the impressive ruins of two linked Early Christian **basilicas** (through the grounds of the Hotel Kórdhistos). The larger has an atrium, narthex and baptistery: there is also a mortuary chapel nearby.

The next resort is **Kamári**. The road climbs up from here through hills pitted with caves to 43.5km **Kéfalos** (106m; 1976 inhab.) which dominates the Bay of Kamáres. On the outskirts of Kéfalos is a castle, used by the Knights but an earlier foundation, with some substantial sections of walling.

From here there is a road to (5km) Limiónas, on the opposite (north) coast of the island, with a small sandy beach and one taverna.

About 1km south of the village are the remains of the ancient capital city of *Astypalaia*. The church of Panayía Palatianí (rebuilt 1988) on a hillock to the left of the road was constructed over a Hellenistic Doric Temple of Demeter; whose stylobate and some column drums remain; many ancient blocks are built into the surrounding walls. Further down are fragments of defence walls, which could be those Alcibiades had built to strengthen the island against the Lacedaimonians in the Peloponnesian War. About 10 minutes further (sign (left): 'Palatia'), delightfully situated among pines, are the remains of a Hellenistic Doric **temple** *in antis* and a **theatre** (two rows of seats survive; others were removed by the Germans).

Immediately beyond, the road forks, left to the **Cave of Asprípetra**, 3.5km southeast, which has yielded Neolithic objects and evidence for cult activity; in the 4–3C BC Pan and the Nymphs were venerated there. This road also gives access to the **monastery of Ayios Ioánnis** (5km; view).The right branch goes to the coast (5km; beach) and the **monastery of Ayios Ioánnis Theológos** (5km). The two are connected by tracks.

Nísiros

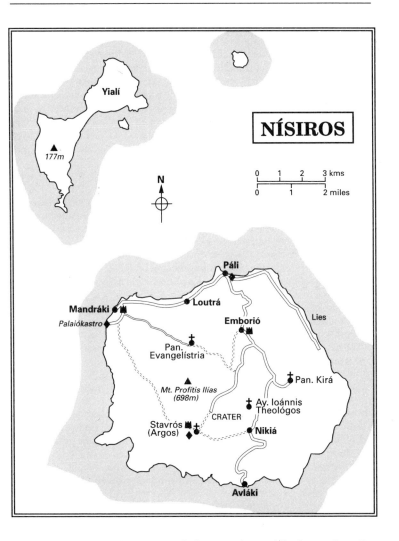

Nísiros is a geological curiosity and often visited as such by day trip from Kos or other islands rather than for longer stays. Formed of an extinct volcano, its crater walls encircle a deep central depression. Although the valley floor and slopes are fertile, the volcanic core is surrounded by a strange, hot, steaming, yellow landscape with sulphurous fumes. Perched on the rim of the crater are two spectacularly situated villages with wonderful views. The volcanic soil is exceptionally fruitful and well-wooded, and there are many species of butterflies and insects. It is particularly pleasant in the spring and there are attractive walks. The island's hot springs gained it a reputation for hydrotherapy even in antiquity and there are substantial modern establishments which, having fallen into disrepair, are now being refurbished. The medieval castles are not as impressive as the Classical citadel, whose walls are as fine as any in Greece. The port has plenty of hotels, rooms and restaurants for its size and there are others in Páli, while Nikiá also offers some rooms. There are excellent, though rather distant, beaches on the west beyond Páli, and other smaller stretches nearer the port.

The island, with a population of 961, is due south of Kos and about the same distance (less than 20km) from the coast of Asia Minor, where the peninsula of Knidos forms the southern arm of the 'Ceramic Gulf'. More or less circular, it is about 10km in either direction and 30sq km in area.

A useful guide by K. Mantoudhákis is available locally, translated into various languages.

History

Mythology provides a context for the creation of *Nisyros* in the battle of Gods and Giants. Poseidon picked up a lump of Kos and used it to bury the giant Polybotes, whose vain efforts to get free explain the activity of the volcano. Virtually nothing is known of the prehistory of the island but it is said by Homer (*Iliad*. II. 676) to have contributed to the contingent which went to Troy under the leadership of the sons of Thessalos. There are vague traditions of colonists from Caria, Kos, Rhodes and Argos. In any case it was a Dorian island.

The main Classical centre was undoubtedly at Palaiókastro, above Mandráki. The existence and nature of other sites (e.g. Argos) is much more problematic, but there was certainly a Roman settlement at Páli. At the time of the Persian Wars, although independent, it was under the control of Artemisia of Halikarnassos, but the ships which went with hers to the battle of Salamis deserted to the other side (Herod. VII. 99). In the Peloponnesian War Nisyros supported first Athens, then Sparta, then Athens again. In the 4C the island issued its own coinage. In the later 3C it was subject to the Macedonians but given back its independence, only to fall under the power of Rhodes. The Nisyran admiral Gnomagoras was honoured for his service in the Rhodian navy. Later it became subject to the Ptolemies and then to Rome.

In the 7C AD the island was plagued by pirates—Arabs, Saracens, Algerians. In 1204 it was incorporated into the Byzantine state and in 1312 taken by the Knights of St. John. From 1315 to 1385 it was controlled by a renegade knight, Assanti, who took to piracy. In 1457 Nisyros was attacked by the Turks and apparently deserted for some time. In 1471 the authority of the Knights was reasserted but piracy remained a problem. Buondelmonti, writing in the 15C, mentions five castles—Mandrachi, Palaeocastro, Pandenichi, Nicia and Argos. From 1533 the island was under Turkish control, its subsequent history following that of the rest of the Dodecanese.

Getting to Nísiros

■ **By boat**. The island is visited once or twice a week in season by **ferries** running between Piraeus (or Rafína) and Rhodes, via some of the Cyclades and most of the Dodecanese. In winter there is not more than one such service a week, sometimes none. These connections are augmented by services (twice weekly in either direction) of the vessel *Nísos Kálimnos* on the run Kálimnos, Kos, Nísiros, Tílos, Sími, Rhodes, Kastellórizo. In summer there are twice daily services between Nísiros and Kardhámaina on Kos; less frequent out of season. There are occasional **hydrofoil** connections with Rhodes and intervening islands.

Getting around Nísiros

■ **By road**. The **bus** route is simple. Starting in Mandráki, it runs along the coast via Loutrá to Páli, then climbs to Emborió and continues to Nikiá. There are two basic services daily (early morning and lunchtime) with some additional trips in summer. Excursion buses meet boats from Kos for trips to the volcano and inland villages. There is only one **taxi**. **Scooters** are available for hire in Mandráki.

■ There are **boat trips** to a good beach on the island of Yialí.

■ **Travel agent. Nísiros Tours**; tel. 0242 31254.

Mandráki

Hotels and restaurants in Mandráki (area code 0242)

C **Kháritos** (11); NPA. Tel. 31322.
C **Porfíris** (38); 8600–11,300 drs.
Tel. 31376. April–Oct.
Also (unclassified) **Romántso** (tel. 31340), **Tría Adhélfia** (tel. 31344).
   Rooms: Nísiros, tel. 31052;

Karáva, tel. 31375; **Dhrosiá**, tel. 31328; **Ipapandí**, tel. 31185; **Foúkiaxi**, tel. 31453

Restaurants: Karáva (waterfront), **Nísiros** and **Sfakianoú** (in the village).

Mandráki (pop. 661) is the port and main centre of the island, with a fair range of accommodation and tavernas. The quay, with several hotels, is plain. From it the village straggles westward along the coast. The nicest part is the original core at the far end. Here the older houses are squeezed into a narrow valley reaching inland, where they would have been partly hidden from the sea. There is a small Folk Museum and a curious open air display of traditional objects. The public tank is an indication of the need to conserve water, and many houses have their own cisterns.

On the headland where the valley reaches the shore is an interesting Venetian castle (1312) reached by 180 steps: the structure includes some ancient masonry. Within the castle is the 14C **church of the Panayía Spilianí** (officially Koímisis tis Theotókou), named after the cave from which the church is formed. Originally part of a wealthy monastery, with its own boat and issuing its own coinage, the church has a fine wooden carved templon (1725) and numerous votives. The ancient icon of the patron was sheathed in silver in 1798. There is a side altar to Ayios Kharálambos. Amongst the offerings a silver boat is said to have been dedicated by a pirate who was obstructed by the Virgin from robbing the monastery and subsequently repented.

Some 4–2C BC graves have been excavated at Ayios Ioánnis. Also near Mandráki (at Misokhóri) is the 13C chapel of Ayios Mámas.

About 20 minutes walk inland from the castle, following signs to 'Kastro' through the village on to a pleasant path along the side of the valley, you come

to one of the most impressive Classical sites in Greece, the massive fortifications of the **ancient city** of *Nisyros* (Palaiókastro). You can enter through a superb gateway at the southeast corner by a tower with bolt holes for its two doors. Inside, flights of steps give access to the ramparts. The exterior of the first tower seaward of the gate bears the 4C inscription ΔΑΜΟΣΙΟΝ ΤΟ ΧΩΡΙΟΝ ΠΕΝΤΕ ΠΟΔΕΣ ΑΠΟ ΤΟ ΤΕΙΧΕΟΣ (the space for five

Walls of the ancient town at Palaiókastro

feet from the wall is public property): intended to keep the area in front of the wall free from any constructions that might help an enemy. This line of wall probably continued to the site of the later Venetian castle at the sea. Of the southern series of towers, the second from the west is preserved in places to its original 19 courses, with some sections of the guttering. There has been no excavation within the fortifications.

From the roadway outside the site it is is possible to continue walking to Stavroú monastery and Nikiá or, on foot or by road, to the Evangelístria monastery (for both see below).

Mandráki to Loutrá, Palí, Emborió and Nikiá

By road, 15km.

Hotels and restaurants in Páli (area code 0242)	
C White Beach (47); 6000–9000 drs. Tel. 31497/8; fax 31389. May–Oct. 1km outside village. **C Ellenís** (10); 7100–9500 drs.	Tel 31453. Also **Rooms**. Several **restaurants** on the harbour.

The flat coast road to the east soon passes (1km) **Loutrá**, with a desalination plant, a small harbour, and a hydrotherapeutic establishment in the process of reconstruction, which makes use of the hot springs. Further on, by the large White Beach Hotel, a by-road leads immediately to (4km) **Páli**, ancient *Pale*, an attractive small fishing village with some accommodation and three or four restaurants fronting the harbour. Beyond the village is a narrow sandy beach then an enormous hydro building, again being repaired. Behind the hydro the tiny 19C church of Panayía Thermianí is installed in a corner of the substantial remains of a **Roman bath** complex. Part of the vault survives and the pool at the far end (coins) may be part of the original construction, although the original floor of the building must have been considerably lower. Dawkins and Wace (BSA 1906) visited a site called Elliniká 'close by at the northeastern cape of the island' which they considered medieval.

Beyond Páli the narrow concrete track continues to the flat stone and shingle beaches of **Yialiskári** and **Liés**, eventually ending in fine sand at Pakhiámmos.

Returning to the main road and turning left, the road climbs, through rich landscape with views to the sea, and passes near to **Emborió**. The little village—occupying the site of one of the medieval castles of Nísiros (possibly Pandenichi), which was largely destroyed by an earthquake in 1933—perches on the edge of the crater's rim (views). An old stepped trackway descends to the crater bottom and another, in the opposite direction, provides a better route for walkers back in the direction of Páli. The population has shrunk to 41. The main church was built in the 19C and reconstructed with aid from New Yorkers of Nisiran descent in 1965. At the highest point of the village is the little **church** of the Taxiárkhis of c 1300.

Past Emborió a branch off the main road leads down into the **crater** and can be taken as far (c 5km) as the **volcanic deposits** at the southern edge. Hot, steaming and sulphurous, in a lunar landscape, it is an intriguing rather than a pleasant excursion but one which is regarded as obligatory by most visitors.

About half way between Emborió and Nikiá a turn to the left leads down to the monastery of **Kirá Panayía** on the hillside high above Liés. This was probably an early 18C foundation but was rebuilt in 1863 and again after the 1933 earthquake. Also between the two villages is a medieval **fort**, in good position for a lookout post, called Parlettia. Just before Nikiá, to the right of the road, is the **church of Ayios Ioánnis Theológos** (1925), possibly on the site of an earlier monastery, nestling under a crag overlooking the crater.

Past Nikiá a road winds down to the coastal hamlet of Avláki (no facilities). The area called Khorió, on this road not far below Nikiá, is said to have some Roman remains. **Nikiá** itself, although bereft of much of its original population (now 61), is a charming, friendly and well kept village (some rooms available; tel. 0242 31401 or 31367). The church has a sculptured marble templon and other furniture; ornate capitals and other architectural members and reliefs must come from an earlier building. Its situation offers spectacular views, over the crater itself, back to Emborió and south over the sea to Tílos.

Visible from a terrace at the top of the village, on a hill between the volcano and the sea, gleam the white buildings of the **monastery of the Cross** (tou Stavroú). You can follow paths (keep to the south side of the intervening hill; the road visible from the village comes up from the volcano and Emborió and does not connect with Nikiá, in spite of appearances) down to the monastery (c 50 minutes) which is situated in the area known as *Argos*, the site of one of the ancient towns of Nísiros, an Early Christian basilica and a medieval castle. The monastic complex is modern though seems to incorporate some older material (altar and floor of church). The archaeology of the place deserves study.

From the monastery you can continue on foot round Mt Profítis Ilías and down to Mandráki. It is a pleasant entirely rural route, not difficult after an initial climb, and takes a total time of about three hours (from Nikiá to Mandráki). There are several small churches by the wayside. Two of these, above the road to the right about an hour and a half hours from Stavrós, although dilapidated, have some elaborate architectural elements in marble. The higher has a cylindrical drum supporting the dome; the lower appears to be on the site of a Hellenistic or Roman temple. Also accessible from this track (ask directions before leaving) is the interesting if humble monastic complex of **Siónes** (1733; the dedication is to the Yénnisis tis Theotókou), with considerable surviving frescoes. On the way down you can pick out the fortifications of the Classical site at Palaiókastro which is the point where you return to Mandráki.

Mandráki, via Evangelístria monastery to Emborió/the volcano

On foot, an hour and a half from Mandráki to the monastery; a further 1 hour to Emborió direct, or 2 hours to the volcano; vehicles can be taken on the dirt road as far as the monastery (6km).

Behind the Hotel Romántso near the quay the road (signed Kástro, Panayía) at first simply skirts the upper edge of Mandráki (the road can also be joined from the west end of the village, or via the Kástro path), then turns inland and uphill. On the climb to the monastery there are good retrospective views of both the Classical and the Venetian kastros. The dirt road can in places be avoided by taking the older track. Some distance off this road to the right (ask directions) is the small deserted monastery of Ayios Ioánnis Pródhromos, usually called **Armás**, with extensive, though dilapidated, fresco decoration (mid 17C) and a more recent (20C) carved wooden templon. The church was refurbished in 1647 but the date of the original foundation is uncertain.

The modest **monastery of the Panayía Evangelístria** occupies a clean and pleasant compound in an attractive orchard setting, high on the hillside, with the central peak of Profítis Ilías, the cone of the volcano, looming above. Although probably a 17C foundation most of the complex is more recent. Follow the path along a wire fence and you come out above a deep valley which intervenes between the mountain of Profítis Ilías to the right and the rim of the crater to the left. If you keep right, then descend into and cross the valley to follow the path visible on slopes of the mountain opposite, you will eventually descend by a rather overgrown path to the bed of the crater. From that point there is a road to the volcano proper (right) or a steep stepped path (left) up to Emborió. The easier route to Emborió is to keep along the left side of the valley at the level of the monastery.

Island of Yialí

The small island of Yialí, 5km north of Nísiros and between it and Kos, is also of volcanic origin. The shape of the island has been radically altered by the quarrying of pumice which is a major industry. Yialí is also a source of obsidian, which was sometimes used for the manufacture of vases in later prehistoric times. Several ancient sites have been discovered, from the Neolithic period onwards. Visits to the island are not encouraged other than by excursion boats which run from Mandráki to its good beaches (tavernas).

The volcano

Léros

Léros (Λέρος; anc. *Leros*) is imbued with a strong sense of history, but here it is recent rather than Classical, and its many rich and widely travelled merchant families, whose benefactions are recorded everywhere, have given the place a cosmopolitan air. The grand Italianate buildings of Lakkí, belonging to the island's period as an Italian naval headquarters, contrast with the contemporary Greek neoclassical houses of Alinda. There is a fine historical museum.

The deep bays from which the island's naval importance derives make for an interesting coastline. The scenery is impressive, even theatrical, though the interior is rather bare and not very good for walking. But the coastal plains can be fertile and there are one or two pleasant resorts (Alinda and Xirókambos); the beaches, however, are not special. Quiet and relatively undeveloped, Léros has many devotees, especially among discerning Greek families several of whom have established themselves here in recent years. The mental hospital installed here in buildings vacated by the Italians, and for which the island as a whole has undeservedly become notorious, is not obtrusive.

Léros lies 40km from the coast of Turkey. Lipsí is to the north, Pátmos to the northwest, and Kálimnos immediately to the south. It is 15km long, northwest—southeast, and 1.2–6.5km wide; the population is 8061. Like Pátmos, Léros both has a highly indented coastline and consists of three peninsulas joined by two narrow isthmuses. Covering 54sq. km, the gently mountainous island rises to a peak at Mt Klidhí (320m) at the east end of a mountain range which spans the northernmost peninsula of the island. While the mountains are generally barren, the valleys have some trees and produce olives, carobs, figs and other fruit, tobacco and wine. The extensive network of military roads constructed by the Italians has been well maintained and covers a much greater area than in the islands to the north.

History

Archaeological finds from the north of the island, near Parthéni, show that *Leros* was inhabited in Neolithic times. Historical traditions variously mention Carians, Leleges, Phoenicians, Lycians and Eteocretans as early colonisers, followed by Dorians and finally the Ionians of Miletos. *Leros* is thought by some to have been one of Homer's 'Kalydnian isles', providing ships for the expedition against Troy under the leadership of Pheidippos and Antiphos, sons of Thessalos and grandsons of Herakles. The name *Leros* is first used of the island in an epigram of Phokylides, the 6C BC Milesian poet. The name also appears in Herodotos (V. 125), Thucydides (VIII. 26–7) and these sources, together with inscriptions, make it clear that by the 5C BC *Leros* had become a deme of *Miletos*. The island retained this status until the Roman period. Occupied by the Persians in the early 5C, Leros was later part of Athens' Delian League.

Pherekydes, who wrote a lost history of *Leros*, and Demodokos the philosopher both came from the island. *Leros* was also famed for its honey; and its inhabitants for being unprincipled. The main settlement in Classical times was probably at Broúzi, just east of Ayía Marína. The renowned

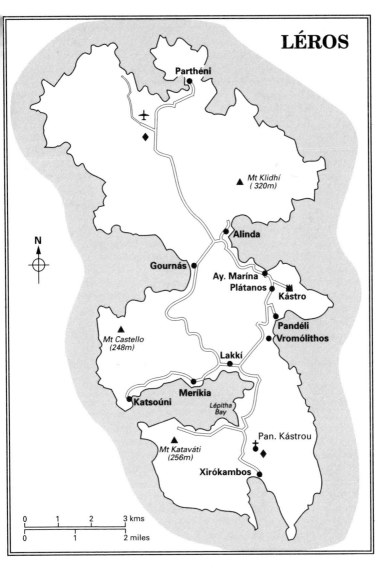

temple of Artemis, where the grieving sisters of Meleager were transformed into guinea-fowl, was in the north of the island, presumably near the modern Parthéni. In his account of the Peloponnesian War, Thucydides mentions the strategic value of *Leros'* deep gulfs, and Plutarch its significance in navigation. Both these features have had a strong influence on the island's subsequent history.

Leros was inhabited continuuously into medieval times, when it was also known as *Lernos*. In 1088 Alexis I Comnenus, Emperor of Byzantium, ceded large parts of the island to the Blessed Christodoulos along with Leipsoi and Patmos. The inhabitants protested and, according to local tradition, threw the monk into the sea, whereupon he spread his habit across the surface of the water and floated to Patmos. On another visit to *Leros*, the Blessed Christodoulos was responsible for the construction of the 11C church of Ay. Ioánnis Theológos in the area of modern Lakkí, now overlain by its late 19C successor. Like Kos and Rhodes, *Leros* was acquired by the Knights in 1306. They enlarged and reinforced the existing Byzantine castle at Plátanos. In 1522 the island fell to the Turks after persistent raids and attacks throughout the 15C. The Venetian admiral Foskolos temporarily occupied *Leros* in 1648.

During the War of Independence, Leros' bays and surrounding seas were the scene of much naval action but, along with the rest of the Dodecanese, the island was returned to Turkey in 1830. The Italian occupation followed in 1912, and the British Royal Navy set up a base in Lakkí in 1917. This centre was greatly developed by the Italians after 1923, when their possession of the Dodecanese was internationally recognised. On 3 February 1926, Admiral de Pinedo ended his pioneer flight from Australia here. The Italians also redesigned Lakkí in a grand city style, and implemented a policy of Italianisation. After the Italian armistice in the Second World War, British forces occupied the island, but were heavily defeated by German troops in the battle of November 1943. British, along with Greek forces, returned in 1945 to terminate the German occupation. The island was reunited with Greece in 1948. More recently it has been a place of internment for political prisoners.

A useful study of the ancient history of the island is J.L. Benson, *Ancient Leros*, 1963.

■ **Festivals.** During the pre-Lenten Carnival men and women compose satirical verses which children, dressed as monks, recite at parties given in houses where a marriage has taken place during the previous year. This custom has been linked to ancient ceremonies in honour of Dionysos at Eleusis.

Other major festivals on the island, featuring traditional songs and dancing, are those of Ay. Marína (17 July, Ay. Marína), Panayía Kástrou (15 Aug, Plátanos), Ay. Ioánnis Theológos (26 Sept, Lakkí) and Ay. Kirá (19 Oct, Parthéni). At Alinda there are a wine festival and sports competitions in the first half of August. A peculiarity of local law, shared with Pátmos, is that all real property passes in the female line, with the result that nearly all the houses and landed property belong to women.

Getting to Léros

■ **By air**. There are daily **flights** between Athens and Léros by Olympic Airways (offices at the airport (tel. 0247 22777) and Plátanos, on the Lakkí road (tel. 0247 22844)).

■ **By sea**. By sea the major **ferries** make daily connections to and from

Kálimnos, Kos and Rhodes to the south, Pátmos and Piraeus, often making stops in the Cyclades en route, to the north and west. In winter these services are kept up four times weekly.

Small **local boats** also run a daily service between Xirókambos on Léros and Mirtiés on Kálimnos, and between Lakkí, or Parthéni in bad weather, and Lipsí. These services are maintained all year, weather permitting. In the summer months the MV *Nísos Kálimnos* provides a twice weekly **service** from Rhodes through the Dodecanese to Sámos and back, and **hydrofoils** ply the same route daily.

Getting around Léros

■ **By road**. As in other islands in the north Dodecanese, Léros has only one **bus**. The driver is also a fisherman, which results in occasional services (usually the evening run) being cancelled without notice. The normal service provides four trips daily from Plátanos via Alinda to Parthéni and back; five daily from Plátanos via Lakkí to Xirókambos and back. On each route there is one early evening service, all others running between early morning and early afternoon.

There are plenty of **taxis**, with ranks in Lakkí (tel. 0247 22550; at the junction of the Plátanos road with the waterfront), Ay. Marína (tel. 0247 23340), and Plátanos (tel. 0247 23070; below the plateia, towards Lakkí. The bus staion is also here).

Scooters are very widely available (Xirókambos, Lakkí, Plátanos, Ay. Marína, Alinda), and **bicycles** can be hired; also **cars** (Lakkí, Ay. Marína).

■ **Travel Agent. Kastís Agency**, 9 Vasiléos Yioryíou, Lakkí. Tel. 0247 22872, 225 00; also in Ayía Marína, tel. 0247 22140; fax 0247 23500; and one or two others.

■ **Police**. Tel. 0247 22222.

■ **First aid**. Tel. 0247 23251.

Lakkí

Hotels and restaurants in Lakkí (area code 0247)	
C Paradhosiakó Agélou (7); 5000–7000 drs. Tel. 22514. April–Oct. **D Miramáre** (16); 6000–6800. Tel. 22053, 22469; fax 22053.	**E Katerína** (10); 6000 drs. Tel. 22460. **Rooms: Pension Zórzou**. Tel. 22338. **Restaurants: Goudhís, Sótos**.

Boats pass through a channel 400m wide into the broad **Bay of Pórto Lagó** and dock at the west side of Lakkí, with its prominent and now infamous mental asylum. The grandly designed town, with wide boulevards and streets and large buildings constructed in the 1920s and 1930s to accommodate the numerous Italian personnel, now seems oversized for its 2366 inhabitants. Many buildings are deserted and decaying. The town is not a great tourist centre, and even the OTE and Olympic Airways offices here have shut down in recent years, although the **post office** remains open (on Vas. Pávlou, by the junction with 7th Martíou; open Mon–Fri, 07.30–14.00). There is a **tourist information office** on the quay (tel. 0247 22937).

Various relics of the Italian occupation include the fortified lookouts on the heights east of the mouth of the bay, and on the knoll immediately west of the ferry pier. From here a road leads west through pine trees round the coast, passing a small beach and ruined gateways, tunnels, lookouts and other buildings from the Italian occupation before reaching (1km) **Meríkia** (taverna, beach). It continues to (4km) **Katsoúni**, on the headland enclosing Pórto Lagó bay on the west.

East of the ferry pier at Lakkí, the broad and impressive waterfront has **war memorials**, particularly that commemorating the Greek warship *Queen Olga*, sunk here by the Germans on 26 September 1943, with the loss of its crew of 71. The **plateia**, a few streets inland and rather subdued, has been renamed Eleftherías, and contains a bust of Paris Roussos (1875–1966), an islander prominent in the struggle against the foreign occupation of the Dodecanese. From the plateia a road leads north to the Bay of Goúrna, with beaches and summer tavernas.

Lakkí to the north: Alinda and Parthéni

13km by road.

Hotels and restaurants in Alinda, Plátano and Vromólithos (area code 0247)

■ **Alinda**
C **Alinda** (24); 5500–7000 drs. Tel. 23226. May–Oct.
C **Arkhontikó Angélou** (9); 8080–12,800 drs. Tel. 22749, 22514.
C **Khrissoúla** (F/A) (31); 8000–13,000 drs. Tel. 22452.
C **Rodhiá** (F/A) (42); 11,000–14,000 drs. Tel. 24070, 23883.
  Rooms: **Yiánna**, tel. 23153.
  Restaurants: **Panórama, Fínikes, Kostarás** (fish).

■ **Plátanos/Ayía Marína**
Rooms: **Rosangélika & Argó**, tel. 24448; **Plátanos**, tel. 22608.
  Restaurants: **Lemonís, Kioúpia, Gláros, Kapilió**.

■ **Vromólithos**
A **Filoxenía** (F/A); NPA. Tel. 24364.
C **Gláros** (F/A) (28); NPA. Tel. 24358, 23438.
C **Tony's Beach** (F/A); NPA. Tel. 24742.

The main road out of town leads north from the east end of the waterfront to the island's capital Plátanos/Ay. Marína—and is lined with houses and hardware shops all along the way. At 1km you pass the turning (right) for **Vromólithos** and (2km) another for **Pandéli**, both in the same bay.

At 3km, **Plátanos** is now merged with (3.5km) its coastal sibling **Ayía Marína** (pop. 2493), prettier and more appealing than Lakkí, and with better shops. In contrast to the Italianate architecture of Lakkí, here, and also at Alinda, there are many neoclassical buildings from the late 19C and early 20C. These, including the public buildings, were mostly funded by expatriate bene-factors. Turning left after the taxi rank in Plátanos you come to the busy plateia. Like the plateia in Lakkí, this is named after a member of the prominent Roussos family, this time Nikítas, a shipowner and benefactor.

The road to **Ayía Marína** leads down to the left (north) and has the **post office** (open Mon–Fri 08.00–14.00) and **OTE** (open Mon–Fri 07.30–15.00), housed in the same building. From the plateia in Plátanos you can also continue straight uphill for the kastro, well signposted for both the shorter route (800m of concrete steps laid over old cobbles) and the longer (2km by road, passing a row of disused windmills).

The **kástro** (open daily 07.00–19.00, free entry), originally Byzantine and rebuilt by the Knights, was substantially restored after heavy damage by bombing in the Second World War. It incorporates ancient blocks, and is situated on a height inaccessible from the east and precipitous on the other sides. The outer walls are particularly impressive. There are good views of the central and southern parts of the island, including the three main bays of Pórto Lagó, Goúrna and Ayía Marína, of the mountains of Kálimnos to the south, and as far east as Turkey. The central lookout at the top of the castle is reserved for use by the army and locked.

The stepped path from Plátanos leads up to the kastro to enter at the west through a small doorway overlooked by a bastion at the southwest corner of the outer walls. Following the pathway you come first to a broad courtyard in the angle of the western and northern circuit walls, and the **church of Panayía Kástrou**, originally the castle's armoury. According to local tradition, the armoury was converted into a church after a miraculous icon which had arrived at the island repeatedly transported itself there overnight. The church has an impressive iconostasis and a small wooden pulpit. Annexed to it is a small **museum of Byzantine antiquities** (no charge), with icons, church furniture and equipment, vestments, etc. Church and museum are open daily (08.30–12.30; also 16.00–20.00, on Wed, Sat, Sun).

On the north and west sides of the kastro only the outer fortification wall still stands, although you can make out the outlines of rooms built onto the wall's inner face. From the north wall two cisterns, c 8m by 6m by 7m deep, and with interiors still plastered, can be see on the slopes below. At the south side of the kastro steps climb into an arched passageway which covers a stretch of the orig-inal cobbled road, lit by two openings in the ceiling. In this area you can best understand the construction and appearance of the interior of the Knights' castle. To the left, a few steps lead to a (locked) series of rooms. To the right, as you pass out of the passageway, is another small room with a pointed vault. Leave the passageway and step up to the southeast and east sides of the fortifi-cation wall. On the east side, at a point where both bedrock and fortification wall drop away, steps descend to a small partially restored **Byzantine chapel** of Ay. Nikólaos which still features some original brickwork, particularly in the apse. It is a building full of character.

From Ayía Marína the coast road leads north around the bay to (6km) **Alinda**; again the two settlements converge.

Alinda has grown considerably in recent years and its houses are better maintained than those of Ayía Marína/Plátanos or Lakkí. Its growth is related to tourism, focused on the long narrow **beach** which lines the bay (tavernas; pedal boats, windsurfers, canoes for hire). However, the town has yet to develop good public amenities: there is no post office, OTE or bank. Behind the busy shops and attractions of the front, the residential area is of little interest.

Just off the waterfront is the **British Military Cemetery**, well maintained, and marked by a large cross. Here lie 179 Britons, two Canadians and two South Africans, most of them victims of the fierce fighting on Léros and elsewhere in the Dodecanese in late 1943. The War Graves Commission and visitors' books are stowed in one of the gateposts.

Further along the waterfront is the **Museum of History and Folklore** (open daily 10.00–12.00, 18.00–21.00; Drs 300 entrance fee), which should not be missed by those interested in the history of Léros, and in Greek culture and tradition generally. Most of the displays are labelled only in Greek, but there are short English biographies of Lerian notables featured in the displays, and notes on the traditional song, music, dance, and dress of the island. A kind of literary companion to the museum which gives particular insight into the pre-Second World War exhibits and other aspects of Lerian history and culture, drawing heavily on the memories and mementoes of Léros' oldest living inhabitants, is available in English. The helpful guide will give a brief tour in passable English and answer questions before leaving visitors to browse.

The museum is housed in a remarkable **tower** which itself ranks as one of the exhibits. The building, constructed between 1923 and 1925, takes the form of a tall three-storeyed mansion with one round and one square turret, both crenellated. The walls are of stone brought from Cairo, and the mansion is described as being built in the 'English' style. An out-house stands at either end of the front wall of the wooded gardens, which contain a bust of the builder, Parisis Bellenis (1871–1957). Bellenis, like many Lerians, spent most of his life in Egypt, where he was chairman of the Lerian Brotherhood of the Greek Community of Cairo. Also a patriotic islander, he was banned from visiting Léros during the years of Italian rule. He financed the building of the high school in Ayía Marína (1955–56), which still bears his name.

The **exhibits** are grouped by subject on the ground and first floors. On the ground floor are kitchen and household utensils, early typewriters and sewing machines, traditional dress and musical instruments (sandoúri, tsamboúna, and laoúto); photographic plates and other equipment used for printing early newspapers in Léros and elsewhere in Greece, and editions of these newspapers dating back to 1790; printing presses.

On the steps up to the **first floor** are displayed some early photographs of the towns and ports of Léros. The first floor landing has a detailed display, including maps and photographs, of the battle of Léros in 1943. The rooms off the landing have: salvaged remains of the warship *Queen Olga*, with exhibits relating to the history of the ship and her crew; memorabilia from the Italian occupation and the Second World War; old maps of the island; photographs and paintings of notable Lerian artists, politicians, heroes, and benefactors and their families; personal effects, furniture and family photographs of Manouil Gedeon (1851–1943), a Lerian publisher and writer on Hellenic and ecclesiastical affairs and ideals.

From Alinda the road heads inland and over the mountains of the island's bare, sparsely populated and largely inaccessible northern peninsula, to the **airport**, military camp, and fishing community at (13km) **Parthéni**, also a former Italian base. Near the airport are the remains of a Hellenistic **watch-tower** on a small hill. From the tower there are commanding views over the bay to the north. The shoreline was considerably closer to the tower before reclamation of land for an extension to the airfield. To reach the tower from the main road you take a track off to the left just before the airport, signposted to the Temple of Artemis. Popular tradition insists that these are the remains of the famed temple, which seems sure to have been in this area, but the remains *in situ* cannot represent the plan of a Greek temple. Square blocks are laid in regular courses (up to three survive to a total height of 1.5m) to form a square with sides c 8.5m long. Nearby is a ruined but still functioning chapel, incorporating some ancient blocks from the tower.

Lakkí to the south (Xirókambos)

5km by road.

Hotels and restaurants in Xirókambos (code area 0247)

A Villa Aléxandros (F/A); NPA. Tel. 24220.
C Efstathía; NPA. Tel. 24099.

Rooms: Georgíanna. Tel. 22747.
Restaurant: Tsitsifiés.

From the east end of the waterfront the road continues round the bay, turning inland from the deeply recessed Lépitha cove towards (5km) **Xirókambos**, on a deep gulf on the south coast of the island. In the middle of the plain between Lépitha and Xirókambos bays, just to the left of the road, rises a small hill known as Palaiókastro. You take a turning up this hill, about 100m before the Xirókambos **campsite** (May–Sept; tel. 0247 23372) and a taverna on the main road, and follow the track to the summit. On the way you pass an Italian gateway and sentry box, with graffiti dating back to the 1920s.

On top of the hill is the modern **church of Panayía Kástrou**, set in the middle of a large walled enclosure, itself of the same careful stone construction as the church. The church stands on top of an **Early Christian chapel** which had a mosaic floor. Slight remains of the mosaic survive in front of the church, in black, red, white, yellow and blue. Immediately behind the church are the remains of an early **Hellenistic tower** (late 4C?), whose squared blocks with dressed edges stand up to four courses high (over 1.5m). The walls were two blocks deep and a metre thick. Like the fort at Parthéni, the tower had a commanding view of the bay below which can now be seen equally well from the church. Both forts may well have been built by the Milesians to help keep control of the sea lanes around the island.

The houses of **Xirókambos** are spread out along the valley between Palaiókastro and the sandy **beach**. The village, with a small fishing fleet, is not overwhelmed by its tourism. Simple, unaffected tavernas and kafeneíons preserve a sociable atmosphere of local intimacy, and prices are modest. Local boats provide a daily service to Mirtiés on the west coast of Kálimnos, leaving early in the morning. On the rocky summit of a high hill to the southwest is another fortified look-out. This dates from the Italian occupation, and faces inland, towards the north.

Léros is surrounded by numerous **islets**. About 19km to the east is **Farmakó**, or Farmakoúsa, where Julius Caesar, returning from his notorious stay in Bithynia, was captured by pirates and detained for 38 days until his ransom arrived; he later caught and crucified his captors.

Kálimnos

KÁLIMNOS

N

Emborio

Paliónisos

Skália

589m

Kastélli

Ay. Konstandínos

458m

Aryinónda

Massoúri

Stiménia   609m

Télendos

Mirtiés

Metókhi   Taxiarkhis
Mikhaíl

Platí Yialós

Ay. Ioánnis

Profítis Ilías
(680m)   Plátanos

Dhaskaliós

Pánormos

Vathí (Rhína)

Kamári

Dhámos

Péra Kástro

Kantoúni

Khristós tes Ierousalém   Khorió

Evangelístria   Pothiá

Ay. Aikateríni   Argos   Khrisokhirá

Kefalás   Vothíni

0   1   2   3 kms

0   1   2 miles

Kálimnos (Κάλυμνος; anc. *Kalymnos*) is an island of great character and contrasts. The starkly dramatic mountains on the west back the narrow coastal strip and Télendos rises sheer from the sea; but between the mountains are fertile valleys. There are attractive places for swimming, though no major beaches, and walking is good, if sometimes strenuous. The community was strongly influenced by the sponge-fishing industry which brought international connections and a lively trade. Kálimnos was a focus of resistance to Italian authority during the occupation. This strong local character is still evident and keeps the influence of tourism within bounds. Apart from the capital Pothiá, which is the commercial centre, visitors patronise particularly the resorts in reach of the bay of Linariá, some of which have become too busy. Places to the north are progressively quieter, like much of the rest of the island, which has interesting sights—especially its castle, caves, and Byzantine remains.

Kálimnos, pop. 15,706, is due south of Léros and west of the Turkish peninsula of Bodrum (*Halikarnassos*). It is 21km long, 13km wide, and has an area of 109sq. km. The main part of the island consists of three mountain ranges separated by two valleys, running roughly (north)west–(south) east. From the middle of the northern-most of these three ranges, a fourth juts out into the sea, forming a narrow, rocky peninsular extension of the island to the northwest. This point is only 2.5km from Léros. The mountains are composed mainly of folded sedimentary rocks, particularly limestone. The mountains are rocky and barren, and crossed only by poor footpaths, but the valleys are fertile and well-wooded, producing figs, olives, grapes, citrus fruits, nuts and cereals. As a result there are many caves, few of them fully explored and some of considerable size. Only the cave of Kefalás, on the south coast, has been developed as a tourist attraction, with regular taxi-boat services and guides. The others are unlit and difficult to locate: local help (e.g. taxi drivers) is needed. From south to north, the ranges rise to 498m, 680m (Profítis Ilías), 608m, and 589m.

The coast is highly indented, and rises steeply inland, especially on the west, where the cliffs face the **island of Télendos** (458m) across a channel only 700m wide. Télendos was probably once joined to Kálimnos.

Kálimnos used to be famous for its honey, which rivalled that of Attica, and some is still produced. Of the two main valleys, that of Vathí, to the north, is the more intensely farmed and generally greener. It stretches from the east coast inland, and most of the way across the island. The valley of Pothiá/Brostá, to the south, cuts right across the island from east coast to west. Consequently the island's main settlements and communication routes are concentrated there. From Pothiá, through the various towns in the Pothiá/Brostá valley to the tourist resorts which stretch northwards up the west coast to Massoúri, the main road is lined with houses and other buildings, with few breaks between the settlements.

Until recently, the fishing and marketing of sponges was the main industry. Although this is now a shadow of its former self, the island still has a sponge fleet which sets out the week after Easter, with great festivities, to return at the end of the summer. Although the divers used to operate as far away as North Africa, most operations are now are in the Aegean; the processing industry is also fed with imported sponges. Fish farming in the bays is now developing as an alternative source of income. Two-thirds of the population live in the island's capital, Pothiá.

History

Archaeological excavations at various sites, including the caves of Kefalás, Ay. Varvára, Khiromándres, and Vathí, have produced evidence of substantial activity in the Neolithic period. The caves were also used later, in Mycenaean times. Carians, Leleges, Phoenicians and Cretans are all cited as early inhabitants of the island. *Kalymnos* is believed to have been one of the 'Kalydnian isles' of the Homeric Catalogue of Ships, joining the expedition against Troy under the leadership of Pheidippos and Antiphos, sons of Thessalos, himself a son of Herakles, and said to have colonised the island from Kos. After the Mycenaeans came Dorian colonists from the Argolid. According to Diodoros, Agamemnon ran aground here on his way home from Troy.

The main centres of occupation in ancient times seem to have been in the valley of Vathí, and around the modern towns of Khorió and Dhámos. During the Persian Wars, *Kalymnos*, and her nearby southerly neighbour, Kos, were controlled by Artemisia, the pro-Persian queen of Halikarnassos. In the 5C BC, *Kalymnos* was a member of Athens' Delian League. In general, the fortunes of ancient *Kalymnos* tended to follow those of Kos, to whom she was annexed, with deme status, by 200 BC.

In AD 554 the island was struck by a terrible earthquake which lasted 14 days. It is described by the historian Agathias, who witnessed the event. In the 7C Saracens and Seljuks plundered the island. Venetian rulers in the latter half of the 13C were followed by the Knights, who controlled the island from 1313 to 1522, and were in turn superseded by the Turks. Kálimnos was most actively opposed to Italian rule, using blue and white (the Greek national colours) everywhere. In 1935 there were riots against an attempt to suppress Greek in schools and to set up an autocephalous Church of the Dodecanese. In the Second World War, most of the Kalimnians took refuge in the Turkish peninsula opposite the island, and then dispersed to various places, including Gaza in Israel.

Getting to Kálimnos

■ **By sea**. In high season, there are at least six services weekly on the major **ferry** routes to Kos and Rhodes (two of which also stop at Nísiros and Tílos), and eight weekly to Piraeus (roughly half stop at Pátmos, Léros, and in the Cyclades; one stops at Astipália, one at Lipsí.).

Hydrofoils also provide daily connections with Rhodes, Sími, and Kos to the south; Léros, Lipsí, Pátmos, and Sámos (with occasional stops at Foúrni and Agathonísi) to the north, in high season. Also in high season, there are **day trips** from Pothiá to Bodrum, and to Léros, Pátmos and Lipsí.

In low season, the ferry services terminating at Rhodes and Piraeus run four times weekly, supplemented by the regular boat trips from Pothiá to Psérimos and Kos (Kos town, Mastikhári), and from Mirtiés to Léros (Xirókambos), which run all year round, weather permitting.

Ferries en route from Rhodes to Piraeus or vice versa tend to reach Kálimnos between midnight and 07.00. There is an all-night café on the ferry pier.

Getting around Kálimnos

■ **By road**. There are daily **bus** services from Pothiá as far as Vathí (3 daily), Vothíni (2), Argos (2) and Massoúri (8, occasionally continuing as far as Emborió).

Taxis are also widely available, with ranks in Pothiá (Plateía Kíprou) and Massoúri.
Bicycles and **scooters** can be hired in Mirtiés, and **cars** in Pothiá.

■ **By sea**. There are **motorboat trips** (35minutes) to the cave of Kefalás, near the southwest promontory of the island. The cave (admission fee) produced objects from the Neolithic period onwards, and in Classical times was a sanctuary of Olympian Zeus.

Boats also provide **day trips** from Pothiá to nearby **beaches** and to **Psérimos** and **Nerá**, an islet to the south with a taverna and a monastery. From **Mirtiés** boats make regular trips to the beach at Emborió and across the channel to the islet of **Télendos** (c 10 minutes).

■ **Travel agent**. Ariston, Pothiá; tel. 0243 47734, 47988; fax 0243 47524; and one or two others.

■ **Bookshop**. **Koukouvás**, inland from National Bank of Greece.

■ **Police**. Tel. 0243 29301.

■ **First aid**. Tel. 0243 28851.

Pothiá and environs

Hotels and restaurants in Pothiá (area code 0243)

C **Arkhontikó** (10); 8000 drs. Tel. 24051, 24149.
C **Evanik** (28); 7500 drs. Tel. 22057.
  Rooms are offered on the quay.
  Restaurants: **Yacht Club** (Naftikós Omilos; by exit from main dock); **Tropicána** (inland); **Acrópolis** (ouzerí; east end of seafront), **Minóre tis Avgís**, **Libéris** (fish), at Paralía Vouváli (far east of seafront, beyond the fishery station).

Boats dock at the busy capital Pothiá, officially Kálimnos, the island's chief port and commercial centre, on the south coast of the island (10,543 inhabitants). The large harbour is well-protected and there is a sizeable fishing fleet. Rising tightly packed above the waterfront the houses of the town, blue and white with red tiled roofs, theatrically frame the deep curving bay. Their regularity is broken by the more colourful churches and by dilapidated or half-constructed buildings. The town is expanding where it can, up and along the slopes of the valley, which stretches inland, rising only gently but with steep sides. These are made more accessible by narrow flights of steps interconnecting with the winding streets of the town.

The broad and very noisy **waterfront** (no beach) is dominated by travel agents, shops and kafeneíons. The facilities are good, especially the shopping, and there is a fruit and vegetable market on the front by the main square.

In one of the streets behind the west end of the waterfront is a **sponge treatment factory** (signs), which offers tours and a video show (open daily 09.00–14.00; admission fee).

Further along is the small **tourist office** (tel. 0243 28583), behind a bronze statue of Poseidon by the sculptor Michael Kokkinos. This statue, as well as the nearby diver, and a Nike set on a plinth which holds four panels with scenes relating to sponge fishing, are among 43 **sculptures** by Kokkinos and his daughter Irene which adorn the island, mainly the capital.

The **main square**, Pl. Ethnikís Antístasis, cramped and often full of traffic, lies just off the east end of the waterfront. Here are the **bus station** and the impressive 18C **church of Christ the Saviour**, with a marble templon by Halepas. Next to the church's freestanding bell-tower is a bust of Georgios Magkos, a leader of resistance to the Italian occupation. From here the main street, Venizélou, leads inland to Plateía Kíprou and the town's **taxi rank**. Up the right branch are the **post office** (open Mon–Fri 07.30–14.00) and **OTE** (open Mon–Fri 07.30–15.00). The road continues to Khorió and the west coast of the island (see below).

Pothiá also has an interesting museum tucked away in the streets north of Pl. Ethnikís Antístasis and east of Od. Venizélou, from which it is well signposted. The **museum** (open Tues–Sun 10.00–14.00; admission free) is housed in the late 19C house of Nikólaos Vouvális (1841–1918), a leading figure in the island's sponge industry, and a local benefactor who built the town hospital. After the death of his wife (29 years his junior) in 1959, the house was turned into a museum. Some of the family possessions were kept as exhibits, now filling three rooms: the dining room, fully equipped; the study, with family photographs; the upstairs drawing room, with oil paintings and portraits of family members and of William Gladstone. In the last room the family's wealth can also be seen in the gilt decor. A fourth room, downstairs, holds Neolithic and Bronze Age finds from the caves of Vathí, Ay. Varvára, and Khiromándres: pottery, flint, bone and other tools, and a few figurines. In the hallway are larger pieces of pottery (amphorae) recovered from the sea.

In the garden is an assortment of ancient stones, including inscriptions, capitals and other architectural blocks, altars and Byzantine slabs with crosses; one piece has a sphinx. The largest object is a Hellenistic torso, thought to be of Asklepios. By the gate stands an old rusting cannon. The guide gives tours (no unaccompanied viewing) in Greek and, more briefly, in other European languages.

South of Pothiá is a modern hydrotherapeutic establishment with hot springs. The **monastery of Ay. Pántes** (access by road or path), with a huge cross and freestanding bell-tower, overlooks the town from the heights to the west. The monastery houses the reliquary of Ay. Sávvas. From here the road continues southwest to (3km) **Vothíni** and (5km) the monastery of Ay. Ekateríni, from where a path leads a further 2km to the **cave of Kefalás** (see above).

Pothiá to Emborió

20km by road.

Leaving Pothiá you head inland and climb gently up the valley. On the outskirts of town a hill on the left with three disused windmills on its slopes has, on the summit, a ruined **Castle of the Knights**, known as the Khrisokheriá. Little of the castle is preserved, apart from the outer walls, but these and the situation, which dominates the valley at its narrowest point, make it impressive. Inside are rock-cut Mycenaean tombs and two chapels. The lower chapel, of **Panayía Khrisokheriá**, is the older of the two, with decaying frescoes including depictions of the Last Supper, and St George. The castle is strategically positioned where the valley narrows considerably to pass between two rocky spurs protruding from the hills to north and south. The castle holds a commanding position on top of the southern spur; on the northern spur opposite, known as Tsoútsoulo, is the church of Ay. Varvára and, on the slopes above, the **cave** of Ay. Varvára, where Neolithic and Mycenaean remains were found.

At (3km) **Khorió** (3259 inhabitants) is the former capital of Kálimnos, built below a castle (views) on the slopes to the north which served as a refuge in the Middle Ages, and remained occupied into the 18C. Behind the main road are narrow winding residential streets. The inland situation keeps it largely free of visitors. The solid and well preserved walls of the **castle**, known as the Péra Kástro and also quiet, trace an irregular polygonal circuit several hundred metres long around the summit of a rocky hill which is linked to the mountains at the north by a steep narrow ridge. The hill is precipitous on all sides except the south, where steps lead up from Khorió to the entranceway. Like that of Khrisokheriá the situation is commanding, though the valley wider here. The walls are of rubble, with some monumental blocks, and are over 1m thick in most places. Inside are nine whitewashed chapels and the extensive ruined remains of numerous houses. A cistern in the centre has been restored with a concrete roof, and is still in use.

On the fortification wall to the east, looking out over a precipitous height towards Pothiá, are two coats of arms; the upper are those of Fabrizio del Carretto, Grand Master of the Knights from 1513 to 1521, quartered with those of the Order. There is a further coat of arms on the south wall.

You leave Khorió, following the signs for Pánormos. The valley narrows. Past a small roundabout and a large cemetery, with a huge sculpture of Christ on the cross by Michael Kokkinos, you reach the signpost for the track (left; 3km) to **Argos**, a farming community situated on a high fertile plateau to the south, with an airstrip (no civilian commerical flights) and an attractive monastery.

A little further along the main road, a footpath leads off (left) through a field to the considerable but unspectacular remains of the three-aisled Byzantine **basilica of the Evangelístria** (and a small church of Ay. Sofía). The basilica is in a fenced enclosure (open). Only the east apse is standing to any height (2m), with one small patch of red-painted stucco. In the sanctuary (c 6 x 8m) parts of the floor and the foundations of a screen wall are still in place, and the walls incorporate many ancient blocks from the nearby sanctuary of Apollo (see below). The rest of the complex ground-plan of the basilica can be made out. In the field between it and the main road are more ancient blocks from the sanctuary of Apollo.

Thirty metres further along the road, 200m from the turning for Argos, some white steps lead over a low wall to the more interesting Early Christian **basilica of Christós tis Ierousalém**. Only the apse and part of the floor are preserved but, unusually, the former is structurally complete, standing 8–9m high and roofed. More blocks from the sanctuary of Apollo are incorporated into the floor and side walls. There are ancient inscriptions (Apollo is mentioned) on five re-used blocks at the bottom of the wall on the north side, and four more on the opposite side of the apse. The church is said to have been built by the Emperor Arcadius (ruled AD 395–403) in thanksgiving for his deliverance from a storm at sea while passing Kálimnos on his return to Byzantium from Jerusalem. About 20m to the south, away from the road, are some foundations of the original **sanctuary of Apollo**. The sanctuary had a Hellenistic Ionic temple, a theatre, and contained many statues, but has only been partially excavated. The cult dates back to the Archaic period, and from the 4C BC onwards public decrees and documents were displayed here, suggesting that this was the principal sanctuary of ancient *Kalymnos*. Scattered building blocks lie around but much of the stone was reused in the basilicas and elsewhere and it is hard now to imagine the site in its original state.

You return to the main road, now a tree-lined avenue, for (4km) **Dhámos**, which merges with the nearby village of **Pánormos**, also known as Eliés for its olive groves, near the west end of the Pothiá/Brostá valley. On the coast is Kamári.

At the plateia of Dhámos you pass turnings (left) for the coastal resorts of **Kandoúni** and **Platí Yialós**. From the former you can climb the slopes to the south in c 30 minutes to reach the **Monastery of the Cross**, whose walled gardens with dense green vegetation precipitously overlook the valley.

From Dhámos the main road begins to climb, and turns towards the right (north), reaching the west coast at (7km) **Mirtiés** (small beach; boats to Télendos, also Xirókambos on Léros), a fairly quiet and not over-developed resort.

Near the top of the slopes in a pleasant situation overlooking the south side of Mirtiés bay are the well-preserved remains of the Byzantine **basilica of Ay. Ioánnis Melitsakhás**. The basilica is in a small walled cemetery, with a modern church of the same saint built over its southeast corner. The foundations of the external and internal walls are still in place, as are parts of the marble paving, and it is easy to make out the original form of the building. Doorways lead from the narthex into each of the basilica's three aisles. Sections of the screen panels (*thorakia*) and columns which separated the aisles are still *in situ*, as are the bases of the pilasters which ran along the inside of the outer walls. The foundations of another screen wall, separating the central aisle from the sanctuary, can also be seen, and the apse itself stands to c 3m. The walls were built of rubble and mortar, and some stucco with decoration in red still survives on the north side. Various religious motifs, particularly chalices, double peacocks and Byzantine crosses, are carved in relief on surviving elements of the basilica, which covered an area of c 20 x 12m.

Island of Télendos

From Mirtiés you can take one of the small boats which spend the day running across the (700m) strait to the island of Télendos (Τέλενδος) in 10–15 minutes (Drs 200–300).

It seems likely that Télendos was once joined to Kálimnos, and only became separated in the disastrous earthquake of AD 554. Remains of the houses which once stood on the isthmus between Kálimnos and Télendos are said to still be visible beneath the waters which now separate the two islands.

The modern village of **Télendos** (Rooms; restaurants)—its white houses, interspersed with olive trees, sloping gently down to a small bay—lies at the base of a low neck of land which forms a southern extension to the main part of the island. The north of the island is a precipitous limestone ridge rising directly from the sea to a peak of 458m, its slopes everywhere steep and rocky, especially on the southwest face.

Only the flatter coastlands facing Kálimnos are inhabited and exploited: here are most of the beaches, the village, and the remains of a once-thriving **Roman and Early Christian settlement**. There are many small **beaches**, most of them along the coast to the north of the village; others on the opposite side (west) near the Early Christian cemetery. The most conspicuous and substantial archaeological remains are those of a large **basilica** and other buildings, roughly 100m north of the pier. The three-aisled basilica covered an area c 40 x

25m, with a row of rooms adjoining to the south and west. Architrave blocks, one bearing a Byzantine cross, and column fragments lie scattered in the vicinity. The walls are of mortared rubble, with large squared ancient blocks in the foundations and at the corners. On the exterior, at the northeast corner of the central apse, the walls stand over 7m high.

On the hillside below the basilica are the remains of a house, while terraces stretch roughly 50m to the northwest. In the second-highest terrace wall is part of a barrel-vaulted **cistern** c 4 x 2.5m, with stucco still adhering to the interior walls. Forty metres to the south of the basilica, behind the houses of the settlement, stand the remains of another building, c 30 by 20m, probably a **bath complex**. Parts of its walls, including a complete arched doorway, are substantially intact. There are also slight remains of more buildings in the next field to the north of the basilica. The site deserves more than its present small quota of visitors.

About 100m further north along the coast, behind houses and tavernas, are parts of a second **bath complex**, now incorporating the chapel of Ay. Kharálambos. South of the settlement is a modern cemetery with the sketchy remains of a second basilica. Beyond this, through a pine grove, you come to the remains of an Early Christian **cemetery**. Here there are eight freestanding tombs with low doors, widely dispersed around a central basilica. While the rubble remains of the basilica are barely recognisable as such, the walls and roofs of the tombs are generally well preserved. All of the tombs are between 4–6m long, 3–4m wide, and barrel vaulted, apart from one which is c 4m sq, and cross vaulted. The walls are of rubble and mortar, with the vaults in brick. Some of the tombs still have stucco on their interior walls.

The most extensive area of archaeological remains on Télendos, and the most impressive in terms of position, is also the least accessible. The Early Christian **settlement** of **Ay. Konstandínos** lies near the north point of the island, on the craggy heights facing over the channel to Kálimnos, not far below the end of a tall ridge of cliffs. There are no easy tracks or even footpaths to the site, but the setting and views—down the steep slopes and across the blue channel to Kálimnos—are the most rewarding on the island. Good shoes are essential for the climb, and at least three hours should be allowed for the round trip. An early start is also to be recommended, to avoid the heat of the day. The ascent is often very steep, and there is much loose scree.

There are two possible routes.

1. Follow the footpath northwards around the coast from the modern village. Beyond the last of the beaches the whitewashed walls of Ay. Konstandínos are visible above you. Turn inland and start to climb the slopes from a point directly below the basilica (at this stage out of sight). Above you see the high cliffs tailing off, with a rocky spur trailing down northeast towards the sea. You head directly upwards, through the one gap in the rocky spur, and climb up to the left to reach the lowest buildings of the settlement.

2. Follow the coastal path only a short distance out of the modern village, to a small beach with benches and parasols. From here climb uphill, making use of long stretches of flat exposed bedrock to gain height quite easily. You head for a slight dip in the spur to the right, c 30m above a small cave visible from the coast. Crossing the spur, you follow a poor footpath across the slopes, rising only slightly, to reach the next spur, where the whitewashed church of **Ay. Konstandínos** comes into sight. Continue climbing across the rocky slopes, either up to a difficult passage across the base of the cliffy heights (look for blue painted crosses marking the route, which will lead down to the basilica from above), or across to cut below the wall-lined rocky spur which tails off well above the sea on the slopes to the north. On the far side of this spur, you turn upwards and finish the climb to the lowest buildings of the settlement.

The **basilica**, snugly fitted onto the flat top of a rocky outcrop, lies at the top end of what was a substantial settlement. Its apse and north aisle are largely intact, although all but the lowest courses of the aisle's arched roof is missing. The apse, still in use as a modern chapel, is mostly whitewashed, but original frescoes are visible on the ceiling, fragmentary and faded. The remains of the **settlement** and its **fortification wall** stretch up to 200m across the slopes to the north, as far as three stepped low cliffs running down the hillside. However, the most extensive remains are on the rocky spur falling directly away from the basilica towards the sea. Here are more traces of defensive walling, and many houses and cisterns, often visible only from near at hand despite being often nearly complete. The walls of the cisterns and houses are made of rubble, brick and mortar; plaster in plain colours is extensively preserved on the insides of most walls. There are thick scatters of sherds and roof tiles across the site.

Back on Kálimnos, you continue roughly northwards out of Mirtiés, up the west coast, along a strip of land wedged in between the sea and the cliffs, which here rise abruptly to over 500m. This massive wall of limestone shades much of the west coast, from Mirtiés as far as Kastélli, from the morning sun, providing about three cool hours of daylight after dawn in which there is no direct sunlight. An early start to catch this period is especially worthwhile if your day is likely to be physically strenuous. The rocks in this area also contain a great many caves, and there are occasional flashes of a striking purple stone which also appear across the strait in Télendos.

You follow the main road through (8.5km) **Massoúri**, with its taxi rank, car and scooter rental, beach and watersports. Beyond Massoúri the tourist belt comes to a distinct halt. After 10km you reach a rocky spur known as **Kastélli**, which juts out into the sea and is connected to the mainland by a low neck of land.

Significant remains of a fortification wall cross the seaward end of the neck of land, protecting the settlement which used to stand on the spur. A stretch of the wall c 40m long survives, running down the south flank of the hill. The settlement was considerably smaller than the one at Ay. Konstandínos on Télendos, but the two sites are otherwise similar—and face each other, across the channel. Again there are considerable remains of cisterns and houses with walls of rubble, brick and mortar, with plaster in plain colours on the interior. Here too are thick scatters of plain pottery and roof tiles. Both sites seem to represent walled **Roman or Early Byzantine settlements** (perhaps on the sites of predecessors) in high, defensive positions with commanding views of the Télendos Channel.

Returning to the main road, you soon round the headland and continue along the steep coast into the deep **Bay of Aryinónda**, with fish farms. At (12.5km) the head of the bay, with a good sandy **beach**, lies the wooded village of

Aryinónda (**Rooms** include **Akroyialí** (tel. 0243 47521), with restaurant), quiet and undeveloped. From the back of the houses a stiff footpath leads to the valley of Vathí. The path leads inland, up the ravine-like valley floor, and then mounts the slopes to the right (south) to a pass over the heights, where the mountains of the northern peninsula of Kálimnos join the main part of the island. From the pass the footpath leads to the northern slopes of the valley of Vathí (see below), which can be reached, via Stiménia, in c 3 hours.

From Aryinónda, you can start up the northern peninsula, following the road around the north side of Aryinónda Bay to (17km) the hamlet of **Skália**, gradually leaving town life, tourism, even agriculture further and further behind. About 1km before the village, 200m up the slopes, is one of the island's most impressive caves, with a chamber 20 x 45m, and 10m high, containing stalagmites and stalactites. The **cave** is hard to locate and difficult to enter; the proprietor of the Skália periptero will act as a guide for a negotiable fee. From Skália a footpath leads over the barren mountain ridge to the hamlet of Paliónisos on the opposite side of the peninsula.

The metalled road continues as far as (20km) **Emborió** (Rooms; restaurants), set in a bay protected by the islet of Kalavrós. In the area between Skália and Emborió there are plentiful signs of ancient occupation. Ancient squared blocks are built into many of the older houses and terrace walls, and potsherds are common in areas where the subsoil has been exposed—along roadsides and at the coast. Mycenaean burials have been found here, but the only substantial ancient remains to be seen on the ground are those of **Kastrí**, a small but intriguing **fortification** at the foot of the cliffs inland from Emborió, probably dating from the Hellenistic period. It looks down over the settlement and bay to Télendos. Access is as follows.

Approaching Emborió from the east, you pass the first few houses of the town, and then the road turns inland (north) for c 50m. As it turns west again to descend into the bay of Emborió, a rough track continues inland and uphill. Follow this track, and head up the right side of the river bed; pass through the goat enclosure by the gate on its right-hand (east) side. Here the ancient rock-cut steps lead up to the doorway, also rock-cut, of the fortification. The defences consist of a 20m screen wall linking two bastions in rough coursed masonry. The north wall of the east tower stands to c 4m, as does the connecting wall. Behind the defences, at the foot of the precipitous cliffs, are traces of rock-cut rooms and a cistern, still lined with stucco. From the fortification there is a great view of the mouth of Aryinónda Bay, of the Télendos Strait, and of the sea to the east, i.e. the sea approaches to the town, all of which suggests that this compact site was a refuge for the local population when threatened by pirates.

Pothiá to Vathí

13km by road.

Leaving Pothiá, you head east and then north, twisting with the line of the highly indented coast. Most of the inlets are rocky but accessible for swimming if you are willing to scramble up and down the slopes. Two have small sandy **beaches** and better access; the first a set of concrete steps, the second a motorable concrete track, also a small taverna. The inlets now house a growing number of fish farms. Only a few herbs, grasses, and weeds manage to cling tenuously to the steep stony slopes.

There are good views of the **Valley of Vathí** as you descend its steep southern side. Stretching inland from the east coast, almost through to the west, it provides stark contrasts. While the slopes are precipitous and barren, the valley floor is flat, lush, and green. The open sea is invisible from the head of Vathí Bay, which is narrow and cliff-bound. The three quiet farming villages in the valley, **Vathí** (or Rhína), the harbour and most developed, **Plátanos** and **Metókhi** successively further inland, merge loosely into one another.

The road approaches from the southern slopes of the bay. On the north side is the **Grotto of Dhaskaleiós** (boats from Pothiá), the largest of the caves in the island. Even from the sea the approach is difficult. Immediately inside is a chamber 25m long, from which opens on the right another chamber, at a lower level, with stalactites and stalagmites and a cavity full of brackish water. Many prehistoric objects were found here, ranging in date from the Neolithic to the Bronze Age.

The ancient remains in the **area of Vathí**, while nowhere spectacular, are thick enough on the ground to suggest that the valley was an important focus of settlement in past times, especially the Early Christian era, since there are remains of four or five **basilicas**. Three of these lie on the slopes of the bay, indicating that the harbour was as important to the Early Christian community as the fertility of the valley's well watered and volcanic soil.

A basilica on the southern slopes of the bay can be reached via a path which starts from some steps just in front of the last house on the southeast side of (12km) **Vathí** (Rhína) (**Hotel Galíni**, tel. 0243 31241. **Restaurants** round the harbour).

The modern church of Ay. Anastásios, below that of Ay. Yióryios and standing on top of the triple-apsed Early Christian '**Basilica of the Resurrection**', is c 200m from the head of the bay on its southern slopes. The southern and central apses of the basilica are preserved, although the latter now lies below the modern church. The south outer wall stands to c 3m, and above is visible the springing of the arch over the south aisle. At the base of the north wall of the modern church, on top of the remains of the basilica wall, is a rounded slab with a Byzantine cross in relief, now whitewashed. Further up these slopes there are considerable but uninspiring remains of unidentified ruined structures and walls, probably from the medieval town.

Further out towards the sea, on the opposite (northern) slopes of the bay, lies a second three-aisled Early Christian **basilica**. The modern church of Ay. Iríni stands over the northern aisle of the basilica, which dates from 5–6C AD and is built of the rough local volcanic stone. Along the south side of the outer wall and around the central apse, the walls are preserved to over 2m. Just beyond are the remains of another apsed structure, either a third basilica or a martyrion. Plaster survives on the inner wall of the apse.

Moving west (inland) from Vathí, you take the left (south) road, following the one-way system. The two parts of the one-way system meet at (8.5km) the small quiet plateia of **Plátanos**, marked by a huge plane tree, a modern relief with Nike holding a wreath, a petrol station, and shops. On the return road to Vathí, along the northern fork, c 50m up the slopes to the left (north), are a few courses of well squared and set ancient blocks. These are probably the remains of a square Hellenistic **watchtower**. Inside, decaying blue stucco adorns the walls.

Continuing inland from the plateia of Plátanos, a low ridge soon develops to the right (north), also c 50m from the road. On the ridge stand two churches and, immediately beyond them, are the considerable remains of an ancient circuit wall, visible from the road c 200m beyond the plateia of Plátanos and the most substantial and interesting of the local antiquities. A path, initially of concrete, leads up to the wall, of an irregular circuit, well constructed of squared blocks in regular courses, and supporting a flat terrace c 50 x 40m. On the terrace are the remains of further ancient structures, only one of which, in the northeast of the terrace, is reasonably-well preserved. This is a triple-apsed Early Christian **basilica**, on top of which is the 13–14C **church of Taxiárkhis Mikhaíl** (locked). A clay incense burner stands outside the church, a typical feature of the churches in this area. The basilica is c 20m north–south, 15m east–west, and parts of its walls are preserved to two storeys. The outline of its exonarthex, with a central doorway into the interior, can be seen on the west side, as can those of the side aisles to the north and south. The vault of the north aisle is partially preserved, as are the central and south apses, on either side of the modern church. 500m to the north are the remains of the other Early Christian basilica in the vicinity. Further inland are the still smaller hamlets of **Metókhi** and **Stiménia**, beyond which steep paths can give access to Aryinónda and Massoúri on the opposite coast (see above).

Islet of Néra
The islet of Nerá, off the south coast of Kálimnos, has a taverna and a small **Monastery of the Cross**, with a festival on 14 September.

Island of Psérimos
The islet of Psérimos (19sq km; Rooms, restaurant), with a **monastery** and 79 inhabitants, lies between Kálimnos and Kos, and is served by daily boat trips from both, in c 1 hour.

The settlement has a beach, often crowded. Smaller quieter inlets can be found elsewhere around the islet, which rises to 268m. Visitors throng to the island on 15 August for the monastery's celebration of the festival of the Assumption of the Virgin Mary.

Astipália

Astipália (Αστυπάλαια; anc. *Astypalaia*) (pop. 1034) is sometimes known locally as Astropalaiá. The usual version of the name can be accented on any of the last three syllables. With its pretty cubic houses, and a Venetian kastro overlooking the harbour, Astipálaia feels more like one of the Cyclades. Rather isolated from the rest of the Aegean, geographically and in terms of communications, it is a good place for a quiet holiday, so long as you are happy with walking and swimming. Although not without its quota of summer visitors, the island is largely deserted beyond the settlements and has a spacious feeling. Quite mountainous, apart from the central isthmus and a fertile valley behind the accessible beach of Livádhia, it is nonetheless good for walking, especially since there is little traffic. Even the furthest beach or monastery can be visited on foot in a day, and a taverna is usually to be found, at Vathí and Kaminákia for example.

The most westerly of the Dodecanese, it lies 40km southeast of Amorgós and about the same distance west of Kos. About 18km long and 97sq km in area, it consists of two peninsulas, the smaller to the northeast rising to 366m, joined by a narrow isthmus, c 6km long and in places only a few hundred metres wide. Erosion of the island's sedimentary rock has left a highly indented coastline with high cliffs and numerous caves. The bedrock, often heavily folded, frequently lies exposed at the surface, with little topsoil.

The water supply is poor and generally brackish. The cliffy heights in the southwest, rising to the island's peak of 482m, have a fair number of springs, which are exploited for agriculture, but the main farming centre is around Maltezána, on the peninsula. Corn, garden vegetables, grapes and citrus fruits are the principal produce, though the decline in agricultural activity is reflected in the decaying terraces which can be seen all over the island. Large freestanding ovens, built of brick and whitewashed, are still common features of the rural farmsteads. Astipaláia is said to be the only Aegean island which has no snakes, a fact popularly connected with the annual passage of migratory cranes.

History

In ancient times the island was known as *Ichthyoessa*, from its rich fishing grounds, which still provide a livelihood for some islanders, and recreation for visitors. Pliny mentions the island's edible snails, which were supposed to have medicinal uses. Another ancient name, 'The Table of the Gods', came from Astipália's abundant flowers and fertility, which must have been more evident then. The island was called *Stampalia*, by the Venetians in the Middle Ages, and again during the later Italian occupation.

An interesting though unproven theory (M. Ovenden in *The Philosophical Journal* 3 (1966)) puts the origin of the constellations here in the Early Bronze Age—he concluded that only at that period and in this area would the constellations have appeared in shapes close enough to justify the descriptions applied to them. Astral navigation was certanly used in antiquity and local names, including 'Astropaliá' (άστρον = star) seem to give some support.

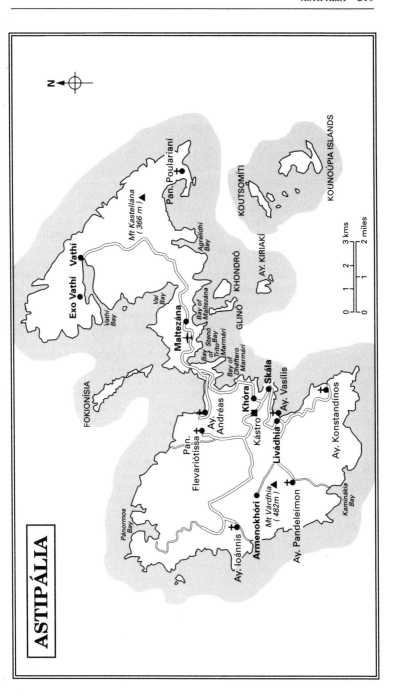

Mycenaean burials have been found at Stenó, Tríto Marmári, and Ay. Ioánnis, and there is evidence of a Mycenaean settlement at Vathí. *Astypalaia* was of some importance in antiquity. Although by tradition a Megarian colony, later colonists came from Epidauros. Material built into the houses and churches of the modern town, together with inscriptions and coins found in the vicinity, show that the **ancient city** stood on the same site, and had a prytaneion, an agora, a theatre, and sanctuaries of Athena, Asklepios, Apollo and Artemis, although no remains of these have been found *in situ*.

The most colourful ancient Astypalaian was the strong-man Kleomedes, who killed his opponent Ikkos of Epidauros in a boxing match during the 71st Olympiad and was disqualified. He returned mad with rage and grief to Astypália and pulled down the local school about its children's ears, killing them all. Kleomedes took refuge in the sanctuary of Athena, but when the islanders broke up the chest in which he had hidden, they found it empty. From then on, in obedience to an oracle from Delphi, Kleomedes was worshipped as a hero. Astypalaia also has claims to be the birthplace of Phalaris, the cruel tyrant of Acragas, and of Onesikritos, historian and chief pilot of the fleet sent by Alexander the Great from the Indus to the Persian Gulf under Nearchos.

A member of Athens' Delian League from 454 to 424 BC, and later controlled by the Ptolemies, the island achieved an alliance with Rome in 105 BC, because of her good harbours and central position in the Aegean, both important in operations against pirates. In the Imperial period, Astypalaia had autonomous status until the reign of the Emperor Gordian.

The island was never controlled by the Knights. The Quirini family of Venice took control from the local leader, Markos Sanoudos, in 1207, after the fall of Constantinople to the Latins. The Byzantine admiral Libarios captured the island in 1269, but it was retaken by John II Quirinus in 1333, and from then on was shared with the Grimani family. After being sacked by Omar Bey Marbasha in 1341, it lay deserted until 1413, when John IV Quirinus introduced settlers from Mikonos and Tinos, renaming the island 'Astinea' (nea = new). This long Venetian presence, and Cycladic influence from the settlers, is still said to be discernible in the dialect and in the local style of embroidery. The traditional women's costumes are varied and elaborate. In 1537 Astypalaia fell to the Turks, who slightly altered the name to Ustrupalaia. Except during the Cretan War (1648–68) and from 1821–28, they held it until 1912, when it was the first of the Dodecanese to be occupied by the Italians and the springboard for their expedition to Rhodes. Lócal accentuation of English betrays the fact that Australia has been the most popular destination for emigrants from Astipália in the 20C.

Getting to Astipália

■ **By air**. The island has a small **airport**, with three flights weekly to/from Athens (c 65 mins).

■ **By sea**. In high season, **ferries** stop at the port in Skála five times weekly en route from the Dodecanese to the Cyclades and the Piraeus (one service connecting with Crete), three times weekly in the opposite direction, to Kálimnos (one service (and a hydrofoil) continuing on to Kos and Rhodes). In winter these services are reduced to one or two ferries weekly in each direction.

Getting around Astipália

■ **By bus.** The bus service consists of one small vehicle which spends the day running continuously along the island's limited extent of metalled road. There are ten services daily between Khóra and Livádhia, seven between Khóra and Maltezána, some of which continue on to the small pier at Váï bay.

■ **By taxi.** There are a few taxis which will travel out across the tracks covering the island, but no organised tours of any kind. Day trip access to beaches and unpopulated offshore islets in summer is by **taxi-boats.** These leave Skála (and Maltezána) between 10.00 and 11.00 in the morning, returning late in the afternoon.

■ **By car.** Some hire cars are available in Khóra, but with the predominance of dirt tracks on the island, travel by **scooter** prevails. They are easily hired in Skála and Khóra.

■ **On foot.** The islanders still make use of donkeys, and older female passengers often sit side-saddle on these, and on motorcycles. The tracks covering the island's two peninsulas tend to follow ridges or other high contours, giving good cooling breezes and clear views over the island and the Aegean. This, and the lack of traffic, makes **walking** a very rewarding experience; from the central isthmus, a return trip on foot can be made to most points on the island in a day.

■ **Travel agent. Astipália Tours,** Skála; tel. 0243 61328, 61292; fax 0243 61328.

■ **Facilities** (see further below). Accommodation and restaurants in Skála, Livádhia, Maltezána. Camping site (summer) at Dhéftero Marmári. Transport and main services in Skála.

■ **Police.** Tel. 0243 61207.

■ **First aid.** Tel. 0243 61222.

Skála and Khóra

Hotels and restaurants in Skála and Khóra (area code 0243)

C Astinéa (18); 7000–8500 drs. Tel. 61040/4.	**D Parádhissos** (17); 5000–8000 drs. Tel. 61224, 61256, 61276.
D Aigaíon (20); 4500–6000 drs. Tel. 61236, 61218.	**Restaurants** around the harbour.

The capital lies on the southeast coast of Astipália's western peninsula, and consists of an upper 'citadel', known as Khóra, and the lower port of Skála. Such an arrangement is typical of Aegean islands which have often known the threat of pirate raids, but the two settlements are now practically one, with a network of concrete staircases, direct and therefore often very steep, connecting the upper and lower parts of the town. It is a quiet relaxed place, little developed and with a pleasant rather rural feel.

On the waterfront at Skála are the quay—with facilities and officials—also the **OTE** (open Mon–Sat 07.30–15.00), and a small sandy beach, overlooked by a promenade with kafeneíons and tavernas. The main church (**Ay. Nikólaos**) with an impressive silver dome, is at the inner end of the bay, near the angle between quayside and beach, and set back a little from the main road. Between this church and the Hotel Parádhisos is a block with the arms of the Quirini, set into an old wall. From either end of the beach, roads (one-way) soon join and climb inland to Khóra, its narrow curving streets and little houses clinging to the slopes of the southwestern end of the bay, crowned by the castle.

Most of the town's other facilities and amenities lie on the stretch of road from the pier end of the beach to Khóra. First you pass the small **Archaeological Museum** which has inscriptions, pottery and sculpture found on the island. The museum is not normally open to visitors. The key is held by Nikólaos Gournás, both physically and socially an imposing figure of the local community. He can be hard to locate, but most people know his name, and have some idea where and when he can be found.

Beyond the museum are the **Olympic Airways** office, the agent for the **National Bank** (by the Hotel Aegean), and then, turning left up to Khóra, the **pharmacy**, the **post office** (open Mon–Fri 07.30–14.00), and the **petrol station**.

At the top of the road, by Khóra's little elongated plateia, are a small public **library** (open Mon, Wed, Fri, Sat 18.00–20.00, Sun 10.00–12.00), a war memorial, and a row of disused windmills.

From here you can take a metalled road leading around the valley. This rises theatrically above Skála, to the last building of Khóra, on the left, the **church of Ay. Anáryiri**. It is built over an Early Christian basilica (5C), whose threshold can be seen in the ground in front of the modern church. Here there are also large parts of the basilica's **mosaic floor**, with geometric patterns in black, white and red. Above, on the summit of the ridge separating the bays of Skála and Livádhia, is a **church of Ay. Nikólaos**. The other, larger church of the same saint, with its distinctive dome, can be seen below, in Skála. The picturesque view of the town is marred only by the number of half-finished buildings on its outskirts which testify to a growing attention to tourism.

The oldest houses, many dilapidated, and a maze of narrow lanes, lie on the slopes of Khóra, around the Venetian kastro, easily the most impressive local monument, which stands clear of the town at its summit, visible from afar.

Kástro

The Kástro (castle; open all day; free) is surprisingly little visited and rarely busy. Substantial parts of the structure are preserved, and wooden fittings in some of the rooms. It was built by John Quirinus in the 13C AD, over a 9C AD fortification. On one occasion the defenders of the castle are said to have repelled assailants round the gate by throwing beehives full of deliberately maddened bees down on them. Set into the vaulted **entranceway**, on the west side of the castle, are an ancient inscription, now upside-down, and the arms of the Quirini family, now whitewashed. Above the gateway is the restored **church of the Madonna of the Castle** (locked). Set on its side in the wall of the courtyard, immediately to the left as you enter the castle, is a squared block with the arms of John Quirinus.

The **interior** of the castle is occupied by a series of narrow lanes, dilapidated houses and covered passageways, the whole set around an open central courtyard. Many of the rooms still have decaying painted stucco on their walls, and the walls often contain ancient blocks, some brought from Agrelídhi Bay. Other ancient material, including Doric capitals, a small round altar and a square base with recesses for the feet of a statue, lie scattered on the ground. In the houses by the south side of the courtyard, near the modern church of Ay. Yióryios (locked), some of the original carved wooden decoration on the walls and ceilings can still be seen.

Below the castle to the southeast is the impressive **church of the Panayía Portaḯtissa** (normally locked; grounds open), with a pebble mosaic courtyard and an intricate wooden iconostasis. In the pleasant and colourful gardens is the sepulchre of the founder.

Khóra to the Monastery of Ay. Ioánnis

11km by road.

Leaving Khóra by the signposted road, which almost immediately becomes a rough but motorable track, you pass between the churches of Ay. Nikólaos (above) and Ay. Anáryiri (below), and skirt the curving ridge which commands Skála Bay. Slowly climbing up the open hillside, and veering round to the left, you get a good view of the central isthmus and the northeastern part of the island, and of nearby islets. The road now heads roughly west, and soon you see to the left the lush, green valley of Livádhia—in striking contrast to the brown and barren slopes elsewhere—with a dam and reservoir at its head.

As the road levels out, and the far side of the island comes into sight, you pass an army camp on a height, and continue to (4km) a right turn (fallen signpost) for the **monastery of Panayía Flevariótissa**. The secluded church, no longer home to a living community, is beautifully maintained by a farmer and his wife, who live there and will provide the key. A few disused cells can be used for overnight accommodation. From the same turning a branch of the track goes down towards the coast.

At 6.5km the road forks, just below a pair of churches. The left branch zigzags up the slopes to an isolated chapel and farmstead at the pass through the stark and cliffy limestone ridge in front (potential for rock climbing). For Ay. Ioánnis, you follow the right branch, which leads across the slopes below the ridge and heads towards the north end of the west coast of the island. Tracks (right) head for farms on the valley slopes, their crops olives and grain, before you reach (9.5km) a pass at the end of the ridge, with a church on a small rise to the right. Here you turn left through a gate, and follow the track down to (11km) the monastery, at the head of a steep gorge-like valley. The limestone ridge is now to the east.

On the rocky height to the west, overlooking the bay, the sparse remains of a medieval **fort** occupy a craggy spur accessible only from the east. Inside its ruined rubble and mortar walls, c 100m by 70m, are the remains of cisterns and wall foundations.

The **monastery of Ay. Ioánnis** itself is small, consisting of a church with some minor ancillary buildings nearby. On the upper slopes of the valley below, there are extensive lush and fertile gardens, watered by a strong spring which fills numerous cisterns, and producing fruit and vegetables as well as offering welcome shade. The monastery's three-day festival begins with a feast on 29 August, with traditional songs, dancing and dress. The ravine between the monastery and fort leads down (c 30 minutes' walk) to a **beach** in the bay.

Khóra to the Bay of Kaminákia

8km by road plus 2km walk.

From Khóra you can walk or take the metalled road to (1.5km) **Livádhia** (Rooms) in the next bay to the south, with a long, not terribly clean, sandy beach and little of interest except its waterfront.

The main road inland from the waterfront also occasionally serves as a riverbed for water released from the dam, and therefore is walled high on either side, and with few side streets. On the way out of Livádhia you cross the low rise of Poundári, which encloses the bay to the south. Here the **church of Ay. Vasílios** stands over the scant remains of an Early Christian basilica, of which some floor slabs and parts of two mosaics survive. Fragmentary geometric patterns in red, white, and black tesserae, can be seen by the church and, a few metres away, a panel of interlocking circles.

Leaving Livádhia, the road loses its metalled surface, and winds further on down the coast: footpaths lead down left to some secluded beaches. At 4km you take the signposted turning (right) for Kaminákia, leaving the coast road which carries on down (2km) to the popular **beach** of Ay. Konstandínos.

As you head inland the road rises steeply, with the southeast part of the island soon coming into view. At about 5km you pass a farmhouse (left), with a white-washed chapel to the right. Behind the chapel are the substantial remains of a much older and ruder predecessor which incorporates ancient blocks. The door-frame is made entirely of dressed marble, and includes a column drum over 1m high. Further on (6km) you pass a right turn which leads to the Khóra–Ay. Ioánnis road (see above) and skirt around a deep ravine to the right, catching glimpses of the isolated chapel of Ay. Elefthérios below.

Heading towards the limestone ridges of the west part of the island, you pass various farm tracks before reaching (8km) the **monastery of Ay. Pandeleímon**, just short of the pass, over a gap between the ridges, into the valley of Kaminákia. The brilliantly whitewashed monastery, of an appealing simplicity, consists of a chapel with a chequered tile floor, a storeroom, and a hall and forecourt, where the patronal festival (2 July), when many villagers wear local costume, is celebrated with the traditional communal meal and dancing. The chapel and hall are well positioned to provide shade in the fore-court. This and the pleasant view down the relatively fertile valley, make it an ideal spot for a break or some lunch.

Over the pass the road quickly deteriorates and most visitors park four-wheeled vehicles at the beginning of the descent to (10km) the **bay of Kaminákia**. On the way down you pass a ruined double-apsed chapel, now a farmer's storehouse. The lintel of the left doorway is an ancient marble drum. The sheltered bay has a clean **beach** of mixed sand and pebbles and a makeshift bar where you can buy bottles of chilled water to make the stiff 30-minute walk back up the valley a little easier. An alternative way back, in high season, is on one of the caiques which ferry day-trippers to this bay from Skála on most days.

Skála to the northeast of the island and Vathí

You take the twisting coast road (metalled) out of the port, pass a petrol station and an electricity plant, and reach (3km) the bay of **Dhéftero Marmári**, with the island's **campsite** (June–Sept; tel. 0243 61338) and a pebble **beach**. Round the next bay, **Tríto Marmári**, with **beach** and makeshift taverna, you come to (5km) the signposted left turn for Ay. Andréas.

Here a 1.5km detour by rough but motorable track cuts across the isthmus to the bay of **Ay. Andréas**, with only a pier, used by a few fishermen, and the isolated taverna where some of their catch is served. The secluded location and charming view across the bay to the northeast of the island make this a splendid place for an evening meal.

The main road levels out, crosses to the north coast of the isthmus, and then (8km) returns to the south coast at a point where the isthmus is only about 100m wide. Circling **Stenó Bay**, with a narrow sandy beach, which is quiet but very close to the road, and refreshments, you reach (10km) **Maltezána** (offi-cially Análipsi; Rooms), said to be named after the Maltese pirates who once used the bay and its surrounding offshore islets as their lair. This farming village of fairly modern houses is the only significant centre of occupation and tourism apart from Skála/Khóra and Livádhia. Here is the turning (left) for the island's small **airport**.

Arriving at the pier, home to a small fishing fleet, you turn left along the waterfront, with a small beach. In the second field on the left, opposite the beach and just before the first of the pensions on the waterfront, are the considerable remains (unsigned) of **Roman baths**, with a fine mosaic in tesserae of orange, yellow, blue, maroon, pink and white. This covers the floor of a room c 6m by 8m, at the far end of the complex. Geometric patterns frame ten faces. In the centre is a square with a face in each corner (seasons?) and an inset circle which has the twelve signs of the zodiac arranged around a central figure, probably Fortune or a planetary deity.

Leaving Maltezána, the metalled road becomes a motorable track. A footpath leads along a small headland to a **monument** dedicated to some French marines involved in action near here on 6 November 1827, during the War of Independence. A short distance further along the footpath, you find some more mosaics (fenced off), said to have belonged to a 5C AD Early Christian **basilica**, although the building might well have had a residential function. Off a long porch two preserved thresholds give access to a pair of rooms. The larger, c 12m x 5m, has remains of some geometric patterns in black, white, and blue. The porch mosaic (red also) is much better preserved. Two dolphins, originally part of the wide border, are still intact. You return to the main road.

At (10km) the east end of the isthmus the road forks. The turning to the left leads down to the **Bay of Váï**: from here caiques ferry passengers the short distance round the coast to Vathí; the journey by road being considerably longer. Ignoring this turning, you follow the road up across the hillside and look down over Váï Bay, on the far slopes of which lie the scant remains of a medieval **fort**, similar to that at Ay. Ioánnis. At (11km) a fork in the track you go left, and continue straight on to return to the south coast of the island above (13km) the picturesque **Agrelídhi Bay.** The road starts to turn north and inland. You pass more tracks uphill to the left before reaching (16km) a disused military camp and a turning off to the right which leads southeast to the isolated **monastery** of Panayía Poulariani. The slopes are particularly stony and dusty, and fairly barren but, beyond the military camp, you begin to descend into the more fertile valley of Vathí, with views also down to the small bays on the northeast coast of the island.

The road ends at the head of **Vathí Bay** and the small, scattered farming community of **Méso Vathí**: from here there is a caique service (12.00, 13.00 and 17.00 daily) to the far end of the north shore of the bay and the even smaller community of **Exo Vathí** (Rooms; taverna) with a small beach. The quiet and sheltered inlet in which Exo Vathí is situated is protected from the south by a rocky spit sticking out into the bay. On the eastern extremity of the spit are the remains of a Hellenic **fort**, overlain by a later round structure. Up to three courses of the original fort's walls remain *in situ*, over 1m thick, in squared blocks of local stone.

Pátmos

Pátmos (Πάτμος; anc. *Patmos*), home of the Revelation of St John the Divine, is dominated by its spectacular monastery, which draws pilgrims and sightseers, especially Greeks. This lends the island a certain sobriety and reserve, although it is popular with visitors. The upper village has numerous small churches and its tiny white houses cram the narrow streets. Ecclesiastical 'seats' throughout the island are a good focus for excursions, and are often green and cultivated. Walking is not too arduous as the landscape is hilly rather than mountainous and the island is criss-crossed with paths. The long sandy beach at Gríkou is accessible but the more distant ones (Psilí Ammos in the south) are quieter and can be reached by boat, on foot, or by a combination of means.

The island is the most northerly of the Dodecanese. As a holy place, the religious laws concerning nudism and proper dress officially apply to the whole island, but they are widely ignored. Its total area is only 39sq. km, but the coastline is long and irregular, with many little bays, hemmed in by the hilly slopes. The three distinct sections, decreasing in size from north to south, are linked by two narrow isthmuses. The central isthmus is the focal point of the island, with the modern port, Skála, dominated on the south by Khóra with the monastery of St John on its fortified crag. Here too was the ancient city. The total population is 2715, most of whom live in Skála and Khóra. The only other significant centres of occupation are at Kámbos, to the north of Khóra, and Gríkou, to the southeast.

Pátmos has much volcanic rock—in fact the island reflects the northern and western sides of a volcanic crater—and is moderately hilly, rising to 237m in the south (Prassóvouno) and 228m in the north (Khondró Vounó), but reaches its peak of 269m at Profítis Ilías, not far south of Khóra. The climate is good but the water is poor and brackish and the soil arid, yielding only modest quantities of cereals, vegetables and wine. This produce is supplemented by fishing and rearing chickens and goats. The dry-stone walls are topped with layers of dry brushwood to deter the ravages of wandering goats which have savaged the vegetation here as in many parts of Greece. Sponge fishing used to be the main occupation, but is now defunct.

History

First inhabited by Mycenaeans, then Dorians and, later, Ionian colonists, *Patmos*, briefly mentioned by Thucydides (III.33.3), Strabo (X.5.13), and Pliny (IV.70), was of little importance in the ancient Greek world. However, potsherds and the remains of fortifications on the acropolis of Kastélli (see below) suggest that there was a sizeable settlement here in the Hellenistic period. Later, however, the island became depopulated, and the Romans made it a place of exile for political prisoners. Here, in AD 95, during the reign of Domitian, St John the Divine was banished from Ephesos. Traditonally the saint is identified with the apostle John, though this has been disputed. The last book of the New Testament describes the Revelation to St John on Patmos of instructions for the churches of Asia followed by a

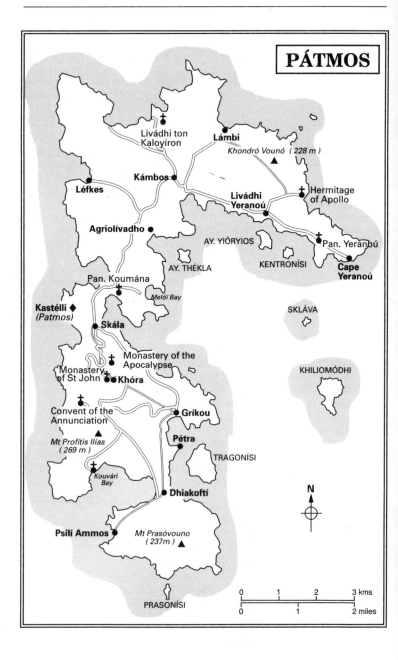

PÁTMOS

Livádhi ton Kaloyíron

Lámbi

Khondró Vounó (228 m)

Kámbos

Léfkes

Livádhi Yeranoú

Hermitage of Apollo

Agriolívadho

AY. YIÓRYIOS

Pan. Yeranbú

Pan. Koumána

AY. THÉKLA

KENTRONÍSI

Cape Yeranoú

Meloï Bay

Kastélli (Patmos)

SKLÁVA

Skála

Monastery of the Apocalypse

Monastery of St John

KHILIOMÓDHI

Khóra

Convent of the Annunciation

Gríkou

Mt Profítis Ilías (269 m)

Pétra

TRAGONÍSI

Kouvári Bay

N

Dhiakoftí

Psilí Ammos

Mt Prasóvouno (237m)

0   1   2   3 kms

0   1   2 miles

PRASONÍSI

vision of the nature of heaven, the punishment of evil and the ultimate creation of the heavenly kingdom.

For centuries the island was deserted because of the incursions of Saracen pirates. In 1088, after founding monasteries in Kos and Leros, the Blessed Christodoulos, a Bithynian abbot, obtained permission from the Byzantine Emperor Alexis I Comnenus to establish the monastery on Pátmos in honour of St John. In 1207 the island was captured by the Venetians. In 1461 Pope Pius II took both island and monastery under his protection. The Turks took Pátmos in 1537, and exacted an annual tribute. In spite of this the island community survived, and to some extent prospered, thanks to its mercantile fleet. In 1669 Venetian refugees arrived from Candia in Crete. The theological Seminary was founded in 1713. Independence came in 1821, only for Turkish control to be reimposed in 1830. This lasted until the Italian annexation of the Dodecanese in 1912. Reunification with Greece came in 1948. The pottery and ceramics of Pátmos, like those of Kos and Rhodes, followed Byzantine traditions, but with distinctive individual features.

Getting to Pátmos

■ **By sea**. In high season, Pátmos has daily **ferries** to the Piraeus and the larger Dodecanesian islands to the south (Léros, Kálimnos, Kos, Rhodes). About half of the boats to/from the Piraeus stop at some of the larger Cyclades en route. There are services to Sámos almost every day, via either Agathonísi or Ikaría and Foúrni. There is also a weekly connection to the northwestern Aegean islands and Thessaloníki.

Hydrofoils provide further transport (daily) to Sámos (both routes) and to Léros, Kálimnos, and Kos. Pátmos is regularly visited by **cruises**.

In low season, there is only one regular service, four times weekly, from the Piraeus to Pátmos via Sámos, continuing through the Dodecanese to Rhodes, and returning by the same route to the Piraeus. This reduced service reflects the absence of tourism on the island out of season: only two hotels remain open through the winter, both in Skála.

Getting around Pátmos

■ **By bus**. The island's one bus divides its time between a route from Skála north to Kámbos and back (four times daily, early morning to early evening), and another circular route linking Skála, Khóra, and Gríkou (twelve times daily, four of which do not include Gríkou).

■ **By road**. **Bicycles**, **scooters** and a few **cars** are available for rent, mainly in Skála (some also in Gríkou) and there is a fleet of **taxis** based in Skála's plateia (tel. 0247 31225).

■ **By boat**. Small boats provide day trips to some of the island's **beaches** (Psilí Ammos to the south, Lámbi, Agriolívadho, Kámbos and others to the north) in high season. There are daily boats to the nearby islet of Arkí, and its smaller neighbour Márathi (both popular with day-trippers for their beaches), and to Lipsi.

■ **On foot**. Most points on the island can be reached on foot in an hour from some point on the bus routes and there are many paths which make for pleasant, traffic-free excursions.

■ **Travel agent**. Astória Travel, Skála. tel. 0247 31205, 31208; fax 0247 31975; and one or two others.

■ **Police**. Tel. 0247 31303.

■ **First aid**. Tel. 0247 31577.

Skála

Hotels in Skála (area code 0247)	
B Romiós (56); 10,000–17,600 drs. Tel. 31070, 31962. April–Oct. Also F/As 20,350 drs.	Tel. 31217, 31498, 31798; fax 01 9231311. April–Oct.
B Skála (78); 10,500–15,600 drs. Tel. 31343, 31344. April–Oct.	**C Villa Kassándra** (F/A) (13); 7400–12,400 drs. Tel. 31523, 31610. April–Oct.
C Blue Bay; 11,100–13,900 drs. Tel. 31165. May–Oct.	**D Dhiethnés** (15); 6400–7870 drs. Tel. 31357.
C Captain's House (13); 8600–14,500 drs. Tel. 31793; fax 31663. April–Oct. Also F/As 15,500 drs.	**D Kástro** (16); 7500–9350 drs. Tel. 31554.
C Pláza (14); 10,000–12,000 drs.	**Rooms** (also a few in Kástro) from representatives on quay, or travel agents.

Boats dock towards the more attractive southeast end of Skála, the commercial and social centre of the island, situated in a large sheltered bay facing east. Opposite the ferry quay is the **bus station** and, between two rusted cannon, a small public garden with a **bust of Immanuel Xanthos**, co-founder of the anti-Turkish Filikí Etairía. Turning right (west) along the quay, you pass the **customs office** and **police station** before reaching the animated **plateia**, with arcaded buildings in the Italian colonial style. Here are the **taxi rank, banks**, and **post office** (open 08.00–13.30; closed Sat, Sun), behind which is the **tourist office** (open daily 09.00–14.00, 18.00–20.30; tel. 0247 31666). On the road out of the southeast corner of the plateia is an impressive twin-domed **church of St John** and, c 150m further on, the **OTE** (open 07.30–21.45; closed Sun). Further along the open, bustling waterfront are boats which offer day trips to beaches and to nearby islands, in season. Most leave between 10.00 and 11.00 in the morning. Opposite are two streets of **bars, tavernas**, and

shipping agents. Next is Skála's small and sandy **beach**, running along the shallow west side of the bay.

The limited but nonetheless interesting remains of the **acropolis** of ancient *Patmos* are reached from the first road running inland from the south end of the beach. After about 100m you turn right and follow a series of steps uphill to the outskirts of the town. From here a footpath leads round the terraced slopes and up to a saddle which approaches the rocky height of Kastélli from the north. On the climb you can see the north and northeast towers of the city's compact but sturdy fortifications and, between them, the best preserved section of the curtain wall, about 3m high. The northwest tower is still out of sight, just above a church of Ay. Konstandínos.

The **fortifications** (largely depleted but the surviving elements in a good state of repair) are in isodomic blocks with tightly fitting dressed edges, probably of the 3C BC. The northeast tower is the best preserved, c 5.5m wide and standing up to 3.5m high. The exterior of the northwest tower (9m sq.) is poorly preserved, but it retains six steps of an internal staircase. Elsewhere on the heights are further slight traces of the fortification walls and many worn potsherds. There are good, clear views of Skála and Khóra, and across the water to the west and north of the island.

If you return to Skála's beach and continue around the bay, you pass a small fenced enclosure, said to be the site of St John's **baptistery**. Beyond the turning (left) for Kámbos, and the island's only **petrol station** (open daily 07.00–13.00, 15.30–19.00) the road turns inland, dividing at the church of Ay. Pandeleímon and Ay. Rafaíl. The left branch takes you to the beach at **Melóï Bay**.

The right branch leads c 200m along the winding concrete road to the **Seat of Panayía Koumána** (open daily 10.00–15.30; 17.00–20.00), one of the many gardened cells or 'Holy Seats' of the main monastery of St John in Khóra, which lie dotted around the hills of Pátmos. These originated as hermitages and/or small farms. Standing on the promontory which borders Skála Bay on the northeast and Melóï Bay on the southwest, its colourful and attractive gardens contain fruit, vegetables and ornamental plants, a small aviary, a number of cells, and two chapels, sumptuously decorated with maroon velvet and gilt finishes. The floor of one of the chapels has a slab with the Byzantine double-headed eagle in relief. The stairs by the spring lead to a large cross and a belvedere with a fine view over Skála Bay to Khóra and the monastery, also to the islands of Arkí and Lipsí to the east.

From Skála the roads inland from east of the ferry pier lead to Khóra (2km). Walkers can take the ancient **mule path** which runs close to the asphalt road, starting from the upper reaches of Skála. Its large cobbles are uneven and polished by continual use, and some steps are now almost completely worn away.

On the way up there are fine views of the surrounding islands and rocks. You pass the island's **hospital** on the right; to the left tracks lead through a grove of fir trees to the **Pátmos Theological Seminary** and the **Convent of the Apocalypse**. The convent is the best known and most distinctive Seat of the main monastery. In a landscape with plants and flowers, but no formal gardens, are three small churches and narrow steps leading down to the large, dimly lit **Cave of St Anne**, its interior heavy with incense. Here, by tradition, St John related the **Revelation** to his disciple, Prochoros. The saint's headrest and writing place, recessed into the rock, are shown set in silver, and there is a 17C iconostasis, with other icons and church furniture.

■ The convent (entrance free) is open Mon, Wed, Fri, Sat 08.30–14.00; Tues, Thurs 08.30–13.00; 16.00–18.00; Sun 09.00–12.30; 16.00–18.00; but opening hours are revised frequently. Modest dress is essential (trousers, long sleeves) and is provided free if needed.

Khóra

Khóra (Rooms limited; attractive restaurants in the plateia) has pleasant 16–17C houses, and some 37 churches dating from the 16C onwards (names and locations are marked on a tourist map published by the monastery). Most lie tightly clustered below the monastery, above the car park which also acts as Khóra's bus station. The streets here are narrow, paved with flat, irregularly-shaped stones, and zigzag gradually up the steep slope to the monastery. To the east and south newer and more spacious houses, with gardens, are gradually but steadily extending down the slopes.

The fortified **MONASTERY OF ST JOHN**, 152m above sea level, has the appearance of a great polygonal castle with towers, buttresses, and battlements. It is visited by the faithful in great numbers on 21 May, the saint's day, and celebrates Easter Week with elaborate ceremonial, including a re-enactment of the Last Supper. Its ritual of the Washing of the Feet on Holy Thursday is shared only with Jerusalem. Other festivals include 16 March (death of the Blessed Christodoulos) and 21 October (return of the Blessed Christodoulos' bones from his deathplace on Evvia).

■ The monastery is open Mon, Wed, Fri, Sat 08.30–14.00; Tues, Thurs 08.30–13.00, 16.00–18.00; Sun 09.00–12.30, 16.00–18.00; but opening hours are frequently revised. An entrance fee is charged only for the library/treasury. Modest dress (trousers, long sleeves) is required, and is provided free of charge at the entrance, if needed. An excellent illustrated guide is available in English.

You approach the monastery from the north, passing stalls and shops selling icons and various religious paraphernalia and mementoes. A stepped passageway leads through the outer wall and past the church of Ay. Yióryios Yirokomeío, and around the north, east, and south sides of the church of Ayy. Apóstoli, to come out on a bench-lined terrace with fine views to the north.

To the left, as you enter by the **fortified gate**, is the tomb of Gregory of Kos, Bishop of Dhidhimótiko (died 1693; closed). The attractive **entrance court**, built in 1698, is distinguished by its striking floor of pebbles and large flat slabs, and its variety of columns and arches. The east side forms the exonarthex of the church, which incorporates elements from a 4C chapel and perhaps from the ancient temple of Artemis. Between the arches hangs a huge wooden simantron. The exonarthex has 17–18C frescoes, including scenes from the life of St John. Its right-hand door (closed) leads to the **Founder's Chapel**. You enter the narthex from the left hand doors of the exonarthex.

To the right is a low medieval door into the Founders's Chapel, also closed. The **narthex** has smoke-blackened early 19C frescoes, and is lined with rows of wooden seats.

The church proper, dimly lit, is a Greek inscribed cross. The floor, of grey and white marble, dates to the time of the foundation. The **iconostasis** (1820) is heavy and ornate, and some of the furniture has inlaid work in a Saracen style. Above the door of the **outer treasury** is an icon on a gold ground, signed by Immanuel Tzanes (1674). The small 12C **Chapel of the Theotokos**, to the south, has an early 17C iconostasis and outstanding 12C frescoes, revealed in 1958 when the 17C frescoes which had covered them were stripped away after damage by earth tremors. Behind the altar are the Holy Trinity, represented as three angels being given hospitality by Abraham; below, the Virgin, flanked by the archangels Michael and Gabriel, wearing Byzantine imperial robes.

Outside the south door of the Chapel of the Theotokos, and accessible from the southeast corner of the entrance court, is the smaller inner courtyard. From here opens the rectangular **refectory**, an 11C structure, the ceiling and dome modified in the 12–13C. It contains two long stone tables, placed end to end; the monks' places marked by indentations. The walls have remains of 12C frescoes, executed in two phases. They represent scenes of Christ's Passion, his miracles, and an illustration of Psalm 102. A passageway (closed) leads to the kitchen.

Stairs climb from the southwest corner of the entrance court to the **treasury**, which has a large and quite remarkable display of items from the monastery's **library** (3000 volumes, 1000 MSS), archives (13,000 documents) and sacristy (more than 200 icons, 300 silver items, and 600 gold embroideries). The complete **monastic collection** is the most important in Greece outside Mt Athos, and can only be visited by appointment. However, some of the most significant and impressive pieces are on display: 33 leaves of the Codex Porphyrius, comprising most of Mark's gospel, written in the early 6C on purple vellum, in uncials (similar to capitals, rounded and unjoined) of silver, with holy names in gold. A further 182 pages are in Leningrad, four in the British Museum, and others in Vienna, the Byzantine Museum in Athens, and the Vatican. Important texts include an 8C Book of Job, with commentaries drawn from 19 scholars; the Discourses of St Gregory, written in 941 in Calabria, and one of the works listed in 1201 in a surviving catalogue of the library. Some exquisite illumination in the Byzantine tradition is contained in various gospels and cartularies, including miniatures of the Evangelist Matthew (1345) and of St Luke (12C).

Also on display are charters and deeds, including the foundation chrysoboul of Alexis I Comnenus (1088) granting bestowal of the island, the use of a ship, and exemption from taxes; icons, notably a miniature mosaic, framed in silver, of St Nicholas (11C) and a famous St Theodore; church furniture, including a handsome chalice (1676) by Panagos, adorned with multi-coloured glass and representations in niello; the superb crozier of Dionysios IV, Patriarch of Constantinople, embellished with filigree ornament, enamels and diamonds, by Mikhalakis Frantzis (1677); and a silver-gilt mitre of the Patriarch Cyprian (early 18C), encased in filigree ornament, precious gems, enamel and embossed plaques; benediction crosses in wooden filigree; pendant model ships (16C) in enamelled silver set with precious stones, worn by the wives of rich ship-owners. The windows have an excellent view of Skála, and the west roof terrace, when open, a wonderful panorama of of the Aegean.

Khóra to the south of the island

By road 4km, plus 30 minute walk.

Hotels in Grikou and Kámbos (area code 0247)	
■ **Grikou**	**C Silver Beach** (16);
B Xenía (35); 13,000–16, 000	9000–12,000 drs. Tel. 32652 .
drs. Tel. 31219.	May–Sept.
C Grikos (18); 8650–11,900 drs.	**C Panórama** (F/A) (20);
Tel. 31294, 31167; fax 31783.	15,000–25,000 drs. Tel. 31209,
May–Oct.	31709; fax 32129. April–Oct.

You leave Khóra from the car park and skirt the east side of the town. On the outskirts a rough and stony footpath, descending from the last taverna on the left, provides a steep short-cut to Grikou. From there the beach extends intermittently all the way (c 20–30 mins on foot) south to the **bay of Dhiakoftí** at the isthmus of Stavrós. 1km along the main road, just before it bends to the left (east) and downhill for Grikou, take a road off to the right (signposted), then immediately turn right again at a fork, for a 1km detour to the **Convent of the Annunciation**. The convent, with an active community, is set in its own gardens. Founded by the monk Amphilokhios Makris in 1937, it stands on the site of the former St Luke's Hermitage (1613). It is open to suitably dressed visitors between 09.00 and 11.00.

Returning, you go sharp right at the fork just before the main road, to descend to **Grikou**, a lively popular resort (watersports, tennis, etc) with a long narrow beach of mixed pebbles and sand.

The main road continues south, and divides 2km further on. The right fork soon becomes a dirt track leading to **Kouvári Bay** and another Seat of the monastery in an attractive situation; unfortunately the Seat is fenced off and closed to the public. The left fork, signposted to Psilí Ammos, takes you down a dirt track to (4km) the **isthmus of Stavrós**, both sides of which have long **beaches**. These are just as good as other beaches on the island but, lacking accommodation, refreshments and shade, are usually much quieter. Vehicles must stop here, but there is a footpath (1.5km) down the west coast to **Psilí Ammos** on the southwest tip of the island, with a fine sandy **beach** (c 30 minutes' walk; also accessible by boat from Skála).

Skála to the north of the island; Kámbos and the Seat of Apollo

By road 8km.

Hotel in Kámbos (area code 0247)	
■ **Kámbos** **B Patmos Paradise** (35); pool. 12,000–26,000 drs. Tel. 32624;	fax 32740. May–Oct. Also F/As 51,000 drs.

You leave Skála on the Kámbos road, which heads inland from the north side of the bay, and pass (2km) the turn (sign) for **Agriolívadho Bay** with its long narrow sandy beach (pedal boats, canoes and windsurfers for hire; taverna). Skirting the bay, at 3km you pass a signposted turning (left) which leads 1.5km down through a fertile terraced valley to **Léfkes** on the west coast, with a beach.

Passing a few houses, you reach (4km) the plateia of **Kámbos** (503 inhabitants), the main settlement and centre of communications in the north of Pátmos. Here are tavernas, an attractive triple-domed church, a playground, and roads leading off to the northwest and northeast. Houses with large rich gardens line the roads leading off the plateia.

For (4km) Livádhi ton Kaloyíron in the northwest of the island, you continue 500m beyond Kámbos until the road forks. Take the right branch which soon becomes an unmetalled track. After another 1km you pass a turn (left) to Ay. Nikólaos Bay, and take the right, signposted to Livádhi Kaloyíron. As you descend slowly over bare slopes towards the north the islands of Ikaría, Foúrni, and Sámos are visible ahead. The monastic Seat of **Livádhi ton Kaloyíron**, has a chapel and cells set in a garden with figs, olives and a well (gardens open, buildings locked), looking down to the beach in the bay. The Seat was founded in 1700 by two monks from Mt. Athos, whose cloisters it is said to resemble.

From the plateia of Kámbos, the northeast road descends past houses dispersed among terraced fields to (5km) Kámbos' popular long, narrow beach, the site of most of the town's accommodation and tavernas. The road leads past the beach and forks, left to Lámbi, right to the northeast peninsula of the island.

Lámbi (pronounced locally Lábbi) has a popular beach of red and yellow pebbles, with two tavernas. To reach the northeast of the island and the Seat of Apollo, drivers must go back to the right turn at the north end of Kámbos beach, and follow the road round to and past (7km) Livádhi Bay (*not* the same as Livádhi ton Kaloyíron). Walkers, however, may take a footpath (rocky but not too difficult) leading off the main road at the top of the valley above Lámbi Bay. The path leads around a taverna, up the slope, and then east into a grove of trees, quickly leaving behind the relatively busy tourist routes to the beaches and tavernas. Here the red and yellow pebbles, for which Lámbi beach below is known, appear in the form of larger stones and rocky outcrops. Their colours intensify when moistened, and provide a striking contrast with the thick green of the vegetation.

As you approach the end of the grove of trees, there is a gate in a wall. Keeping to the right of the wall, a path leads up a few hundred metres and turns towards the south, descending to Kámbos. Ignoring that, you pass through the gate, scramble over some scree and through the pass, with a well. A half-hour walk leads across the north slopes of the valley, joining a motorable track about two-thirds of the way down. Eventually you turn left onto the asphalt road above Livádhi Bay, joining the motor route from Kámbos. You pass through a gate across the road, and come to a second, with a left turn just before it. Through the second gate, the track leads down to **Cape Yeranó**, and the chapel of Panayía Yeranoú, at the northeast tip of the island.

The left turn before the gate leads down the steep slopes above the sea to (8km) the **Seat of Apollo**, named after its founding monk, arguably the most attractive of the various Seats of the monastery dotted around the island. There are cells and a chapel set in lush gardens with a spring. The fertility of the gardens, the simple and fascinating layout of the cells, and the isolated coastal situation of the Seat are all outstanding. The monks, if present, may give a brief tour of the buildings.

Island of Arkí

Arkí (Αρκί), or Arkó, northeast of Pátmos and north of Lipsí, is a dependent islet 5km long and rising to 277m. Its 50 inhabitants, who subsist on fishing and rearing goats and chickens, are based in the single village, which has a few **rooms** to rent and an **OTE**, but no other facilities. Fresh water has to be shipped in from nearby islands. There are various even smaller islets around Arkí, one of which, **Maráthi** (Μαράθι), is popular for its beach (with taverna). In season, caiques provide day trips to both Arkí and Maráthi from Pátmos and Lipsí, though there is no boat connection between the two islets.

Island of Agathonísi

Agathonísi (Αγαθονήσι), further east, and to the south of Sámos, is as long as Arkí and slightly wider, rising to 208m. Two or three ferries (plus hydrofoils in summer) stop at the island each week, connecting with Sámos to the north, and Lipsí, Pátmos, and other Dodecanesian islands to the south. In the past the island has been known as *Netousa* and *Tragea*. Its population now stands at 122, in two villages, Megálo Khorió, by the port, and Mikró Khorió, further inland. **Megálo Khorió** has some rooms to rent, and a few tavernas and shops. There is no post office or OTE. The water supply is poor and, as with Arkí, supplies are shipped in from Sámos.

Lipsí

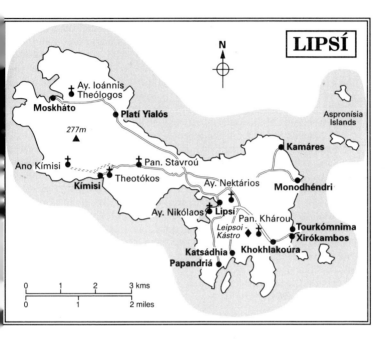

Lipsí (Λειψοί; anc. *Leipsoi*), is a delightful place for quiet relaxation in simple surroundings, with an almost complete absence of cars and metalled roads. Facilities are basic but adequate; walking is pleasant and easy; and there are good beaches.

Also known increasingly as Lipsós, the island lies east of Pátmos and north of Léros. One of the smallest of the Dodecanese, it is 9km long (roughly north-west–southeast) and 15.5sq. km in area. Mt Skafí in the west rises to 277m. The 36km of coastline is irregular and indented, especially in the south, where the island's port is set at the east end of a deep bay. This is the only settlement of any size, contains most of the 606 inhabitants, and all of its public facilities, offices and shops. There is some fishing and, in the southeast, relatively intense agriculture. A sweet dark wine is produced, and celebrated in a three-day festival in the first half of August. The northwest of the island is less farmed, and home mostly to goats. The only other source of income is a modest level of tourism.

The only accommodation is in Lipsí town. Tavernas at Platí Yialós and Katsádhia allow **camping** free of charge under nearby olive trees, but have no facilities.

History

Not surprisingly, *Leipsoi* was of little importance in antiquity; its only reference in ancient literature is in Pliny (NH V. 133). From the 5C BC, *Leipsoi* was part of the state of Miletos, on the Anatolian mainland, though without the deme status granted to nearby Léros. For 566 years from the foundation of the Monastery of St John the Divine on Pátmos in 1088, *Leipsoi* belonged to that institution, with a beneficial effect on the island's prosperity. The monastery still owns some property here. This close connection with the religious community on Pátmos and the relative isolation of the island have lent strength to the people's maintainance of the Orthodox tradition. There are over 40 churches dotted over the island, all regularly visited, well maintained, and rarely locked, with more under construction.

The simple island existence becomes most animated during religious festivals. Wedding celebrations, which start mid-evening in the town plateia, can carry on around the relatives' houses until the following midday. Lipsí's most important festival, and the only one which attracts worshippers from outside the island, is at the church of the Panayía of Kháros, half an hour's walk southeast of the town. Here, on the three days around 24 August, the faithful come to witness the church's dried flowers return to life. Although the population has fallen through emigration, the community has been maintained and there is a large secondary school, with grounds and playing fields.

Getting to Lipsí

■ **By boat**. The larger **ferries** stop at Lipsí, en route for Pátmos and Piraeus to the west, and the Dodecanese to the south as far as Rhodes, twice weekly (in each direction) in high season, once weekly in low season. In addition, **smaller craft** operate near daily services to Arkí, Pátmos, Sámos, and Léros all year, weather permitting (plus **hydrofoils** in summer), and to nearby islets in high season.

Getting around Lipsí

■ Lipsí has no formal **bus** or **taxis**; the islanders rely heavily on donkeys, also ponies and small horses. For larger loads, open-topped pick-ups are used, as these are far better suited to the island's stony dirt tracks than cars. Two municipal minibuses and some of the pick-ups provide a taxi service for tourists, running from the quayside in the town out to the island's beaches. Alternatively **scooters** can be hired near the southeast end of the waterfront, or visitors may enjoy simply exploring this small and quiet island **on foot**. Tough shoes are generally required, especially on the routes to Monodhéndri, Kamáres, and Kímisi. All of the islands's main beaches are easily accessible from Lipsí town, taking between 30 minutes and an hour to reach on foot.

■ **Travel agent. John and Rena's Agency**; tel. 0247 41254 (leaflet on island walks available).

■ **Police**. Tel. 0247 41222.

■ **First aid**. Tel. 0247 41204.

Lipsí town

From the northeast corner of the harbour (**police** and the useful **travel/tourist agency**), steps lead a short way up to the small and busy plateia, location of the Dhimarkhíon and most of the island's amenities. In the narrow winding streets radiating from it are various shops. The island has a doctor, and at weekends a dentist is available. Also in the plateia are the principal **church** (Ay. Ioánnis Theológos), built in the 1930s with funds from expatriates in America; **post office**; **OTE** (a long-distance telephone is also available in the tourist office); and shaded kafeneíos. Here too are a bust of the Patmian Immanuel Xanthos, local hero of the struggle against the Turks, after whom the plateia is named, and the museum.

The **Nikeforeíon Ecclesiastical Museum** is a repository for all sorts of natural objects and curiosities preserved and discovered by the islanders at home and abroad. Some have considerable historic or artistic significance, others none; but, as a whole, the collection offers fascinating insights into the island's cultural history. On display are small ancient altars of Zeus and of Artemis, thought to have been found in the area south of the town, around the site of the ancient settlement; amphoras recovered from the sea; a grave relief; ancient and Byzantine inscriptions and architectural blocks, including part of a large Ionic corner capital; traditional island costumes, lace, embroidery and other needle-work; a collection of rocks from around the world; a collection of holy water, oils, crosses and stones from different holy sites; old and ageing icons; coins, dating back to the reign of Justinian and beyond; an illustrated copy of the gospels produced in 1775; a collection of official letters, certificates, and medals received by the islanders, including two letters from Andreas Miaoulis, dated 21 and 23 August 1824, concerning Lipsí's role in the War of Independence.

It is as well to bear in mind that there is no bank (money can be changed at the tourist office in the plateia, the post office and in the hotel) and that opening hours are in general irregular and erratic. The plateia's tourist office (in the Dhimárkhíon) does however adhere to its hours of Mon–Fri 09.30–13.30, 16.30–20.30; Sat–Sun 10.30–13.30, at least in summer.

Lipsí town to the southeast

1. About 30 minutes on foot. 2. About 50 minutes (without sightseeing and detours).

1. The church of Ay. Nikólaos stands above the headland which separates the waterfront of Lipsí town from the next small bay to the south. Around this latter bay, in the valley which rises inland behind it, and on the hill to the southeast, stood the **ancient settlement**. Although the only archaeological remains still *in situ* are some traces of the fortification walls on the hilltop acropolis (see below), the site of the town is confirmed by the amount of ancient building material which can be seen in the area, mainly in and around the churches. At Ay. Nikólaos ancient blocks are built into the courtyard wall, with two (one an architrave block) framing the gateway. Lying in front of the church are a slender column drum, c 1.5m long, and a repainted Byzantine capital. The church may stand on the site of the temple of Apollo Leipsieus.

Following the road into the valley to the south, you soon come to another church, **Panayía Kouséliou**. The wall in front of the church door contains a fluted column drum, while a block with an inscription and a later Byzantine cross is built into a corner of the church. The inscription, which mentions one Apollodoros, son of Herakleitos, clearly refers to the public affairs of *Leipsoi*, further evidence that the ancient town was in this vicinity. One minute further on is the **church of Ay. Markélla**, with a rusting shell case, once used as a bell, a column drum in the southeast corner of the courtyard wall, and another Byzantine capital. Carrying on up the road, you find (left) **Ay. Nektários**, the island's baptistery, with a small aviary and another chapel below. An inscription records the construction of the church in the 1980s. The next church along the road has another old shellcase-bell.

Just beyond is a **crossroads** where you turn right (south). About 100m past another church, Ay. Anáryiri, you can go through a wide wooden gate to the left. This opens onto a small footpath up to the summit of the hill on which stand the scant remains of the ancient **acropolis**, known as Kástro. Stretches of the **fortification wall** can be traced, especially on the east side of the hill, just below the line of the flat summit. Many roughly squared ancient blocks are also visible in the dry-stone walls across the upper stretches of the hill. There is a commanding view of the island below, and of the sea approaches.

From the bottom of the hill, the road continues down to the two sandiest and most sheltered **beaches** in the southeast of the island, **Papandriá** and **Katsádhia**. At the latter are two tavernas and the church of Ay. Pandeleímon and Ay. Spiridhón. A Byzantine capital, with a cross in relief, stands outside the door of the church.

2. Returning to the crossroads you turn right (east). The metalled road leads to the **church of Panayía Khárou**, and a small farming settlement. The triple-apsed church, a Greek inscribed cross, has a water tap and a large courtyard to cater for its popular festival. In the courtyard in front of the church, set in concrete, is an ancient fluted column drum. The road continues down to **Khokhlakoúra beach**, with small caves. From here on the beaches get progressively less sheltered and sandy as you continue northeastwards around the coast to Xirókambos, Tourkómnima, Monodhéndri and Kamáres. The first two can be reached by rough track from Khokhlakoúra, and are separated from each other by a small headland. From the headland the remains of a mole, just underwater, project into Tourkómnima Bay. As the name suggests, this was once the first port of call for travellers from Asia Minor, clearly visible from here.

Monodhéndri and **Kamáres**, the last and most northerly of the beaches in the southeast part of the island, can be reached by following the coast (pathless but walkable) northwards, or by returning to the crossroads and turning right (north). Past another church with a shellcase bell you join the road from Lipsí town. A 150m stretch of this road just outside the town consists of an old paved mule path, very similar to that between Skála and Khóra on Pátmos, but here far better preserved. The road divides about 1km from the coast, left for Kámares, right for Monodhéndri, and turns into a footpath, through rough open slopes, for the last stretch. Monodhéndri's one tree stands on a headland protecting the bay. Both pebble beaches are small and isolated and attractive mainly for their seclusion.

Lipsí to Platí Yialós and Moskháto

6km by road.

Leaving town to the west, you pass two small sandy beaches frequented by the locals. The road then rises inland and soon reaches the opposite (north) coast of the island. Following the coast you pass (2km) the turning for Kímisi (see below), beyond the island's sprawling and malodorous rubbish tip. The detour (2km) is a hard climb, only motorable for the initial ascent. The hilly slopes running down to the north coast are covered in scrub, with little terracing or agriculture.

At (4km) **Platí Yialós** there is, as the name suggests, a fine sandy **beach**, the most popular on the island, in a bay with taverna and chapel. The road continues to (6km) the bay of **Moskháto**, with a very small beach, a fish farm, and the **church** of Ay. Ioánnis Theológos. Beneath the apse of the church, traces of the foundations of the original 17C chapel can be seen. The chapel is prominent on old nautical maps, despite the fact that it cannot be seen from the open sea. This, combined with the veneration of St John the Theologian here, suggests that Moskháto was once the first port of call for ships coming from Pátmos.

Lipsí to Kímisi

Approx 4 hours on foot (round trip).

Apart from the routes to the beaches described above, there is one footpath which crosses the northwestern half of the island and is not to be missed, if you enjoy walking away from roads and habitation. It give access to the best views on the island, covering 180 degrees, in various directions. Although the round trip can be done in about four hours, a more leisurely excursion might be planned to take up a whole day. The tracks are rough, but fairly easy to follow.

The path leads off to the left about 1km out of Lipsí town on the Platí Yialós/Moskhátou road (see above), at the point where it starts to descend to the north coast. You climb, keeping to the right of a stone wall, and soon reach a stretch of the path which seems to include some old paving. Crossing the northern slopes of the island's central range, you come to the first of three small **hermitages**, each consisting of a church with simple adjoining cells. **Panayía Stavroú** has a spring and small shrine.

About 200m further on you come to the road which connects the north coast/Platí Yialós road with Kímisi Bay to the south. Turn left here, noting a **footpath** which leads off to the right across the hillside at the beginning of the descent to **Kímisi Bay**, with the second of the hermitages and a small beach.

The **hermitage** consists of the church of the **Theotókos** with adjoining cell (usually occupied), and a spring which feeds a small but productive garden. The bones of monks are said to have been buried in the rocks round about, especially during the Turkish occupation. From the far side of the beach a footpath runs up across the hillside. Both this path and the one noted above lead to the third hermitage, known simply as **Ano Kímisi**, again with church and cell. All three are exceptionally peaceful and isolated, well suited for a short rest before carrying on the journey.

From the third church you turn about for Lipsí town. At the end of the footpath you can cut straight across the main road back to the town, and follow the motorable track opposite, which passes a ruined windmill before curving back round to the northern side of Lipsí.

Glossary

AEGIS. Cuirass or shield with Gorgon's head and ring of snakes.

AGORA. Public square, often including market-place.

AKATHIST HYMN. Twenty four verses (or *oikoi*), each beginning with a different letter of the alphabet, sung in Lent. The subjects (aspects of the incarnation, twelve of them particularly connected with the Panagia) are regularly depicted in frescoes.

AMAZONOMACHIA, GIGANTOMACHIA, TITANOMACHIA. Battle between Gods and Amazons, Giants, Titans.

AMBO (pl. ambones). Pulpit in a Christian basilica; two pulpits on opposite sides of a church from which the gospel and epistle were read.

AMPHIPROSTYLE. Façade columns set forward of the façade of a building, at both ends (only).

ANTHEMION. Flower ornament.

APOTROPAION. A protective symbol to turn away evil.

BATTER. Sloping apron in front of wall or tower (also called talus).

BASTION. Part of fortification wall projecting from the wall itself.

BEMA. Raised platform (anc.); sanctuary of church (Byz.)

BRECCIA. A composite rock (pudding-stone).

CAVEA. Auditorium of a Greek or Roman theatre.

CHITON. A tunic.

CHLAMYS. Light cloak worn by epheboi.

CHOROS. A hanging circle in metal or wood for the display of icons.

CHTHONIC. Dwelling in or under the ground.

CLOISONNÉ. Building technique where stones are individually framed with bricks or tiles.

CONCH. The quarter of a sphere which forms the top part of an apse.

COROPLAST. Maker of small figurines, usually of terracotta.

CUNEUS (pl. cunei). Lit: 'wedge'. Wedge shaped block of seats, formed by the intersecting vertical and horizontal passages in the cavea of a theatre.

CYMA (recta or reversa). A wave moulding with double curvature.

DEISIS. (Byz.) (i) Supplication; (ii) (in scholarship from 19C onwards) scene showing Christ with hand raised in blessing to the Virgin and John the Baptist supplicating to either side.

DIACONICON. (Byz.) Sacristy for sacred vessels on south side of sanctuary (cf. prothesis).

DODEKAORTO. The twelve major feasts of the Orthodox church (frequently represented in paintings): Annunciation (mod. Evangelismós), Nativity (Yénnisis), Presentation (Ipapandí), Baptism (Váptisis), Transfiguration (Metamórfosis), Raising of Lazarus (Eyersi tou Lazárou), Entry into Jerusalem (Vaïofóros), Crucifixion (Stávrosis), Resurrection (Anástasis), Ascension (Análipsis), Pentecost (Pentekostí), Dormition (Koímisis).

DRAFTED (of masonry). Stone with chisel-dressed band round the edges as a guide for the levelling of the rest of the surface.

EISODIA (TIS THEOTOKOU).

Presentation (of the Virgin Mary).

EPHEBOS. Greek youth under training (military, or university).

EPITAPHIOS. Ceremonial pall.

EROTES. Figures of Eros, god of love.

ESCHARA. Sacred hearth.

EXEDRA. Semicircular recess in a classical or Byzantine building.

FORICA. Latrine.

FOSSE. Ditch, in fortifications.

GLACIS. Broad sloping area of natural rock, or of earth, in front of defences, on which attackers are exposed.

HERM. Quadrangular pillar, usually adorned with a phallus, and surmounted by a bust.

HEROÖN. Shrine or chapel of a demigod or mortal.

HIMATION. An oblong cloak thrown over the left shoulder, and fastened over or under the right.

HOPLITE. Heavily armed foot-soldier.

HYPAETHRAL. Open to the sky.

HYPAPANTE (mod. Ipapandí). Presentation of Christ in the temple.

ICONOSTASIS. Screen bearing icons. See templon.

ISODOMIC (of masonry). Set in courses of equal height.

KATHOLIKON. Main church in a monastery.

KORE. Maiden; Archaic female figure.

KOIMISIS (TIS THEOTOKOU). Lit: 'falling asleep'. Dormition (of the Virgin Mary).

KOUROS. Boy; Archaic male figure.

LESCHE. Club-house.

MACHICOLATION. Opening in floor of projecting gallery, for dropping missiles on attackers.

MARTYRION. Shrine to martyr.

MEGARON. Hall of a Mycenaean palace or house.

NAOS. Main room of temple, containing cult statue (anc.); central section of church,

between narthex and iconostasis (Byz.).

NARTHEX. Vestibule of a Byzantine church.

NAUMACHIA. Mock naval combat for which the arena of an amphitheatre was flooded.

NYMPHAION. Sanctuary of the Nymphs.

ODEION. A concert hall, usually in the shape of a Greek theatre, but roofed.

OIKOS. A house.

OMPHALOS. A sacred stone, commemorating the centre of the earth where Zeus' two eagles met.

OPUS ALEXANDRINUM. Mosaic design of black and red geometric figures on a white ground.

OPUS SECTILE. Pieces of marble cut to form a pattern.

PANAGIA (mod. Panayía). Lit: 'all-holy'. The Virgin Mary.

PANTOKRATOR. The Almighty.

PARECCLESION. Chapel added to a Byzantine church.

PENDENTIVE. Spherical triangle formed by intersection of dome with two adjacent arches below.

PEPLOS. A mantle in one piece, worn draped by women.

PERIBOLOS. A precinct, but often archaeologically the circuit round it.

PETASOS. Broad-brimmed felt hat worn by epheboi.

PHIALE. Saucer or bowl.

PINAX. Flat plate, tablet, or panel.

PODIUM. Low wall or continuous pedestal carrying a colonnade or building.

POLYANDREION. Communal tomb.

POROS. A soft, coarse, conchiferous limestone (tufa).

PRODROMOS. Lit: 'forerunner'. Usual epithet of St. John the Baptist.

PROPYLON, PROPYLAEA. Entrance gate to a temenos; in plural form when there is more than one door.

PROTHESIS. (anc.) Laying out of a corpse; (Byz.) The setting forth of the oblation, or the chamber north of the sanctuary where this is done.

PUTEAL. Ornamental well-head.

QUADRIGA. Four-horsed chariot.

RAVELIN. Freestanding, usually triangular, fortification outside and separate from main wall.

REDAN. Triangular bastion projecting from main fortification wall.

SCARP. Retaining wall of moat or fosse nearest fortification wall; retaining wall on far side is counterscarp.

SIMANTRON. Block of wood or metal bar beaten as a call to divine service.

SKENE. Stage-building of a theatre.

SPHENDONE. The rounded end of a stadium.

SQUINCH. Straight or arched structure across angle of square building, to support dome.

STELE (pl. stelai). Stone slab, often with sculptural decoration and usually either marking a grave or set up as an offering (votive) in a sanctuary.

STOA. A porch or portico not attached to a larger building.

SYNOIKISM. Union of separate communities in a single city-state.

SYNTHRONON. Seat for bishop or elders in apse of a Byzantine church.

TALUS. See batter.

TEMENOS. A sacred enclosure.

TEMPLON. Stone screen separating bema from naos. Later became iconostasis.

TERREPLEIN. Space behind parapet, rampart or bastion, itself consisting of inner and outer walls with an earth or rubble filling.

TETRASTYLE. With four columns.

THEME. (Byz.) A province.

THEOLOGOS. Lit: 'theologian'. Usual epithet of St. John the Evangelist.

THEOTOKOS. Lit: 'God - bearing'. Usual epithet of the Panagia.

THOLOS. A circular building.

THORAKION. Panel (to waist height), component of lower part of templon.

THYMELE. Altar set up in a theatre.

TRANSENNA. Openwork grille at the entrance to a Byzantine chapel.

TRICONCH. Building plan using three hemispherical units arranged as a trefoil.

TRILITHON. Gateway made up of two jambs and a lintel.

TRIREME. Greek galley rowed by 3 banks of oars.

TURBEH. (Ott.) Mausoleum.

XOANON. Wooden image or idol.

XYSTOS. Roofed colonnade in gymnasium, often equipped with starting blocks, for indoor athletic training.

Modern terms frequently used in the text

DHIMARKHÍON. Town hall.

LIMENARKHÍON. Port authority.

PLATEÍA. Square or open space in a town or village.

YIMNÁSION. (= Gymnasium) Secondary school.

Index

There are two indexes. The general index includes people, practical information, subjects, and places outside the Dodecanese. The other is an index of the inlands

General index

Proper names and ancient sites are given in *italic*.

Index to the islands of The Dodecanese

Proper names and ancient sites are given in *italic*.

If you would like more information about
Blue Guides please complete the form below and
return it to

Blue Guides
A&C Black (Publishers) Ltd
Freepost
Eaton Socon
Huntingdon
Cambridgeshire
PE19 3BR
or fax it to us on
0171-831 8478

Name . . . .
. . . .
Address . . . .
. . . .
. . . .
. . . .
. . . .